S0-AXU-171

enVisionMATH 2.0

Scott Foresman · Addison Wesley

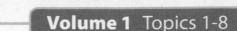

Volume 1 Topics 1-8

Authors

Randall I. Charles
Professor Emeritus
Department of Mathematics
San Jose State University
San Jose, California

Janet H. Caldwell
Professor of Mathematics
Rowan University
Glassboro, New Jersey

Juanita Copley
Professor Emerita, College of Education
University of Houston
Houston, Texas

Warren Crown
Professor Emeritus of Mathematics Education
Graduate School of Education
Rutgers University
New Brunswick, New Jersey

Francis (Skip) Fennell
L. Stanley Bowlsbey Professor of Education and Graduate and Professional Studies
McDaniel College
Westminster, Maryland

Stuart J. Murphy
Visual Learning Specialist
Boston, Massachusetts

Kay B. Sammons
Coordinator of Elementary Mathematics
Howard County Public Schools
Ellicott City, Maryland

Jane F. Schielack
Professor of Mathematics
Associate Dean for Assessment and Pre K-12 Education,
College of Science
Texas A&M University
College Station, Texas

Mathematicians

Roger Howe
Professor of Mathematics
Yale University
New Haven, Connecticut

Gary Lippman
Professor of Mathematics and Computer Science
California State University East Bay
Hayward, California

PEARSON

Glenview, Illinois   Boston, Massachusetts   Chandler, Arizona   Upper Saddle River, New Jersey

Contributing Authors

Zachary Champagne
District Facilitator, Duval County
Public Schools
Florida Center for Research in
Science, Technology, Engineering,
and Mathematics (FCR-STEM)
Jacksonville, Florida

Jonathan A. Wray
Mathematics Instructional
Facilitator
Howard County Public Schools
Ellicott City, Maryland

ELL Consultants

Janice Corona
Retired Administrator
Dallas ISD, Multi-Lingual
Department
Dallas, Texas

Jim Cummins
Professor
The University of Toronto
Toronto, Canada

Texas Reviewers

Theresa Bathe
Teacher
Fort Bend ISD

Chrissy Beltran
School Wide Project Coordinator
Ysleta ISD

Renee Cutright
Teacher
Amarillo ISD

Sharon Grimm
Teacher
Houston ISD

Esmeralda Herrera
Teacher
San Antonio ISD

Sherry Johnson
Teacher
Round Rock ISD

Elvia Lopez
Teacher
Denton ISD

Antoinese Pride
Instructional Coach
Dallas ISD

Joanna Ratliff
Teacher
Keller ISD

Courtney Jo Ridehuber
Teacher
Mansfield ISD

Nannie D. Scurlock-McKnight
Mathematics Specialist
A.W. Brown Fellowship-Leadership
Academy
Dallas, TX

Brian Sinclair
Math Instructional Specialist
Fort Worth ISD

Copyright © 2015 by Pearson Education, Inc., or its affiliates. All Rights Reserved. Printed in the United States of America. This publication is protected by copyright, and permission should be obtained from the publisher prior to any prohibited reproduction, storage in a retrieval system, or transmission in any form or by any means, electronic, mechanical, photocopying, recording, or likewise. For information regarding permissions, write to Rights Management & Contracts, Pearson Education, Inc., One Lake Street, Upper Saddle River, New Jersey 07458.

Pearson, Scott Foresman, Pearson Scott Foresman, and enVisionMATH are trademarks, in the U.S. and/or in other countries, of Pearson Education Inc., or its affiliates.

ISBN-13: 978-0-328-76722-9
ISBN-10: 0-328-76722-0

Digital Resources

Look for these digital resources in every lesson!

Go to PearsonTexas.com

Solve
Solve & Share problems plus math tools

Learn
Visual Learning Animation Plus with animation, interaction, and math tools

Glossary
Animated Glossary in English and Spanish

Tools
Math Tools to help you understand

Check
Quick Check for each lesson

Games
Math Games to help you learn

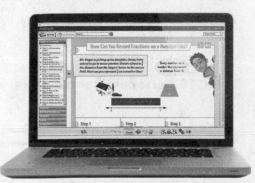

eText
The pages in your book online

PearsonTexas.com
Everything you need for math anytime, anywhere

Key

Number and Operations
Algebraic Reasoning
Geometry and Measurement
Data Analysis
Personal Financial Literacy

Mathematical Process Standards are found in all lessons.

Digital Resources at PearsonTexas.com

Solve   Learn   Glossary

Check   Tools   Games

And remember, the pages in your book are also online!

Contents

Topics

TOPIC 1 — Numeration

Hi, I'm Daniel. Here are different ways to show 47,062.

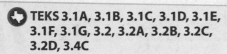

expanded form: $40{,}000 + 7{,}000 + 60 + 2$
standard form: 47,062
word form: forty-seven thousand, sixty-two

TEKS 3.1A, 3.1B, 3.1C, 3.1D, 3.1E, 3.1F, 3.1G, 3.2, 3.2A, 3.2B, 3.2C, 3.2D, 3.4C

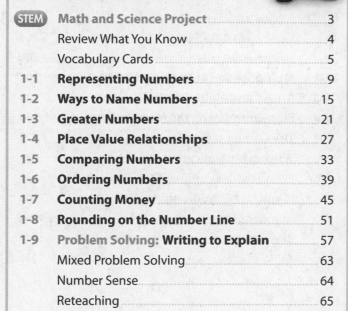

TOPIC 2 — Number Sense: Adding and Subtracting Whole Numbers

Hi, I'm Marta. This number line shows how to find $54 + 81 - 100$.

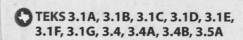
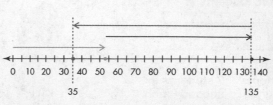

TEKS 3.1A, 3.1B, 3.1C, 3.1D, 3.1E, 3.1F, 3.1G, 3.4, 3.4A, 3.4B, 3.5A

Volume 1

TOPIC 3 Developing Proficiency: Adding and Subtracting Whole Numbers

Hi, I'm Alex.
This strip diagram can help you write and solve the equation
$458 - 221 = \square$.

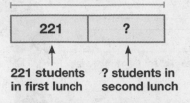

458 students

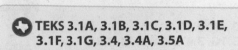

221	?

221 students in first lunch   ? students in second lunch

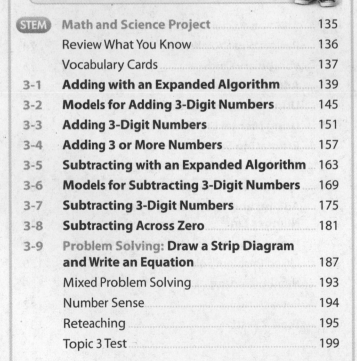

TEKS 3.1A, 3.1B, 3.1C, 3.1D, 3.1E, 3.1F, 3.1G, 3.4, 3.4A, 3.5A

TOPIC 4 Multiplication Meanings

Hi, I'm Jada.
These show multiplication as repeated addition.

20 squares

4	4	4	4	4

An addition sentence or multiplication sentence can represent the total number of squares: $4 + 4 + 4 + 4 + 4 = 20$
$5 \times 4 = 20$.

TEKS 3.1A, 3.1B, 3.1C, 3.1D, 3.1E, 3.1F, 3.1G, 3.4D, 3.4E, 3.4F, 3.4K, 3.5B, 3.5C

TOPIC 5

Multiplication Facts: Use Patterns and Known Facts

Hi, I'm Carlos. You can use a hundred chart to find multiples of 2, 5, and 9.

○ multiples of 2   ☐ multiples of 5   △ multiples of 9

TEKS 3.1A, 3.1B, 3.1C, 3.1D, 3.1E, 3.1F, 3.1G, 3.4, 3.4E, 3.4F, 3.4K, 3.5B, 3.5C

TOPIC 6

Meanings of Division

Hi, I'm Emily. A strip diagram can help you find how many groups there are or how many are in each group.

12 Toys

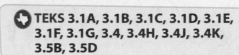

4 toys for each friend

TEKS 3.1A, 3.1B, 3.1C, 3.1D, 3.1E, 3.1F, 3.1G, 3.4, 3.4H, 3.4J, 3.4K, 3.5B, 3.5D

TOPIC 7

Division Facts

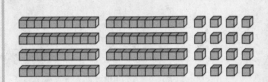

Hi, I'm Jackson. This array shows a division fact.

30 drums in 3 equal rows
$30 \div 3 = 10$
10 drums in each row

TEKS 3.1A, 3.1B, 3.1C, 3.1D, 3.1E, 3.1F, 3.1G, 3.4F, 3.4I, 3.4J, 3.4K, 3.5B, 3.5D

TOPIC 8

Number Sense: Multiplying 2-Digit by 1-Digit Numbers

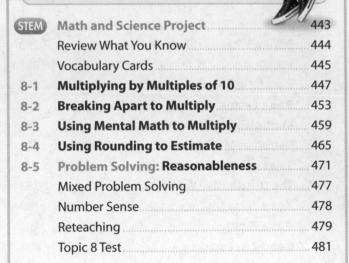

Hi, I'm Marta. This array of place-value blocks shows 4×24. Another way to think of 4×24 is $(4 \times 20) + (4 \times 4)$.

TEKS 3.1A, 3.1B, 3.1C, 3.1D, 3.1E, 3.1F, 3.1G, 3.4, 3.4G

Volume 2

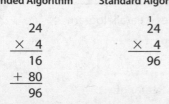
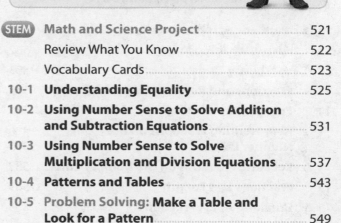

Volume 2

TOPIC 11 — Understanding Fractions

Hi, I'm Carlos. You can break $\frac{2}{3}$ apart into unit fractions and write $\frac{2}{3}$ as the sum of its parts.

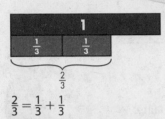

$$\frac{2}{3} = \frac{1}{3} + \frac{1}{3}$$

TEKS 3.1A, 3.1B, 3.1C, 3.1D, 3.1E, 3.1F, 3.1G, 3.3, 3.3A, 3.3B, 3.3C, 3.3D, 3.3E, 3.3F, 3.3G, 3.3H, 3.4A, 3.4K, 3.7A

TOPIC 12 — Shapes and Solids

Hi, I'm Jada. A quadrilateral is a polygon with four sides. These are different quadrilaterals.

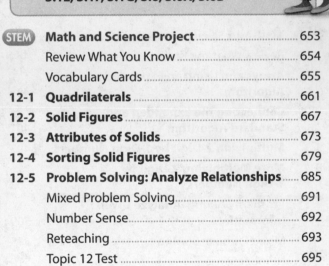

Trapezoid   Square   Parallelogram

Rhombus   Rectangle

TEKS 3.1, 3.1A, 3.1B, 3.1C, 3.1D, 3.1E, 3.1F, 3.1G, 3.6, 3.6A, 3.6B

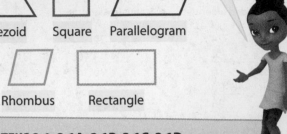

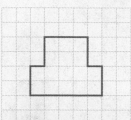

TOPIC 13

Measurement: Perimeter and Area

Hi, I'm Zeke. You can find the area of a shape by counting square units.

TEKS 3.1A, 3.1B, 3.1C, 3.1D, 3.1E, 3.1F, 3.1G, 3.3C, 3.4E, 3.4K, 3.6C, 3.6D, 3.6E, 3.7B

TOPIC 14

Measurement: Capacity, Weight, Mass, and Time

Hi, I'm Marta. This balance scale shows that this apple weighs about 9 ounces.

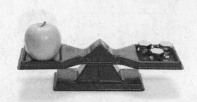

TEKS 3.1A, 3.1B, 3.1C, 3.1D, 3.1E, 3.1F, 3.1G, 3.7, 3.7C, 3.7D, 3.7E

TOPIC 15 — Data Analysis

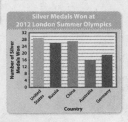

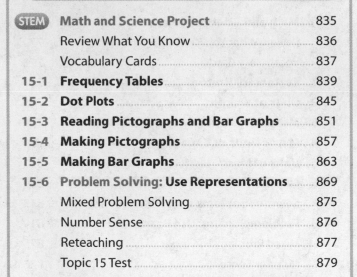

Hi, I'm Daniel. You can use a pictograph or a bar graph to compare data.

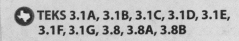

⭐ TEKS 3.1A, 3.1B, 3.1C, 3.1D, 3.1E, 3.1F, 3.1G, 3.8, 3.8A, 3.8B

TOPIC 16 — Personal Financial Literacy

Hi, I'm Emily. This table shows income earned from doing work.

DATA

Money Connie Earns	
Job	**Money Earned Each Hour**
Giving piano lessons	$9
Walking dogs	$7

⭐ TEKS 3.1A, 3.1B, 3.1C, 3.1D, 3.1E, 3.1F, 3.1G, 3.9, 3.9A, 3.9B, 3.9C, 3.9D, 3.9E, 3.9F

Volume 2

Step Up to Grade 4

These lessons help you prepare for Grade 4.

Have a great year!

⭐ **TEKS 3.1A, 3.1B, 3.1C, 3.1D, 3.1E, 3.1F, 3.1G, 4.2A, 4.2E, 4.3B, 4.3E, 4.4, 4.4C, 4.4E, 4.4H, 4.6A, 4.7A, 4.7B**

Problem-Solving Handbook

Applying Math Processes

Analyze
- How does this problem connect to previous ones?
- What am I asked to find?
- What information do I know?

Plan
- What is my plan?
- What strategies can I use? (See the list of some helpful strategies.)
- How can I use tools?
- How can I organize and record information?

Solve
- How can I use number sense?
- How can I estimate?
- How can I communicate and represent my thinking?

Justify
- How can I explain my work?
- How can I justify my answer?

Evaluate
- Have I checked my work?
- Is my answer reasonable?

Use this Problem-Solving Handbook throughout the year to help you solve problems.

Some Helpful Strategies

- Represent the Problem
  - Draw a Picture or Strip Diagram
  - Write an Equation
  - Make a Table or List
- Look for a Pattern
- Use Reasoning
- Analyze Given Information
- Analyze Relationships

Problem-Solving Tools

Real Objects

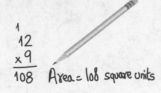

Manipulatives
Distance Walked

Lexi   50 yards

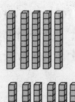

Michael   75 yards

Paper and Pencil

$$\begin{array}{r} 1 \\ 12 \\ \times\,9 \\ \hline 108 \end{array}$$

Area = 108 square units

Technology

Problem-Solving Techniques

Mental Math
Money Earned

Jeannie........$27
Kevin............$45
Wilson..........$37

$27 + 45 + 37 = ?$
$30 + 50 + 40 = 120$
$120 - 11 = 109$
$109

Estimation

A bamboo plant can grow 36 inches in a day.

There are 7 days in a week.
$7 \times 36 = ?$
About $7 \times 40 =$ 280 inches in a week.

Number Sense

Each number is between 100 and 200. The total will be between 400 and 800.

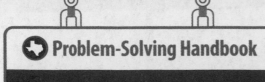

Problem-Solving Handbook

Strip Diagrams

You can draw a **strip diagram** to show how the quantities in a problem are related. Then, you can write an equation to solve the problem.

Part-Part-Whole: Addition and Subtraction

Draw this **strip diagram** for situations that involve joining different-sized parts of a whole or separating a whole into different-sized parts.

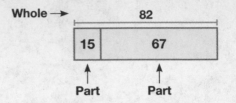

Problem 1

Greg had $43 and used it all to buy a baseball glove and a baseball. How much did he pay for the baseball?

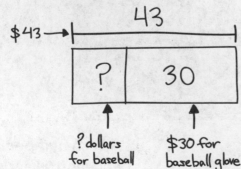

$43 - 30 = ?$ or $43 - ? = 30$

Greg paid $13 for the baseball.

Problem 2

Robin had some rings. She gave 56 of them to her sister. The rings below were left. How many rings did Robin have to begin with?

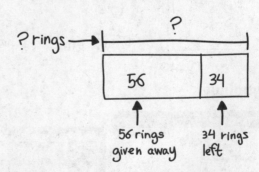

$56 + 34 = ?$ or $? - 56 = 34$

Robin had 90 rings to begin with.

Pictures help you understand.
Don't trust key words in a problem.

Comparison: Addition and Subtraction

Draw this **strip diagram** for comparison situations involving how much more one quantity is than another quantity.

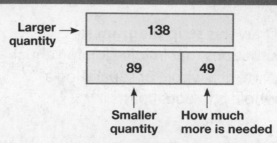

Larger quantity → 138

| 89 | 49 |

↑ Smaller quantity   ↑ How much more is needed

Problem 1

Two dogs together weigh 102 pounds. The smaller dog weighs 6 pounds. How many more pounds does the larger dog weigh?

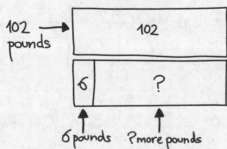

102 pounds → | 102 |

| 6 | ? |

↑ 6 pounds   ↑ ? more pounds

$102 - 6 = ?$

The larger dog weighs 96 more pounds.

Problem 2

Pedro has a collection of 30 postage stamps. Tim has 12 more postage stamps than Pedro. How many postage stamps does Tim have?

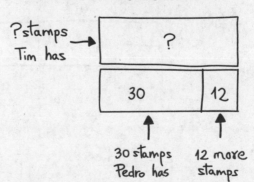

? stamps Tim has → | ? |

| 30 | 12 |

↑ 30 stamps Pedro has   ↑ 12 more stamps

$30 + 12 = ?$

Tim has 42 postage stamps.

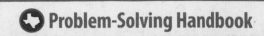
More Strip Diagrams

The **strip diagrams** on these pages can help you solve problems involving multiplication and division.

Equal Parts: Multiplication and Division

Draw this **strip diagram** for situations that involve joining equal parts of a whole or separating a whole into equal parts.

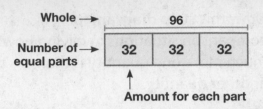

Whole → 96

Number of → 32 | 32 | 32
equal parts

↑ Amount for each part

Problem 1

Jack spent $40 on tickets to a movie for himself and some friends on Saturday. How many tickets did Jack buy?

Admit One — **$8** — Admit One

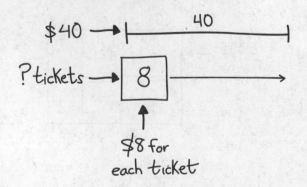

$40 → |——— 40 ———|

?tickets → [8] →

↑
$8 for each ticket

$40 \div 8 = ?$ or $8 \times ? = 40$

Jack bought 5 tickets.

Problem 2

Marie put all of her marbles in bags of 9 each and was able to fill 4 bags. How many marbles does Marie have?

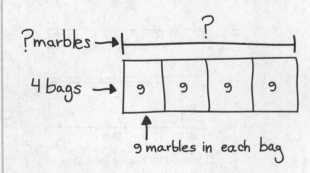

?marbles → |——— ? ———|

4 bags → | 9 | 9 | 9 | 9 |

↑
9 marbles in each bag

$4 \times 9 = ?$ or $? \div 4 = 9$

Marie has 36 marbles.

Multiplication and division are similar to addition and subtraction.

Comparison: Multiplication and Division

Draw this **strip diagram** for comparison situations involving how many times one quantity is of another quantity.

Larger quantity →
72		
24	24	24

3 times as many

Smaller quantity →
24

Problem 1

Kendra has a box with 60 toys in it. She has 5 times as many toys as Kent. How many toys does Kent have?

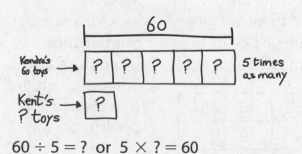

Kendra's 60 toys →
60				
?	?	?	?	?

5 times as many

Kent's ? toys →
?

$60 ÷ 5 = ?$ or $5 × ? = 60$

Kent has 12 toys.

Problem 2

The bar graph shows how far Lana drove her car for 3 days. On Tuesday, Kelly drove 5 times as far as Lana. How far did Kelly drive on Tuesday?

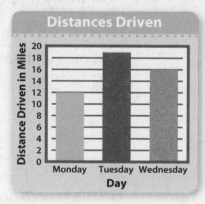

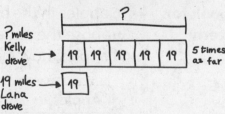

? miles Kelly drove →
?				
19	19	19	19	19

5 times as far

19 miles Lana drove →
19

$5 × 19 = ?$

Kelly drove 95 miles.

More Problem-Solving Strategies

Creating a solution plan involves choosing and trying a strategy and then sometimes trying a different strategy.

Strategy	Example	When I Use It
Draw a Picture	Marcia made a quilt. The width of the quilt is 6 feet. The perimeter of the quilt is 26 feet. What is the length of Marcia's quilt? Opposite sides of a rectangle have the same length. $26 = 6 + 6 + ? + ?$ $26 = 12 + ? + ?$ $14 = ? + ?$ $14 = 7 + 7$? ft 6 ft P = 26 ft The length of the quilt is 7 feet.	A **representation** of the problem can help you visualize the facts and identify relationships.
Write an Equation	Anu is putting 49 action figures on shelves. The figures are placed equally on 7 shelves. How many figures does Anu put on each shelf? Find $49 \div 7 = ?$. Anu puts 7 action figures on each shelf.	You can **communicate ideas** by writing an equation to describe a situation involving an operation or operations.
Make a Table and Look for a Pattern	Donna buys a box of apples. There are 16 apples in the box, and 4 of them are green. Suppose the pattern continues. If Donna buys 64 apples, how many of them will be green? <table><tr><td>Apples</td><td>16</td><td>32</td><td>48</td><td>64</td></tr><tr><td>Green Apples</td><td>4</td><td>8</td><td>12</td><td>?</td></tr></table> If Donna buys 64 apples, she will get 16 green apples.	Make a table and look for a number **relationship** when there are 2 or more quantities that change in a predictable way.

Strategy	Example	When I Use It
Use Reasoning	Carla's piano lesson lasted 30 minutes. Then, she walked to the library and spent 60 minutes studying. If Carla spent 105 minutes on all of her activities, how long did it take her to walk to the library? $\begin{array}{r} 30 \text{ minutes} \\ + 60 \text{ minutes} \\ \hline 90 \text{ minutes} \end{array}$ $\qquad$ $\begin{array}{r} 105 \text{ total minutes} \\ - 90 \text{ minutes} \\ \hline 15 \text{ minutes} \end{array}$ It took Carla 15 minutes to walk to the library.	**Reason** with the facts you know to find what actions cause the end result.
Analyze Given Information	Toni spent \$10 on art supplies. She bought two of one item and one of another item. What three items could Toni have bought? $\$3 + \$3 + \$2 = \$8$ Not enough $\$4 + \$4 + \$3 = \$11$ Too much $\$4 + \$4 + \$2 = \$10$ Perfect! Toni bought 2 scissors and 1 glue stick.	**Analyze given information** to help find a solution. 
Analyze Relationships	A necklace has green and blue beads. It has 2 times as many green beads as blue beads. The necklace has 5 blue beads. How many beads does the necklace have?  The necklace has 5 blue beads. It has 2 times 5 or 10 green beads. $10 + 5 = 15$ So, the necklace has 15 beads.	You can **analyze relationships** in information you are given to find unknown information.

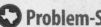
Problem-Solving Recording Sheet

This sheet helps you organize your work and make sense of problems.

Name **Gene**

Teaching Tool
1

Problem-Solving Recording Sheet

Problem:
Each week, for 5 weeks, Laura walked 18 miles. How many total miles did Laura walk?

ANALYZE		PLAN
Need to Find	**Know**	**Strategies**
How many total miles Laura walked.	Laura walked 18 miles each week for 5 weeks.	☐ Represent the Problem 　☑ Draw a Picture or Strip Diagram 　☑ Write an Equation 　☐ Make a Table or List ☐ Look for a Pattern ☐ Use Reasoning ☑ Analyze Given Information ☐ Analyze Relationships

SOLVE and JUSTIFY

Show Your Work and Answer.

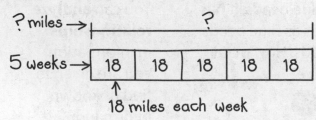

? miles → |⎯⎯⎯⎯⎯⎯⎯ ? ⎯⎯⎯⎯⎯⎯⎯|

5 weeks → | 18 | 18 | 18 | 18 | 18 |
　　　　　　↑
　　　18 miles each week

5 × 18 = ?

5 × 18 = 90

In 5 weeks, Laura walked 90 miles.

EVALUATE

Check Your Work. Is Your Answer Reasonable?

I can estimate. 18 is about 20. 5 × 20 = 100. The estimate, 100, is close to 90, so 90 is reasonable.

TT1

Copyright © Pearson Education, Inc., or its affiliates. All Rights Reserved. 3

Numeration

Essential Question: How are numbers read, written, compared, ordered, and rounded using place value?

The weather changes from day-to-day and from location-to-location.

Did you know the highest temperature ever recorded in Texas was 120 degrees Fahrenheit?

Give me some cold water because I think I'm melting! Here is a project on weather changes and ordering numbers.

Math and Science Project: Temperature Changes

Do Research Use the Internet or other sources to find and compare temperatures from different locations in Texas. Find temperature changes during each day and from day-to-day. To make your report more interesting, find record high and low temperatures from the same locations.

Journal: Write a Report Include what you found. Also in your report:

- Use the newspaper or a thermometer to find the temperature in your city for three days in a row.

- Record the temperatures in a table.

- Order the temperatures from least to greatest. Then, order them from greatest to least.

Review What You Know

Vocabulary

Choose the best term from the box. Write it on the blank.

> • equal shares
>
> • divide
>
> • division sentence
>
> • multiply

1. You can use ÷ to write a

_____ .

2. Dividing apples so everyone gets the same amount is an example of

_____ .

3. You can _____ to make equal groups.

Division as Sharing

4. Chen has 16 model cars. He puts them in 4 rows. Each row has an equal number of cars. How many model cars are in each row?

5. Julie has 24 glass beads to give to 4 friends. Each friend gets an equal share. How many glass beads does each friend get?

Division as Repeated Subtraction

Subtract until you reach 0 to solve the problem. Show your work.

6. Tony has 15 apples. He gives 3 apples to each friend. How many friends does Tony share the apples with?

Relating Multiplication and Division

7. There are 12 team members. They line up in 3 equal rows. How many are in each row?

8. Which multiplication sentence helps you solve the problem in Exercise 7?

A $2 \times 6 = 12$
B $1 \times 12 = 12$
C $3 \times 4 = 12$
D $3 \times 12 = 36$

9. **Explain** There are 20 bottles of juice lined up in 4 equal rows. Explain how you can use a multiplication sentence to find out how many bottles of juice are in each row.

My Word Cards

Use the examples for each word on the front of the card to help complete the definitions on the back.

digits

0, 1, 2, 3, 4, 5, 6, 7, 8, 9

place value

3,946

↑

hundreds

standard form

3,845

expanded form

2,476 = 2,000 + 400 + 70 + 6

word form

9,325 = nine thousand, three
hundred twenty-five

period

421,356,798

period

compare

42 < 50 or 42 is less than 50.

68 > 42 or 68 is greater than 42.

order

least to greatest
12, 57, 89

greatest to least
89, 57, 12

Complete each definition. Extend learning by writing your own definitions.

_____ is the value given to a place a digit has in a number.

The symbols used to write the numbers 0, 1, 2, 3, 4, 5, 6, 7, 8, and 9 are called

_____.

A number written as the sum of the values of its digits is written in

_____.

_____ is a way to write a number showing only its digits.

A group of three digits in a number, separated by a comma, is called a

_____.

A number written in words is written in

_____.

When you arrange numbers from least to greatest or from greatest to least, you are putting numbers in

_____.

When you _____ numbers, you decide if one number is greater than or less than another number.

© Pearson Education, Inc. 3

My Word Cards

Use the examples for each word on the front of the card to help complete the definitions on the back.

dollar sign

$6.47

decimal point

$4.11

round

42 rounded to the nearest 10 is 40.

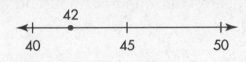

number line

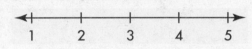

My Word Cards

The dot used to separate dollars from cents in money is called the

_____.

A _____ ($) is a symbol used to indicate money.

A line that shows numbers in order using a scale is called a _____.

When you _____, you replace a number with a number that tells about how much or how many to the nearest ten, hundred, thousand, and so on.

© Pearson Education, Inc. 3

Name _____

☆ ☆
Solve & Share

Use place-value blocks to show 274. Then, record three different ways you can write 274.

You can **create and use representations.** You can represent 274 many ways. *Show your work here and use digital tools to solve the problem.*

⊕ **TEKS 3.2A** Compose and decompose numbers up to 100,000 as a sum of so many ten thousands, so many thousands, so many hundreds, so many tens, and so many ones using objects, pictorial models, and numbers, including expanded notation as appropriate. Also, 3.2: **Mathematical Process Standards** 3.1B, 3.1C, 3.1D, 3.1E

Digital Resources at PearsonTexas.com

Solve   Learn   Glossary   Check   Tools   Games

Look Back!

Tools What other tools could you use to show 274?

How Can You Read and Write 3- and 4-Digit Numbers?

All numbers are made from the digits 0, 1, 2, 3, 4, 5, 6, 7, 8, and 9.

Place value is the value of the place a digit has in a number.

Did you know a two-humped camel weighs between 1,000 and 1,450 pounds?

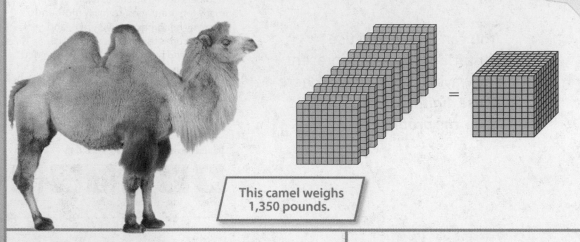

=

This camel weighs 1,350 pounds.

B You can show 1,350 in different ways.

You can use place-value blocks.

1 thousand   3 hundreds   5 tens   0 ones

C A number written in a way that shows only its digits is in standard form.

1,350

Write a comma between the thousands and the hundreds.

A number written as the sum of the values of its digits is in expanded form.

1,000 + 300 + 50

A number written in words is in word form.

one thousand, three hundred fifty

Do You Understand?

Convince Me! John said, "The numbers and pictures below show the number 3,247." Is John correct? Explain.

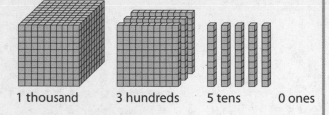

three hundred + 40 +   + 7 ones

© Pearson Education, Inc. 3

Another Example

How can you show 1,350 on a place-value chart?

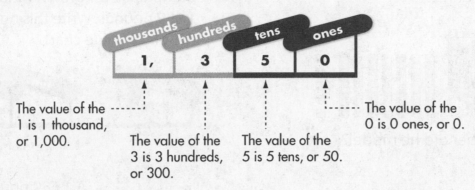

The value of the 1 is 1 thousand, or 1,000.

The value of the 3 is 3 hundreds, or 300.

The value of the 5 is 5 tens, or 50.

The value of the 0 is 0 ones, or 0.

☆ Guided Practice *

In **1** and **2**, write each number in standard form.

1.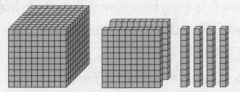

2. **Tools** Write a 4-digit number that has a tens digit of 5, a hundreds digit of 2, and 6 for each of the other digits. Use place-value blocks to help you.

Independent Practice ☆

For **3** and **4**, write each number in standard form.

3.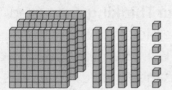

4.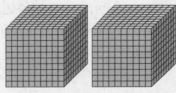

For **5** and **6**, write each number in expanded form and word form.

5. 326 _____

6. 5,163 _____

7. Luis modeled a number using these ⭐ place-value blocks.

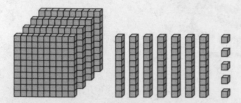

Which number did he model?

A   5,750

B   4,750

C   574

D   475

8. Represent One of the largest pumpkins ever grown weighed 1,689 pounds. Write this number in the place-value chart.

 A 1,689 pound pumpkin weighs almost 1 ton! One ton is 2,000 pounds.

9. Analyze Information Cora sent two thousand, four hundred twenty-five text messages last summer. Evan sent 100 more text messages. Write the number of text messages Evan sent in expanded form.

10. The number 2,406 written in word ⭐ form is two thousand, four hundred six. How do you write the number in expanded form?

A   2,000 + 400 + 10 + 6

B   2,000 + 400 + 60

C   2,000 + 400 + 6

D   2,000 + 40 + 6

11. Leo has 4 toothpicks. He places them as shown. What shape can Leo make if he adds one more toothpick?

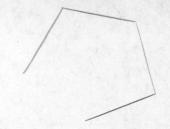

12. Extend Your Thinking Sam used place-value blocks to show the number 3,124. Then, he added two more thousands blocks. What was the new number? Explain.

© Pearson Education, Inc. 3

Name _____

Another Look!

Did you know there are different ways to show 2,365?

place-value blocks:

expanded form: 2,000 + 300 + 60 + 5

standard form: 2,365

word form: two thousand, three hundred sixty-five

In **1** through **3**, write each number in standard form.

1.

2.

3.

In **4** through **7**, write each number in expanded and word form.

4. 1,240 _____

5. 6,381 _____

6. 4,457 _____

7. 7,823 _____

8. Which of the following is 100 more ★ than 8,040?

   A eight hundred forty

   B eight thousand, forty

   C eight thousand, one hundred forty

   D eight thousand, four hundred

9. Tools Jason arranged the digits 4, 7, 2, and 6 to make the greatest possible number. Does the model show Jason's number? Explain.

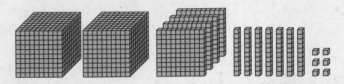

10. Mental Math Emilia has 175 stickers in her collection. She wants to add 500 more stickers. Write the new number of stickers in expanded form.

11. Math and Science In 1936, the temperature was 120 degrees Fahrenheit in Seymour, Texas. Write 1936 in expanded and word form.

12. Analyze Information Will said the number in the place-value chart in expanded form is 6,000 + 300 + 80 + 4. Is he right? Explain.

13. Extend Your Thinking An arena can seat seven thousand, forty-eight people. Two thousand seats are being added. Write the new number of seats in standard form and word form.

14. Write the total number of seats, old and new combined, in expanded form.

Coming Soon! 2,000 More Seats

© Pearson Education, Inc. 3

Name _____

Solve & Share

How can you use place-value blocks to show 1,500 in two different ways? Model each way you find with blocks. Draw a picture of each model and then record each in word form.

You can **create and use representations.** You can represent 1,500 many ways. *Show your work in the space below!*

TEKS 3.2A Compose and decompose numbers up to 100,000 as a sum of so many ten thousands, so many thousands, so many hundreds, so many tens, and so many ones using objects, pictorial models, and numbers, including expanded notation as appropriate. Also, 3.2B. **Mathematical Process Standards** 3.1B, 3.1C, 3.1D, 3.1E, 3.1F, 3.1G

Digital Resources at PearsonTexas.com

Solve   Learn   Glossary   Check   Tools   Games

Look Back!

Connect How are 10 hundreds blocks related to 1 thousands block?

How Can You Name a Number Using Thousands, Hundreds, Tens, and Ones?

The Sunshine Skyway Bridge crosses Tampa Bay, Florida. The length of its longest span is shown in the picture. What are some different ways to name this number?

Place value can be used to name numbers in different ways.

You can use thousands and hundreds.

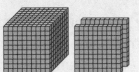

1,200 feet

one thousand, two hundred

B You can use only hundreds.

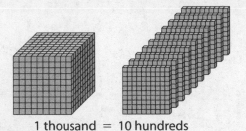

1 thousand = 10 hundreds

twelve hundreds

C You can use only tens.

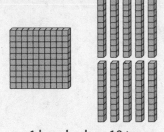

1 hundred = 10 tens

one hundred twenty tens

D You can use only ones.

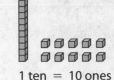

1 ten = 10 ones

one thousand, two hundred ones

Do You Understand?

Convince Me! How would you show 2,500 using only hundreds blocks?
How would you show 2,500 using exactly seven blocks?

© Pearson Education, Inc. 3

☆ Guided Practice ☆

The model shows a number. Name the number in four ways.

1.
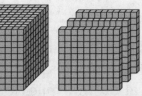

2. **Reason** In the example about the Sunshine Skyway Bridge, how are the four names for 1,200 the same? How are they different?

Independent Practice ☆

For **3** and **4**, the model shows a number. Name the number in four ways.

3.
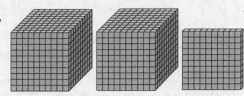

4.
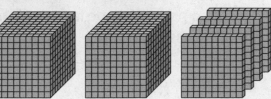

For **5** through **8**, name each number using thousands and hundreds. Then name the number using only hundreds.

5. 5,200 _____

6. 6,500 _____

7. 9,800 _____

8. 1,800 _____

Problem Solving

Use the table at the right for **9** and **10**.

9. **Analyze Information** Beth wrote down the address she heard: three thousand, nine hundred Allen Street. Which place has this address?

10. Write two other names for the address number in the problem above.

DATA	Place	Address
	Ace Sporting Goods	1518 Allen Street
	Central Post Office	15008 Allen Street
	Gibson's Market	3900 Allen Street
	Tops Bowling Center	15108 Allen Street

11. **Explain** Ana said, "I was born in the year two thousand." Write the number to name the year. How does a number that names a year look different from a 4-digit number in standard form?

12. **Number Sense** There are 7,700 lakes in Florida that cover more than ten acres. Write two names for the number of lakes.

13. **Number Sense** Look at the model. ★ Which additional blocks do you need to make the number 2,300?

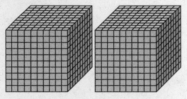

   A 2 hundreds blocks
   B 3 hundreds blocks
   C 4 hundreds blocks
   D 5 hundreds blocks

14. **Extend Your Thinking** The Rio Grande is about 1,900 miles long. The Mississippi River is about 400 miles longer. Write two names for the length of the Mississippi River.

15. **Extend Your Thinking** Miko says she can model 3,200 with 3 thousands blocks and 20 tens blocks. Is Miko correct? Explain.

16. **Personal Financial Literacy** Sheila started a Happy Helpers business. She helps people in her neighborhood. Last week, Sheila helped 3 neighbors pull weeds in their gardens. Sheila was paid $10 by each neighbor she helped. How much did Sheila earn last week?

© Pearson Education, Inc. 3

Name _____

Another Look!

Did you know you can name 1,600 in different ways?

Regroup 1 thousand as 10 hundreds.

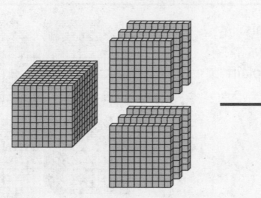

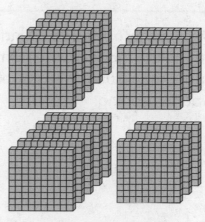

one thousand, six hundred

sixteen hundreds

For **1** and **2**, use thousands and hundreds, then hundreds only to name each number.

1.

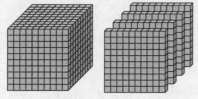

_____ thousand, _____ hundred

_____ hundreds

2.

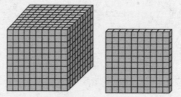

_____ thousand, _____ hundred

_____ hundreds

For **3** through **6**, name each number in two ways.

3. 3,200

4. 5,700

5. 3,600

6. 4,300

7. **Reason** Martin needs two thousand, five hundred toothpicks for a project. He has twenty-three hundred toothpicks. Does he have enough toothpicks? Explain your reasoning.

8. The Coopers live at one thousand, seven hundred South Central Avenue. Write the number for the Coopers' address in standard and expanded forms.

9. **Analyze Information** Henri told his friend the model to the right shows more than 6,000. Is he correct? Explain your reasoning.

10. **Explain** Jonesborough, Tennessee, was founded in 1779. Write this year in word form.

11. **Number Sense** What is one way to write 100 years from the year 1800 in word form?

    A eighteen hundred
    B nineteen hundred
    C nine thousand
    D nineteen thousand

12. **Extend Your Thinking** Darcy uses place-value blocks to show a number. She uses 4 thousands blocks and 5 hundreds blocks. What is the number? How can Darcy use different place-value blocks to show the number another way? Explain.

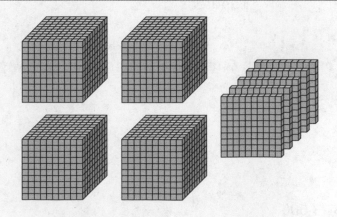

© Pearson Education, Inc. 3

Name _____

☆ ★ ☆
Solve & Share

The news reported 95,687 people watched the parade. Record 95,687 in the place-value chart below. Use the place-value chart to help write the number in word and expanded forms.

TEKS 3.2A Compose and decompose numbers up to 100,000 as a sum of so many ten thousands, so many thousands, so many hundreds, so many tens, and so many ones using objects, pictorial models, and numbers, including expanded notation as appropriate. Also, 3.2B. **Mathematical Process Standards** 3.1B, 3.1C, 3.1D, 3.1E, 3.1G

You can **create and use representations.** You can represent 95,687 many ways.

Digital Resources at PearsonTexas.com

 Solve   Learn   A-Z Glossary   Check   Tools   Games

thousands period
ones period

hundred thousands | ten thousands | one thousands | hundreds | tens | ones

Word form

_____

Expanded form

_____

Look Back!

Tools How does a place-value chart help you write a number in word form?

A

Great Sand Dunes National Park and Preserve in Colorado covers 85,932 acres of land.

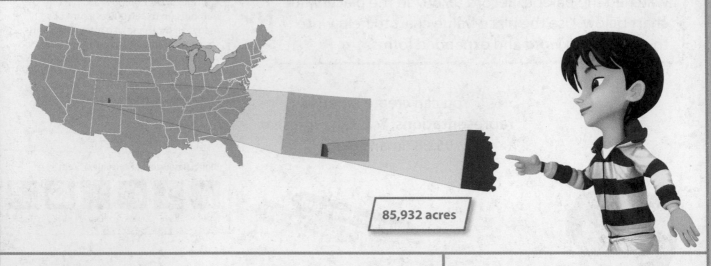

85,932 acres

B How can you read, write, and name 85,932 in different ways?

place-value chart:

A period is a group of 3 digits in a number, starting from the right.

thousands period   ones period

hundred thousands | ten thousands | one thousands | hundreds | tens | ones

| 8 | 5, | 9 | 3 | 2 |

Two periods are separated by a comma.

C **standard form:**
85,932

expanded form:
80,000 + 5,000 + 900 + 30 + 2

word form:
eighty-five thousand, nine hundred thirty-two

Do You Understand?

Convince Me! What number is shown below? Write the number in standard form. Use a place-value chart to help.

six hundred + 3 ones + 8 thousand + 70 + forty thousand

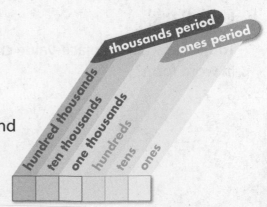

© Pearson Education, Inc. 3

Another Example

You can name 800,000 in different ways.

800,000 is 8 hundred thousands.

800,000 is 80 ten thousands.

800,000 is 800 thousands.

800,000 is 8,000 hundreds.

800,000 is 80,000 tens.

800,000 is 800,000 ones.

☆ Guided Practice *

In **1** through **4**, write each number in standard form.

1. forty-two thousand, six hundred seven

2. ninety-eight thousand, three hundred twenty

3. 20,000 + 600 + 90 + 3

4. 70,000 + 8,000 + 700 + 40 + 2

5. **Check for Reasonableness** Raymond says the value of the digit 5 in 65,420 is 50,000. Do you agree? Why or why not?

6. **Explain** Describe how 30,434 and 43,403 are alike and how they are different.

Independent Practice

7. Write this number in standard form.

   twenty-seven thousand, five hundred fifty

8. Write this number in expanded form.

   46,374

9. Find the missing number.

   30,000 + _____ + 600 + 3 = 34,603

10. Find the missing number.

    80,000 + 3,000 + _____ + 20 + 1 = 83,921

11. Find the missing numbers.

    20,000 + _____ + _____ = 22,300

12. Find the missing numbers.

    _____ + 400 + _____ = 50,412

13. Analyze Information Write the population of each city in the table in expanded form and word form.

City Populations	
City	**Number of People**
Allen, TX	84,246
Pecos, TX	8,780
Friendswood, TX	35,805

14. Tools What is the time that is halfway between the two times shown on the clocks?

15. Communicate How many flat surfaces, edges, and vertices does a cylinder have?

16. ★ Which is the word form of the number 45,920?

A four thousand, nine hundred ninety-two

B forty thousand, nine hundred twenty

C forty-five thousand, ninety-two

D forty-five thousand, nine hundred twenty

17. Extend Your Thinking Mount Everest is the tallest mountain in the world. It is twenty-nine thousand, thirty-five feet high. Write the height of Mount Everest in standard form. Give the value of each digit.

© Pearson Education, Inc. 3

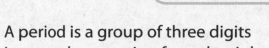

Another Look!

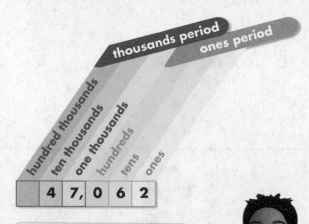

4 7, 0 6 2

A comma is used to separate two periods.

A period is a group of three digits in a number, starting from the right.

Here are different ways to show 47,062.

expanded form: 40,000 + 7,000 + 60 + 2

standard form: 47,062

word form: forty-seven thousand, sixty-two

1. Write 98,326 in a place-value chart, and then write it in expanded, standard, and word forms.

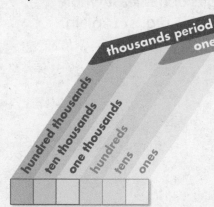

expanded form: 90,000 + _____ + 300 + _____ + 6

standard form: 9 _____, _____, 2 _____

word form: ninety-eight thousand, three hundred

_____

For **2** through **4**, write each number in standard form.

2. 8,000 + 200 + 50 + 1   **3.** 30,000 + 600 + 30 + 2   **4.** twenty-nine thousand, three hundred seventy-eight

For **5** through **7**, write each number in expanded form.

5. 22,438   **6.** 49,281   **7.** 86,752

8. Number Sense The area of Lake Ontario is 18,960 square kilometers. Write the area of Lake Ontario in expanded and word forms.

9. Number Sense ⭐ How many hundreds are in 50,000?

A 0 hundreds
B 50 hundreds
C 500 hundreds
D 5,000 hundreds

10. Draw a Picture Draw the plane shape that all three solid figures have in common.

11. ⭐ Which is the word form of 28,309?

A twenty-eight thousand, three hundred ninety

B twenty-eight hundred, thirty hundred nine

C twenty-eight thousand, three hundred nine

D twenty-eight thousand, thirty-nine

12. Extend Your Thinking Which is greater, the greatest whole number with 4 digits or the least whole number with 5 digits? Explain.

13. Big Bend National Park in Texas covers a large number of acres of land. What is the value of the 8 in the number of acres?

14. Extend Your Thinking Write how many hundred thousands, ten thousands, and thousands there are in the number of acres of land Big Bend National Park covers.

Welcome to Big Bend National Park
801,163 acres

© Pearson Education, Inc. 3

Name _____

Solve & Share

What is the relationship between the value of the first 5 and the value of the second 5 in 5,500? *Solve this problem any way you choose.*

 TEKS 3.2B Describe the mathematical relationships found in the base-10 place value system through the hundred thousands place. Also, 3.2. **Mathematical Process Standards** 3.1B, 3.1C, 3.1D, 3.1F, 3.1G

Digital Resources at PearsonTexas.com

Solve   Learn   Glossary   Check   Tools   Games

You can **analyze relationships.** You can analyze the relationship between place values.

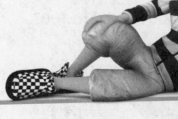

Look Back!

Reason Describe two ways 5,000 and 500 are related. How do you know?

How Are the Digits in a Multi-Digit Number Related to Each Other?

A-Z

Kiana collected 1,100 bottle caps. What is the relationship between the values of the digit 1 in each place?

1,100 bottle caps

B

1,100

The first 1 is in the thousands place. Its value is 1,000.

The second 1 is in the hundreds place. Its value is 100.

How is 1,000 related to 100?

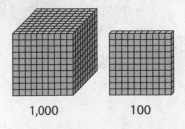

1,000   100

C

1,000 is ten times as much as 100.

The 1 in the thousands place is ten times as great as the 1 in the hundreds place.

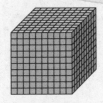

10 hundreds   1 hundred

When two digits next to each other in a number are the same, the digit on the left is always ten times as great as the digit on the right.

Do You Understand?

Convince Me! Is the value of the first 4 ten times as great as the value of the second 4 in 4,043? Explain why or why not.

 © Pearson Education, Inc. 3

Another Example

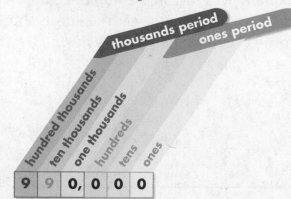

The first 9 is in the hundred-thousands place. Its value is 900,000.

The second 9 is in the ten-thousands place. Its value is 90,000.

The value of the first 9 is ten times as great as the value of the second 9.

☆ Guided Practice *

In **1** through **3**, what is the relationship between the values of the given digits?

1. the 7s in 7,700

2. the 4s in 440,200

3. the 5s in 430,552

4. Reason Is the value of the first 5 ten times as great as the value of the second 5 in 5,045? Explain.

5. Explain Is the value of the 2 in 23,406 ten times as great as the value of the 3 in the same number? Explain.

☆ Independent Practice ☆

For **6** through **9**, name the values of the given digits in each number.

6. the 2s in 6,228   **7.** the 5s in 55,714   **8.** the 4s in 14,423   **9.** the 8s in 880,000

Problem Solving

10. Communicate What can you say about the 3s in the number 43,335?

11. Explain Mia says in the number 5,555, all the digits have the same value. Is she correct? Explain why or why not.

12. ⭐ Which of the following names the value of the 4s in the number 44,492?

A 40,000; 4,000; 400

B 40,000; 400; 40

C 4,000; 400; 4

D 400; 40; 4

13. Name the shape. Tell how many sides, angles, and vertices it has.

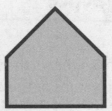

14. Find the area of the shaded rectangle.

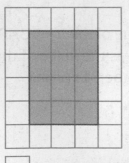

☐ = 1 square unit

15. Number Sense In 1934, there was an extreme drought in the Great Plains. In the number 1934, is the value of the 9 in the hundreds place ten times the value of the 3 in the tens place? Explain.

16. Extend Your Thinking In the number 77,532, if you move from the 7 in the ten-thousands place to the 7 in the thousands place, what happens to the value of the 7?

17. Explain Vin says in the number 4,346, one 4 is 10 times as great as the other 4. Is he correct? Explain why or why not.

© Pearson Education, Inc. 3

Name _____

Another Look!

In the number 3,300, what is the relationship between the value of the digit 3 in each place?

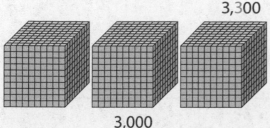

3,300

3,000   300

The first 3 is in the thousands place. Its value is 3,000.

The second 3 is in the hundreds place. Its value is 300.

When two digits next to each other in a number are the same, the digit on the left is always 10 times as great as the digit on the right.

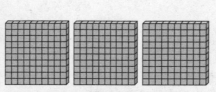

Since 3,000 is ten times as great as 300, the first 3 has a value 10 times greater than the second 3.

1. Write the value of the hundreds and the value of the tens in the number 440. What is the relationship between the value of the digit 4 in each place?

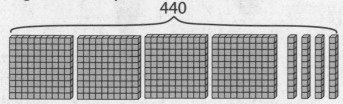

440

_____   _____

The _____ in the hundreds place has a value _____ times greater than the _____ in the _____ place.

For **2** and **3**, name the values of the given digits.

2. the 4s in 4,400

3. the 8s in 88,000

For **4** and **5**, write the relationship between the values of the given digits.

4. the 6s in 6,600

5. the 4s in 44,000

6. Analyze Information What is the relationship between the 6s in the number 660,472?

7. Reason Is the relationship between the 7s in 7,742 and the 7s in 7,785 different in any way? Explain why or why not.

8. Analyze Information List the children in order from the one who sold the most cups of lemonade to the one who sold the fewest cups of lemonade.

9. How many cups of lemonade were sold in all?

10. ★ Which of the following names the value of the 5s in the number 15,573?

   A 500 and 5
   B 500 and 50
   C 5,000 and 50
   D 5,000 and 500

11. Extend Your Thinking In your own words, explain the place-value relationship when the same two digits are next to each other in a multi-digit number.

12. Name the value of each 2 in the number 222,222.

13. Maria said, "The 4 in 400,000 has a value of 400." Is Maria correct? Explain.

© Pearson Education, Inc. 3

Name _____

Solve & Share

The school store has 345 red pens and 380 blue pens. Are there more red or more blue pens?

thousands period

ones period

hundred thousands
ten thousands
one thousands
hundreds
tens
ones

⭐ **TEKS 3.2D** Compare and order whole numbers up to 100,000 and represent comparisons using the symbols >, <, or =. Also, 3.2.
Mathematical Process Standards 3.1B, 3.1C, 3.1D, 3.1F, 3.1G

Digital Resources at PearsonTexas.com

Solve   Learn   Glossary   Check   Tools   Games

You can **analyze relationships.** You can analyze the relationship between place values with place-value blocks or a place-value chart.

Look Back!

Tools How do place-value blocks and place-value charts help you compare two different numbers?

How Do You Compare Numbers?

A

Which is taller, the Statue of Liberty or its base?

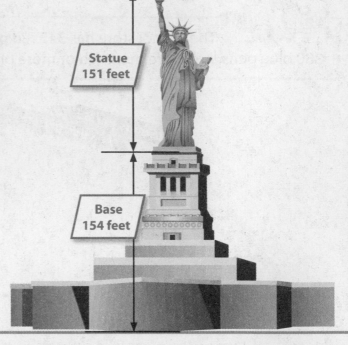

Statue
151 feet

Base
154 feet

When you compare two numbers you find which number is greater and which number is less.

You can use symbols to compare numbers.
< is less than
> is greater than
= is equal to

B You can compare 151 and 154 with place value.

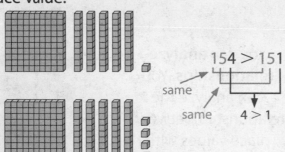

The place-value blocks also show 151 is **less than** 154.

151 < 154

C On the number line, 151 is to the left of 154. So, 151 is **less than** 154.

151 < 154

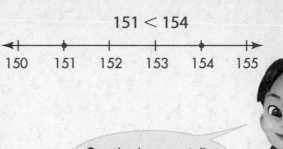

So, the base is taller than the statue!

Do You Understand?

Convince Me! Write one of the numbers below on each line to make true statements. Can you do it a different way? Explain.

2,314   2,413   1,234   4,321

_____ > _____   _____ < _____

34

© Pearson Education, Inc. 3

Another Example

To compare 23,456 and 23,482 on a place-value chart, line up the digits by place value. Compare the digits starting from the left.

Both numbers have a 2 in the ten-thousands place, a 3 in the thousands place, and a 4 in the hundreds place. 23,456 has 5 tens while 23,482 has 8 tens.

23,456 < 23,482

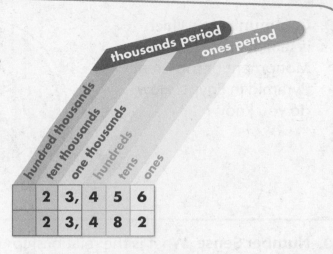

☆ Guided Practice *

For **1** through **4**, compare the numbers. Use <, >, or =.

1.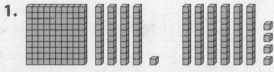

   141 ◯ 64

2.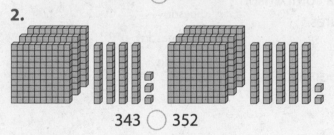

   343 ◯ 352

3. 2,561 ◯ 2,261   4. 23,458 ◯ 32,458

5. **Check for Reasonableness** Cara says since 4 is greater than 1, the number 496 is greater than the number 1,230. Do you agree? Why or why not?

6. Draw a number line to compare the numbers.

   1,462 ◯ 1,521

Independent Practice ☆

Leveled Practice In **7** and **8**, compare the numbers. Use <, >, or =.

7.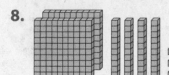

   93 ◯ 120

8.

   243 ◯ 234

Problem Solving

9. Communicate Which is taller, the Washington Monument or the Great Pyramid in Egypt? How do you know?

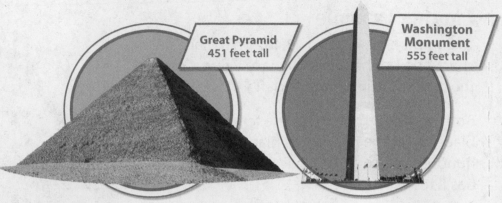

Great Pyramid 451 feet tall

Washington Monument 555 feet tall

---

10. Number Sense What is the relationship between the 5s in the number 75,532?

11. Reason Mark is thinking of a 4-digit number. Rory is thinking of a 5-digit number. Whose number is greater? How do you know?

In **12** and **13**, use the table at the right.

12. Math and Science Gemma recorded the temperatures at noon in Austin, Texas, for five days. Write a comparison between the highest and lowest temperatures.

13. On which days was the temperature at noon less than 89°F?

Temperatures in Austin, Texas	
Day	**Temperature (°F)**
Monday	87°F
Tuesday	92°F
Wednesday	91°F
Thursday	86°F
Friday	89°F

DATA

---

14. Which number sentence is true if the number 1,537 replaces the box?

A 1,456 > ☐

B ☐ = 1,256

C 1,598 < ☐

D ☐ > 1,357

< means less than.
> means greater than.

15. Extend Your Thinking Suppose you are comparing 12,725 and 12,639. Do you need to compare the tens digits? Which number would be farther to the right on the number line? Explain.

© Pearson Education, Inc. 3

Name _____

Another Look!

Use these symbols to compare numbers.

< less than   > greater than   = equal to

Compare 375 and 353.

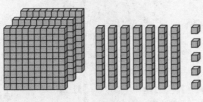   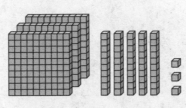

375   353

Both have the same number of hundreds.
Compare the tens. 375 has more tens.

375 is greater than 353.
375 > 353

1. Compare 237 and 273.

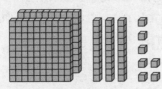

237 _____ 273

2. Compare 1,345 and 1,337.

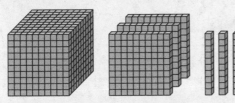

1,345 _____ 1,337

For **3** through **10**, compare the numbers. Use <, >, or =.

3. 842 ◯ 824   **4.** 4,669 ◯ 4,705   **5.** 7,305 ◯ 7,305   **6.** 1,100 ◯ 998

7. 12,586 ◯ 12,568   **8.** 43,567 ◯ 45,567   **9.** 9,654 ◯ 32,654   **10.** 5,436 ◯ 5,436

11. Reason Write a 5-digit number greater than 99,988.

12. Communicate Every digit in 798 is greater than any digit in 4,325. Explain why 4,325 is greater than 798.

13. Explain Which is taller: the Gateway Arch or the Space Needle? How do you know?

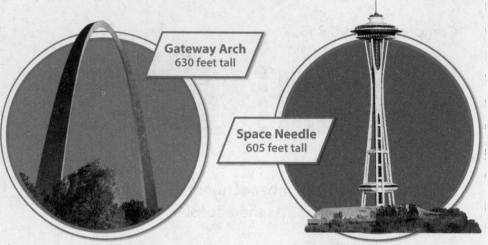

Gateway Arch
630 feet tall

Space Needle
605 feet tall

14. ⭐ Which statement is true about the numbers 56,372 and 56,327?

A 56,372 = 56,327 because the same five digits appear in each number.

B 56,372 > 56,327 because 7 tens > 2 tens.

C 56,372 < 56,327 because 2 tens < 7 tens.

D 56,327 = 56,327 because the numbers are identical.

15. If Mark has a piano lesson 30 minutes after the time shown on the clock, what time is his lesson?

16. Extend Your Thinking Which has a greater distance: Rapid City to Miami or Portland to Little Rock? Which digits did you use to compare?

Distance in Miles	
New York, NY, to Rapid City, SD	1,701
Rapid City, SD, to Miami, FL	2,167
Miami, FL, to Seattle, WA	3,334
Portland, OR, to Little Rock, AR	2,217

© Pearson Education, Inc. 3

Name _____

Solve & Share

Here are heights, in feet, for three of the world's highest waterfalls. Arrange the heights in order from greatest to least, then least to greatest. *Solve this problem any way you choose.*

TEKS 3.2D Compare and order whole numbers up to 100,000 and represent comparisons using the symbols >, <, or =. **Mathematical Process Standards** 3.1B, 3.1C, 3.1D, 3.1E, 3.1G

Digital Resources at PearsonTexas.com

Solve | Learn | Glossary | Check | Tools | Games

You can **formulate a plan.** You can use place value to formulate a plan for comparing and ordering numbers.

From greatest to least

_____

_____

_____

From least to greatest

_____

_____

_____

DATA	Waterfall	Height (in feet)
	Tugela Falls	3,110
	Yosemite Falls	2,425
	Angel Falls	3,212

Look Back!

Explain Will your problem-solving strategy work when comparing numbers such as 55,423 and 5,423? Explain.

How Can You Order Numbers?

Three vehicle weights, in pounds, are recorded in the table.

Vehicle	Weight (in pounds)
Bulldozer	13,500
Garbage Truck	36,000
Ambulance	13,800

DATA

When you order numbers, you write them from greatest to least or from least to greatest.

Write the weights in order from greatest to least.

B You can use a place-value chart to help you.

hundred thousands	ten thousands	thousands	hundreds	tens	ones
	1	3,	5	0	0
	3	6,	0	0	0
	1	3,	8	0	0

3 > 1
so, 36,000
is the greatest
number.

3 = 3

5 < 8
so, 13,500
is the least
number.

C The vehicle weights in order from greatest to least are:

Garbage Truck: 36,000 pounds
Ambulance: 13,800 pounds
Bulldozer: 13,500 pounds

Do You Understand?

Convince Me! Use all of the numerals 3, 4, 5, 6, and 7 to make three 5-digit numbers. Arrange your numbers from least to greatest.

© Pearson Education, Inc. 3

☆ Guided Practice*

Use the place-value chart to order the numbers in Exercise **1** from least to greatest.

1. 11,573   11,137   12,457

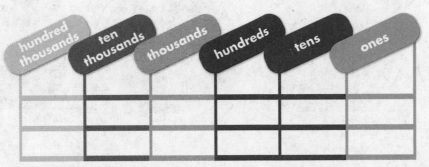

2. Construct Arguments The Colorado River is 1,450 miles long. The length of another river has a 2 in the hundreds place. Can this river be longer, in miles, than the Colorado River? Explain.

3. Reason Show the numbers 315; 305; and 319 in order on the number line below.

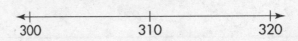
300   310   320

Independent Practice ☆

Leveled Practice In **4** through **7**, order the numbers from greatest to least.

4. 16,743   26,930   16,395

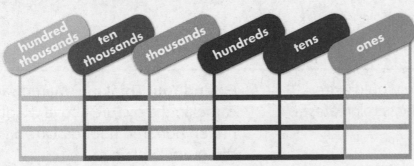

5. 1,293   995   1,932

6. 18,754   17,792   18,700

7. 35,304   35,430   3,403

8. Represent Show 1,020; 965; and 985 in order on the number line below.

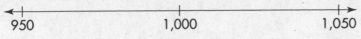
950   1,000   1,050

Problem Solving

For **9** and **10**, use the pictures below.

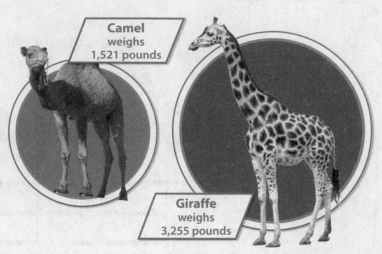

Camel weighs 1,521 pounds

Grizzly Bear weighs 550 pounds

Moose weighs 1,421 pounds

Giraffe weighs 3,255 pounds

9. **Analyze Information** Which animal weighs 100 pounds more than a moose?

10. A ton is equal to 2,000 pounds. Which animals weigh less than 1 ton?

11. **Reason** Corky's truck weighs more than Jane's truck. Jane's truck weighs less than Kinsey's truck. Which of the following could be the truck weights in order from greatest to least?

  A Jane's truck, Kinsey's truck, Corky's truck

  B Kinsey's truck, Jane's truck, Corky's truck

  C Corky's truck, Kinsey's truck, Jane's truck

  D Jane's truck, Corky's truck, Kinsey's truck

12. I have 4 sides. The lengths of all my sides are equal. Which shape am I?

13. **Explain** Describe how you would write the numbers below from least to greatest.

  3,456   3,654   2,375

14. **Extend Your Thinking** Margo says the camel in the picture above weighs about fifteen hundred pounds. Do you agree or disagree? Explain.

© Pearson Education, Inc. 3

Name _____

Another Look!

You can use place value to order numbers.

Order these numbers from least to greatest.

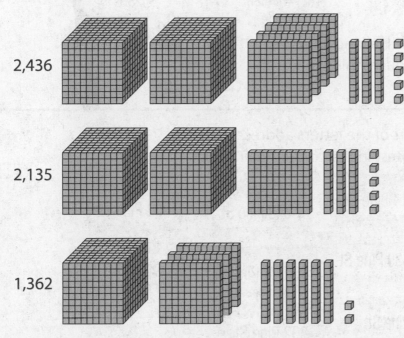

2,436

2,135

1,362

Compare the thousands.
1 thousand < 2 thousands, so 1,362 is the least number.

Compare the hundreds in the remaining two numbers.
4 hundreds > 1 hundred, so 2,436 is the greatest number.

From least to greatest, the order is:

1,362   2,135   2,436
least   greatest

In **1** and **2**, order the numbers from least to greatest.

1. 4,560   4,483   4,652

2. 23,658   23,104   23,367

In **3** and **4**, order the numbers from greatest to least.

3. 5,626   5,636   5,716

4. 12,432   12,198   13,989

In **5** and **6**, use the table at the right.

5. Write the names of the roller coasters in order from shortest to longest.

6. Write the lengths of the roller coasters, in feet, in order from longest to shortest.

Roller Coaster	Length (in ft)
Boss Eureka, Missouri	5,051
Chang Louisville, Kentucky	4,155
Titan Arlington, Texas	5,312

DATA

In **7** and **8**, use the table at the right.

7. Analyze Information New Hampshire has a land area of 8,968 square miles. Which states in the table have a greater land area than New Hampshire?

8. Number Sense Name the state with a land area that is between 7,420 and 7,850 square miles.

Land Areas (in square miles)	
State	**Land Area**
Maryland	9,774
Massachusetts	7,840
New Jersey	7,417
Vermont	9,250

DATA

9. Number Sense Write the numbers of the letters addressed to Pine St. in order from least to greatest in the correct mail bags.

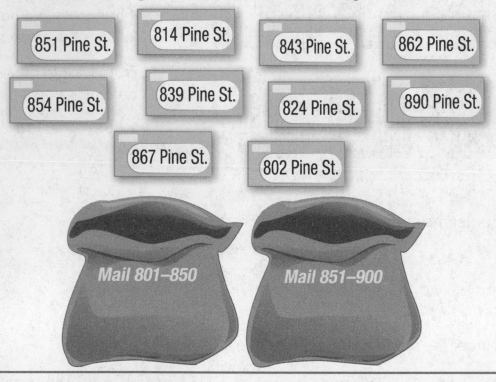

851 Pine St.

814 Pine St.

843 Pine St.

862 Pine St.

854 Pine St.

839 Pine St.

824 Pine St.

890 Pine St.

867 Pine St.

802 Pine St.

Mail 801–850

Mail 851–900

10. You are comparing 4,730 to 4,820. In which places are the digits different?

   A The hundreds place and ones place

   B The thousands place and hundreds place

   C The hundreds place and tens place

   D The thousands place and ones place

11. Extend Your Thinking The Amazon River is 4,000 miles long. The Yangtze River is 3,964 miles long, and the Nile River is 4,145 miles long. Write the steps you would use to order the lengths of the rivers, in miles, from greatest to least.

© Pearson Education, Inc. 3

Name _____

Solve & Share

Lindy bought vegetables for 6 dollars and 91 cents. List ways you can make 6 dollars and 91 cents using bills and coins. *Solve this problem any way you choose.*

TEKS 3.4C Determine the value of a collection of coins and bills. Mathematical Process Standards 3.1A, 3.1B, 3.1C, 3.1D, 3.1E, 3.1F, 3.1G

Digital Resources at PearsonTexas.com

 Solve   Learn   Glossary   Check   Tools   Games

DATA

5 dollars	**1 dollar**	**25 cents**	**10 cents**	**5 cents**	**1 cent**

You can **use representations.** A data table is one way to record the ways you find.

Look Back!

Communicate Examine your solutions. Which combinations are you likely to use to pay a bill?

How Do You Count Money?

A

Greg has the money shown below. Does he have enough money to buy the toy giraffe?

B

A dollar sign shows money amounts.

$1.95

A decimal point separates dollars and cents.

C

Here are some familiar bills and coins.

5 dollars
$5 or $5.00

1 dollar
$1 or $1.00

half dollar
50¢ or $0.50

quarter
25¢ or $0.25

dime
10¢ or $0.10

nickel
5¢ or $0.05

penny
1¢ or $0.01

D

To count money, start with the bill or coin of greatest value. Then count on to find the total value.

$1.00 → $1.50 → $1.75 → $1.85 → **$1.90**

Write: $1.90
Say: one dollar and ninety cents

No, Greg does not have enough money.

Do You Understand?

Convince Me! Shawn says, "I can show $1.75 using only quarters." Is she correct? Explain.

© Pearson Education, Inc. 3

Another Example

How can you show $2.56 in different ways?

One way

$1.00 $2.00 $2.25 $2.50 $2.55   **$2.56**

Another way

$1.00 $1.50 $2.00 $2.25 $2.35 $2.45 $2.55   **$2.56**

☆ Guided Practice*

In **1** and **2**, count on to find the total value.

1.

$0.50 $0.75   _____ _____ _____

2.

$1.00   _____

3. Analyze Information What coins and bills could you use to show $2.65 two ways?

4. Number Sense If you have 195 pennies, do you have enough money to buy the toy giraffe that Greg wanted?

Independent Practice ☆

In **5** and **6**, write the total value in dollars and cents.

5.

6. 1 one-dollar bill, 2 half dollars, 1 quarter, 4 dimes, 4 nickels

Problem Solving

7. Number Sense Order the numbers from greatest to least. Then tell which number is between 44,866 and 45,626.

45,627   44,867   45,927

8. Connect Bob has 3 quarters, 1 dime, and 1 nickel. What coin does he need to make $1.00?

9. Analyze Information Use the table to answer the question. If you were using quarters only, how many quarters would you need for a child's movie ticket?

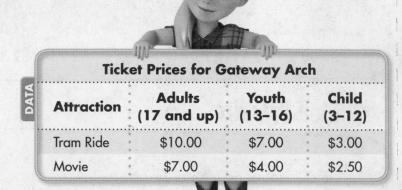

Ticket Prices for Gateway Arch

Attraction	Adults (17 and up)	Youth (13–16)	Child (3–12)
Tram Ride	$10.00	$7.00	$3.00
Movie	$7.00	$4.00	$2.50

10. Tyler has 5 coins worth $0.65. All of the coins are either quarters or dimes. How many of each coin does he have?

A 2 quarters, 3 dimes
B 3 quarters, 2 dimes
C 1 quarter, 4 dimes
D 4 quarters, 1 dime

11. Personal Financial Literacy Sachi saves $5.00 each week for 8 weeks. How much does Sachi save? Explain how you found your answer.

12. Extend Your Thinking Look at page 46. Keisha says Greg needs 5 more coins to have enough to buy the toy giraffe. Reni says he needs only 1 more coin. Explain who is correct.

13. Extend Your Thinking Show two ways to make $2.62. Draw rectangles with numbers to represent bills. Draw circles with numbers to represent coins.

© Pearson Education, Inc. 3

Name _____

Another Look!

To count money, start with the bills. Count on from the greatest to the least value.

Count on: $5.00 $6.00 $7.00

$7.25 $7.35 $7.45 $7.50 $7.51

1. Write the total value in dollars and cents.

For **2** through **5**, draw circles with numbers to represent coins.

2. Show two ways to make $0.75 without using a half dollar or pennies.

3. Show two ways to make $0.60 without using quarters or pennies.

4. Show two ways to make $0.25 without using pennies.

5. Show two ways to make $0.45 without using nickels.

6. I have 0 edges. I do not have any flat surfaces. Which solid shape am I?

Circle the correct solid.

7. Number Sense Mindy has the money shown below in her pocket. Write the total value in dollars and cents.

8. Maria has 2 one-dollar bills, 1 quarter, 7 dimes, 3 nickels, and 4 pennies in her piggy bank. How much money does Maria have?

9. Number Sense Rae has 5 dollars more than the money listed: 1 one-dollar bill, 2 quarters, 2 dimes, 1 nickel, 3 pennies. Write the amount of money Rae has in dollars and cents.

10. Reason What is the least number of coins you can use to show $0.37? What are the coins?

11. Lance buys a notebook at the school store for $1.00. He pays with the exact amount of money. Which coins could Lance have used to buy the notebook?

A 3 quarters and 2 dimes

B 2 quarters, 2 dimes, and 2 nickels

C 1 half dollar, 1 quarter, and 1 dime

D 1 half dollar and 5 dimes

12. Extend Your Thinking Show how you can make $0.60 two different ways using only 3 coins each time.

50

© Pearson Education, Inc. 3

Name _____

☆ **Solve & Share** ☆

Think about ways to find numbers that tell *about* how much or how many. Derek has 27 stickers. How could you describe to someone *about how many* stickers Derek has?

⭐ **TEKS 3.2.C** Represent a number on a number line as being between two consecutive multiples of 10; 100; 1,000; or 10,000 and use words to describe relative size of numbers in order to round whole numbers.
Mathematical Process Standards 3.1A, 3.1B, 3.1C, 3.1D, 3.1F, 3.1G

Digital Resources at PearsonTexas.com

 Solve   Learn   Glossary   Check   Tools   Games

You can **analyze relationships.** You can use phrases such as "is about," "closer to," "almost," or "is nearly" to describe a relationship between numbers.

Look Back!

Justify How do you know the number you chose to describe *about* how many stickers Derek has is a good number to use?

How Can You Round Numbers?

About how many rocks does Tito have? Round 394 to the nearest ten.

When you round, you find a number that is "close to" or "nearly" your number.

To round, replace a number with a number that tells about how many.

Donna
350
rocks

Carl
345
rocks

Tito
394
rocks

B

You can use a number line to round to the nearest ten.

A number line is a line with numbers in order using a scale.

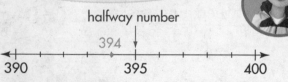

halfway number

394

390   395   400

394 is closer to 390 than 400, so 394 rounds to 390.

Tito has about 390 rocks.

C

Round the number of rocks Donna has to the nearest hundred. You can use a number line.

halfway number

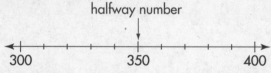

300   350   400

If a number is halfway between, round to the greater number.

350 is halfway between 300 and 400, so 350 rounds to 400.

Donna has about 400 rocks.

Do You Understand?

Convince Me! Susan and Mike are playing a guessing game.

Susan says, "I am thinking of a number that has a four in the hundreds place and a two in the ones place. When you round it to the nearest hundred, it is 500. What is my number?"

Mike says, "I cannot tell. I see five possible answers on the number line." Is Mike correct? Explain.

© Pearson Education, Inc. 3

Another Example

You can use a number line to round to the nearest thousand or ten thousand.

3,945 rounds to 4,000.

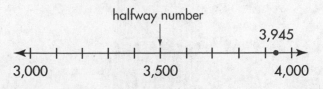

38,500 rounds to 40,000.

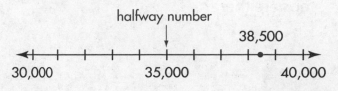

☆ Guided Practice*

In **1** and **2**, round to the nearest hundred.

1.

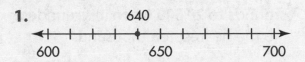

2. 305

In **3** and **4**, round to the nearest thousand.

3.

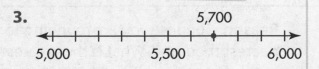

4. 1,490

5. **Number Sense** What number is halfway between 20,000 and 30,000?

6. Round 25,678 to the nearest ten thousand.

7. **Connect** Look back at page 52. If Tito adds one more rock to his collection, about how many rocks will he have, rounded to the nearest ten? Rounded to the nearest hundred? Explain your answer.

☆ Independent Practice ☆

In **8** through **10**, round to the nearest hundred.

8. 428

9. 699

10. 750

In **11** through **13**, round to the nearest thousand.

11. 8,880

12. 5,310

13. 8,500

Problem Solving

14. Number Sense The Leaning Tower of Pisa in Italy has 293 steps. To the nearest ten, about how many steps are there? To the nearest hundred, about how many steps are there?

It took almost 200 years to build the Leaning Tower of Pisa.

---

15. ⭐ To the nearest hundred dollars, a computer game costs $100. Which could **NOT** be the actual cost of the game?

A $89

B $91

C $110

D $150

16. Number Sense Write a number that rounds to 20,000 when it is rounded to the nearest ten thousand.

---

17. Connect Name the least number of coins you can use to show $0.47. What are the coins?

18. Reason Suppose you are rounding to the nearest thousand. What is the greatest number that rounds to 6,000? What is the least number that rounds to 6,000?

---

19. Extend Your Thinking A 3-digit number has the digits 2, 5, and 7. To the nearest hundred, it rounds to 800. What is the number? Show how you found the answer.

20. Emil says, "I am thinking of a number that is greater than 142, rounds to 100 when rounded to the nearest hundred, and has a 5 in the ones place." What is Emil's number?

© Pearson Education, Inc. 3

Another Look!

You can use a number line to round to the nearest ten, hundred, thousand, or ten thousand.

Round 483 to the nearest 10.

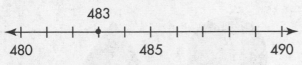

483 is closer to 480 than 490, so 483 rounds to 480.

Round 483 to the nearest 100.

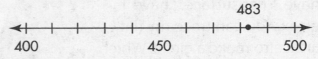

483 is closer to 500 than 400, so 483 rounds to 500.

Round 4,830 to the nearest 1,000.

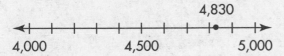

4,830 is closer to 5,000 than 4,000, so 4,830 rounds to 5,000.

Round 48,300 to the nearest 10,000.

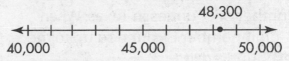

48,300 is closer to 50,000 than 40,000, so 48,300 rounds to 50,000.

1. Round 328 to the nearest ten.

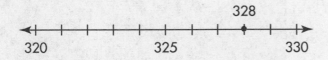

2. Round 630 to the nearest hundred.

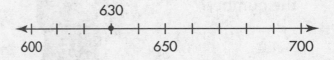

3. Round 6,499 to the nearest thousand.

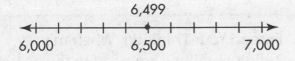

4. Round 15,500 to the nearest ten thousand.

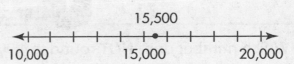

5. Round 429 to the nearest ten and hundred.

6. Round 23,421 to the nearest thousand and ten thousand.

7. Communicate How would you use a number line to round 16,800 to the nearest ten thousand?

8. Check for Reasonableness Tyrell says 753 rounds to 800. Sara says 753 rounds to 750. Who is correct? Explain.

9. I have 1 flat surface. I have 1 vertex. You can trace my flat surface to make a circle. Which shape am I? Circle the correct solid figure.

10. Number Sense Solve this puzzle to find the number of counties in Texas. When this 3-digit number is rounded up to the nearest hundred, it rounds to 300. The digit in the ones place is 4. The sum of the digits in the 3-digit number is 11. What is the number?

11. Which number does **NOT** round to 4,000?

A 3,470
B 3,690
C 4,130
D 4,480

12. Extend Your Thinking When this 3-digit number is rounded to the nearest hundred, it rounds to 900. The digit in the ones place is the fifth odd number you count beginning with 1. The sum of the digits is 22. What is the number?

© Pearson Education, Inc. 3

Name _____

Explain how you know 2,345 is less than 2,371.

Problem Solving

Lesson 1-9
Writing to Explain

TEKS 3.1G Display, explain, and justify mathematical ideas and arguments using precise mathematical language in written or oral communication. Also, 3.2C, 3.2D **Mathematical Process Standards** 3.1B, 3.1C, 3.1D, 3.1E

Digital Resources at PearsonTexas.com

Solve Learn Glossary Check Tools Games

You can **create and use representations.** A place-value chart can help you compare numbers. *Show your work in the space below!*

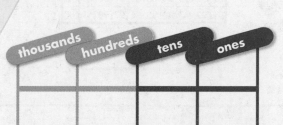

Look Back!

Explain Do you think your written explanation above is a good explanation? Did you include words, pictures, numbers, or symbols? Tell why.

A Analyze

Why does it make sense that 40 + 80 = 120?

Good written explanations communicate your reasoning to others.

Math explanations can use:

- words
- pictures
- numbers
- symbols

45 < 89
45 is less than 89

Emma's Work and Explanation

B Plan and Solve

Find 40 + 80.

$4 + 8 = 12$

$40 + 80 = 120$

"Adding 40 and 80 is the same as adding 4 tens and 8 tens, which makes 12 tens, because $4 + 8 = 12$. Then, if you count by tens 12 times, you get to 120."

C Evaluate

A good math explanation should be:

- correct
- simple
- complete
- easy to understand

Emma's explanation is good!

Do You Understand?

Convince Me! Do you think Emma's explanation could be better? Tell why.

© Pearson Education, Inc. 3

☆ Guided Practice ☆

In **1** through **3**, use words, pictures, numbers, or symbols to write good math explanations.

1. Use words to explain how a number line can help you round 248 to the nearest ten.

2. Explain how a number line can help you round 248 to the nearest ten.

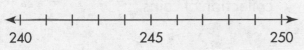

240   245   250

3. **Explain** Use numbers or symbols to explain how you can round 248 to the nearest ten.

Good math explanations use words, pictures, numbers, or symbols in a correct, simple, complete, and easy to understand way.

☆ Independent Practice ☆

Leveled Practice In **4** and **5**, answer each question with complete sentences.

4. Explain why the following sums all end in 0.

40 + 30 = 70   90 + 40 = 130   50 + 60 = 110

5. Explain how to use a number line to show how 300 is 346 rounded to the nearest hundred.

Problem Solving

6. Reason Explain what makes a number even.

7. Which is the word form of 2,340?

A twenty-three thousand, forty

B two thousand, three hundred four

C two thousand, three hundred forty

D twenty-three hundred four

8. Explain How can you order these numbers from least to greatest? Explain.

3,456   2,365   3,465

9. Communicate Mark has a half-dollar, a quarter, a dime, and a penny. Explain how to count on to find the value of Mark's collection of coins.

10. Communicate Explain how to round a 3-digit number to the nearest ten on a number line.

11. Extend Your Thinking Tim says in the number 25,773, one 7 is ten times as great as the other 7. Is he correct? Why or why not?

60

© Pearson Education, Inc. 3

Name _____

Another Look!

A good explanation should be correct, simple, complete, and easy to understand. It can use words, pictures, numbers, or symbols.

Explain how you can write 1,300 two different ways.

I can use place-value blocks to show 1,300 as thousands and hundreds.

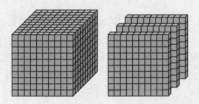

1,300 = one thousand, three hundreds

I can use place-value blocks to show 1,300 as hundreds only.

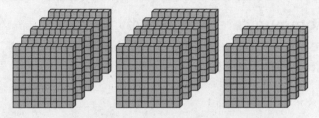

1,300 = thirteen hundreds

---

1. Write 2,700 two different ways. Use thousands and hundreds, then use hundreds only.

   2,700 = _____ thousand, _____ hundreds

   2,700 = _____ hundreds

---

2. Explain how you can write 1,600 two different ways.

---

3. Why is 4,536 less than 4,563? Use the place-value chart in your explanation.

4. Construct Arguments Show and explain why 13,464 is greater than 13,446. Use the place-value chart in your explanation.

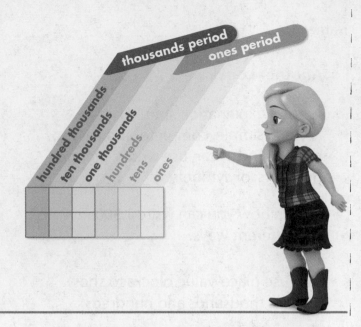

5. Communicate Explain why it makes sense that one of the 3s in 2,334 is ten times greater than the other.

6. Explain How can you order these numbers from least to greatest? Explain.

24,763   24,635   24,685

7. 1,453 in expanded form is written as:

⭐ **A** 1,000 + 400 + 50 + 3

B 1,000 + 450 + 3

C 1,400 + 50 + 3

D 1,000 + 400 + 43 + 10

8. Marisol said, "My number has 2 ten thousands, 4 thousands, 8 hundreds, 6 tens, and 5 ones." Write Marisol's number in standard and expanded form.

9. Extend Your Thinking Explain how to round 765 to the nearest hundred on a number line.

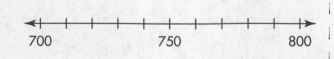

© Pearson Education, Inc. 3

Name _____

1. Reason Write a 4-digit number that has a ones digit of 2, a hundreds digit of 7, and a 4 for the thousands and tens digits.

2. Number Sense Travis scored 45,362 points playing a computer game. What is the score written in expanded and word form?

Applying Math Processes

- How does this problem connect to previous ones?
- What is my plan?
- How can I use tools?
- How can I use number sense?
- How can I communicate and represent my thinking?
- How can I organize and record information?
- How can I explain my work?
- How can I justify my answer?

3. Extend Your Thinking In the number 52,281, if you move from the 2 in the thousands place to the 2 in the hundreds place, what happens to the value of the 2?

4. Draw a Picture What coins and bills could you use to show $5.85 two ways?

5. Explain There are 30 chairs lined up in 6 equal rows. Explain how you can use a multiplication sentence and a strip diagram to find out how many chairs are in each row.

6. Communicate How can you use the number line below to round 562 to the nearest hundred?

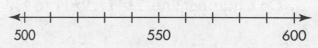

500   550   600

Error Search

For **1** through **4**, circle each statement that is not correct. Then tell why it is not correct.

1. The value of the digit 3 in 36,285 is 3,000.

2. In 3,637, the value of the 3 in the thousands place is ten times as great as the value of the 3 in the tens place.

3. The value of three quarters is the same as 1 half-dollar, 2 dimes, and 1 nickel.

4. The number 750 rounded to the nearest hundred is 700.

Reasoning

For **5** through **9**, write whether each statement is true or false. If you write false, change the numbers or words so the statement is true.

5. 548 rounded to the nearest ten is 540.

6. On a number line, 234 is closer to 230 than 240.

7. The number 32,653 is one thousand less than 33,653.

8. 23,456; 23,546; and 23,645 are in order from greatest to least.

9. 1 quarter, 1 dime, and 2 nickels have the same value as 1 half-dollar.

© Pearson Education, Inc. 3

Set A | pages 9–14

Reteaching

You can use place-value blocks to show 1,324.

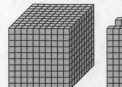

1 thousand   3 hundreds   2 tens   4 ones

Write the number in **standard form**.
1,324

Write the number in **expanded form**.
1,000 + 300 + 20 + 4

Write the number in **word form**.
one thousand, three hundred twenty-four

Remember that place value is the value of the place a digit has in a number.

Write each number in standard form. Use place-value blocks to help.

1.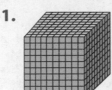

2. $3,000 + 500 + 40 + 2$

3. five thousand, six hundred twelve

Set B | pages 15–20

You can name 1,500 in different ways.

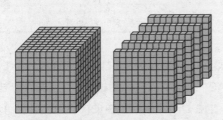

one thousand, five hundreds

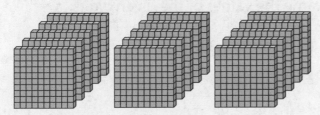

fifteen hundreds

You can name 1,500 using only tens.
one hundred fifty tens

You can name 1,500 using only ones.
one thousand, five hundred ones

Remember that place value can be used to name numbers in different ways.

Name each number in four ways. Use place-value blocks to help.

1.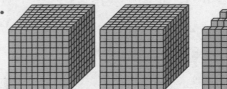

2. 6,500

3. 1,800

Set C pages 21–26

You can use a place-value chart to show 52,793.

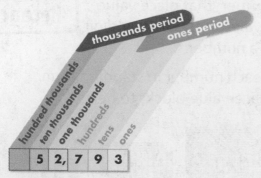

standard form:
52,793

expanded form:
50,000 + 2,000 + 700 + 90 + 3

word form:
fifty-two thousand, seven hundred ninety-three

Remember that a period is a group of 3 digits in a number, starting from the right. Two periods are separated by a comma.

Write each number in standard and expanded forms.

1. eight thousand, two hundred ten

2. ten thousand, six hundred twelve

3. thirty-two thousand, one hundred twenty-two

4. fifty-one thousand, six hundred ninety-five

5. twenty-two thousand, four hundred eleven

Set D pages 27–32

In the number 2,200, what is the relationship between the values of the digit 2 in each place?

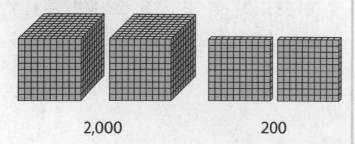

2,000   200

The first 2 is in the thousands place. Its value is 2,000.

The second 2 is in the hundreds place. Its value is 200.

2,000 is ten times as much as 200.

Remember that when two digits next to each other in a number are the same, the value of the digit on the left is always 10 times as great as the value of the digit on the right.

Name the values of the given digits.

1. the 3s in 1,338

2. the 5s in 5,562

3. the 8s in 88,376

4. the 4s in 12,644

5. the 2s in 92,264

6. the 6s in 6,615

7. the 8s in 68,800

8. the 7s in 770,053

© Pearson Education, Inc. 3

Name _____

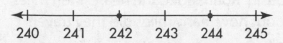

Set E pages 33–38

You can use a number line to compare 242 and 244.

240 241 242 243 244 245

On the number line, 242 is to the left of 244. So, 242 is less than 244.

242 < 244

Remember that you can use symbols to compare numbers: < is less than, > is greater than, and = is equal to.

Write >, <, or = in the circle to make the statement true.

1. 532 ◯ 535   **2.** 1,679 ◯ 1,686

3. 5,358 ◯ 5,158   **4.** 34,674 ◯ 34,392

Set F pages 39–44

You can use a place-value chart to order numbers.

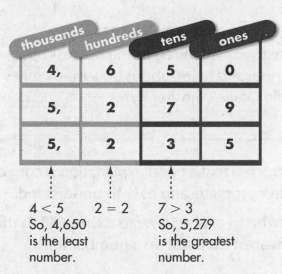

thousands	hundreds	tens	ones
4,	6	5	0
5,	2	7	9
5,	2	3	5

4 < 5   2 = 2   7 > 3
So, 4,650   So, 5,279
is the least   is the greatest
number.   number.

The numbers from greatest to least are:

5,279   5,235   4,650

Remember that when you order numbers, you write them from greatest to least or from least to greatest.

In **1** and **2**, order the numbers from least to greatest.

1. 1,172   1,127   2,053

2. 42,316   42,426   41,601

In **3** and **4**, order the numbers from greatest to least.

3. 5,672   5,795   5,612

4. 78,342   78,234   79,123

Set G pages 45–50

Count on to find the total value.

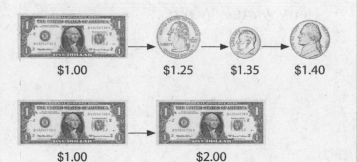

$1.00 $1.25 $1.35 $1.40

$1.00 $2.00

Remember that when counting money, count on from the greatest to the least value.

Write the total value in dollars and cents.

1.

2. 2 one-dollar bills, 1 quarter, 2 dimes

You can use a number line to round.

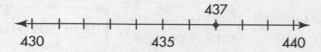

437

Nearest ten: 437 rounds to 440.

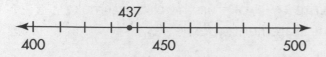

437

Nearest hundred: 437 rounds to 400.

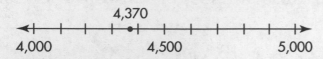

4,370

Nearest thousand: 4,370 rounds to 4,000.

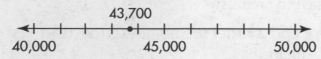

43,700

Nearest ten thousand: 43,700 rounds to 40,000.

Remember that if a number is halfway between, round to the greater number.

1. Mark's family traveled 563 miles to visit his cousin. Rounded to the nearest ten miles, about how many miles did they travel?

2. Sara collected 281 shells. Rounded to the nearest hundred, about how many shells did she collect?

3. Round 5,218 to the nearest thousand.

4. Round 21,942 to the nearest ten thousand.

5. Drake's mother flew 89,214 miles last year. Rounded to the nearest ten thousand miles, about how many miles did Drake's mother fly?

Good written explanations communicate your reasoning to others.

Use digital tools to solve this and other Reteaching problems.

A place-value chart can help you explain why the value of the digit 3 in 3,284 is 3,000.

thousands	hundreds	tens	ones
3,	2	8	4

The digit 3 is in the thousands place. So, it has a value of 3,000.

Remember that a good explanation is correct, simple, complete, and easy to understand.

1. Write to explain how to round 650 to the nearest hundred on a number line.

2. Harry used the digits 4, 7, 9, and 3 to write the least number possible. He wrote 4,379. Explain why the answer Harry wrote is incorrect.

© Pearson Education, Inc. 3

Name _____

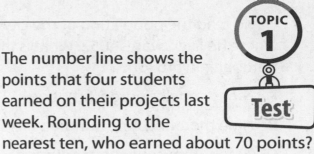
1. Judy read 68,392 people attended a concert last Saturday. What is the value of the 8 in this number?

A 80

B 800

C 8,000

D 80,000

2. In class, Nick saw these place-value blocks on the table. What number do the blocks show?

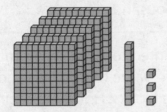

A 5,303

B 533

C 531

D 513

3. On a game show Lindsay watched, one player scored 48,320 points. The second player scored 83,420 points. The third player scored 38,240 points. Which lists these numbers in order from least to greatest?

A 38,240   48,320   83,420

B 48,320   38,240   83,420

C 38,240   83,420   48,320

D 83,420   48,320   38,240

4. The number line shows the points that four students earned on their projects last week. Rounding to the nearest ten, who earned about 70 points?

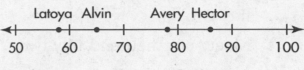

A Alvin

B Latoya

C Avery

D Hector

5. Ariel bought a gift for her younger sister. The gifts she looked at are listed below.

Small red ball: $1.31
Book: $4.49
Small stuffed bird: $3.89
Game: $9.39

Ariel paid for the gift with the bills and coins below. Which gift did she buy?

A Small red ball

B Book

C Small stuffed bird

D Game

6. Chris recorded the value of a set of place-value blocks in standard form. The value is 3,800. How could you write 3,800 in another way?

A Three hundred eight

B Three thousand, eighty

C Thirty-eight hundreds

D Thirty-eight thousands

7. David read the population of the city where he lived was 91,052. What is this number in word form?

  A Ninety-one hundred, fifty-two

  B Nine thousand, one hundred fifty-two

  C Ninety-thousand, one thousand fifty-two

  D Ninety-one thousand, fifty-two

8. Ella said, "One of the following statements is not true." Which of the following statements is **NOT** true?

  A 2,390 > 2,309

  B 8,270 < 8,721

  C 34,612 > 34,611

  D 79,553 < 79,535

9. In December, the local bookstore sold 2,902 fiction books, 2,651 nonfiction books, and 2,811 magazines. List the items sold in order from least to greatest.

  A Magazines, fiction books, nonfiction books

  B Nonfiction books, magazines, fiction books

  C Fiction books, magazines, nonfiction books

  D Nonfiction books, fiction books, magazines

10. The scoreboard reported 37,781 fans attended the game. In the number 37,781, how are the values of the two 7s related to each other?

  A The 7 in the thousands place is 10 times the value of the 7 in the hundreds place.

  B The 7 in the hundreds place is 10 times the value of the 7 in the thousands place.

  C The 7 in the thousands place is 1,000 times the value of the 7 in the hundreds place.

  D The 7 in the hundreds place is 1,000 times the value of the 7 in the thousands place.

11. Angel wanted to show the number 2,000 with place-value blocks. He used only hundreds blocks. How many hundreds blocks did he use?

  A Two

  B Twenty

  C Two hundred

  D Two thousand

12. Eric marked the distance traveled by an explorer named Estevez on a number line. Rounding to the nearest thousand, about how far did Estevez travel?

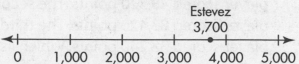

  A About 2,000 miles

  B About 3,000 miles

  C About 3,500 miles

  D About 4,000 miles

© Pearson Education, Inc. 3

Name _____

13. Ian did some chores for his neighbors. He earned 1 five-dollar bill, 2 one-dollar bills, 3 dimes, and 2 pennies. How much money did he earn?

A $5.32

B $6.40

C $6.77

D Not here

14. Darla, Rita, and Lisa are sisters. Darla is 8,089 days old, Rita is 8,911 days old, and Lisa is 8,522 days old. Which of these lists the sisters from youngest to oldest?

A Rita, Darla, Lisa   **C** Darla, Rita, Lisa

B Darla, Lisa, Rita   **D** Lisa, Rita, Darla

15. Ms. Aronson's class is serving pancakes at the school picnic. The number line shows how many pancakes they have served so far. Rounding to the nearest hundred, about how many pancakes have they served so far?

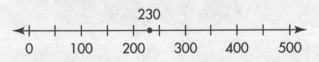

A About 100   **C** About 250

B About 200   **D** About 300

16. Beth wrote 90,000 + 6,000 + 20. What is Beth's number in standard form?

A 962

B 90,620

C 96,020

D 96,200

17. In the number 83,356, what are the values of the two 3s?

A Three thousand and three hundred

B Thirty thousand and three thousand

C Three hundred and thirty

D Thirty and three

18. Students at three schools had a contest to see who could pick up the most cans for recycling. At the end of the year, they listed their scores in a chart. Which school came in first in the contest? Which school came in second?

School	Scores
King	96,312
Roosevelt	92,592
Lincoln	96,323

DATA

A 1st place: King; 2nd place: Lincoln

B 1st place: Lincoln; 2nd place: Roosevelt

C 1st place: Roosevelt; 2nd place: Lincoln

D 1st place: Lincoln; 2nd place: King

19. Erin wrote down the heights of several buildings she had read about.

> Building A is 1,381 feet.
>
> Building B is 1,191 feet.
>
> Building C is 1,614 feet.
>
> Building D is 1,205 feet.

Which building is the shortest?

A Building A   **C** Building C

B Building B   **D** Building D

---

20. Shira used place-value blocks to show a number. How should she write the number in expanded form?

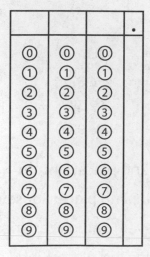

---

21. At the track meet, the coach marked several teams' total scores on a number line. Rounded to the nearest 10 points, about what score did Team 2 earn? Mark your answer in the grid below.

---

22. The city festival had 38,854 participants. What is the value of the 5 in 38,854?

A 50

B 500

C 5,000

D 50,000

---

23. Gary's number has a 6 in the thousands place, a 7 in the hundreds place, and a 5 in the ones place. When rounded to the nearest ten, the number is 6,760. What is Gary's number?

---

24. Jackie has these coins. When she adds the values of the coins together, how many cents does she have? Mark your answer in the grid below.

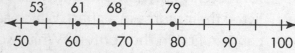

© Pearson Education, Inc. 3

Number Sense: Adding and Subtracting Whole Numbers

Essential Questions: How can sums and differences be estimated and found mentally? Can addition and subtraction be done on the number line?

The sun is a star that provides heat for the water cycle.

Did you know about 70 percent of the earth's surface is covered by water? The sun heats the water, and then the water cools and falls to the earth as rain or snow.

The sun must get tired, heating up all that water. Here's a project on the water cycle, comparing data, and using addition.

Math and Science Project: The Water Cycle

Do Research Use the Internet or other sources to find out about the water cycle and average yearly rainfall in your city. Compare the average yearly rainfall in your city to other cities around the country or around the world!

Journal: Write a Report Include what you found. Also in your report:

- Choose three cities. Make a table and record the average yearly rainfall for these cities and your city.

- Round the numbers and compare the yearly rainfall data. Which cities had more rain than yours?

- Write and solve addition problems using your data. Use estimation to check for reasonableness.

Review What You Know

Vocabulary

Choose the best term from the box. Write it on the blank.

> • number line
>
> • compare
>
> • standard form
>
> • sum

1. A number written in a way that shows only its digits is in

   _____.

2. When you _____ two numbers, you find which number is greater and which number is less.

3. The answer in addition is the _____.

Naming Numbers

Name each number in two ways.

4. 7,100

5. 8,600

6. 3,700

Rounding

7. Round 375 to the nearest hundred.

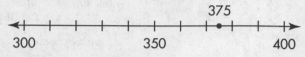

Round each number to the nearest ten.

8. 137   9. 1,806

Round each number to the nearest thousand.

10. 975   11. 95,345

12. Which number is 4,613 rounded to the nearest hundred?

    A 4,600
    B 4,610
    C 4,700
    D 5,000

Counting Money

13. **Explain** Tony has the money shown below. Does he have enough money to buy a toy car that costs $2.86? Explain.

  © Pearson Education, Inc. 3

My Word Cards

Use the examples for each word on the front of the card to help complete the definitions on the back.

A-Z

Commutative (Order) Property of Addition

$$5 \quad + \quad 7 = 12$$

Identity (Zero) Property of Addition

$$4 + 0 = 4$$

Associative (Grouping) Property of Addition

$$(4 + 3) + 8 = 15$$
$$4 + (3 + 8) = 15$$
$$(4 + 3) + 8 = 4 + (3 + 8)$$

estimate

$$255 \longrightarrow 300$$
$$+ \; 322 \longrightarrow 300$$
$$600$$

$255 + 322$ is about 600.

compatible numbers

$$255 \longrightarrow 250$$
$$322 \longrightarrow 325$$

inverse operations

addition	subtraction
$14 + 12 = 26 \longleftrightarrow 26 - 12 = 14$	

multiplication	division
$8 \times 9 = 72 \longleftrightarrow 72 \div 9 = 8$	

My Word Cards

The _____

_____ states that the sum of any number and zero is that same number.

Numbers can be added in any order and the sum remains the same because of

the _____

_____

_____.

To give an approximate number or

answer is to _____.

Addends can be regrouped and the sum remains the same because of the

_____

_____

_____.

Two operations that undo each other

are called _____

_____.

Numbers that are easy to add, subtract, multiply, or divide mentally are called

_____.

© Pearson Education, Inc. 3

Name _____

Solve & Share

Use the pictures of the cups below. Is the total of the numbers on the two cups on the left the same as the total of the numbers on the two cups on the right? Explain your answer.

TEKS 3.4A Solve with fluency one-step and two-step problems involving addition ... within 1,000 using strategies based on ... properties of operations.... Also, 3.5A. Mathematical Process Standards 3.1C, 3.1D, 3.1G

Digital Resources at PearsonTexas.com

Solve | Learn | Glossary | Check | Tools | Games

You can **communicate.** How can you use symbols, numbers, drawings, and words to explain your answer?

Look Back!

Reason What is different about the numbers on the left cups and the numbers on the right cups?

What Are Some Ways to Think About Addition?

A

You can use addition to join groups.

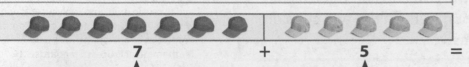

?

7   +   5   =   12

Addends are numbers added together to give a sum.

The sum is the answer to an addition problem.

Properties of Addition

B Commutative (Order) Property of Addition: You can add numbers in any order and the sum will be the same.

$$7 + 5 = 5 + 7$$

Identity (Zero) Property of Addition: The sum of zero and any number is that same number.

$$5 + 0 = 5$$

C Associative (Grouping) Property of Addition: You can group addends in any way and the sum will be the same.

(3 + 4)   +   5   = 12

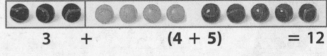

3   +   (4 + 5)   = 12

$$(3 + 4) + 5 = 3 + (4 + 5)$$

Parentheses, (), show what to add first.

Do You Understand?

Convince Me! Draw a line from each addition property to the number sentence example of the property.

Associative (Grouping) Property of Addition $17 + 0 = 17$

Identity (Zero) Property of Addition $22 + 6 = 6 + 22$

Commutative (Order) Property of Addition $(9 + 5) + 2 = 9 + (5 + 2)$

© Pearson Education, Inc. 3

☆ Guided Practice *

In **1** and **2**, identify each property.

1. $4 + (15 + 26) = (4 + 15) + 26$

2. $173 + 0 = 173$

In **3** through **5**, write each missing number.

3. ____ $+ 90 = 90$

4. $426 + 239 = 239 +$ ____

5. $(2 +$ ____$) + 6 = 2 + (3 + 6)$

6. Explain Why is the Commutative Property of Addition also called the *order* property?

7. Reason Ralph says you can rewrite $(4 + 5) + 2$ as $9 + 2$. Do you agree? Why or why not?

Independent Practice

In **8** through **10**, identify each property.

8. $9 + 3 = 3 + 9$ **9.** $18 + 0 = 18$ **10.** $6 + (4 + 3) = (6 + 4) + 3$

In **11** through **22**, write each missing number.

11. $4 + (2 + 3) = 4 +$ ____

12. ____ $+ 25 = 25$

13. $125 + 262 =$ ____ $+ 125$

14. $(170 + 130) +$ ____ $= 300 + 150$

15. $(75 +$ ____$) + 87 = 100 + 87$

16. $(225 + 325) + 250 =$ ____ $+ (225 + 325)$

17. $23 +$ ____ $+ 11 = 23 + 11$

18. $100 + (45 + 138) = ($____ $+ 45) + 138$

19. $($____ $+ 0) + 14 = 7 + 14$

20. $(12 + 2) + 20 =$ ____ $+ 20$

21. $34 + (2 + 28) = ($____ $+ 28) + 34$

22. $(50 + 30) +$ ____ $= 50 + (30 + 20)$

For another example, see Set A on page 127.   **Topic 2** │ Lesson 2-1   **79**

Problem Solving

23. Number Sense Group the addends below in a different way to get the same sum. Write the new number sentence.

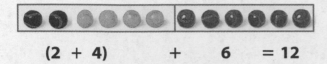

$$(2 + 4) \quad + \quad 6 \quad = 12$$

24. Draw a Picture Draw objects of 2 different colors to show $4 + 3 = 3 + 4$.

25. Construct Arguments Barry said, "The sum of $3 + (6 + 5)$ is the same as $(6 + 5) + 3$." Don said, "The sums are different." Who is correct? Explain.

26. ⭐ Below is an example of a property of addition. Both sides of the sentence equal 22. What is the missing number for each ☐?

$$8 + \boxed{} = \boxed{} + 8$$

A 14
B 18
C 24
D 30

27. Extend Your Thinking A lionfish has 13 spines on its back, 2 near the middle of its underside, and 3 on its underside near its tail. Using a property of addition, write two different number sentences to find how many spines a lionfish has. What property did you use?

28. Extend Your Thinking Gino found the sum of his pencils. He wrote the sum in expanded form as $20 + 10 + 3$. Do you agree with him? Why or why not?

DATA

Gino's Pencils	
Color	Number of Pencils
Red	4
Blue	3
Green	7
Yellow	9

© Pearson Education, Inc. 3

Name _____

Another Look!

Ali planted 2 blue flowers, 4 orange flowers, and 2 red flowers in her garden. How many flowers did Ali plant?

Addition properties make it easier to add numbers.

Commutative (Order) Property of Addition

You can add numbers in any order and the sum will be the same.

$2 + 4 + 2 = 8$ $2 + 2 + 4 = 8$

Associative (Grouping) Property of Addition

You can group numbers in any way and the sum will be the same.

$(2 + 4) + 2 = 8$ $2 + (2 + 4) = 8$

Identity (Zero) Property of Addition

The sum of any number and zero equals that same number.

$0 + 4 = 4$

1.

$(\_\_\_ + 3) + \_\_\_ = 6$ $\_\_\_ + (\_\_\_ + \_\_\_) = \_\_\_$

In **2** through **7**, write each missing number.

2. $300 + 400 = 400 + \_\_\_\_$ **3.** $\_\_\_\_ + 32 = 32$

4. $(8 + 7) + 3 = \_\_\_\_ + (7 + 3)$ **5.** $9 + (2 + 7) = (9 + 2) + \_\_\_\_$

6. $89 + \_\_\_\_ = 89$ **7.** $35 + 49 = \_\_\_\_ + 35$

8. This number sentence shows the Commutative Property of Addition:

$$25 + (30 + 5) = (30 + 5) + 25$$

Which shows how the number sentence can be changed to show the Associative Property of Addition?

A $(30 + 5) + 25 = 25 + (30 + 5)$

B $25 + (30 + 5) = (25 + 30) + 5$

C $0 + 60 = 60$

D $30 + 25 = 25 + 30$

9. Reason Draw lines onto the hexagon below to show how you can cut it into new shapes. What are the shapes you made?

10. Construct Arguments Jake says adding 0 to an addend does not change a sum. Is he correct? Explain. Include a number sentence in your explanation.

11. The Great Belt Bridge in Denmark is 5,328 feet long. The Mackinac Bridge in Michigan is 3,800 feet long. Use the < and > symbols to write two different comparisons of the lengths.

12. Draw a Picture Show an example of the Commutative Property of Addition by drawing a picture. Use the addends 2 and 3.

13. Minnie has 16 old posters and 25 new posters. Amanda has 25 old posters and 16 new posters. Both girls keep their posters in plastic storage cases. Who has more posters? Explain.

14. Extend Your Thinking Troy wants to buy a pair of pants, a pair of socks, and a cap. Use the Associative Property of Addition to show two ways he can add the prices to find the total cost.

DATA	Clothing Sale	
	Pants	$15
	Cap	$5
	Socks	$6

© Pearson Education, Inc. 3

Name _____

Solve & Share

A school store sold 36 pencils last week and 28 pencils this week. Use mental math to find how many pencils were sold both weeks. Explain how you found your answer.

⭐ **TEKS 3.4A** Solve with fluency one-step … problems involving addition … within 1,000 using strategies based on place value, properties of operations…. Also, 3.5A. **Mathematical Process Standards** 3.1B, 3.1C, 3.1D, 3.1G

You can use **mental math.** How can what you know about place value help you solve this problem? *Show your work in the space below!*

Digital Resources at PearsonTexas.com

Solve Learn Glossary Check Tools Games

Look Back!

Mental Math What is another way you can find 36 + 28 using mental math?

How Can You Add with Mental Math?

Dr. Gomez recorded how many whales, dolphins, and seals she saw. How many whales did she see during the two weeks?

Find 25 + 14.

You can use mental math to add and solve this problem.

DATA

Marine Animals Seen		
Animal	Week 1	Week 2
Whales	25	14
Dolphins	28	17
Seals	34	18

B One Way

- Break apart 14.
  14 = 10 + 4
- Add 10 to 25.
  25 + 10 = 35
- Add 4 to 35.
  35 + 4 = 39

25 + 14 = 39

Dr. Gomez saw 39 whales.

C Another Way

- Break apart both addends.
  25 = 20 + 5   14 = 10 + 4
- Add the tens. Add the ones.
  (20 + 10) = 30   (5 + 4) = 9
- Then add the tens and ones.
  30 + 9 = 39

25 + 14 = 39

Dr. Gomez saw 39 whales.

Properties of Addition let you reorder and group the tens and ones this way.

Do You Understand?

Convince Me! Suppose the problem above was 35 + 22. Show how you could use the same two ways above to solve the problem.

© Pearson Education, Inc. 3

Another Example

You can make a ten to add mentally. Find 228 + 117.

- Break apart 117. $117 = 100 + 15 + 2$
- Add 2 to 228 to make a ten. $228 + 2 = 230$
- Add 100 to 230. $230 + 100 = 330$
- Add 15 to 330. $330 + 15 = 345$

So, $228 + 117 = 345$.

> You can use mental math to add 3-digit numbers.

☆ Guided Practice *

1. Make a ten to add 38 + 26.

$38 + 26$

$26 = 2 + 24$

$38 + \underline{\quad} = 40$

$40 + \underline{\quad} = 64$

So, $38 + 26 = \underline{\quad}$

2. Use breaking apart to add 325 + 212.

$325 + 212$

$212 = 200 + 10 + 2$

$325 + 200 = \underline{\quad}$

$525 + 10 = \underline{\quad}$

$\underline{\quad} + 2 = 537$

So, $325 + 212 = \underline{\quad}$

3. Number Sense Compare the One Way and Another Way examples on page 84. How are they the same? How are they different?

4. Mental Math Use addition properties to find how many animals Dr. Gomez saw during Week 1. Show your work.

☆ Independent Practice ☆

> In **5** through **8**, find each sum using mental math.

5. 52 + 44   **6.** 36 + 43   **7.** 651 + 150   **8.** 378 + 542

Problem Solving

9. **Mental Math** You can use mental math to find the number of people who attended a movie Friday and Saturday. Which shows how to reorder and group the tens and ones to find the sum?

A (60 + 20) + (4 + 1)
B 64 + 21
C 21 + (60 + 4)
D (64 + 1) + 20

DATA	Day	Friday	Saturday
	Number of People	64	21
	Boxes of Popcorn Sold	25	10

10. The Tigers scored 35 points in the first half and 48 points in the second half of a basketball game. The Dolphins scored 32 points in the first half of the same game. Which numbers can you add to find the total number of points the Tigers scored?

A 35 + 48 + 32
B (30 + 40) + (5 + 8)
C (30 + 30) + (2 + 5)
D 37 + 48 + 2

11. **Explain** Explain how the solids shown in Group A and Group B could have been sorted.

Group A   **Group B**

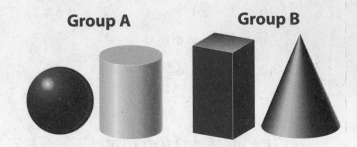

12. **Extend Your Thinking** The Rodriguez family drove 229 miles on Friday and 172 miles on Saturday. Explain how you can break apart both addends to find the total number of miles the Rodriguez family drove.

13. **Check for Reasonableness** Is Bill's work correct? If not, tell why and write a correct answer.

Find 38 + 7.
I'll think of 7 as 2 + 5.
38 + 2 = 40
40 + 7 = 47
So, 38 + 7 is 47.

© Pearson Education, Inc. 3

Name _____

Another Look!

> You can add numbers using mental math.

You can break apart numbers to make them easier to add mentally.

Add $31 + 45$ by breaking apart numbers.	Add $457 + 138$ by breaking apart numbers to make a ten.

Break the numbers into tens and ones.

		tens		ones
31	=	30	+	1
45	=	40	+	5

Add the tens: $30 + 40 = 70$.

Add the ones: $1 + 5 = 6$.

Add the sums: $70 + 6 = 76$.

So, $31 + 45 = 76$.

Break 138 into $100 + 35 + 3$

Add 3 to 457 to make a ten.
$457 + 3 = 460$

Add 100 to 460.
$460 + 100 = 560$

Add 35 to 560.
$560 + 35 = 595$

So, $457 + 138 = 595$.

---

1. $24 + 71 =$ _____

		tens		ones
24	=	20	+	____
71	=	70	+	____

Add the tens: $20 + 70 =$ _____

Add the ones: $4 + 1 =$ _____

Add the sums: _____ + _____ = _____

2. $628 + 237 =$ _____

Break 237 into $200 + 35 +$ _____

$628 + 2 =$ _____

$630 + 200 =$ _____

$830 + 35 =$ _____

In **3** through **14**, use mental math to add.

3. $36 + 43$ **4.** $29 + 36$ **5.** $218 + 274$ **6.** $325 + 437$

7. $58 + 73$ **8.** $91 + 64$ **9.** $167 + 244$ **10.** $482 + 88$

11. $95 + 27$ **12.** $138 + 248$ **13.** $13 + 54$ **14.** $675 + 237$

15. Personal Financial Literacy In 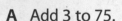 November, Juanita saved $42 of the amount she needs to buy a saddle for her horse. If she saves $10 less than this amount in December, how much will she have saved?

16. Number Sense Todd wants to round 352 to the nearest ten. Use the number line below to show how he can round the number. What is 352 rounded to the nearest ten?

17. Justify Explain how you can break apart one of the addends to make a ten to find the number of points Jeannie and Kevin scored.

SCORES	
Name	Score
Jeannie	245
Kevin	227

18. Jeff wants to use mental math to see if he can afford the computer and printer shown at the right. First, he makes a ten by adding 527 + 3. What does Jeff have to do next before finding the sum of the costs of both items?

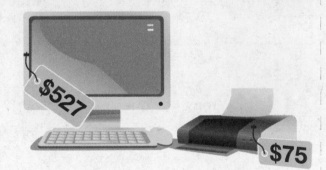

$527

$75

A Add 3 to 75.

B Add 5 to 75.

C Subtract 3 from 75.

D Subtract 5 from 75.

19. Cathy entered 22,741 + 100 = 22,841 into her notebook computer. Write the sum of the number sentence Cathy entered in expanded form and word form.

20. Extend Your Thinking Find the sum of 301 + 73 + 27, mentally, using the Associative Property of Addition. Show how you can use the property to group two of the addends. Explain how you found the sum.

© Pearson Education, Inc. 3

Name _____

Solve & Share

You want to buy an item that originally costs $63. If you get the discount shown on the sign below, what will the sale price be? Use mental math to find the sale price. Explain how you found your answer.

DISCOUNT:
$17 off
original price

⭐ **TEKS 3.4A** Solve with fluency one-step and two-step problems involving addition and subtraction within 1,000 using strategies based on place value, properties of operations.... Also, 3.4, 3.5A. **Mathematical Process Standards** 3.1C, 3.1D, 3.1G

Digital Resources at PearsonTexas.com

 Solve Learn Glossary Check Tools  Games

You can use **mental math.** How can what you know about place value help you solve this problem? *Show your work.*

Look Back!

Mental Math What is another way you could use mental math to solve the problem?

A

A store is having a sale on jackets. A jacket is on sale for $17 less than the original price. What is the sale price?

Find 52 − 17.

$52
$17 off!

You can use mental math to subtract and solve this problem.

The difference is the answer when subtracting two numbers.

B ## One Way

52 − 17 = ?

It's easier to subtract 20.
52 − 20 = 32

If you subtract 20, you subtract 3 more than 17. You must add 3 to the answer.

32 + 3 = 35

52 − 17 = 35

The sale price is $35.

C ## Another Way

52 − 17 = ?

Make a simpler problem by changing each number in the same way.

You can change 17 to 20 because it's easy to subtract 20. So, add 3 to both 17 and 52.

52 − 17 = ?
↓ + 3   ↓ + 3
55 − 20 = 35
52 − 17 = 35

The sale price is $35.

Do You Understand?

Convince Me! Suppose the problem above was 62 − 28. Show how you could use the same two ways above to solve the problem.

© Pearson Education, Inc. 3

Another Example

You can count on to subtract mentally. Find $300 - 155$.

$155 + 5 = 160$
$160 + 40 = 200$
$200 + 100 = 300$

$5 + 40 + 100 = 145$

So, $300 - 155 = 145$.

You can use mental math to subtract 3-digit numbers.

Guided Practice

In **1** through **4**, find each difference using mental math.

1. $46 - 18$
   $48 - 20 = $ _____

2. $34 - 19$
   $35 - 20 = $ _____

3. $73 - 16$
   $77 - 20 = $ _____

4. $82 - 47$
   $85 - 50 = $ _____

5. Find $400 - 138$ mentally by counting on.

   $138 + $ _____ $= 140$

   $140 + $ _____ $= 200$

   $200 + $ _____ $= 400$

   _____ $+$ _____ $+$ _____ $=$ _____

6. **Reason** In the One Way example on page 90, why do you add 3 to 32 instead of subtract 3 from 32?

7. **Communicate** Suppose a computer costs $515, and a printer costs $85. If you buy both, you can save $130. What is the sale price for both items? Show how to use mental math to solve.

Independent Practice

In **8** through **19**, find each difference using mental math.

8. $28 - 19$

9. $87 - 18$

10. $39 - 17$

11. $68 - 24$

12. $84 - 15$

13. $97 - 54$

14. $53 - 39$

15. $72 - 38$

16. $400 - 250$

17. $430 - 216$

18. $705 - 255$

19. $687 - 323$

Problem Solving

20. Mental Math The giant Rafflesia flower can be as wide as shown in the picture. One petal can be 18 inches wide. How can you use mental math to find how much wider the whole flower is than one petal?

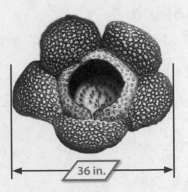

36 in.

---

21. Number Sense Nina wrote the following number pattern. Describe the pattern rule. What are the next three numbers in the pattern?

653   553   453   353

22. ★ Of the students at Paul's school, 270 are girls and 298 are boys. There are 354 students at Alice's school. How many more students are there at Paul's school than at Alice's school?

A 104
B 114
C 204
D 214

---

23. Extend Your Thinking What is the sale price of the jeans? If Sarah has $50, how much change will she receive after buying the jeans at the sale price? Describe how you can use mental math to find each part of the answer.

$46 SALE! Take $18 off the original price.

---

24. Extend Your Thinking To find 57 − 16, Tom added 4 to each number, and then subtracted. Saul added 3 to each number, and then subtracted. Will both ways work to find the correct answer? Explain.

25. Number Sense Suppose you are comparing 3,698 and 3,821. Which place-value digits do you need to compare? Which number would be farther right on a number line? Explain.

© Pearson Education, Inc. 3

Name _____

Another Look!

You can use mental math and properties of operations to help solve subtraction problems.

Megan has 372 buttons. She used 14 buttons to make a collage and 49 buttons to make an ornament. How many buttons does Megan have now?

You can use properties of operations to change numbers to make subtraction easier.

First find $372 - 14$.

You can add 6 to both 372 and 14.

$$\begin{array}{r} 372 + 6 \rightarrow 378 \\ -\ 14 + 6 \rightarrow\ \ 20 \\ \hline 358 \end{array}$$

So, $372 - 14 = 358$.

Then find $358 - 49$.

You can add 1 to both 358 and 49.

$$\begin{array}{r} 358 + 1 \rightarrow 359 \\ -\ 49 + 1 \rightarrow\ \ 50 \\ \hline 309 \end{array}$$

So, $358 - 49 = 309$.

Adding the same amount to each number does not change the difference.

Megan has 309 buttons.

In Exercises **1** to **8**, use mental math to subtract.

1. $32 - 17$

$\begin{array}{r} 32 + 3 \rightarrow 35 \\ -\ 17 + 3 \rightarrow \underline{\quad} \end{array}$

2. $94 - 19$

$\begin{array}{r} 94 + 1 \rightarrow \underline{\quad} \\ -\ 19 + 1 \rightarrow 20 \end{array}$

3. $281 - 112$

$\begin{array}{r} 281 + 8 \rightarrow 289 \\ -\ 112 + 8 \rightarrow \underline{\quad} \end{array}$

4. $309 - 195$

$\begin{array}{r} 309 + 5 \rightarrow \underline{\quad} \\ -\ 195 + 5 \rightarrow 200 \end{array}$

5. $56 - 27$

$59 - 30 = \underline{\quad}$

6. $81 - 36$

$85 - 40 = \underline{\quad}$

7. $228 - 119$

$229 - 120 = \underline{\quad}$

8. $647 - 355$

$652 - 360 = \underline{\quad}$

In Exercises **9** to **20**, find the difference.

9. $53 - 37$

10. $77 - 35$

11. $84 - 28$

12. $76 - 18$

13. $59 - 15$

14. $64 - 46$

15. $54 - 13$

16. $97 - 24$

17. $90 - 55$

18. $460 - 212$

19. $800 - 325$

20. $769 - 428$

21. **Explain** A box of tiles contains 225 tiles. Mai needs 163 tiles for her art project, and her friend Beth needs 72 tiles for her project. If they buy one box of tiles, do they have enough for both projects? Explain.

22. **Number Sense** Gillian started to find $88 - 29$. This is what she did.

$$88 - 29 = ?$$
$$88 - 30 = 58$$

What should Gillian do next?

23. ⭐ Romi saw the following example of an addition property. It has a missing number.

$$(3 + 2) + 1 + \boxed{} = 3 + (2 + 1)$$

Which is the missing number in the example?

A 0   C 2
B 1   D 3

24. **Math and Science** The average yearly precipitation for three Texas cities is Austin, 34 inches; Dallas, 38 inches; and Longview, 48 inches. Use mental math to find how much more average yearly precipitation Longview has than Austin.

25. Cary wants to print 36 pictures from his digital camera and 6 pictures from his computer. So far, he has printed 19 of all the pictures. How many more pictures does Cary need to print?

26. **Number Sense** Martin has 1 quarter, 5 dimes, 2 nickels, and 4 pennies. Tim has 2 quarters, 2 dimes, and 3 nickels. How much money does each boy have? Who has more money?

27. **Extend Your Thinking** Use mental math to find how many total raffle tickets Ms. Hudson's and Mr. Nealy's classes sold. How many more tickets did their classes sell than Mrs. Robertson's class?

Change each number the same way when subtracting mentally.

DATA

Raffle Tickets Sold

Class	Number of Tickets
Ms. Hudson	352
Mr. Nealy	236
Mrs. Robertson	429

© Pearson Education, Inc. 3

Name _____

Solve & Share

Look at the table below. Is the weight of a female and male sun bear together more or less than the weight of one female black bear? Without finding an exact answer, explain how you can decide. **Solve this problem any way you choose.**

✚ **TEKS 3.4B** Round to the nearest 10 or 100 or use compatible numbers to estimate solutions to addition and subtraction problems.
Mathematical Process Standards 3.1C, 3.1D, 3.1E, 3.1G

Digital Resources at PearsonTexas.com

| Solve | Learn | Glossary | Check | Tools | Games |

You can **communicate.** How can you use symbols, numbers, and words when you write an explanation? **Show your work in the space below!**

Type of Bear	Weight	
	Female	**Male**
Sun Bear	78 pounds	95 pounds
Black Bear	215 pounds	345 pounds

Look Back!

Estimation Why is an exact answer not needed to solve the problem?

How Can You Estimate Sums?

Do the two pandas together weigh more than 500 pounds?

Estimate 255 + 322.

Female
255 pounds

Male
322 pounds

You can estimate to find out about how much the two pandas weigh.

B One Way

Round to the nearest hundred.

$$255 \rightarrow 300$$
$$+\ 322 \rightarrow 300$$
$$600$$

255 + 322 is about 600.
600 > 500

The pandas together weigh more than 500 pounds.

C Another Way

Use compatible numbers.

Compatible numbers are numbers that are close to the addends, but easy to add mentally.

$$255 \rightarrow 250$$
$$+\ 322 \rightarrow 325$$
$$575$$

255 + 322 is about 575 and 575 > 500.
The total weight is more than 500 pounds.

Do You Understand?

Convince Me! Sandy said, "Just look at the numbers. 200 and 300 is 500. The pandas weigh over 500 pounds because one panda weighs 255 pounds and the other weighs 322 pounds." What do you think she means?

© Pearson Education, Inc. 3

Another Example

Suppose one panda ate 146 pounds of bamboo in a week and another ate 143 pounds. About how many pounds of bamboo did the two pandas eat?

You can estimate 146 + 143 by rounding to the nearest ten.

$$146 \rightarrow 150$$
$$\underline{+\ 143 \rightarrow 140}$$
$$290$$

The pandas ate about 290 pounds of bamboo in a week.

☆ Guided Practice*

Round to the nearest ten to estimate.

1. 28 + 46   ____ + ____ = ____

2. 108 + 223   ____ + ____ = ____

Round to the nearest hundred to estimate.

3. 514 + 258   ____ + ____ = ____

4. 198 + 426   ____ + ____ = ____

5. **Reason** If both addends are rounded to greater numbers, will the estimate be greater than or less than the actual sum?

6. **Construct Arguments** By rounding to the same place to estimate sums, everyone gets the same addends. Is this true if compatible numbers are used instead? Explain.

Independent Practice ☆

In **7** through **10**, round to the nearest ten to estimate.

7. 18 + 43   **8.** 75 + 72   **9.** 39 + 102   **10.** 376 + 295

In **11** through **14**, round to the nearest hundred to estimate.

11. 403 + 179   **12.** 462 + 251   **13.** 64 + 403   **14.** 539 + 399

In **15** through **18**, use compatible numbers to estimate.

15. 75 + 26   **16.** 167 + 27   **17.** 108 + 379   **18.** 145 + 394

*For another example, see Set D on page 128.

Problem Solving

Use the table to answer **19** and **20**.

19. Estimation Ms. Tyler drove from Austin to Dallas, and then from Dallas to Corpus Christi. To the nearest ten miles, about how many miles in all did she drive?

20. Estimation Ms. Tyler drove from Dallas to Lufkin and back again. To the nearest hundred miles, about how many miles did she drive?

Distance from Dallas, TX

City	Miles Away
Austin	195
Corpus Christi	413
Houston	247
Lufkin	182
Victoria	307

DATA

---

21. What plane shape do you make when you trace the flat surface of a cylinder?

22. Represent Ralph has 75¢. How much more money does he need to buy a pencil for 90¢? Complete the diagram.

90¢

75¢	

Money
Ralph has

Money
needed

---

23. Number Sense ★ Emma uses compatible numbers to estimate the sum of two addends. Her estimate is 125. Which are the actual addends of Emma's problem?

A 27 + 54 **C** 76 + 28

B 102 + 49 **D** 54 + 77

___ + ___ = 125

---

24. You want to add 16 + 12 + 18. Explain how you can use the Associative Property of Addition to group two of the numbers that are compatible. What is the sum of the addends?

25. Extend Your Thinking Susan wants to drive from Los Angeles to Monterey, and then from Monterey to San Francisco. From Los Angeles to Monterey is 326 miles. From Monterey to San Francisco is 113 miles. About how far will Susan drive? Explain the method you used to estimate, and give the actual distance Susan will drive.

© Pearson Education, Inc. 3

Name _____

Another Look!

There is more than one way you can estimate.

The students at your school are saving cereal box tops.

136
box tops

152
box tops

About how many box tops have the students saved?
When you find *about* how many, you estimate.

Estimate by rounding each addend. Then, add the rounded numbers.

Round to the nearest ten.	Round to the nearest hundred.
136 → 140	136 → 100
+ 152 → 150	+ 152 → 200
290	300

The students have saved about
290 box tops.

The students have saved about
300 box tops.

In **1** through **4**, round to the nearest ten to estimate.

1.   44 → ____
  + 98 → ____

2.   71 → ____
  + 87 → ____

3.   225 → ____
  + 64 → ____

4.   351 → ____
  + 104 → ____

In **5** through **8**, round to the nearest hundred to estimate.

5. 91 + 268

6. 378 + 136

7. 436 + 309

8. 365 + 487

9. Construct Arguments Sun-Yi estimated 270 + 146 and got 300. Is her estimate reasonable? Explain.

10. Construct Arguments Miguel has 325 baseball cards and 272 football cards. He said he has 597 cards in all. Is his answer reasonable? Explain using estimation.

11. ★ Which of the following shows estimating 283 + 496 + 72 by using compatible numbers?

A 200 + 500 + 100 = ☐

B 300 + 400 + 100 = ☐

C 280 + 400 + 25 = ☐

D 280 + 500 + 75 = ☐

12. Represent In the space below, draw a flat shape that has 5 equal sides. Then, write the number of vertices your shape has.

13. Tools Paige and her friend Karla planted 4 types of rosebushes for the Dundee Community Center. The bar graph at the right shows the color and number of each bush the girls planted. How many more red and pink rosebushes were planted than yellow and white rosebushes?

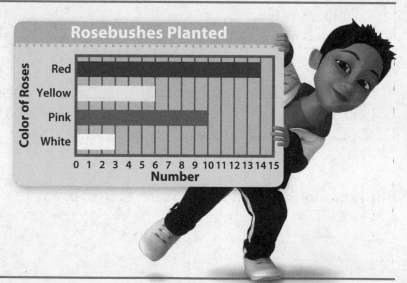

Rosebushes Planted

Color of Roses: Red, Yellow, Pink, White

Number: 0 1 2 3 4 5 6 7 8 9 10 11 12 13 14 15

14. Extend Your Thinking Cheryl drove from Kansas City to Austin, and then from Austin to Fort Worth. Estimate the number of miles she drove. How many actual miles did Cheryl drive? How can you tell if your answer is reasonable? Explain.

DATA

Distances from Austin, TX	
City	Number of Miles Away
Memphis, TN	643
Fort Worth, TX	189
Kansas City, MO	692

© Pearson Education, Inc. 3

Name _____

Solve & Share

Sara collected 356 aluminum cans to recycle. Pierre collected 112 cans. About how many more cans did Sara collect? *Solve this problem any way you choose.*

⭐ **TEKS 3.4B** Round to the nearest 10 or 100 or use compatible numbers to estimate solutions to addition and subtraction problems. **Mathematical Process Standards** 3.1B, 3.1C, 3.1G

Digital Resources at PearsonTexas.com

Solve   Learn   Glossary   Check   Tools   Games

You can **select and use tools.** What tool can you use to help you estimate? *Show your work in the space below!*

Look Back!

Justify Will rounding to the nearest ten or to the nearest hundred give an estimate that is closer to the exact answer? Explain.

All of the tickets for a concert were sold. So far, 126 people have arrived at the concert. About how many people who have tickets have not arrived?

Estimate 493 − 126 by rounding.

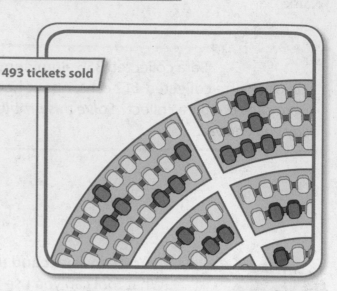

493 tickets sold

You can estimate to find *about* how many.

One Way

Round each number to the nearest hundred and subtract.

$$493 \rightarrow 500$$
$$\underline{-\ 126 \rightarrow 100}$$
$$400$$

About 400 people have not yet arrived.

Another Way

Round each number to the nearest ten and subtract.

$$493 \rightarrow 490$$
$$\underline{-\ 126 \rightarrow 130}$$
$$360$$

About 360 people have not yet arrived.

Do You Understand?

Convince Me! Suppose 179 people have arrived at the concert. Use the two ways above to estimate how many people have not arrived.

© Pearson Education, Inc. 3

Another Example

You can use compatible numbers to estimate differences.

Estimate 372 − 149.

$$
\begin{array}{rcl}
372 & \rightarrow & 375 \\
- \; 149 & \rightarrow & 150 \\
\hline
& & 225
\end{array}
$$

375 and 150 are compatible numbers for 372 and 149.

☆ Guided Practice *

In **1** and **2**, round to the nearest hundred to estimate.

1. 321 − 112   **2.** 655 − 189

In **3** and **4**, round to the nearest ten to estimate.

3. 76 − 42   **4.** 216 − 97

5. Justify In the problem at the top of page 102, which way of rounding gives an estimate that is closer to the actual difference? Explain why.

6. Estimation A theater sold 415 tickets to a show. So far, 273 people have arrived. About how many more people are expected to arrive? Explain.

☆ Independent Practice ☆

In **7** through **10**, round to the nearest hundred to estimate.

7. 186 − 89   **8.** 461 − 216   **9.** 891 − 686   **10.** 724 − 102

In **11** through **14**, round to the nearest ten to estimate.

11. 79 − 61   **12.** 149 − 87   **13.** 241 − 117   **14.** 994 − 610

In **15** through **18**, use compatible numbers to estimate.

15. 79 − 26   **16.** 355 − 177   **17.** 481 − 105   **18.** 794 − 556

Problem Solving

19. Justify About how many feet longer was a *Brachiosaurus* than a *T. rex*? Use compatible numbers to estimate. Explain your answer.

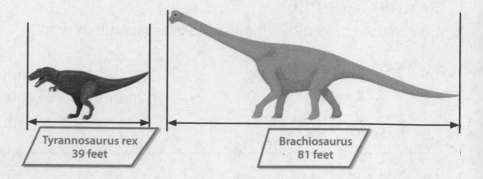

Tyrannosaurus rex
39 feet

Brachiosaurus
81 feet

For **20** and **21**, use the table at the right.

20. Estimation 100 more tickets were sold on Sunday than on Friday. About how many fewer tickets were sold on Sunday than the number of tickets sold on Wednesday and Friday?

Grand Concert Hall	
Day	**Number of Tickets Sold**
Wednesday	506
Thursday	323
Friday	251
Saturday	427
Sunday	☐

21. Communicate Write a number sentence using the Commutative Property of Addition to show two ways to find the total number of tickets sold on Thursday and Friday.

---

22. ★ Anna and Joe are writing reports for their science class. Anna's report is 827 words long. Joe's report is 679 words long. Which will give the closest estimate for how many more words Anna wrote than Joe?

A $800 - 700 =$ ☐

B $830 - 680 =$ ☐

C $830 - 670 =$ ☐

D $900 - 700 =$ ☐

23. Extend Your Thinking To earn some extra money, Mrs. Runyan helps a carpenter. One week she earned $486, and the next week she earned $254. About how much did Mrs. Runyan earn during the two weeks? If she wanted to earn $545, about how much extra money did she earn? Show how you used estimation to find your answers.

© Pearson Education, Inc. 3

Name _____

Another Look!

You can use rounding to estimate differences.

Members of the Biology Club caught 288 butterflies and 136 grasshoppers in their nets. About how many more butterflies than grasshoppers did the club catch?

When you find *about* how many, you estimate. You can estimate by rounding.

Round to the nearest hundred.

$$288 \rightarrow 300$$
$$-136 \rightarrow 100$$
$$\overline{\hspace{2em}200}$$

There were about 200 more butterflies than grasshoppers caught.

Round to the nearest ten.

$$288 \rightarrow 290$$
$$-136 \rightarrow 140$$
$$\overline{\hspace{2em}150}$$

There were about 150 more butterflies than grasshoppers caught.

In **1** through **8**, round to the nearest hundred to estimate.

1. $584 \rightarrow$ _____
   $-347 \rightarrow$ _____

2. $274 \rightarrow$ _____
   $-\ 97 \rightarrow$ _____

3. $615 \rightarrow$ _____
   $-523 \rightarrow$ _____

4. $831 \rightarrow$ _____
   $-143 \rightarrow$ _____

5. $442 - 112$

6. $725 - 278$

7. $682 - 224$

8. $363 - 187$

In **9** through **16**, round to the nearest ten to estimate.

9. $49 \rightarrow$ _____
   $-17 \rightarrow$ _____

10. $468 \rightarrow$ _____
    $-\ 32 \rightarrow$ _____

11. $588 \rightarrow$ _____
    $-461 \rightarrow$ _____

12. $351 \rightarrow$ _____
    $-106 \rightarrow$ _____

13. $65 - 55$

14. $355 - 86$

15. $274 - 207$

16. $592 - 330$

17. Construct Arguments Duncan says since 5 is greater than 2, the number 565 is greater than 2,344. Do you agree? Explain.

18. Estimation On Friday, 537 people attended a play. On Saturday, 812 people attended the same play. About how many more people attended the play on Saturday than on Friday? How did you estimate? Show your work.

19. Justify Andrew has been saving the bills and coins shown at the right. He wants to buy a new bicycle seat bag. The bag costs $3.59, including tax. Will Andrew have enough money? If not, how much more money will he need to save?

20. ⭐ Which shows about how many more feet Dallas's elevation is than Waco's using estimation by rounding to the nearest ten?

Waco 405 feet
Dallas 463 feet
Austin 489 feet

A 460 − 400 = 60

B 460 − 410 = 50

C 400 − 400 = 0

D 500 − 400 = 100

21. Analyze Information Lori lives 272 miles from her grandparents, 411 miles from her favorite aunt, and 39 miles from her cousins. About how much closer does Lori live to her grandparents than to her favorite aunt? Show your work.

22. Extend Your Thinking Carl is estimating 653 − 644. His work is shown below.

700 − 600 = 100

What is the actual difference? Is Carl's estimate reasonable? If not, how could he have made a closer estimate?

© Pearson Education, Inc. 3

Name _____

Solve & Share

The Eat Healthy Café prepared 326 breakfasts and 584 lunches during one month. Some lunches were salads and some were sandwiches. There were 253 salad lunches. How many lunches were sandwiches? After solving, show a way to check your work.

⭐ **TEKS 3.4A** Solve with fluency one-step and two-step problems involving addition and subtraction within 1,000 using strategies based on … the relationship between addition and subtraction. **Mathematical Process Standards** 3.1B, 3.1C, 3.1D, 3.1E, 3.1G

You can **create and use representations.** How can you show what you know about addition and subtraction to help solve this problem? *Show your work in the space below!*

Digital Resources at PearsonTexas.com

Solve   Learn   Glossary   Check   Tools   Games

Look Back!

Construct Arguments Ryan solves the problem by finding 584 − 253. He says 330 of the lunches were sandwiches. Is Ryan's answer correct? Show a way to check his work.

How Can the Relationship Between Addition and Subtraction Help You Check Your Work?

A company has already asked 253 people the same question. How many more people need to answer the question to reach the goal?

Goal: 775 people

What is your favorite type of cereal?

☐ Hot cereal
☐ Cold cereal

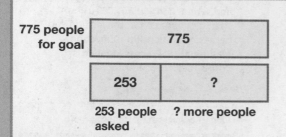

775 people for goal | 775

253 | ?

253 people asked | ? more people

Subtract to find how many more people.

Step 1

Find 775 − 253.

Estimate: 780 − 250 = 530

```
  775
− 253
  522
```

Begin by subtracting ones, then tens, then hundreds.

Step 2

Operations that undo each other are inverse operations. Subtracting 253 and adding 253 are inverse operations.

Add to check a subtraction problem.

```
  522
+ 253
  775
```

The numbers match the subtraction.

522 more people must answer the question.

The answer is reasonable since 522 is close to the estimate, 530.

Do You Understand?

Convince Me! Thomas solved the subtraction problem below and added to check. He said, "The check didn't work. I must have subtracted wrong." What would you tell him?

```
  586          221
− 365        + 365
  221          486
```

© Pearson Education, Inc. 3

☆ Guided Practice *

In **1** and **2**, subtract. Then, add to check.

1.
```
   7 8              □ □
 − 2 3   ────→   + 2 3
   □ □              □ □
```

2.
```
   6 8 7            □ □ □
 − 3 6 5  ────→   + 3 6 5
   □ □ □            □ □ □
```

In **3**, add. Then, subtract to check.

3.
```
   4 3 2            □ □ □
 + 3 5 7  ────→   − 3 5 7
   □ □ □            □ □ □
```

4. **Reason** In Step 2 of the example on page 108, how do you know which numbers to add?

5. Ron added 75 + 24 and got 98. He used subtraction to check the sum.
```
    98
  − 24
    74
```

What should the difference be? Why is this important for Ron to know?

☆ Independent Practice ☆

Leveled Practice In **6** through **11**, estimate, then add or subtract. Use the inverse operation to check your answer.

6.
```
   7 9           □ □
 − 4 2         + 4 2
   □ □           □ □
```

7.
```
   2 6           □ □
 + 5 2         − 5 2
   □ □           □ □
```

8.
```
   8 3           □ □
 − 5 1         + 5 1
   □ □           □ □
```

9.
```
   4 1 7         □ □ □
 + 2 6 1       − 2 6 1
   □ □ □         □ □ □
```

10.
```
   3 6 9
 − 1 5 9
   □ □ □
```

11.
```
   3 2 5
 + 5 4 3
   □ □ □
```

Problem Solving

For **12** and **13**, use the table at the right.

You can use the relationship between addition and subtraction to check your work for these problems.

12. How many more votes did John Bell receive than Stephen Douglas? Draw a strip diagram to solve.

13. Analyze Information How many more votes did Abraham Lincoln receive than the total votes of the other three candidates? Explain how you found your answer.

DATA

1860 Electoral Votes

Candidate	Number of Votes
Abraham Lincoln	180
Stephen Douglas	12
John Breckinridge	72
John Bell	39

14. Communicate Write a story problem that can be solved using the fact $15 - 9 = 6$ or $6 + 9 = 15$.

15. Mandi's class has recess at the time shown on the clock. What time does her class have recess? Use A.M. or P.M. in your answer.

16. Robert has 311 baseball cards in a box and 217 baseball cards in a book. Robert's goal is to have 840 baseball cards. How many more cards does Robert need to reach his goal? Use mental math to solve.

After solving, use the relationship between addition and subtraction to check your calculations.

A 212
B 222
C 312
D 322

17. Extend Your Thinking Shoshone Falls in Idaho is 212 feet high. Nevada Falls in California is 382 feet higher than Shoshone Falls. What is the height of Nevada Falls? Explain how you found your answer. Show how you can use an inverse operation to check your answer.

© Pearson Education, Inc. 3

Name _____

Another Look!

You can use addition to check subtraction and subtraction to check addition.

Subtract 672 − 421.
Estimate: 670 − 420 = 250

Step 1

Subtract.

Step 2

Check your work.
Since you subtracted, use addition to check.

```
    672          251   Use the difference as one addend.
  − 421        + 421   Use the number you subtracted as the other addend.
    251          672   The sum should match the number you subtracted from.
```
Since the difference 251, is close to the estimate, 250, the difference is reasonable.

In **1** through **8**, estimate, then add or subtract. Use the inverse operation to check your answer.

1.
```
   4 5
  −2 1        □□
             +2 1
              □□
```

2.
```
   1 6
  +6 3        □□
             −6 3
              □□
```

3.
```
   6 5 6
  −2 4 3      □□□
            +2 4 3
             □□□
```

4.
```
   4 7 6
  +2 0 3      □□□
            −2 0 3
             □□□
```

5.
```
   5 3 4
  +1 5 2      □□□
            −1 5 2
             □□□
```

6.
```
   7 5 8
  −4 2 7      □□□
            +4 2 7
             □□□
```

7.
```
   9 7 7
  −4 5 2      □□□
            +4 5 2
             □□□
```

8.
```
   2 6 3
  +5 2 2      □□□
            −5 2 2
             □□□
```

For **9** and **10**, use the table at the right.

9. **Tools** How many more customers did the Daily Diner have on Wednesday than on Monday?

10. **Mental Math** The diner had 50 fewer customers on Friday than on Tuesday and Thursday combined. How many customers did the diner have on Friday?

Daily Diner Customers	
Day	**Number of Customers**
Monday	275
Tuesday	210
Wednesday	395
Thursday	240

11. **Explain** How can you check that your answer for Exercise 9 is correct? Explain your process.

12. **Math and Science** In February 1956, a total of 61 inches of snow fell in Vega, Texas. During that same time, 24 inches of snow fell in Plainview, Texas. Use mental math to find how many inches of snow fell in Vega and Plainview in February 1956.

13. ★ Suzanne has 168 berets. She gave 28 berets to her cousin and 44 berets to her sister. How many berets does Suzanne have left?

    A 96
    B 104
    C 230
    D 240

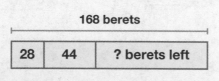

14. **Draw a Picture** Draw a picture that models the Commutative Property of Addition where the sum of the addends on each side of the number sentence is 10.

15. **Represent** Draw lines into the circle and rectangle below to divide each of them into four equal parts.

16. **Extend Your Thinking** Becky added 273 + 416 and got 688. Then she checked her answer by adding 688 + 416. What error did Becky make? Was the sum she found for the original problem correct? Explain.

© Pearson Education, Inc. 3

Name _____

Solve & Share

The school chorus had $86. They spent $40 for music. Then they held a car wash and earned $72. How much money does the school chorus have now? You may use the number line below if you like.

⭐ **TEKS 3.5A** Represent one-and two-step problems involving addition and subtraction of whole numbers to 1,000 using pictorial models, number lines, and equations. Also, 3.4A.
Mathematical Process Standards 3.1C, 3.1D, 3.1E

You can **create and use a representation.** A number line can be used to show addition and subtraction. *Show your work in the space below!*

Digital Resources at PearsonTexas.com

Solve   Learn   Glossary   Check   Tools   Games

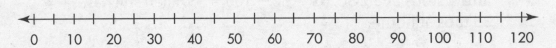

0   10   20   30   40   50   60   70   80   90   100   110   120

Look Back!

Estimation Use estimation to find about how much the school chorus has now. Explain how you estimated.

How Can You Use a Number Line to Add and Subtract?

B

Ellen collected can tabs for a charity. Last week, she collected 53 tabs. This week, she collected 82 tabs. Then, she mailed a package of tabs to the charity. How many can tabs does Ellen still have at home? Find 53 + 82 − 100.

100 tabs sent to charity

I can show this problem on a number line. The number line helps me see the relationship between addition and subtraction.

Step 1 Draw a number line from 0 to 140. Show the 53 tabs Ellen collected last week. Draw a green arrow from 0 to 53.

Step 2 Add the 82 tabs Ellen collected this week. Draw a red arrow that starts at 53 and goes to the right 82 units. The red arrow stops at 135.

In this problem, the green arrow and the red arrow show addition. The blue arrow shows subtraction. I can see the relationship between addition and subtraction on the number line.

Step 3 Subtract the 100 tabs Ellen mailed. Draw a blue arrow that starts at 135 and goes to the left 100 units. The blue arrow stops at 35. So, 53 + 82 − 100 = 35. Ellen still has 35 tabs at home.

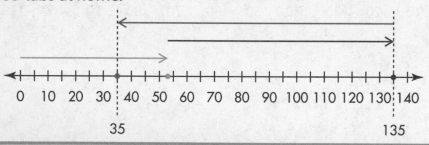

Do You Understand?

Convince Me! This number line shows 238 − 175 − 22 = 41. What is the length of the red arrow? What is the length of the blue arrow? How do you know?

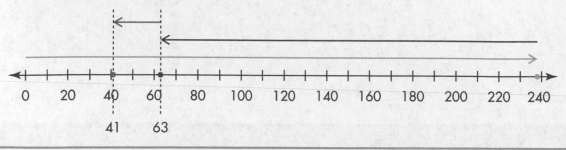

© Pearson Education, Inc. 3

☆ Guided Practice *

In **1** and **2**, use the number line to solve the problem.

1. $58 + 26$

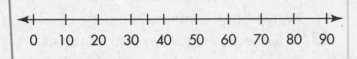

0   10   20   30   40   50   60   70   80   90

2. $42 - 22$

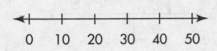

0   10   20   30   40   50

3. Reason In the example on page 114, why are 3 colors used for the arrows above the number line?

4. Tools Joel, Greg, and Lenny have 52 sports cards. Lenny has 28 cards. Greg has 10 cards, and Joel has the rest of the cards. Draw a number line to find how many cards Joel has.

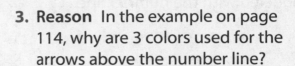

0   10   20   30   40   50   60

Independent Practice ☆

Leveled Practice In **5** through **8**, use the number line to solve the problem.

5. $60 - 15 + 20$

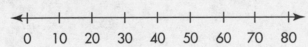

0   10   20   30   40   50   60   70   80

6. $112 + 30 - 47$

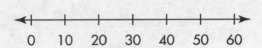

0   10   20   30   40   50   60   70   80   90   100 110 120 130 140 150

7. $200 - 40 + 20$

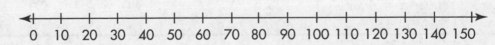

0   20   40   60   80   100   120   140   160   180   200

8. $110 + 40 - 10$

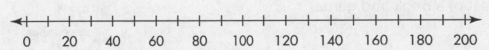

0   10   20   30   40   50   60   70   80   90   100 110 120 130 140 150

Problem Solving

9. Tools Write and solve a word problem that is modeled with the number line.

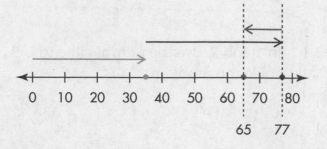

10. The new media center at Stacey's school is in the shape of the polygon shown below. What is the name of this polygon?

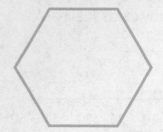

11. Nelly's book contains 280 pages. She read 115 pages on Monday and 45 pages on Tuesday. How many pages does Nelly have left to read?

280 pages

115	45	? pages left

A 120   C 395
B 160   D 440

12. Use the tally chart to complete the pictograph. How many maple trees are in the park?

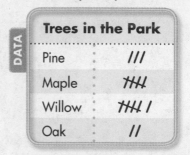

Trees in the Park

Pine	///
Maple	卌
Willow	卌 /
Oak	//

Trees in the Park

Pine

Maple

Willow

Oak

Each 🌳 = 1 tree

13. **Extend Your Thinking** Create a number line to find how much more a pair of sneakers costs than the cost of a book and game.

Item	Cost
Book	$15
Sweatshirt	$28
Game	$23
Sneakers	$65

© Pearson Education, Inc. 3

Name _____

Another Look!

There are 65 boys, 65 girls, and 7 teachers at school.
How many more students are there than teachers at school?
Find $65 + 65 - 7$.

Show the number of boys by drawing a green arrow from
0 to 65. Show the number of girls by drawing a red arrow
that starts at 65 and goes to the right 65 units to 130.

Subtract 7 teachers by drawing a blue arrow that starts
at 130 and goes to the left 7 units to 123.

I can show this
problem on a
number line.

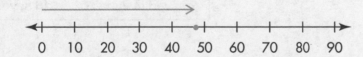

Use mental math to check your work.
$65 + 65 = (60 + 60) + (5 + 5) = 120 + 10 = 130$
$130 - 7 = 123$ There are 123 more students than teachers at school.

In **1** through **4**, use the number line to solve the problem.

1. $47 + 30$

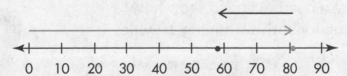

2. $81 - 23 - 16$

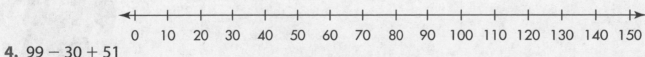

3. $77 + 48 + 20$

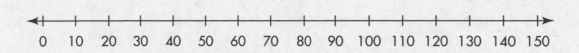

4. $99 - 30 + 51$

5. Tools Write and solve a word problem that is modeled with the number line.

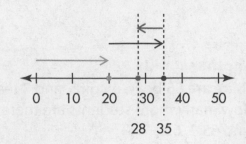

28 35

---

6. Circle the solid figure or figures that have flat surfaces or faces you can trace to make the same shape as the red square that is shown.

---

7. Heather had a board that measured 60 inches long. She cut the board into three pieces. One piece measures 16 inches. A second piece measures 12 inches. What is the length of the third piece?

A 28 inches
B 32 inches
C 76 inches
D 88 inches

8. Personal Financial Literacy Igor opened a savings account in June. The total amount in Igor's new savings account after he made deposits in June and July is $26.

Solve ☐ + 15 = 26 to find the amount Igor saved in June.

$26 total in savings	
? saved in June	$15 saved in July

---

9. Extend Your Thinking Create a number line to show how many more campers signed up for both swimming activities than for soccer.

Activity	Number of Campers
Afternoon Swim	15
Arts & Crafts	25
Morning Swim	20
Soccer	30

© Pearson Education, Inc. 3

Name _____

Solve & Share

An aquarium has 58 rosy red minnows and 77 goldfish in it. How many fish live in the aquarium? Draw a representation to help you solve this problem.

⭐ **TEKS 3.1E** Create and use representations to organize, record, and communicate mathematical ideas. Also 3.4A, 3.5A.
Mathematical Process Standards 3.1B, 3.1C, 3.1D

Digital Resources at PearsonTexas.com

Solve Learn Glossary Check Tools Games

You can **create and use representations.** How could a strip diagram or some other representation help you solve this problem? *Show your work in the space below!*

Look Back!

Draw a Picture What operation did you model with the representation you drew for the problem? Explain how you know.

How Can You Draw a Representation to Help You Solve a Problem?

A Analyze

David wants to buy some soccer souvenirs. How much money does David need to buy a pair of shorts and a shirt?

Pennant $12

Poster $10

Shirt $19

Shorts $15

Add to find the total amount David needs.

B Plan and Solve

Draw a strip diagram to show addition.

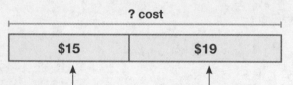

? cost

$15	$19

↑ $15 for shorts   ↑ $19 for shirt

You know the parts. Add to find the total.

$15 + $19 = ?   Think: $15 + $20 = $35
$15 + $19 = $34 $20 is $1 more than $19.

David needs $34 to buy shorts and a shirt.

C Justify and Evaluate

Make sure the answer is reasonable.

Estimate.

$15 + $19 is about $20 + $20, or $40.

The answer is reasonable because $34 is close to $40.

Do You Understand?

Convince Me! Draw a strip diagram to solve this problem: How much money will David need if he wants to buy a pennant and a poster?

© Pearson Education, Inc. 3

Another Example

You can draw a strip diagram to show subtraction.

Harris's office building has 126 windows. First Financial Bank has 146 windows. How many more windows does the bank have than the office building?

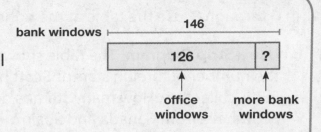

$146 - 126 = ?$

$146 - 126 = 20$ The bank has 20 more windows.

☆ Guided Practice*

1. Regina's Bakery baked 34 pies on Monday and 28 pies on Tuesday. Complete the strip diagram to find how many pies Regina's Bakery baked during both days.

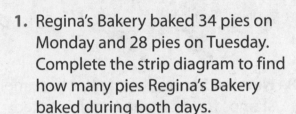

____ pies

| 34 | 28 |

34 pies on ____   28 pies on ____

For **2** and **3**, use the strip diagram for Problem 1.

2. What does each box show?

3. **Reason** What does the line above the two rectangles show?

Independent Practice ☆

In **4** and **5**, complete the strip diagram and solve.

4. Alexander spent $27 for tickets to a baseball game. He also spent $24 on food. How much did he spend on tickets and food?

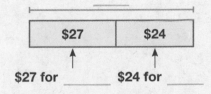

| $27 | $24 |

$27 for ____ $24 for ____

5. A pilot flew a total of 635 hours carrying mail in Alaska during this year and last year. Last year, she flew 295 hours. How many hours did she fly this year?

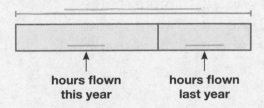

hours flown this year   hours flown last year

Problem Solving

In **6** through **8**, use the table at the right.

6. **Use a Strip Diagram** The table shows the number of foreign stamps Scott has in his collection. How many stamps does Scott have from Canada and Spain?

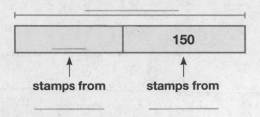

stamps from   stamps from

Scott's Stamp Collection	
Country	**Number of Stamps**
Canada	125
France	60
Mexico	85
Spain	150
United Kingdom	175

7. **Represent** How many more stamps does Scott have from the United Kingdom than from Mexico? Draw a strip diagram to solve.

8. **Number Sense** Scott said, "I have more stamps from Canada and the United Kingdom than I have from France, Mexico, and Spain combined." Is Scott correct? Explain.

9. **Analyze Information** At the aquarium, Janet counted 12 sand sharks, 9 zebra sharks, and 11 nurse sharks. About how many more zebra and nurse sharks did Janet count than sand sharks?

   A   About 5 more sharks
   B   About 10 more sharks
   C   About 20 more sharks
   D   About 30 more sharks

10. **Extend Your Thinking** In Traci's third-grade class, 18 students own cats, 22 students own dogs, and 2 students own snakes. How many students own cats, dogs, or snakes? Draw a strip diagram to solve the problem.

© Pearson Education, Inc. 3

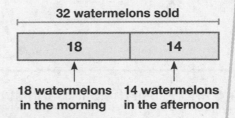

Another Look!

Add the numbers in the parts of the strip diagram to find how many.

Don sold 18 watermelons in the morning and 14 watermelons in the afternoon. How many watermelons did he sell?

You can draw a strip diagram to show addition.

$18 + 14 = 32$
Don sold 32 watermelons.

32 watermelons sold

| 18 | 14 |

18 watermelons in the morning   14 watermelons in the afternoon

In **1** through **3**, complete the strip diagram and solve.

1. Two buses are carrying students to a field trip. There are 36 students on one bus and 30 students on the other. How many students are on both buses?

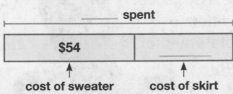

_____ students

| _____ | 30 |

students on Bus #1   students on Bus #2

2. Vanessa buys a skirt and a sweater for $91. The sweater costs $54. How much does the skirt cost?

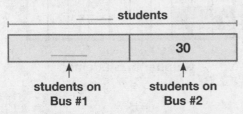

_____ spent

| $54 | |

cost of sweater   cost of skirt

3. A male giant panda at a zoo in Washington D.C. weighed 221 pounds in February. A female giant panda weighed 145 pounds during that same month. How much did the two pandas weigh all together?

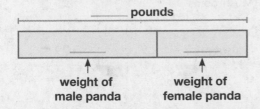

_____ pounds

| | |

weight of male panda   weight of female panda

4. **Represent** Kelly spends $28 on a mug and a book. The mug costs $15. How much does the book cost? Draw a strip diagram to solve the problem.

5. **Communicate** Jane sold 25 raffle tickets Monday, 30 raffle tickets Tuesday, and 40 raffle tickets Wednesday. How many raffle tickets did Jane sell all together? Use the Associative Property of Addition to solve this problem. Explain how you solved the problem.

For **6** and **7**, use the bar graph at the right.

6. Which way do most students take to get to school?

7. Which is the most likely reason why only ★ 2 students walk to school?

   A   Walking is a good way to exercise.

   B   Walking is more popular than riding a bike.

   C   More students live too far away to walk.

   D   Students who walk could ride a bike.

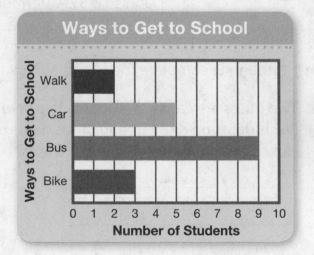

8. **Extend Your Thinking** The table shows the number of votes received from students for four different pizza toppings. How many more votes were received for meatless toppings than meat toppings? Describe a property you used to solve the problem.

You can use the Associative Property of Addition to help find the total votes for meatless toppings.

Favorite Pizza Toppings

DATA

Topping	Number of Votes
Green Peppers	45
Mushrooms	55
Cheese	134
Sausage	129

© Pearson Education, Inc. 3

Name _____

1. Estimation Jason estimated 762 − 237 by using 800 − 200. Carrie estimated 762 − 237 by using 760 − 240. Whose method will give an estimate closer to the actual answer? Tell how you decided.

Applying Math Processes
- How does this problem connect to previous ones?
- What is my plan?
- How can I use tools?
- How can I use number sense?
- How can I communicate and represent my thinking?
- How can I organize and record information?
- How can I explain my work?
- How can I justify my answer?

2. Number Sense Is Lynn's work correct? If not, tell why and write a correct answer.

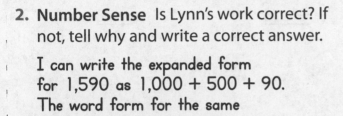

I can write the expanded form for 1,590 as 1,000 + 500 + 90. The word form for the same number is one thousand, five hundred nine.

3. Use a Strip Diagram Write a word problem that can be modeled with the strip diagram. Solve your problem.

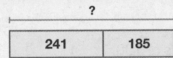

?	
241	185

4. Explain Kyle wrote the sentence $4 + (6 + 7) = (4 + 6) + 7$ to model an addition property. What property did he model? Explain.

5. Represent On Friday, 138 people showed up on time for a play. 10 more people came late, and 56 people left early. How many people stayed until the end? Model the problem below.

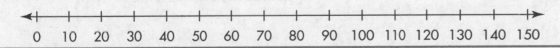

0 10 20 30 40 50 60 70 80 90 100 110 120 130 140 150

6. Extend Your Thinking Jamal wants to solve 400 − 228. Explain how Jamal can count on to find the difference.

Error Search

For **1** through **4**, find each answer that is not correct. Circle the problem that is wrong. Rewrite the problem so it is correct.

1.	47	2.	90	3.	325	4.	272
	+ 29		− 36		+ 236		− 78
	62		54		651		206

Compatible Numbers

In **5** and **6**, draw circles around two or more numbers next to each other, across or down, with a sum of 50 or 100. Look for compatible numbers (numbers that are easy to compute with mentally).

5. Find sums of 50.

4	46	25	25	45
29	15	35	33	3
21	19	31	17	2
49	10	40	14	36
1	24	26	20	30

6. Find sums of 100.

94	6	40	92	25
50	50	10	8	75
36	19	50	45	55
40	31	75	41	59
24	50	25	78	22

© Pearson Education, Inc. 3

Name _____

Set A pages 77–82

You can use properties of addition to help solve addition problems.

The Commutative Property of Addition

$12 + \square = 15 + 12$

$12 + 15 = 15 + 12$

You can order addends in any way, and the sum will be the same.

The Associative Property of Addition

$3 + (7 + 4) = (3 + \square) + 4$

$3 + (7 + 4) = (3 + 7) + 4$

You can group addends in any way, and the sum will be the same.

The Identity Property of Addition

$306 + \square = 306$

$306 + 0 = 306$

The sum of any number and zero is that same number.

Remember that both sides of the equal sign must have the same value.

Write each missing number.

1. $18 + \underline{\quad} = 18$

2. $14 + (16 + 15) = (\underline{\quad} + 16) + 15$

3. $\underline{\quad} + 13 = 13 + 17$

4. $28 + (\underline{\quad} + 22) = 28 + (22 + 25)$

5. $62 + 21 + 0 = 62 + \underline{\quad}$

6. $\underline{\quad} + (263 + 178) = (314 + 263) + 178$

7. Use the numbers 178 and 34 to write a number sentence that models the Commutative Property of Addition.

Set B pages 83–88

Use mental math to find $57 + 25$.

Break apart 25. $25 = 20 + 5$

Add 20 to 57. $57 + 20 = 77$

Add 5 to 77. $77 + 5 = 82$

So, $57 + 25 = 82$.

Use mental math to find $374 + 238$.

Break apart 374 and 238.

$300 + 70 + 4$ and $200 + 30 + 8$

Add hundreds, tens, and ones.

$(300 + 200) + (70 + 30) + (4 + 8)$

$500 + 100 + 12 = 612$

So, $374 + 238 = 612$.

Remember that you can break apart both addends when finding sums mentally.

1. $30 + 56$ 2. $463 + 418$

3. Leo scored 257 points in Game 1, 315 points in Game 2, and 325 points in Game 3. Show how to use addition properties to find the total number of points Leo scored.

Use mental math to find 83 − 16.

It's easier to subtract 20.
83 − 20 = 63

If you subtract 20, you subtract 4 more than 16, so you add 4 to the answer.
63 + 4 = 67

So, 83 − 16 = 67.

Use mental math to find 400 − 168.

Count on.

168 + 2 = 170
170 + 30 = 200
200 + 200 = 400
2 + 30 + 200 = 232

So, 400 − 168 = 232.

Remember to change each number in the same way when subtracting mentally.

1. 52 − 16   **2.** 84 − 37

3. 768 − 259   **4.** 282 − 125

5. A pair of pants costs $34. The pants are on sale for $8 off. If Matt has $50, how much change will he get after buying the pants at the sale price? Describe how you can use mental math to solve the problem.

Estimate 478 + 134.

Round each addend to the nearest ten.

$$\begin{array}{r} 478 \rightarrow 480 \\ + 112 \rightarrow 110 \\ \hline 590 \end{array}$$

Round each addend to the nearest hundred.

$$\begin{array}{r} 478 \rightarrow 500 \\ + 112 \rightarrow 100 \\ \hline 600 \end{array}$$

Use compatible numbers.

$$\begin{array}{r} 478 \rightarrow 475 \\ + 112 \rightarrow 110 \\ \hline 585 \end{array}$$

Remember that compatible numbers are numbers close to the actual numbers and are easier to add mentally.

Estimate each sum.

Round to the nearest hundred.

1. 367 + 319   **2.** 732 + 127

Round to the nearest ten.

3. 98 + 42   **4.** 459 + 85

Use compatible numbers.

5. 372 + 123   **6.** 211 + 164

7. Will rounding to the nearest ten or the nearest hundred give a closer estimate of 314 + 247? Explain your answer.

© Pearson Education, Inc. 3

Set E pages 101–106

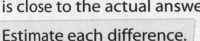

Estimate 486 − 177.

Round each number to the nearest hundred.

$$486 \rightarrow 500$$
$$-\ 177 \rightarrow 200$$
$$\overline{\ \ 300}$$

Round each number to the nearest ten.

$$486 \rightarrow 490$$
$$-\ 177 \rightarrow 180$$
$$\overline{\ \ 310}$$

Use compatible numbers.

$$486 \rightarrow 475$$
$$-\ 177 \rightarrow 175$$
$$\overline{\ \ 300}$$

Remember that an estimate is close to the actual answer.

Estimate each difference.

Round to the nearest hundred.

1. 527 − 341   **2.** 872 − 110

Round to the nearest ten.

3. 87 − 35   **4.** 659 − 241

Use compatible numbers.

5. 472 − 228   **6.** 911 − 347

7. Will rounding to the nearest ten or the nearest hundred give a closer estimate of 848 − 231? Explain your answer.

Set F pages 107–112

Find 679 − 128.

Find the difference.

> You can check a subtraction problem using addition.

$$\begin{array}{cc} 679 & 551 \\ -\ 128 & +\ 128 \\ \hline 551 & 679 \end{array}$$

The numbers in the addition and subtraction match, so 551 is the correct difference.

Remember that you can check an addition problem using subtraction.

Add or subtract. Check your work.

1.
$$\begin{array}{r} 7\ 4\ 6 \\ -\ 5\ 3\ 2 \\ \hline \square\square\square \end{array} \qquad \begin{array}{r} \square\square\square \\ +\ 5\ 3\ 2 \\ \hline \square\square\square \end{array}$$

2.
$$\begin{array}{r} 2\ 3\ 7 \\ +\ 4\ 1\ 2 \\ \hline \square\square\square \end{array} \qquad \begin{array}{r} \square\square\square \\ -\ 4\ 1\ 2 \\ \hline \square\square\square \end{array}$$

3. Toni read 131 pages on Monday and 158 pages on Tuesday. How many pages did Toni read in all? Check your work.

Find 45 + 35 + 17.

Use a number line to add.

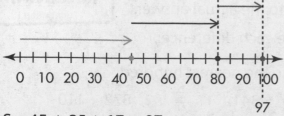

So, 45 + 35 + 17 = 97.

Find 95 − 40 − 30.

Use a number line to subtract.

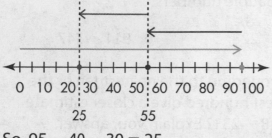

So, 95 − 40 − 30 = 25.

Remember to move to the right to add, and move to the left to subtract.

Add or subtract. Use the number line to help.

1. 43 + 29

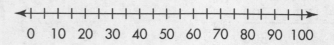

2. 52 − 12

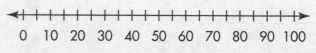

3. 85 + 10 − 51

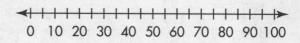

Kim spent $45 on a shirt and $25 on a skirt. How much did she spend?

You can draw a strip diagram to show addition.

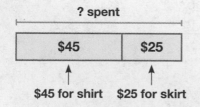

? spent

$45 $25

$45 for shirt $25 for skirt

Each part of the rectangle in the bottom part of the diagram shows an addend.

$45 + $25 = ?

$45 + $25 = $70
So, Kim spent $70.

Remember that strip diagrams can also show subtraction.

Draw a strip diagram and then solve.

1. Sue has 54 trading cards. Then she buys 27 more. How many trading cards does Sue have?

2. Mr. Wong drove 332 miles. He drove 184 miles before stopping for gas. How many miles did he drive after stopping for gas?

© Pearson Education, Inc. 3

1. Amber modeled an addition property below. Which is the missing number?

$(2 + 1) + 3 = 2 + (\boxed{} + 3)$

A 0

B 1

C 2

D 3

4. In June, Jackie sold 638 pounds of vegetables. In July, she sold 776 pounds of vegetables. Which estimate uses rounding numbers to the nearest ten to find how many more pounds of vegetables she sold in July than June?

A $800 - 600 = 200$

B $780 - 640 = 140$

C $775 - 650 = 125$

D $800 - 625 = 175$

2. A mother elephant at the zoo ate 171 pounds of food one day. A baby elephant ate 69 pounds of food that day. Which is **NOT** a reasonable estimate for how much they ate all together?

A $175 + 70 = 245$

B $170 + 70 = 240$

C $175 + 75 = 250$

D $130 + 70 = 200$

5. Kayla wants to use mental math to add 32 and 54. Which of these shows how to break apart the numbers into tens and ones?

A Break 32 into $20 + 12$. Break 54 into $25 + 29$.

B Break 32 into $30 + 2$. Break 54 into $32 + 22$.

C Break 32 into $16 + 16$. Break 54 into $27 + 27$.

D Break 32 into $30 + 2$. Break 54 into $50 + 4$.

3. Brianna wants to subtract $82 - 48$ mentally. Which of the following should she do first to find the difference mentally?

A Add 2 to 48 and add 2 to 82.

B Add 2 to 48 and subtract 2 from to 82.

C Subtract 8 from 48 and subtract 2 from 82.

D Subtract 12 from 82 and add 12 to 48.

6. Amy subtracts 342 from 456 and gets 114. Which number should she add to 114 to check her answer?

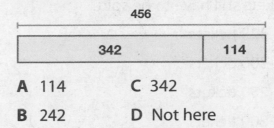

A 114   **C** 342

B 242   **D** Not here

7. Christopher's school has 704 students. 528 students live within two miles of school. Which is the most reasonable estimate for how many students live farther than two miles from school?

  A About 160

  B About 170

  C About 190

  D About 200

8. Michael modeled the Associative Property of Addition using a number sentence below. Which number sentence did he use?

  A $32 + 56 + 10 = 10 + 56 + 32$

  B $(49 + 28) + 5 = 49 + (28 + 5)$

  C $56 + 890 = 890 + 56$

  D $82 + 0 = 82$

9. Abigail's school had 491 tickets to sell for the talent show. So far, they have sold 235 tickets. Which is the most reasonable estimate for how many tickets still have to be sold?

  A 325 tickets

  B 300 tickets

  C 250 tickets

  D 200 tickets

10. Jessica counted 127 seats on the left side of the assembly hall at school. She counted 105 seats on the right side. She uses mental math to find how many seats there are. Which shows a way she can do this?

  A $(100 + 100) + 20 + (7 + 5) =$ $200 + 20 + 12 = 232$

  B $127 + 105 = 323$

  C $130 + 100 = 230$

  D $100 - 100 = 0; 27 - 5 = 22$

11. José subtracted 57 from 169. His work is shown below. How can he check his work using inverse operations?

$$\begin{array}{r} 169 \\ -57 \\ \hline 112 \end{array}$$

  A Add 57 and 169.

  B Add 112 and 169.

  C Subtract 112 from 169.

  D Add 112 and 57.

12. Kara wanted to round to the nearest ten to estimate the sum of 405 and 385. She wrote $400 + 400 = 800$. Which best explains what she did incorrectly?

  A Kara used compatible numbers.

  B Kara's estimate is not reasonable.

  C Kara rounded to the nearest hundred.

  D Kara's addition is wrong.

© Pearson Education, Inc. 3

Name _____

13. Gina's estimate for 214 + 157 was close to the actual sum. She rounded to the nearest ten. Which was Gina's estimate?

A 210 + 160 = 370

B 300 + 100 = 400

C 200 + 160 = 360

D 210 + 155 = 365

14. Adrian wants to buy a tablet computer for $350 and a storage case for $62. Which strip diagram can be used to find the total cost of the items?

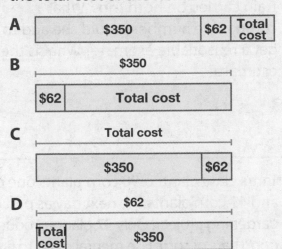

15. Margot wants to find the sum of 41 + 50 + 150. Which shows a way she can find the sum mentally using the Associative Property of Addition?

A 41 + (50 + 150) = 241

B 241 + 0 = 241

C 41 + 50 + 150 = 150 + 50 + 41

D 41 + 50 + 150 = 241

16. Allie wants to subtract 341 − 97 mentally. First, she adds 3 to 97 to get 100. What should Allie's next step be? What is the difference?

A Add 6 to 341. The difference is 247.

B Add 200 to 100. The difference is 100.

C Subtract 3 from 341. The difference is 238

D Add 3 to 341. The difference is 244.

17. David cycled 74 miles one week and 55 miles another week. David's friend Marc cycled 126 miles during the same two weeks. Which man cycled more miles and how many more miles did he cycle?

A David cycled 2 miles more than Marc.

B David cycled 3 more miles than Marc.

C Marc cycled 3 more miles than David.

D Both men cycled the same number of miles.

18. A store had 354 pounds of fruit Monday morning. By Monday night, it had sold all but 146 pounds of fruit. Bill rounded to the nearest 10 before he estimated how much fruit was sold. Which is Bill's estimate for how many pounds of fruit the store sold on Monday?

A About 180 pounds

B About 200 pounds

C About 220 pounds

D About 240 pounds

19. Emil found 693 − 231. The difference he got was 464. What should he do to check his answer, and what will he find?

A Subtract 639 − 300 = 339; His original answer was incorrect.

B Subtract 464 − 231 = 233; His original answer was incorrect.

C Add 693 + 231 = 924; His original answer was correct.

D Add 464 + 231 = 695; His original answer was incorrect.

---

20. What problem did Joel model on the number line below?

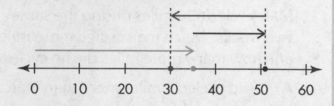

---

21. While Joshua was waiting for the bus, he counted the trucks and cars that passed. He counted 5 vans, 24 trucks, and 38 cars. Use mental math to find the sum of the vehicles Joshua counted. Mark your answer in the grid below.

---

22. Hamza wrote this number sentence. What property or properties are modeled?

$51 + 8 + 0 = 51 + 8$

A The Associative (Grouping) Property

B The Identity (Zero) Property

C The Commutative (Order) Property

D The Commutative (Order) Property and the Identity (Zero) Property

---

23. A train came into Dallas carrying 392 passengers. Leaving Dallas, it had 259 passengers. Erin wants to estimate the total number of passengers the train carried on both trips. What compatible numbers could she add to get a reasonable estimate? What is the estimate?

---

24. Tara's class planted 90 corn plants one day and 47 corn plants the next day as part of a gardening project. Only 97 plants produced good ears of corn. Use mental math to find how many plants did not produce good ears of corn. Mark your answer in the grid below.

© Pearson Education, Inc. 3

Developing Proficiency: Adding and Subtracting Whole Numbers

Essential Question: What are standard procedures for adding and subtracting whole numbers?

Water is matter and can be in the form of a liquid, solid, or gas.

Did you know water freezes at 32 degrees Fahrenheit?

That's really cool! Here is a project on water and subtraction.

Math and Science Project: Hot and Cold!

Do Research Use the Internet or other sources to find out about water in the form of a solid, liquid, and gas. List examples of each and where you find them. Also, find the temperature at which water boils.

Journal: Write a Report Include what you found. Also, in your report:

- Include the temperatures at which water freezes and boils. Explain how this affects the form of water.

- Choose one or two of your examples and relate them to a recent real-world event.

- Make up two subtraction problems based on temperature and how it affects water.

Review What You Know

Vocabulary

Choose the best term from the box. Write it on the blank.

> • Commutative Property of Addition
>
> • Associative Property of Addition
>
> • compatible numbers
>
> • inverse operations

1. _____ are numbers that are easy to add or subtract with mentally.

2. According to the _____

   _____, the grouping of addends can be changed, and the sum will remain the same.

3. Addition and subtraction are

   _____.

Estimating Sums

Use compatible numbers to estimate each sum.

4. $27 + 12$ 5. $133 + 102$

6. $74 + 345$ 7. $52 + 87$

8. $293 + 278$ 9. $119 + 426$

Estimating Differences

10. **Explain** Tony and Kim play a video game. Tony scores 512 points. Kim scores 768 points. About how many more points does Kim score than Tony? Which estimation method did you use?

11. Which number sentence shows the most reasonable estimate for $467 - 231$?

    A $425 - 250 = 175$
    B $500 - 200 = 300$
    C $400 - 300 = 100$
    D $470 - 230 = 240$

Associative Property of Addition

12. **Explain** Megan and Sophia went shopping. Megan bought a pair of shoes for $45. At another store she bought a necklace for $32 and a bracelet for $29. Sophia bought two pairs of shoes at the same store. One pair cost $45 and the other cost $32. Sophia bought pants for $29 at another store. Use the Associative Property of Addition to explain why each girl spent the same amount. Then find how much Megan and Sophia spent in all.

© Pearson Education, Inc. 3

My Word Cards

Use the examples for each word on the front of the card to help complete the definitions on the back.

---

regrouping

28 = 28 ones

28 = 1 ten 18 ones

28 = 2 tens 8 ones

---

equation

addition	subtraction
$2 + 5 = 7$	$7 - 5 = \square$

multiplication	division
$2 \times 5 = 10$	$10 \div\ ? = 2$

---

unknown

$3 + 4 = ?$ $310 - \square = 270$

↑   ↑

unknown   unknown

My Word Cards

Complete each definition. Extend learning by writing your own definitions.

A number sentence that uses an equal sign (=) to show the value to its left is the same as the value to its right is

called an _____.

When you are _____ numbers, you are naming whole numbers in a different way.

A symbol that stands for a number in an

equation is called an _____.

138

© Pearson Education, Inc. 3

Name _____

Solve & Share

Find the sum of 327 + 241. Think about place value. *Solve this problem any way you choose.*

⭐ **TEKS 3.4A** Solve with fluency one-step … problems involving addition … within 1,000 using strategies based on place value…. Also, 3.4.
Mathematical Process Standards 3.1B, 3.1C, 3.1D, 3.1E, 3.1F, 3.1G

Digital Resources at PearsonTexas.com

Solve   Learn   Glossary   Check   Tools   Games

You can **formulate a plan.** Part of your plan for solving this problem could be to show each of the numbers in expanded form. *Show your work in the space below!*

Look Back!

Connect How can using place value help you solve this 3-digit addition problem?

How Can You Break Large Addition Problems into Smaller Ones?

Find the sum of 243 + 179. Each digit in the numbers can be modeled with place-value blocks.

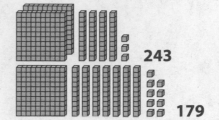

243

179

You can use place value to add the numbers.

B ## Step 1

Break 243 + 179 into smaller problems. Think about the place values of each number.

Hundreds	Tens	Ones
200	40	3
+ 100	+ 70	+ 9
300	110	12

C ## Step 2

Then, add the sums of all the places.

```
  300
  110
+  12
-----
  422
```

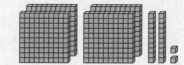

So, 243 + 179 = 422.

Do You Understand?

Convince Me! Lexi says, "To solve 243 + 179, I can just count on with place-value blocks to find the answer: 100, 200, 300, another hundred from the 11 tens is 400, one more ten and 12 ones is 422!" How is Lexi's way like Steps 1 and 2 above?

© Pearson Education, Inc. 3

Guided Practice*

In **1**, use place value to find the sum.

1.

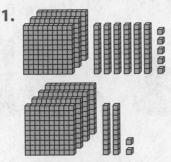

Find 365 + 422.

Hundreds	Tens	Ones	Total
300	60	5	
+ 400	+ 20	+ 2	

2. Communicate Suppose you were adding 527 + 405. What would the tens problem be? Why?

3. Write the smaller problems you could use to find 623 + 281. What is the sum?

Independent Practice

Leveled Practice In **4** through **11**, find each sum.

4.

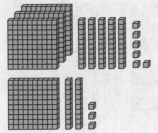

356 + 123

Hundreds	Tens	Ones	Total
300	50	6	
+ 100	+ 20	+ 3	

5.

550 + 423

Hundreds	Tens	Ones	Total
500	50	0	
+ 400	+ 20	+ 3	

6. 185 + 613

7. 730 + 168

8. 546 + 143

9. 362 + 524

10. 644 + 101

11. 463 + 315

*For another example, see Set A on page 195.

Problem Solving

12. Represent John read a book with 377 pages. Jess read a book with 210 pages. How many pages did John and Jess read? Draw a strip diagram to model and solve the problem.

13. Explain Explain how the solids shown in Group A and Group B could have been sorted.

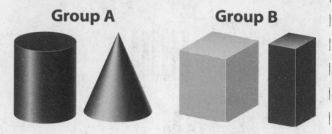

Group A **Group B**

14. Max wants to add 331 + 516 using place value. He begins by breaking the problem into smaller problems. He writes (300 + 500) + (30 + 10) + (1 + 6). Which shows the correct hundreds, tens, and ones?

A 800 + 40 + 6

B 800 + 40 + 7

C 700 + 40 + 8

D 400 + 80 + 8

15. Formulate a Plan Bill needs to find 318 + 230. Into what three smaller problems can Bill break this addition? What is the sum?

You can use place value to add.

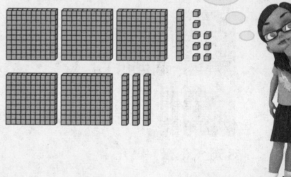

16. Construct Arguments Henry believes the sum of 275 + 313 is 598. Is Henry correct? Explain.

?	
275	313

17. Extend Your Thinking A school cafeteria sold 255 lunches on Monday, 140 lunches on Tuesday, and 226 lunches on Wednesday. Did the cafeteria sell more lunches on Monday and Tuesday or on Tuesday and Wednesday? Explain.

© Pearson Education, Inc. 3

Another Look!

You can use place-value blocks to model each number.

Find 234 + 451.

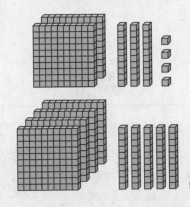

Break the problem into smaller problems.

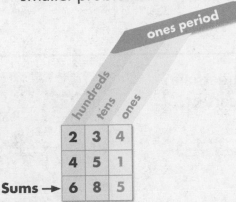

ones period

hundreds tens ones

| 2 | 3 | 4 |
| 4 | 5 | 1 |

Sums → | 6 | 8 | 5 |

Add the sums.   **Total**

Hundreds ────→ 600
Tens ──────→ 80
Ones ──────→ + 5
234 + 451 =   685

In **1**, complete the steps to find the sum.

1.
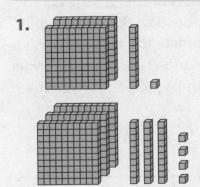

Hundreds	Tens	Ones	Total
200	10	1	_____
+ 300	+ 30	+ 4	
		+	_____

For **2** through **10**, find each sum.

2. 516 + 142

3. 439 + 520

4. 721 + 176

5. 631 + 245

6. 580 + 315

7. 714 + 144

8. 128 + 441

9. 214 + 253

10. 661 + 127

11. **Mental Math** Estimate first, then use counting on to solve mentally. How many more students are in eighth grade than sixth grade at North Middle School? Is your answer reasonable? Explain.

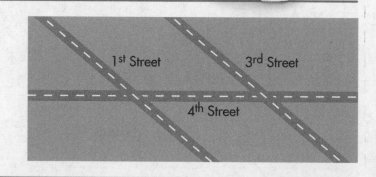

Students at North Middle School	
Grade	Students
6th	352
7th	379
8th	421

12. Lisa concludes 1st and 3rd Streets are parallel to each other. Is she correct? Explain.

1st Street   3rd Street

4th Street

13. ⭐ Katrina uses place value to find the sum of 627 + 361. She begins by breaking the problem into smaller problems. She writes (600 + 300) + (20 + 60) + (7 + 1). Which shows the correct hundreds, tens, and ones?

  A 800 + 80 + 9   C 900 + 80 + 8
  B 800 + 90 + 8   D 900 + 90 + 8

14. **Number Sense** Ryan read 127 pages of a book on Monday and 172 pages of the same book on Tuesday. Use compatible numbers to estimate the number of pages Ryan read on Monday and Tuesday. What is the actual number of pages Ryan read?

15. **Extend Your Thinking** The Smith family took a vacation. They drove 256 miles on the first day and 287 miles on the second day. If they drove the same number of total miles on their return trip, how many miles did they drive on their entire trip?

16. **Construct Arguments** Is Dale's work correct? If not, tell why and write a correct answer.

Find 64 − 27.
I can add 3 to 27 to get 30.
64 − 30 = 34
34 − 3 = 31
So, 64 − 27 = 31.

© Pearson Education, Inc. 3

Name _____

☆ ☆
Solve & Share

Find the sum of 146 + 247. **Solve this problem any way you choose.**

✪ **TEKS 3.4A** Solve with fluency one-step and two-step problems involving addition ... within 1,000 using strategies based on place value.... Also, 3.5A.
Mathematical Process Standards 3.1C, 3.1D, 3.1E, 3.1F, 3.1G

Digital Resources at PearsonTexas.com

Solve   Learn   Glossary   Check   Tools   Games

You can **communicate.** Using place-value blocks and drawing pictures of the blocks can show how you found the sum. **Show your work!**

Look Back!

Number Sense When you add numbers, how do you know if you need to regroup?

How Can You Add 3-Digit Numbers with Place-Value Blocks?

Find 143 + 285.

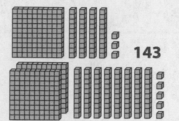

143

285

You can add whole numbers by using place value to break them apart.

Add the ones, tens, and hundreds.

B

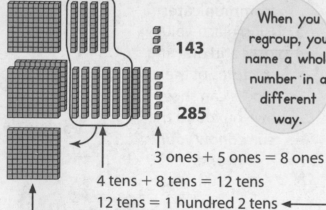

143

285

When you regroup, you name a whole number in a different way.

3 ones + 5 ones = 8 ones

4 tens + 8 tens = 12 tens

12 tens = 1 hundred 2 tens ← Regroup.

1 hundred + 1 hundred + 2 hundreds = 4 hundreds ← Add the hundreds.

C

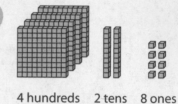

4 hundreds   2 tens   8 ones

428

143 + 285 = 428

Do You Understand?

Convince Me! Mr. Wu drove 224 miles yesterday. He drove 175 miles today. Use place-value blocks or draw pictures of blocks to find how many miles Mr. Wu drove.

© Pearson Education, Inc. 3

Another Example

You may have to regroup twice when you add. Find 148 + 276.

Step 1

Add the ones.
8 ones + 6 ones = 14 ones

Regroup.
14 ones = 1 ten 4 ones

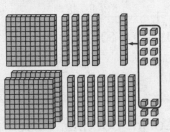

Step 2

Add the tens.
1 ten + 4 tens + 7 tens = 12 tens

Regroup.
12 tens = 1 hundred 2 tens

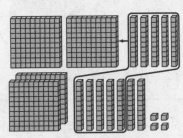

Step 3

Add the hundreds.
1 hundred + 1 hundred + 2 hundreds = 4 hundreds

So, 148 + 276 = 424.

☆ Guided Practice *

In **1**, use the model to write the problem and find the sum.

1.

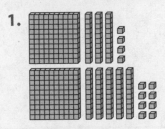

2. **Connect** How do you know when you need to regroup?

3. **Tools** Use place-value blocks to find 247 + 168.

Independent Practice ☆

In **4** through **6**, write the problem and find the sum.

4.

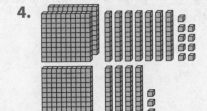

5.

6.

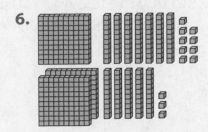

Problem Solving

7. Draw a Picture Mike wants to use place-value blocks to show 237 + 153. Draw a picture of the blocks Mike should use. What is the sum?

8. Represent Josh plays basketball and scores 15 points in game one, 9 points in game two, and 18 points in game three. How many points did Josh score? Use the number line to model and solve the problem.

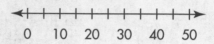

9. Which number sentence do the place-value blocks show?

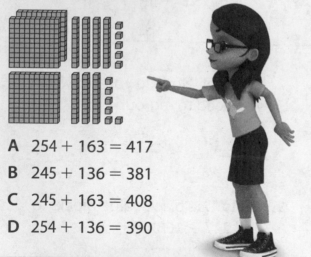

A 254 + 163 = 417

B 245 + 136 = 381

C 245 + 163 = 408

D 254 + 136 = 390

10. Represent Mrs. Collins bought a $256 plane ticket in March and a $125 plane ticket in April. Use place-value blocks or draw pictures to find out how much Mrs. Collins spent on the plane tickets.

11. Extend Your Thinking Heather is saving money to buy a new television that costs $750. Last month she saved $427, and this month she saved $325. Does Heather have enough money saved to buy the television? Use place-value blocks to help you solve the problem. Explain.

12. Explain Bill and John were playing a computer game. Bill scored 256 points in the first round and 345 points in the second round. John scored 325 points in the first round and 273 points in the second round. Who scored more points and won the game? Explain.

© Pearson Education, Inc. 3

Name _____

Another Look!
Find 152 + 329.

Show each number with place-value blocks.

152

329

Step 1 Add the ones.
2 + 9 = 11

Step 2 Add the tens.
50 + 20 = 70

Step 3 Add the hundreds.
100 + 300 = 400

Step 4 Add the sums.
400 + 70 + 11 = 481

In **1**, use place-value blocks to find the sum.

1. 235 + 186

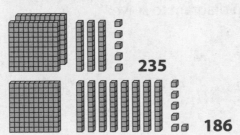

235

186

Add the ones.
_____ + 6 = _____

Add the tens.
_____ + _____ = 110

Add the hundreds.
_____ + _____ = _____

Add the sums.
_____ + 110 + _____ = 421

In **2** through **4**, find each sum. Use place-value blocks or draw pictures to help.

2. 635 + 222

3. 337 + 152

4. 359 + 548

5. **Estimation** About how many tickets were sold for the three rides on Saturday? About how many tickets were sold for the three rides on Sunday? Round to the nearest ten to estimate.

Number of Tickets Sold		
Ride	Saturday	Sunday
Ferris Wheel	368	302
Roller Coaster	486	456
Swings	138	154

6. One kind of pecan tree produces about 45 pecans in each pound of nuts. If you have one pound of these pecans and one pound of the kind of pecan shown at the right, how many pecans do you have?

There are about 60 pecans in one pound of this kind of nut.

7. **Reason** Ed wants to model 137 + 429 with place-value blocks. He has enough hundreds and ones blocks, but only has 5 tens blocks. Is this enough to show the sum? Explain.

8. **Represent** At a busy airport, 228 flights landed between noon and 3:00 P.M. On the same day, 243 flights landed between 3:00 P.M. and 6:00 P.M. How many flights landed between noon and 6:00 P.M.? Draw a strip diagram to solve.

9. Larry was playing a board game. He scored 248 points in the first game and 273 points in the second game. How many points did Larry score?

? points	
248 points	273 points

A 411

B 421

C 511

D 521

10. **Extend Your Thinking** There are 230 seats on an airplane, but 15 of the seats are empty. There are 175 seats on another airplane, but 20 of the seats are empty. How many passengers are on both of the airplanes?

© Pearson Education, Inc. 3

Name _____

☆ **Solve & Share** ☆

Suppose a bus travels 276 miles on Monday and 248 miles on Tuesday. How many miles does the bus travel? *Solve this problem any way you choose.*

 TEKS 3.4A Solve with fluency one-step and two-step problems involving addition … within 1,000 using strategies based on place value…. Also, 3.5A. **Mathematical Process Standards** 3.1A, 3.1B, 3.1C, 3.1D, 3.1E, 3.1F, 3.1G

Digital Resources at PearsonTexas.com

Solve Learn Glossary Check Tools Games

You can **connect ideas.** You know how to use place-value blocks to show regrouping. Is there another way you can show regrouping to solve this problem? *Show your work!*

Look Back!

Estimation Why would it be a good idea to estimate first before you solved this problem?

How Can You Use Addition to Solve Problems?

Jason's family drove from Niagara Falls to Albany. They drove 119 miles in the morning and 187 miles in the afternoon. How far did Jason's family drive?

Find 119 + 187.

Estimate by rounding to the nearest hundred.
100 + 200 = 300
So, 119 + 187 is about 300 miles.

187 miles

Niagara Falls

Albany

NEW YORK

119 miles

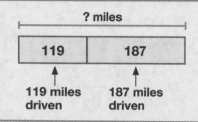

? miles

119	187

119 miles driven   187 miles driven

An estimate can help you check whether or not your answer is reasonable.

Add the ones, tens, and hundreds.

B ## Step 1

9 ones + 7 ones = 16 ones

Regroup.
16 ones = 1 ten 6 ones

$$\begin{array}{r} ^{1} \\ 119 \\ + 187 \\ \hline 6 \end{array}$$

C ## Step 2

1 ten + 1 ten + 8 tens
= 10 tens

Regroup.
10 tens = 1 hundred 0 tens

$$\begin{array}{r} ^{11} \\ 119 \\ + 187 \\ \hline 06 \end{array}$$

D ## Step 3

1 hundred + 1 hundred + 1 hundred = 3 hundreds

$$\begin{array}{r} ^{11} \\ 119 \\ + 187 \\ \hline 306 \end{array}$$

Jason's family drove 306 miles.

The answer is reasonable since 306 is close to 300.

Do You Understand?

Convince Me! Draw or use place-value blocks to show how Steps 1, 2, and 3 above work. What did you find out?

© Pearson Education, Inc. 3

☆ Guided Practice *

In **1** through **4**, estimate by rounding to the nearest ten. Then find each sum. You may use place-value blocks or drawings to help.

1.   1 2 6
       + 1 7 1
       ─────
       2 ☐ ☐

2.   5 3 8
       + 4 2 9
       ─────
       ☐ ☐ 7

3.   4 1 5
       + 1 6 8
       ─────
       ☐ 8 ☐

4.   3 9 1
       + 6 0 9
       ─────
       ☐ ☐ ☐ 0

5. Check for Reasonableness In Exercise 1, how can you tell if your answer is reasonable?

6. Sue scored 236 points during the first half of her basketball season. She scored 285 points during the second half. How many points did she score during the entire season?

? points

236	285

Independent Practice ☆

For **7** through **22**, estimate by rounding to the nearest ten. Then, find each sum.

7.   1 3 6
       + 2 5 2
       ─────
       3 ☐ ☐

8.   6 7 8
       + 1 2 9
       ─────
       ☐ ☐ 7

9.   5 6 4
       + 2 8 3
       ─────
       8 ☐ ☐

10.   1 1 8
        + 3 3 5
        ─────
        ☐ 5 ☐

11.   172
        + 534

12.   324
        + 508

13.   309
        + 287

14.   465
        + 285

15. 582 + 230

16. 207 + 238

17. 424 + 391

18. 678 + 143

19. 756 + 219

20. 148 + 607

21. 523 + 469

22. 167 + 189

Problem Solving

For **23** through **26**, use the table at the right.

23. Connect How many soup can labels did Grades 1 and 2 collect? Estimate by rounding to the hundred first, then solve. Write a number sentence that represents the problem.

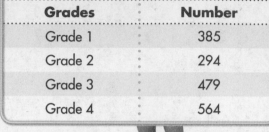

Soup Can Labels Collected	
Grades	**Number**
Grade 1	385
Grade 2	294
Grade 3	479
Grade 4	564

24. Check for Reasonableness Is your answer to Exercise 23 reasonable? Explain.

25. Number Sense Without finding the exact sum, how do you know Grades 2 and 3 together collected more soup can labels than Grade 4?

26. ★ Which number sentence shows how many labels Grades 1 and 4 collected?

A $385 + 497 = 882$

B $385 + 564 = 949$

C $385 + 479 = 864$

D $385 + 294 = 679$

---

27. Number Sense The tallest roller coaster in the world is called Kingda Ka. It is 192 feet taller than the first Ferris wheel. Use the symbols $>$ and $<$ to compare the heights of the two rides in two different ways.

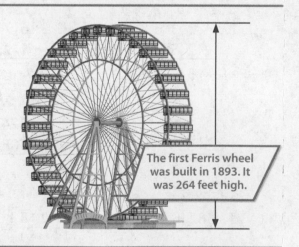

The first Ferris wheel was built in 1893. It was 264 feet high.

---

28. Extend Your Thinking Sharon can run 278 yards in one minute. Pete can run 145 more yards than Sharon in one minute. How many yards can they both run in one minute?

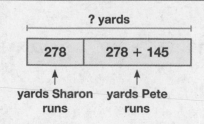

? yards

278	278 + 145

↑ yards Sharon runs   ↑ yards Pete runs

© Pearson Education, Inc. 3

Name _____

Another Look!
Find 237 + 186.

You can use place-value blocks to model each number you are adding.

237

186

Step 1
$$\begin{array}{r} \overset{1}{237} \\ +\ 186 \\ \hline 3 \end{array}$$

Step 2
$$\begin{array}{r} \overset{1\ 1}{237} \\ +\ 186 \\ \hline 23 \end{array}$$

Step 3
$$\begin{array}{r} \overset{1\ 1}{237} \\ +\ 186 \\ \hline 423 \end{array}$$

In **1**, use the place-value blocks to help add.

1. 345 + 276

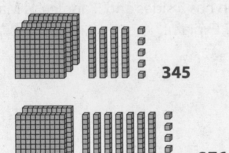

345

276

Add the ones and regroup.
$$\begin{array}{r} \overset{1}{3\ 4\ 5} \\ +\ 2\ 7\ 6 \\ \hline 1 \end{array}$$

Add the tens and regroup.
$$\begin{array}{r} \square\ \square \\ 3\ 4\ 5 \\ +\ 2\ 7\ 6 \\ \hline \square\ \square \end{array}$$

Add the hundreds.
$$\begin{array}{r} \square\ \square \\ 3\ 4\ 5 \\ +\ 2\ 7\ 6 \\ \hline \square\ \square\ \square \end{array}$$

For **2** through **5**, estimate by rounding to the nearest hundred. Then find each sum.

2. $\begin{array}{r} 118 \\ +\ 146 \\ \hline \end{array}$

3. $\begin{array}{r} 283 \\ +\ 147 \\ \hline \end{array}$

4. $\begin{array}{r} 542 \\ +\ 109 \\ \hline \end{array}$

5. $\begin{array}{r} 220 \\ +\ 479 \\ \hline \end{array}$

For **6** and **7**, use the table at the right.

6. **Communicate** How many points were scored by Howie and Theo? Estimate by rounding to the nearest hundred, then solve. Write a number sentence that represents the problem.

Points Scored

Player	Points
Howie	272
Theo	325
Isabel	288

7. **Check for Reasonableness** Is your answer to Exercise 6 reasonable? Explain.

8. **Connect** There were 252 horses in the pasture. The rancher added 163 new horses to the pasture. How many horses are now in the pasture?

A 415   C 667

B 567   D 677

9. **Represent** Lexi is having a party. She decorates with 8 stars. Is the number of stars Lexi uses odd or even? Draw counters in the ten frame to justify your answer.

10. **Construct Arguments** Maria was asked to show $8.85 using the least number of bills and coins. She showed 1 five-dollar bill, 3 one-dollar bills, 2 quarters, 3 dimes, and 1 nickel. Do you agree? If not, what bills and coins should Maria show?

11. **Construct Arguments** Marc concludes a hexagon has 5 sides and 5 angles. Is Marc correct? Explain.

12. **Extend Your Thinking** Sarah and Angela have been collecting coins for a long time. Both girls have a collection of pennies and nickels in their piggy banks. Which girl has more coins in her bank? Explain how you know using numbers and symbols.

Sarah
149 pennies
127 nickels

Angela
173 pennies
105 nickels

© Pearson Education, Inc. 3

Name _____

A pet store has 162 goldfish, 124 angelfish, and 53 pufferfish. How many fish are there? How might an estimate help you solve the problem? *Solve this problem any way you choose.*

TEKS 3.4A Solve with fluency one-step and two-step problems involving addition … within 1,000 using strategies based on place value…. Also, 3.5A.
Mathematical Process Standards 3.1B, 3.1C, 3.1D, 3.1E, 3.1F, 3.1G

You can **connect ideas.** Use what you know about adding two numbers to add three numbers. *Show your work in the space below!*

Digital Resources at PearsonTexas.com

Solve   Learn   Glossary   Check   Tools   Games

Look Back!

Reason How is adding three numbers similar to adding two numbers?

How Can You Use Addition to Solve Problems?

Different kinds of birds are for sale at a pet store. How many birds are for sale?

Find 137 + 155 + 18.

Round to the nearest ten to estimate:
140 + 160 + 20 = 320.

Parrots
18

Canaries
137

Parakeets
155

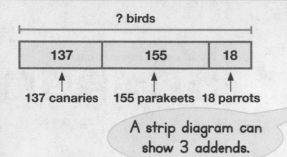

? birds

| 137 | 155 | 18 |

↑ 137 canaries   ↑ 155 parakeets   ↑ 18 parrots

A strip diagram can show 3 addends.

Step 1

Line up ones, tens, and hundreds.

```
  137
  155
+  18
```

Step 2

Add the ones. Regroup.

```
   2
  137
  155
+  18
    0
```

Step 3

Add the tens. Regroup.

```
  1 2
  137
  155
+  18
   10
```

The answer is reasonable since 310 is close to 320.

Step 4

Add the hundreds.

```
  1 2
  137
  155
+  18
  310
```

In all, 310 birds are for sale.

Do You Understand?

Convince Me! Suppose the pet store gets 46 lovebirds to sell. How many birds are for sale at the pet store now? Solve, and then write a number sentence that includes your solution.

© Pearson Education, Inc. 3

Name _____

In **1** through **4**, find each sum.

1.
```
    1
  1 2 3
  1 6 8
+   3 6
  □□7
```

2.
```
  5 1 0
    4 5
+   2 7
  5□□
```

3.
```
  2 4 7
  3 6 2
+   4 9
```

4. 56 + 183 + 269

You can use estimation to check if your sums are reasonable.

For **5** and **6**, look at the example on page 158.

5. Connect Why is there a 2 above the tens place in Step 2?

6. Represent Suppose the pet store gets 28 cockatoos to sell. Complete the strip diagram to show how many birds are for sale now. Solve.

```
|————————— birds —————————|
| 137        | 155       | 18 |    |
```
  ↑   ↑   ↑
137 canaries 155 parakeets 18 parrots

Leveled Practice In **7** through **17**, find each sum.

7.
```
    6 4
    4 2
+   8 8
  □□□
```

8.
```
  3 5 4
    8 5
+   7 2
  □□□
```

9.
```
  3 0 7
    3 7
+ 2 3 4
  □□□
```

10.
```
  7 1 4
  1 6 3
+   9 9
  □□□
```

11.
```
  602
  125
+ 231
```

12.
```
  246
   54
  233
+ 205
```

13.
```
  164
   68
+  35
```

14.
```
  125
   35
  124
+ 239
```

15. 32 + 9 + 56 + 8

16. 481 + 78 + 42

17. 398 + 219 + 23 + 251

Problem Solving

In **18** and **19**, use the calorie information.

18. **Formulate a Plan** Karin had cereal, a glass of milk, and a banana for breakfast. How many calories were in her food? Round to the nearest ten to estimate and then solve. Write a number sentence that includes your solution.

banana: 105 calories
bowl of dry cereal: 110 calories
glass of milk: 150 calories

You can use rounding to estimate.

19. Use your estimate in Exercise 18 to explain why your answer is reasonable.

20. **Number Sense** Compare the numbers 23,212 and 23,209. Use <, >, or =. Explain how you made your comparison.

21. Ramos has 12 one-dollar bills, 225 pennies, 105 nickels, and 65 dimes. How many coins does he have?

   A 385

   B 395

   C 980

   D 3,815

22. **Number Sense** What is the relationship between the 5s in the number 755,371?

23. **Extend Your Thinking** Meg says 95 + 76 + 86 is greater than 300, but less than 400. Is Meg correct? Why or why not?

24. **Analyze Information** Use the picture at the right to find the height of President Washington's head carved in Mt. Rushmore. Write a number sentence that includes the solution to the problem.

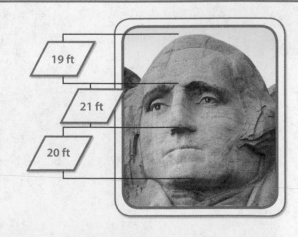

19 ft

21 ft

20 ft

© Pearson Education, Inc. 3

Name _____

Another Look!

Find 137 + 201 + 109.

?		
137	201	109

To add three numbers, you can add two numbers first. Then, add the sum of the first two numbers and the third number.

You can break the problem into two smaller problems.

Step 1

Add 137 + 201.

```
  137
+ 201
  338
```

Step 2

Add 338 + 109.

```
   1
  338
+ 109
  447
```

So, 137 + 201 + 109 = 447.

In **1** and **2**, complete the smaller problems to find the sum.

1. 35 + 63 + 76

```
      3 5
    +
    ─────
```

```
      1
     ☐ ☐
   +  7 6
   ──────
```

2. 149 + 22 + 314

```
      1
    1 4 9
  +  ☐ ☐
  ───────
```

```
   ☐ ☐ ☐
 + 3 1 4
 ───────
```

In **3** through **8**, find the sum.

3.
```
  127
   39
+  87
```

4.
```
  293
  312
+  78
```

5.
```
   25
  238
   75
+ 180
```

6. 150 + 125 + 350

7. 382 + 164 + 267

8. 46 + 461 + 309

9. Explain Justine has 162 red buttons, 98 blue buttons, and 284 green buttons. She says she knows she has more than 500 buttons without finding the exact sum. Do you agree? Explain.

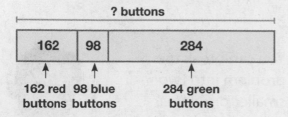

? buttons

162	98	284

162 red 98 blue   284 green
buttons buttons   buttons

10. Justify To subtract 78 − 35 mentally, Carmine added 5 to each number and Karen added 2 to each number. Will both methods work to find the correct answer? Why or why not?

11. ⭐ On Friday, 215 people went to the street fair. On Saturday, 163 more people went to the street fair than on Friday. On Sunday, 192 people went. How many people went to the fair on Friday, Saturday, or Sunday?

A 570

B 685

C 775

D 785

12. Represent Kyle was playing a new video game. He scored 128 points on his first game. He scored 305 points on his second game, and 490 points on his third game. How many points did Kyle score? Draw a strip diagram to model the problem, and then solve. Write a number sentence that also models the problem and includes your solution.

13. Extend Your Thinking Carlos ate or drank all the items listed in the table. How many calories did Carlos consume? What are two ways you can use to find the answer?

Food	Amount	Calories
Bran flakes	1 ounce	90
Banana	1	105
Orange juice	1 cup	110
Milk	1 cup	150

© Pearson Education, Inc. 3

Name _____

Solve & Share

Find the difference of 534 − 108. Think about place value. *Solve this problem any way you choose.*

TEKS 3.4A Solve with fluency one-step and two-step problems involving … subtraction within 1,000 using strategies based on place value.… Also, 3.4. **Mathematical Process Standards** 3.1B, 3.1C, 3.1D, 3.1G

You can **reason.** How could you break this problem into smaller subtraction problems? *Show your work in the space below!*

Digital Resources at PearsonTexas.com

Solve   Learn   Glossary   Check   Tools   Games

Look Back!

Number Sense How can using place value help you solve this subtraction problem?

How Can You Break Large Subtraction Problems into Smaller Ones?

At the end of the fourth round of a game of Digit Derby, Marco's score was 462 points. During the fifth round of the game, Marco loses points. What is Marco's score at the end of the fifth round?

Find 462 − 181.

End of Round 4

Marco has 462 points.

End of Round 5

Marco loses 181 points.

Place value can help you break a subtraction problem into smaller problems.

B Step 1

Start with 462.

Subtract the **hundreds**.
462 − 100 = 362

So far, 100 has been subtracted.

C Step 2

Next, start with 362.

Subtract the **tens**.

You need to subtract 8 tens, but there are not enough tens. So, subtract the 6 tens.
362 − 60 = 302

Then, subtract the 2 tens that are left.
302 − 20 = 282

So far, 100 + 60 + 20 = 180 has been subtracted.

D Step 3

That leaves just 1 to subtract.

Subtract the **ones**.
282 − 1 = 281

100 + 60 + 20 + 1 = 181 has been subtracted.

At the end of the fifth round, Marco's score is 281 points.

Do You Understand?

Convince Me! Find 453 − 262. Use place value to help break the problem into smaller problems. Show your work.

© Pearson Education, Inc. 3

Name _____

Guided Practice*

In **1** and **2**, use place value to help break the problem into smaller problems.

1. Find 374 − 236.

   374 − 200 = ____

   174 − 30 = ____

   144 − 4 = ____

   140 − 2 = ____

2. Find 369 − 175.

   369 − 100 = ____

   269 − 60 = ____

   209 − 10 = ____

   199 − 5 = ____

3. **Explain** Why do you need to record the numbers you subtract at each step?

4. **Reason** Ana is trying to find 634 − 210. She decides to start by subtracting 10 from 634. Do you agree with Ana? Explain.

Independent Practice

Leveled Practice In **5** through **10**, follow the steps to find each difference. Show your work.

5. 738 − 523

   First, subtract 500.

   ____ − ____ = 238

   Then, subtract 20.

   238 − ____ = ____

   Then, subtract 3.

   ____ − 3 = ____

6. 755 − 315

   First, subtract 300.

   755 − ____ = ____

   Then, subtract 10.

   ____ − 10 = ____

   Then, subtract 5.

   ____ − ____ = 440

7. 336 − 217

   First, subtract 200.

   ____ − 200 = ____

   Then, subtract 10.

   ____ − 10 = ____

   Then, subtract 6.

   ____ − ____ = 120

   Then, subtract 1.

   ____ − 1 = ____

8. 455 − 182

9. 865 − 506

10. 794 − 355

Problem Solving

11. Don's book has 316 pages. He read 50 pages last week. He read another 71 pages this week. How many more pages does Don have left to read?

A   121

B   195

C   196

D   245

You can use estimation to remove two answer choices.

12. Analyze Information There are 97 boys and 86 girls in the school lunchroom. Near the end of lunch, 128 students leave. How many students are left in the lunchroom? Show how you can break part of the problem into smaller problems.

13. Personal Financial Literacy Yuri wants to buy a catcher's mitt for $68 and loan his friend Jacob $10. So far, Yuri has made deposits into a new savings account for $23, $16, and $37. Does Yuri have enough money to buy the mitt and loan his friend Jacob $10? Explain.

14. Tools Write the time shown on the clock in 2 different ways.

15. Use a Strip Diagram Beth had a necklace with 128 beads. The string broke, and she lost 43 beads. How many beads does Beth have left?

128 beads

43	?

↑ 43 beads lost   ↑ ? beads left

16. Extend Your Thinking Which weighs more, two adult male Basset Hounds or one adult male Great Dane? Show the difference in pounds between the two Basset Hounds and the Great Dane. Draw strip diagrams to represent and help you solve the problem.

145 pounds

66 pounds

© Pearson Education, Inc. 3

Name _____

Another Look!

Greenwood School has 258 musical instruments. The students use 156 instruments for a concert and 71 instruments for a parade. How many instruments are not used?

Use place value to break the subtraction problem into smaller problems.

First find 258 − 156.

(Subtract hundreds)	258 − 100 = 158
(Subtract tens)	158 − 50 = 108
(Subtract ones)	108 − 6 = 102

Then find 102 − 71.

(Subtract tens)	102 − 70 = 32
(Subtract ones)	32 − 1 = 31

31 instruments are not used.

In **1** through **4**, subtract.

1. Follow the steps to find 365 − 138.

First, subtract 100. 365 − 100 = ____

Then, subtract 30. ____ − ____ = 235

Then, subtract 5. 235 − ____ = ____

Then, subtract 3. ____ − 3 = ____

2. Follow the steps to find 217 − 118.

First, subtract 100. 217 − 100 = ____

Then, subtract 10. 117 − 10 = ____

Then, subtract 7. 107 − 7 = ____

The, subtract 1. 100 − 1 = ____

3. Follow the steps to find 568 − 293.

First, subtract 200. ____ − ____ = 368

Then, subtract 60. ____ − 60 = ____

Then, subtract 30. 308 − ____ = ____

Then, subtract 3. ____ − 3 = ____

4. Follow the steps to find 928 − 374.

First, subtract 300. ____ − 300 = ____

Then, subtract 20. ____ − ____ = 608

Then, subtract 50. ____ − 50 = ____

Then, subtract 4. ____ − ____ = 554

In **5** through **7**, write the steps to show each difference.

5. 756 − 642

756 − 600 = 156

6. 848 − 276

848 − 200 = 648

7. 641 − 139

8. How many vertices does the cube below have?

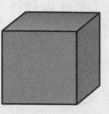

A 4

B 6

C 8

D 12

A vertex is a point where edges meet.

9. Ray has 269 rocks in his collection. He added 134 more rocks. Then, he gave 23 rocks away. Which number sentence shows how many rocks Ray has left?

A $269 + 134 - 23 = 380$

B $269 - 134 + 23 = 158$

C $269 + 134 + 23 = 426$

D $269 - 134 - 23 = 112$

10. Use a Strip Diagram Rachel had 534 pennies. She gave 251 pennies to her sister. How many pennies does Rachel have left?

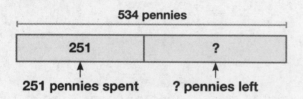

534 pennies

| 251 | ? |

251 pennies spent   ? pennies left

11. Number Sense Tamara needs to find $455 - 364$. Her work is below. Explain what is incorrect and find the correct answer.

$455 - 300 = 155$

$155 - 50 = 105$

$105 - 4 = 101$

12. Math and Science Pure water boils at 212 degrees Fahrenheit. It freezes at 32 degrees Fahrenheit. How many degrees difference is there between these two temperatures? Explain how you found your answer.

13. Extend Your Thinking Tom had 347 marbles. He traded 28 of them for 17 marbles he really wanted. How many marbles does Tom have now? Explain how you found the answer.

14. Tools Students in Mr. Miller's third-grade class were asked which breakfast they like best from the three choices shown in the bar graph. How many more students chose eggs or fruit than cereal?

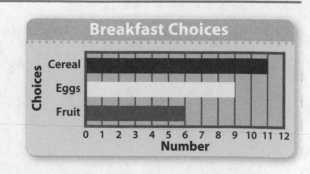

Breakfast Choices

© Pearson Education, Inc. 3

Name _____

Find the difference of 246 − 153.
Solve this problem any way you choose.

Lesson 3-6
Models for Subtracting
3-Digit Numbers

 TEKS 3.4A Solve with fluency one-step and two-step problems involving ... subtraction within 1,000 using strategies based on place value.... Also, 3.5A. **Mathematical Process Standards** 3.1B, 3.1C, 3.1D, 3.1E, 3.1G

Digital Resources at PearsonTexas.com

  A-Z

Solve   Learn   Glossary   Check   Tools   Games

You can **create and use representations.** Drawing pictures of place-value blocks is one way to represent this problem and help you solve it. *Show your work in the space below!*

Look Back!

Check for Reasonableness How can you check to see if the difference you found for 246 − 153 is reasonable?

How Can You Subtract 3-Digit Numbers with Place-Value Blocks?

Fish caught near the Hawaiian Islands can be very large. How many more pounds does a broadbill swordfish weigh than a blue marlin?

Find 237 − 165.

Wild Hawaiian Fish Weights	
Type of Fish	**Weight (in lb)**
Blue Marlin	165
Broadbill Swordfish	237

DATA

Use place value to subtract the ones first, the tens next, and then the hundreds.

Show 237 with place-value blocks.

B Subtract the ones.

7 ones > 5 ones, so no regrouping.

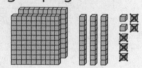

7 ones − 5 ones = 2 ones

```
  2 3 7
− 1 6 5
      2
```

C Subtract the tens.

3 tens < 6 tens, so regroup.
1 hundred = 10 tens

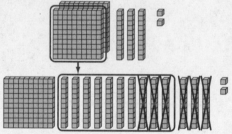

13 tens − 6 tens = 7 tens

```
  ¹ ¹³
  2 3 7
− 1 6 5
    7 2
```

D Subtract the hundreds.

1 hundred − 1 hundred = 0 hundreds

```
  ¹ ¹³
  2 3 7
− 1 6 5
    7 2
```

So, 237 − 165 = 72.
A broadbill swordfish weighs 72 more pounds than a blue marlin.

Do You Understand?

Convince Me! Anderson needs $231 to buy a new bike. He saved $144 from his summer job. How much more does Anderson need to save to buy the bike? Write a subtraction sentence that models the problem. Use place-value blocks to help you solve the problem using the same steps shown above.

☆ Guided Practice *

In **1** through **8**, use place-value blocks or draw pictures to subtract.

1. 249
    − 187

2. 261
    − 134

3. 158
    − 76

4. 384
    − 182

5. 173 − 158

6. 325 − 213

7. 412 − 101

8. 999 − 898

9. **Communicate** In the example on page 170, for 237 − 165, why do you need to regroup 1 hundred into 10 tens?

10. **Represent** Colby saved $256 doing jobs in his neighborhood. He bought a computer printer for $173. How much money did Colby have left? Draw a picture of place-value blocks to help you subtract.

Independent Practice ☆

In **11** through **26**, use place-value blocks or draw pictures to subtract.

You can draw squares to show hundreds, lines to show tens, and dots to show ones. This picture shows 123.

11. 347
     − 263

12. 196
     − 149

13. 218
     − 117

14. 251
     − 132

15. 423
     − 291

16. 539
     − 275

17. 376
     − 153

18. 417
     − 308

19. 123
     − 81

20. 456
     − 329

21. 259
     − 158

22. 437
     − 183

23. 198
     − 124

24. 460
     − 295

25. 375
     − 241

26. 627
     − 135

*For another example, see Set F on page 197.

Problem Solving

For **27** and **28**, use the table at the right.

27. Tools How many fewer miles is it from Cincinnati to Cleveland than from Cleveland to Chicago?

28. Reason Mr. Miller is driving from Washington, D.C. to Cleveland and then to Cincinnati. He has traveled 127 miles. How many miles are left in his trip?

Trip Distances	
Trip	Miles
Cleveland to Chicago	346
Cincinnati to Cleveland	249
Washington, D.C. to Cleveland	372

DATA

29. It is 239 miles from Dallas to Houston and 275 miles from Dallas to San Antonio. How many fewer miles is it from Dallas to Houston than from Dallas to San Antonio?

30. An amusement park ride can hold 120 people. There are already 80 people on the ride and 62 people waiting in line. Which number sentence can be used to find how many people need to wait for the next ride?

A $80 + 62 = 142$

B $80 - 40 = 40$

C $62 - 40 = 22$

D $80 - 62 = 18$

31. Use a Strip Diagram Jenny got $20 for her birthday. She earned $56 babysitting. Then she earned $159 shoveling snow. How much money does Jenny have?

?		
$20	$56	$159

32. Extend Your Thinking Sylvia needs to find $423 - 257$. Will she need to regroup to find the answer? If so, explain how she will need to regroup. What will Sylvia's answer be?

33. Analyze Information Marcy and Sabrina each ran for Junior High student council president. Which girl got more votes? How many more votes did that girl get?

DATA

Student Council President Votes		
	7th Grade Votes	8th Grade Votes
Marcy	172	159
Sabrina	155	167

© Pearson Education, Inc. 3

Name _____

Another Look!

You can use place-value blocks to model subtraction.

Find 234 − 192.

Step 1

Subtract the ones. 4 > 2. No regrouping is needed.

4 ones − 2 ones = 2 ones

$$\begin{array}{r} 234 \\ -\ 192 \\ \hline 2 \end{array}$$

Step 2

Subtract the tens. 3 tens < 9 tens, so regroup 1 hundred as 10 tens.

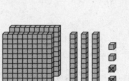

13 tens − 9 tens = 4 tens

$$\begin{array}{r} {}^{1\,13}2\not{3}4 \\ -\ 192 \\ \hline 42 \end{array}$$

Step 3

Subtract the hundreds.

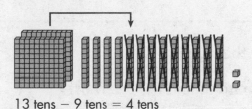

1 hundred − 1 hundred = 0 hundreds

$$\begin{array}{r} {}^{1\,13}2\not{3}4 \\ -\ 192 \\ \hline 42 \end{array}$$

Find the value of the remaining blocks: 4 tens + 2 ones = 40 + 2 = 42.

In **1** through **8**, use place-value blocks or draw pictures to subtract.

1. $\begin{array}{r} 356 \\ -\ 128 \end{array}$

2. $\begin{array}{r} 261 \\ -\ 122 \end{array}$

3. $\begin{array}{r} 321 \\ -\ 176 \end{array}$

4. $\begin{array}{r} 446 \\ -\ 257 \end{array}$

5. $\begin{array}{r} 256 \\ -\ 42 \end{array}$

6. $\begin{array}{r} 374 \\ -\ 188 \end{array}$

7. $\begin{array}{r} 318 \\ -\ 157 \end{array}$

8. $\begin{array}{r} 431 \\ -\ 279 \end{array}$

9. You can compare the differences of subtraction problems using the > or < symbols. Which of the following is **NOT** a true comparison?

   A $634 - 200 > 456 - 100$

   B $532 - 300 < 792 - 500$

   C $225 - 100 > 869 - 800$

   D $552 - 100 < 675 - 300$

10. Explain Brady used place-value blocks to model and find $364 - 247$. Explain what Brady should do next.

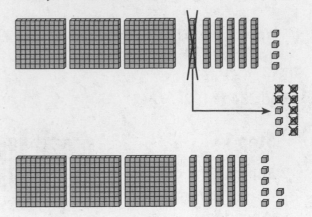

For **11** and **12**, use the table at the right.

11. Mental Math Use mental math to find the total cost of one tent and one sleeping bag. Explain how you found the answer mentally.

12. Extend Your Thinking A sleeping bag usually costs $229. A tent usually costs $265. How much could you save off the regular price for each item? Which item has a larger discount? Explain.

DATA

Camping Equipment Sale	
Sleeping bags	$195 each
Tents	$238 each
Water bottles (box of 12)	$10

13. Tools Marcos measured the length of a crayon. First, he used connecting cubes. Then, he used paper clips. Did Marcos use more connecting cubes or paper clips to measure the length? Explain.

© Pearson Education, Inc. 3

Name _____

☆ **Solve & Share** ☆

Last year, there were 347 houses for sale in Mill County and 289 houses for sale in Hunter County. Of the houses for sale in Mill County, 162 were sold. How many houses in Mill County were not sold?
Solve this problem any way you choose.

✪ **TEKS 3.4A** Solve with fluency one-step and two-step problems involving … subtraction within 1,000 using strategies based on place value…. Also, 3.5A. **Mathematical Process Standards** 3.1A, 3.1B, 3.1C, 3.1D, 3.1F, 3.1G

You can **connect ideas.** You know how to show regrouping with and without place-value blocks when you add. How can you do the same when you subtract? **Show your work in the space below!**

Digital Resources at PearsonTexas.com

Solve   Learn   Glossary   Check   Tools   Games

Look Back!

Draw a Picture How can you show the regrouping of 1 hundred into tens using a picture of place-value blocks?

A

How Can You Use Subtraction to Solve Problems?

Mike and Linda are playing a game. How many more points does Mike have than Linda?

Find 528 − 341.

Estimate by rounding to the nearest ten:
530 − 340 = 190.

MIKE 528   341 LINDA

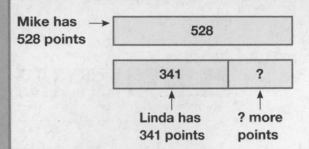

Mike has → 528 points

528

341   ?

Linda has   ? more
341 points   points

B Subtract the ones.

8 ones > 1 one
You do not regroup.
8 ones − 1 ones = 7 ones

$$
\begin{array}{r}
5\ 2\ 8 \\
-\ 3\ 4\ 1 \\
\hline
7
\end{array}
$$

> You can use place value to subtract without using place-value blocks.

C Subtract the tens.

Since 2 tens < 4 tens, regroup
1 hundred into 10 tens.
12 tens − 4 tens = 8 tens

$$
\begin{array}{r}
\overset{4\ 12}{5\ \not2\ 8} \\
-\ 3\ 4\ 1 \\
\hline
8\ 7
\end{array}
$$

D Subtract the hundreds.

4 hundreds − 3 hundreds
= 1 hundred

$$
\begin{array}{r}
\overset{4\ 12}{\not5\ \not2\ 8} \\
-\ 3\ 4\ 1 \\
\hline
1\ 8\ 7
\end{array}
$$

Mike has 187 more points.

187 is close to the estimate, 190. The answer is reasonable.

Do You Understand?

Convince Me! In Box C above, how are 5 hundreds, 2 tens, 8 ones the same as 4 hundreds, 12 tens, 8 ones? Use place-value blocks to show how these are the same.

176

© Pearson Education, Inc. 3

Another Example

You may have to regroup twice when you subtract. Find 356 − 189.

Subtract the ones. Regroup if needed.	Subtract the tens. Regroup if needed.	Subtract the hundreds.
6 ones < 9 ones. So, regroup 1 ten into 10 ones.	4 tens < 8 tens. So, regroup 1 hundred into 10 tens.	

Subtract the ones. Regroup if needed.

6 ones < 9 ones. So, regroup 1 ten into 10 ones.

$$\begin{array}{r} \overset{4\,16}{3\cancel{5}\cancel{6}} \\ -\ 189 \\ \hline 7 \end{array}$$

Subtract the tens. Regroup if needed.

4 tens < 8 tens. So, regroup 1 hundred into 10 tens.

$$\begin{array}{r} \overset{14}{\underset{}{}}\\[-6pt] \overset{2\,4\,16}{3\cancel{5}\cancel{6}} \\ -\ 189 \\ \hline 67 \end{array}$$

Subtract the hundreds.

$$\begin{array}{r} \overset{14}{\underset{}{}}\\[-6pt] \overset{2\,4\,16}{3\cancel{5}\cancel{6}} \\ -\ 189 \\ \hline 167 \end{array}$$

So, 356 − 189 = 167.

☆ Guided Practice *

In **1** and **2**, subtract. Use place-value blocks as needed.

1.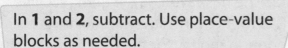
   374
   − 176

2. 856
   − 219

3. **Explain** In the example on page 176, explain how to decide if regrouping is necessary.

Independent Practice ☆

In **4** through **11**, estimate by rounding to the nearest ten. Then, find each difference. Check answers for reasonableness.

4.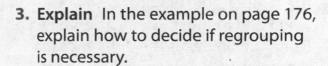
   431
   − 145

5. 276
   − 97

6. 516
   − 402

7. 526
   − 238

8. 574 − 86

9. 629 − 453

10. 979 − 569

11. 764 − 237

Problem Solving

12. Use a Strip Diagram At the end of their game, Lora had 426 points, and Lou had 158 points. How many more points did Lora have than Lou?

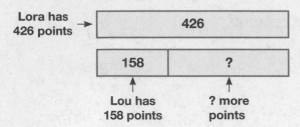

Lora has 426 points → 426

158 | ?

↑ Lou has 158 points ↑ ? more points

13. Ana made 14 hats. After giving some hats to Ty's family and some to Liv's family, she had 3 hats left. If she gave Ty's family 6 hats, which of these shows one way to find how many hats Ana gave to Liv's family?

A $14 + 3 - 6 = \square$

B $14 - 3 - 6 = \square$

C $14 - 3 + 6 = \square$

D $14 + 3 + 6 = \square$

---

14. Math and Science Water boils at 212 degrees Fahrenheit. Marcia measured the temperature of her shower water and found it was 110 degrees Fahrenheit. What is the difference in temperature between boiling water and Marcia's shower water?

15. Personal Financial Literacy Beth is saving for a hiking trip that costs $58. So far, she has saved $37. If Beth receives $15 for her birthday, will she have enough money for the trip? Explain.

---

16. Connect The world's largest basket is the building in this picture. It is 186 feet tall from the base of the building to the top of the handles. What is the height of the handles?

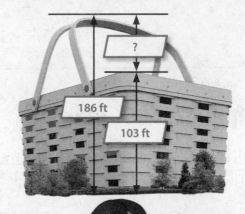

?

186 ft

103 ft

---

17. Extend Your Thinking How many more swimmers signed up for the first session at Oak Pool than the first and second sessions at Park Pool combined? Write a number sentence that represents the problem and includes the solution.

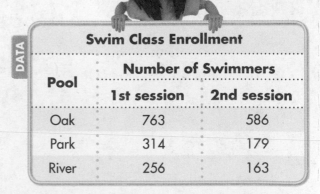

Swim Class Enrollment		
Pool	Number of Swimmers	
	1st session	2nd session
Oak	763	586
Park	314	179
River	256	163

© Pearson Education, Inc. 3

Another Look!

Find 726 − 238.

Estimate by rounding to the nearest ten: 730 − 240 = 490.

Use your estimate to check for reasonableness.

Step 1

First, subtract the ones.
6 ones < 8 ones.
Regroup 1 ten into 10 ones.

```
    1 16
  7 2̶ 6̶
 − 2 3 8
        8
```

Step 2

Subtract the tens.
1 ten < 3 tens.
Regroup 1 hundred into 10 tens.

```
      11
   6 1̶ 16
  7 2̶ 6̶
 − 2 3 8
      8 8
```

Step 3

Subtract the hundreds.

```
      11
   6 1̶ 16
  7 2̶ 6̶
 − 2 3 8
    4 8 8
```

Is your answer reasonable? Yes, because 488 is close to the estimate, 490.

In **1** through **8**, estimate by rounding to the nearest ten. Then, find each difference. Show your regrouping work. Check answers for reasonableness.

1.
```
   9 1 4
 − 4 8 2
 □ □ 2
```

2.
```
   8 8 3
 − 3 8 8
 4 □ □
```

3.
```
   3 7 5
 − 1 8 3
 □ □ 2
```

4.
```
   7 3 6
 − 2 9 5
 4 □ □
```

5.
```
   4 7 8
 − 1 5 2
 □ □ □
```

6.
```
   2 4 6
 − 1 2 7
 □ □ □
```

7.
```
   8 1 6
 − 3 0 4
 □ □ □
```

8.
```
   9 1 9
 − 2 8 4
 □ □ □
```

In **9** through **16**, estimate by rounding to the nearest ten. Then, find each difference.

9.
```
   3 1 8
 − 1 2 3
```

10.
```
   4 4 1
 − 1 8 7
```

11.
```
   3 3 4
 − 2 7 5
```

12.
```
   5 9 7
 − 3 8 4
```

13.
```
   7 3 2
 − 4 5 5
```

14.
```
   4 1 2
 −   8 3
```

15.
```
   8 2 8
 − 6 1 5
```

16.
```
   6 4 9
 − 3 6 7
```

17. Use a Strip Diagram On a field trip, Sara's class counted 276 dandelions, 307 African daisies, and 187 purple coneflowers. How many more dandelions than coneflowers did they count?

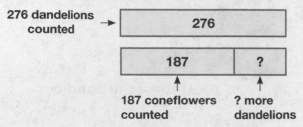

276 dandelions counted → | 276 |

| 187 | ? |

↑ 187 coneflowers counted   ↑ ? more dandelions

18. ⭐ Texas has 254 counties. California has 58 counties and Florida has 67 counties. How many more counties does Texas have than the number of counties in California and Florida combined?

A 125

B 129

C 139

D 196

19. Number Sense Write a three-digit number you could subtract from 749 where you need to regroup hundreds. Then, find the difference.

20. Check for Reasonableness Toby subtracted the numbers below. Is his answer correct? Explain how you know. Show a way to check his answer.

$$\begin{array}{r} \overset{14}{} \\ 6\ \overset{4}{}\ 17 \\ 7\ 5\ 7 \\ -\ 3\ 9\ 8 \\ \hline 3\ 5\ 9 \end{array}$$

In **21** and **22**, use the table at the right.

21. Analyze Information How many miles closer to Omaha is Chicago than Dallas? Use the table and follow the steps below to solve.

  a. Estimate the answer.

  b. Write the solution to the problem in word form.

  c. Explain why your answer is reasonable.

DATA

All Roads Lead to Omaha	
Trip	Miles
Dallas to Omaha	644
Chicago to Omaha	459
Tulsa to Omaha	387

22. Extend Your Thinking Jill is going on a trip from Chicago to Omaha, and then from Omaha to Tulsa. Bill will travel from Dallas to Omaha. How much farther will Jill travel than Bill? Explain how you got your answer.

You can use an inverse operation to check your solution to each part of a problem.

© Pearson Education, Inc. 3

Name _____

Solve & Share

A community center needs to raise $302 to buy a printer. So far, it has raised $164. How much more does the center need to raise? *Solve this problem any way you choose.*

You can **connect ideas.** How is this problem similar to other problems you have solved before? *Show your work in the space below!*

⭐ **TEKS 3.4A** Solve with fluency one-step and two-step problems involving …subtraction within 1,000 using strategies based on place value…. Also, 3.5A. **Mathematical Process Standards** 3.1B, 3.1C, 3.1D, 3.1E, 3.1F, 3.1G

Digital Resources at PearsonTexas.com

Solve   Learn   Glossary   Check   Tools   Games

Look Back!

Number Sense When might you need to think of 302 as 2 hundreds, 10 tens, and 2 ones?

How much more does the Elm School Art Club need?

Find:
$$\begin{array}{r} 305 \\ -\ 178 \\ \hline \end{array}$$

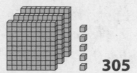
305

Goal →
$305

$178	?

Elm School Art Club Fundraiser!

GOAL — $305

Currently $178

Sometimes you will subtract from a number that has 1 or more zeros.

Subtracting from a number with one zero

B Regroup to subtract the ones. There are no tens in 305 to regroup. Regroup 1 hundred.

305 is the same as 2 hundreds 10 tens 5 ones.

$$\begin{array}{r} \overset{2\ \ 10}{\cancel{3}\ \cancel{0}\ 5} \\ -\ 1\ 7\ 8 \\ \hline \end{array}$$

C Regroup the tens.

305 is the same as 2 hundreds 9 tens 15 ones.

$$\begin{array}{r} \overset{2\ \ \overset{9}{10}\ \ 15}{\cancel{3}\ \cancel{0}\ \cancel{5}} \\ -\ 1\ 7\ 8 \\ \hline \end{array}$$

D Subtract the ones, the tens, and then the hundreds.

$$\begin{array}{r} \overset{2\ \ \overset{9}{10}\ \ 15}{\cancel{3}\ \cancel{0}\ \cancel{5}} \\ -\ 1\ 7\ 8 \\ \hline 1\ 2\ 7 \end{array}$$

The Art Club needs $127.

Do You Understand?

Convince Me! Use place-value blocks to help you solve the problem below.

$$\begin{array}{r} \overset{3\ \ \overset{9}{10}\ \ 14}{\cancel{4}\ \cancel{0}\ \cancel{4}} \\ -\ 2\ 6\ 9 \\ \hline \end{array}$$

© Pearson Education, Inc. 3

Another Example

You may have to subtract from a number that has two zeros. Find 600 − 164.

Subtract the ones.	Now regroup tens.	Subtract the ones, the tens,
0 ones < 4 ones	10 tens 0 ones = 9 tens 10 ones	and then the hundreds.

Subtract the ones.
0 ones < 4 ones
So, regroup.

You can't regroup 0 tens.
So, regroup 1 hundred.
6 hundreds 0 tens =
5 hundreds 10 tens

$$\begin{array}{r} {}^{5}\;{}^{10}\\ \cancel{6}\;\cancel{0}\;0\\ -1\;6\;4 \end{array}$$

Now regroup tens.
10 tens 0 ones = 9 tens 10 ones

$$\begin{array}{r} {}^{9}\\ {}^{5}\;\cancel{10}\;10\\ \cancel{6}\;\cancel{0}\;\cancel{0}\\ -1\;6\;4 \end{array}$$

Subtract the ones, the tens, and then the hundreds.

$$\begin{array}{r} {}^{9}\\ {}^{5}\;\cancel{10}\;10\\ \cancel{6}\;\cancel{0}\;\cancel{0}\\ -1\;6\;4\\ \hline 4\;3\;6 \end{array}$$

So, 600 − 164 = 436.

Guided Practice

In **1** through **4**, find each difference. Use place-value blocks as needed.

1. 402
      −139

2. 820
      −567

3. 300
      −157

4. 607
      −439

5. Construct Arguments Lia says she needs to regroup every time she subtracts from a number with a zero. Do you agree? Explain.

Independent Practice

In **6** through **13**, find each difference. Use place-value blocks as needed.

6.   203
       − 157

7.   401
       − 282

8.   705
       − 123

9.   600
       − 439

10. 570 − 385

11. 809 − 297

12. 200 − 142

13. 740 − 458

Problem Solving

14. Represent The average person eats about 126 pounds of fresh fruit in a year. Draw a strip diagram to find how many pounds of processed fruit the average person eats. Then solve.

The average person eats a total of about 280 pounds of fresh and processed fruit each year.

---

15. Analyze Information Use the graph at the right. How many corn and pea plants are in Tony's garden? Explain how you know.

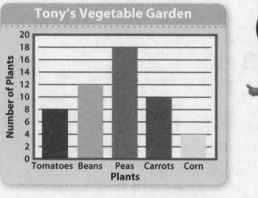

Tony's Vegetable Garden

---

16. Explain Rick is allowed to receive 1,000 text messages each month. How many more text messages did Rick receive this week than last week? Explain how you regrouped to find the answer.

Rick's Text Messages
Last week: 125
This week: 208

---

17. ⭐ Dina counted 204 items on the library cart. There were 91 fiction books, 75 nonfiction books, and some magazines. Which number sentence shows one way to find the number of magazines?

A 204 − 91 − 75 = ☐

B 204 + 91 + 75 = ☐

C 204 − 91 + 75 = ☐

D 204 + 91 − 75 = ☐

18. Extend Your Thinking The Art Club needs 605 paintbrushes. A large bag has 285 brushes. A small bag has 130 brushes. Will one large bag and one small bag be enough paintbrushes? Explain.

© Pearson Education, Inc. 3

Name _____

Another Look!

Find 207 − 98.

```
         207
┌──────────────┐
│   98  │  ?   │
└──────────────┘
```

You need to regroup when you subtract across zeros.

Step 1

Subtract the ones. Since there are 0 tens, you must first regroup the hundreds.

```
  2 0 7
−   9 8
```

Step 2

Regroup the hundreds.

2 hundreds and 0 tens = 1 hundred and 10 tens.

```
  1 10
  2 Ø 7
−   9 8
```

Step 3

Regroup the tens.

10 tens and 7 ones = 9 tens and 17 ones.

Subtract.

```
      9
  1 10 17
  2 Ø 7
−   9 8
  1 0 9
```

In **1** through **20**, find each difference. Use place-value blocks as needed.

1.
```
  3 0 1
−   7 2
  □ □ □
```

2.
```
  5 0 2
− 2 2 5
  □ □ □
```

3.
```
  4 0 0
− 2 2 8
  □ □ □
```

4.
```
  6 0 3
− 4 1 5
  □ □ □
```

5.
```
  7 0 5
− 2 5 9
  □ □ 6
```

6.
```
  3 0 0
− 1 8 2
  1 □ □
```

7.
```
  4 3 0
− 2 1 6
  □ 1 □
```

8.
```
  8 0 0
− 5 4 9
  2 □ □
```

9.
```
  6 0 0
− 3 2 5
```

10.
```
  5 4 0
− 1 3 7
```

11.
```
  2 0 7
− 1 6 6
```

12.
```
  7 9 0
− 4 1 2
```

13.
```
  5 6 0
− 2 8 9
```

14.
```
  3 0 1
− 2 4 3
```

15.
```
  2 0 7
− 1 6 6
```

16.
```
  8 0 0
− 6 2 1
```

17. 400 − 254

18. 708 − 594

19. 500 − 222

20. 640 − 135

21. **Number Sense** Lance has the bills and coins shown at the right. What is the total value of the money he has? How did you find the answer?

Think of the value of each bill and coin as you solve.

22. **Communicate** Write and solve a subtraction problem that involves regrouping and includes Ted having $304 in savings.

23. Write 53,278 in expanded form.

24. **Use a Strip Diagram** There were 600 ears of corn for sale at the produce market. At the end of the day, there were 212 ears left. How many ears of corn were sold? Complete the strip diagram and write a number sentence.

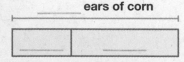

ears of corn

25. **Explain** Darrin has 602 songs on his MP3 player. Dana has 345 fewer songs on her MP3 player than Darrin. How many songs do Darrin and Dana both have on their MP3 players? Explain how you solved the problem.

26. ★ Williams Tower in Houston, TX, is 901 feet tall. The Tower of the Americas in San Antonio, TX, is 622 feet tall. How much taller is Williams Tower than the Tower of the Americas?

A 279 feet

B 289 feet

C 379 feet

D 389 feet

27. **Extend Your Thinking** Party Palace has an order for 505 party favors. It packages 218 favors on Saturday and 180 favors on Sunday. How many more party favors does it still need to package? What is one way you can solve this problem?

© Pearson Education, Inc. 3

Name _____

Solve & Share

Jackson School has 2 floors and 600 students. If 200 students are on the first floor, how many students are on the second floor? Draw a picture or diagram to help you solve this problem.

TEKS 3.1D Communicate mathematical ideas, reasoning, and their implications using multiple representations, including symbols, diagrams, graphs, and language as appropriate. Also, 3.4A, 3.5A. **Mathematical Process Standards** 3.1E, 3.1F, 3.1G

Digital Resources at PearsonTexas.com

Solve   Learn   Glossary   Check   Tools   Games

You can **create and use representations.** Your picture or diagram should include numbers and labels from the problem. *Show your work!*

Look Back!

Represent Suppose you use a strip diagram to represent and solve the problem. How do you know the size of the part for the number of students on the second floor should be larger than the part for 200 students on the first floor?

A **Analyze**

There are two lunch periods at Central School. If 221 students eat during the first lunch period, how many students eat during the second lunch period?

An equation is a number sentence that uses an equals sign (=) to show the value to its left is the same as the value to its right.

Central School
Grades K-6
458 Students

B **Plan**

Draw a strip diagram.

458 students

221	?

↑ 221 students in first lunch   ↑ ? students in second lunch

You know the total and one part. Write a subtraction equation: 458 − 221 = ☐

An unknown is a symbol that stands for a number in an equation.

C **Solve**

$$\begin{array}{r} 458 \\ -221 \\ \hline 237 \end{array}$$

There are 237 students who eat during the second lunch period.

D **Justify and Evaluate**

Make sure the answer is reasonable.

458 − 221 is about 460 − 220 = 240.

237 is close to 240, so 237 is reasonable.

The number 237 is reasonable and the right question was answered.

Do You Understand?

Convince Me! Draw a strip diagram and write an equation to solve this problem:

There are two recess periods at Gifford School. If there are 433 students in the school and 249 students at the first recess period, how many students are at the second recess period?

© Pearson Education, Inc. 3

Another Example

There are 40 boys and 45 girls in Grade 2. That is 17 more students than in Grade 3. How many students are in Grade 3?

Find and solve the hidden question. How many students are in Grade 2?

? students in Grade 2

40	45

↑ 40 boys   ↑ 45 girls

$40 + 45 = \square$

$$\begin{array}{r} 40 \\ + 45 \\ \hline 85 \end{array}$$

Grade 2 has 85 students.

Use the answer to the hidden question to solve the problem.

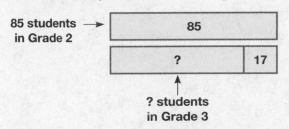

85 students in Grade 2 →

85

?	17

↑ ? students in Grade 3

$\square + 17 = 85$

$$\begin{array}{r} \overset{7}{\cancel{8}}\,\overset{15}{\cancel{5}} \\ - 1\ 7 \\ \hline 6\ 8 \end{array}$$

Grade 3 has 68 students.

☆ Guided Practice*

1. A total of 254 people entered a bicycle race. So far, 135 people have finished. How many people are still riding? Draw a strip diagram and write an equation to solve.

2. **Connect** How do you know what operation to use to solve the problem at the top of page 188?

3. What symbols can you use for unknowns in an equation?

☆ Independent Practice ☆

4. In 1789, there were 65 members in the U.S. House of Representatives. Now, there are 370 more members. Draw a strip diagram and write an equation to find how many members there are now.

Problem Solving

5. Nancy had $375 in the bank. She took $145 out to help pay for a scooter that costs $185. Which equation can you solve to find how much money Nancy has left in the bank?

A $345 − $185 = ☐

B $375 − $145 − $185 = ☐

C $375 − $145 = ☐

D $357 + $185 + $145 = ☐

6. Represent Gordy drew this hexagon to decorate his book cover. Then, he drew 3 lines to divide the hexagon into 6 triangles. Show the lines Gordy could have drawn.

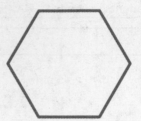

7. Max exercised 38 minutes on Monday and 25 minutes on Tuesday. On Wednesday, he exercised 15 minutes less than he did on Monday. Which equation can you solve to find how many minutes Max exercised during these 3 days?

A 38 + 25 + 15 = ☐

B 38 + 25 + 10 = ☐

C 38 + 25 = ☐

D 38 + 25 + 23 = ☐

8. Represent Waco has an elevation of 405 feet above sea level. Texarkana has an elevation of 324 feet above sea level. How many feet greater is Waco's elevation than Texarkana's? Draw a strip diagram and write an equation to solve.

9. Extend Your Thinking The number of representatives in Texas and Michigan is 28 more than the number of representatives in Illinois. How many representatives are in Illinois? Draw strip diagrams and write equations to solve.

U.S. Representatives as of 2012

State	Number
California	53
Florida	25
Michigan	15
Texas	32

© Pearson Education, Inc. 3

Name _____

Another Look!

The distance from Cleveland to Pittsburgh is 129 miles. From Cleveland to Detroit is 170 miles. How many more miles are there from Cleveland to Detroit?

| 170 miles to Detroit → | 170 miles |
| | |

| | 129 | ? |
| | 129 miles to Pittsburgh | ? more miles |

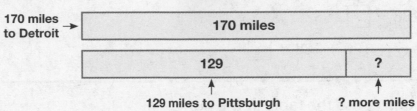

Write an equation to solve:

$129 + \boxed{} = 170$

$$\begin{array}{r} \overset{6}{\cancel{1}}\overset{10}{\cancel{7}}\,\cancel{0} \\ -1\ 2\ 9 \\ \hline 4\ 1 \end{array}$$

There are 41 more miles from Cleveland to Detroit.

In **1** through **3**, complete each strip diagram and write an equation to solve.

1. Honolulu, HI, has an area of 86 square miles. Corpus Christi, TX, has an area 69 square miles greater than the area of Honolulu. How many square miles is Corpus Christi?

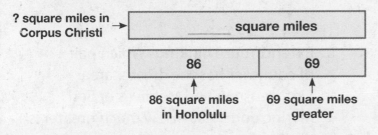

? square miles in Corpus Christi → _____ square miles

| 86 | 69 |

86 square miles in Honolulu   69 square miles greater

2. Bakersfield, CA, has an area of 113 square miles. Its area is 64 square miles greater than the area of Anaheim, CA. What is the area, in square miles, of Anaheim?

113 square miles in Bakersfield → 113 square miles

| 64 | _____ |

64 square miles greater   ? square miles in Anaheim

3. Marc asked some students in his school how they wake up in the morning. 47 students said by alarm, 68 students said by clock radio, and 35 students said they wake up naturally. How many more students said they wake up by clock radio than naturally?

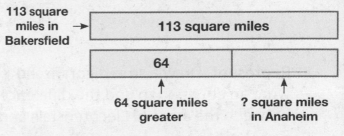

68 wake up by clock radio → 68 students

| 35 | _____ |

35 students wake up naturally   ? more students

4. There are 120 men and 117 women who work at an office in New York. There are 188 people who work at a factory in Dallas. Which equation can you solve to find how many more people work at the office than the factory?

A $237 + 188 = \square$

B $188 + \square = 237$

C $188 - \square = 52$

D $117 + 120 + 188 = \square$

5. **Construct Arguments** Nico says the value of the 5 in 97,459 is greater than the value of the 4 in the same number because 5 is greater than 4. Is Nico correct? Explain.

In **6** through **8**, use the table at the right.

6. **Use a Strip Diagram** How many square miles greater is the area of Maldives than the area of San Marino? Complete the strip diagram and write an equation to solve the problem.

116 square miles in Maldives →

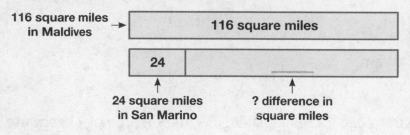

116 square miles

24

24 square miles in San Marino

? difference in square miles

Area of Countries	
Country	Area (in square miles)
San Marino	24
Liechtenstein	62
Maldives	116
Palau	177

DATA

7. **Represent** Draw a strip diagram and write an equation to find the difference between the areas of Liechtenstein and San Marino.

8. **Extend Your Thinking** Which pair of countries has the greater area: Liechtenstein and Maldives or San Marino and Palau? How much greater is the area?

© Pearson Education, Inc. 3

Name _____

1. **Extend Your Thinking** Jerome has the bills and coins shown below. Jen has the same amount of money. Describe a different group of bills and coins Jen could have.

Applying Math Processes

- How does this problem connect to previous ones?
- What is my plan?
- How can I use tools?
- How can I use number sense?
- How can I communicate and represent my thinking?
- How can I organize and record information?
- How can I explain my work?
- How can I justify my answer?

2. **Communicate** Arnold received 145 text messages during September and October. He received 69 texts in September. How many texts did he receive in October? Write an addition equation that represents the problem.

145 text messages

69	?

↑   ↑
69 September texts   ? October texts

3. **Represent** Sammy has 236 shells in his collection. He collected 125 of them last week. How many shells did Sammy have before last week? Write an equation and draw a strip diagram to solve.

For **4** and **5**, use the table at the right.

4. **Mental Math** Troy's Nature Club counted different kinds of trees in a nearby state park. How many trees did the club count?

5. How many more oak trees were counted than maple trees?

Trees in State Park	
Tree	**Count**
Elm	74
Oak	206
Maple	115

Error Search

For **1** through **4**, circle each problem that is not correct. Then, tell why it is not correct.

1.	315	2.	672	3.	705	4.	278
	+ 96		− 325		− 457		+ 392
	401		357		248		560

Compatible Numbers

In **5** and **6**, draw circles around two or more numbers next to each other, across or down, with a sum of 50 or 100. Look for compatible numbers (numbers that are easy to compute with mentally).

5. Find sums of 50.

25	25	25	2	48
21	38	15	40	29
29	12	10	6	11
9	45	30	4	10
41	5	20	23	27

6. Find sums of 100.

40	35	25	21	79
50	45	55	8	92
50	68	32	35	24
25	40	60	65	36
75	81	9	10	40

© Pearson Education, Inc. 3

Name _____

TOPIC
3

Find the sum of 257 + 186.

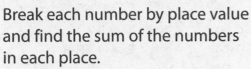

You can break 257 + 186 into smaller addition problems.

Break each number by place value and find the sum of the numbers in each place.

Hundreds	Tens	Ones
200	50	7
+ 100	+ 80	+ 6
300	130	13

Then, add the sums.

```
  300
  130
+  13
  443
```

So, 257 + 186 = 443.

Reteaching

Remember you can use place value to add numbers by breaking large addition problems into smaller addition problems.

In **1** through **4**, find each sum. Break each problem into smaller problems.

1. 135 + 152   **2.** 650 + 138

3. 535 + 423   **4.** 475 + 264

5. Mike's Café sold 137 sandwiches on Friday. It sold 248 on Saturday. How many sandwiches were sold on both days?

Set B pages 145–150

Find 163 + 254. Use place-value blocks.

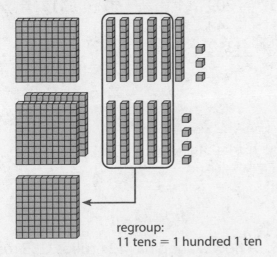

regroup:
11 tens = 1 hundred 1 ten

4 hundreds   1 ten   7 ones

So, 163 + 254 = 417.

Remember to regroup if the sum of the digits in a column is 10 or more.

In **1** through **6**, find the sum. Use place-value blocks or draw pictures.

1. 213 + 172   **2.** 411 + 256

3. 536 + 251   **4.** 347 + 235

5. 196 + 243   **6.** 465 + 357

Set C pages 151–156

Find 235 + 187.

Estimate by rounding to the nearest ten:
240 + 190 = 430.

Add the ones.
Regroup if needed.

$$\begin{array}{r} \overset{1}{2}35 \\ +\ 187 \\ \hline 2 \end{array}$$

Add the tens.
Regroup if needed.

$$\begin{array}{r} \overset{1\ 1}{2}35 \\ +\ 187 \\ \hline 22 \end{array}$$

Add the hundreds.

$$\begin{array}{r} \overset{1\ 1}{2}35 \\ +\ 187 \\ \hline 422 \end{array}$$

The answer is reasonable since 422 is close to 430.

So, 235 + 187 = 422.

Remember that an estimate can help you check whether your answer is reasonable.

For **1** through **4**, estimate by rounding to the nearest ten. Then, find each sum.

1. $\begin{array}{r} 236 \\ +\ 217 \\ \hline \end{array}$

2. $\begin{array}{r} 407 \\ +\ 436 \\ \hline \end{array}$

3. 235 + 59

4. 584 + 326

5. Chad has a new video game. He scored 368 points on his first try. He scored 486 points on his second try. How many points did Chad score?

Set D pages 157–162

Find 124 + 32 + 238.

Estimate by rounding to the nearest ten:
120 + 30 + 240 = 390.

Add the ones.
Regroup if needed.

$$\begin{array}{r} \overset{1}{1}24 \\ 32 \\ +\ 238 \\ \hline 4 \end{array}$$

Add the tens.
Regroup if needed.

$$\begin{array}{r} \overset{1}{1}24 \\ 32 \\ +\ 238 \\ \hline 94 \end{array}$$ Tens do not need regrouping.

Add the hundreds.

$$\begin{array}{r} \overset{1}{1}24 \\ 32 \\ +\ 238 \\ \hline 394 \end{array}$$

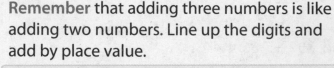

The answer is reasonable since 394 is close to 390.

So, 124 + 32 + 138 = 394.

Remember that adding three numbers is like adding two numbers. Line up the digits and add by place value.

For **1** through **4**, estimate by rounding to the nearest ten. Then, find each sum.

1. $\begin{array}{r} 209 \\ 48 \\ +\ 312 \\ \hline \end{array}$

2. $\begin{array}{r} 412 \\ 273 \\ +\ 139 \\ \hline \end{array}$

3. 146 + 86 + 53

4. 125 + 224 + 306

5. A flower shop has 124 tulips, 235 roses, and 85 carnations. How many flowers does the flower shop have?

© Pearson Education, Inc. 3

Name _____

Set E pages 163–168

Use place value to help find 548 − 263.

Subtract the   548 − 200 = 348
hundreds.

Subtract the tens.   348 − 40 = 308
Start with 348.
There are not enough
tens. So, subtract the
4 tens there are.

Then, subtract 2   308 − 20 = 288
more tens.

Subtract the ones.   288 − 3 = 285

So, 548 − 263 = 285.

Remember that place value can help you break a subtraction problem into smaller problems.

For **1** through **4**, find each difference. Break each problem into smaller problems.

1. 489 − 253   2. 544 − 162

3. 856 − 328   4. 349 − 98

5. Jason's book has 238 pages. He read 87 pages on Monday and 32 pages on Tuesday. Use place value to find how many pages Jason has left to read.

Set F pages 169–174

Find 346 − 172.

Subtract the ones.

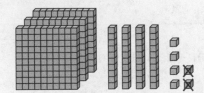

Subtract the tens.

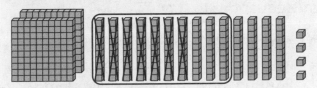

Regroup 1 hundred as 10 tens.

Subtract the hundreds.

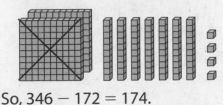

So, 346 − 172 = 174.

Remember to use place value to subtract the ones first, the tens next, and then the hundreds.

For **1** through **4**, find the difference. Use place-value blocks or draw pictures.

1.   678   2.   458
    − 435   − 273

3.   275   4.   526
    − 84   − 207

5. The Smith family is driving to Dallas. The trip is 450 miles. So far, they have driven 315 miles. How many miles are left in the trip?

Set G pages 175–180

Find 416 − 243.

Estimate by rounding to the nearest ten:
420 − 240 = 180.

Subtract the ones.
Regroup if needed.

Subtract the tens.
Regroup if needed.

$$\begin{array}{r} 416 \\ -243 \\ \hline 3 \end{array}$$

$$\begin{array}{r} {}^{3\,11}\!\!\not4\not1 6 \\ -243 \\ \hline 73 \end{array}$$

Subtract the hundreds.

$$\begin{array}{r} {}^{3\,11}\!\!\not4\not1 6 \\ -243 \\ \hline 173 \end{array}$$
The answer is reasonable since
173 is close to 180. So, 416 − 243 = 173.

Remember to regroup if necessary.

For **1** and **2**, estimate by rounding to the nearest ten. Then, find each difference.

1. $\begin{array}{r} 458 \\ -176 \\ \hline \end{array}$ 2. $\begin{array}{r} 236 \\ -79 \\ \hline \end{array}$

3. Damian's conservation club has 235 tree seedlings to plant. They have planted 172 seedlings so far. How many seedlings do they have left to plant?

Set H pages 181–186

Find 400 − 257.

Regroup the hundreds and tens.

Subtract ones, tens, and hundreds.

$$\begin{array}{r} {}^{3\ \overset{9}{\cancel{10}}\ 10}\!\!\not4\not0\not0 \\ -257 \\ \hline \end{array}$$

$$\begin{array}{r} {}^{3\ \overset{9}{\cancel{10}}\ 10}\!\!\not4\not0\not0 \\ -257 \\ \hline 143 \end{array}$$

Remember you have to regroup when subtracting across zeros.

For **1** and **2**, find the difference.

1. $\begin{array}{r} 400 \\ -227 \\ \hline \end{array}$ 2. $\begin{array}{r} 306 \\ -198 \\ \hline \end{array}$

Set I pages 187–192

Mike has to read a 256-page book. In Week 1 he read 82 pages. In Week 2 he read 100 pages. Draw a strip diagram and write an equation to find how many more pages he has to read.

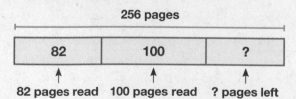

256 pages

| 82 | 100 | ? |

82 pages read   100 pages read   ? pages left

82 + 100 = 182

256 − 182 = ☐

$$\begin{array}{r} {}^{1\ 15}\!\!2\not5 6 \\ -182 \\ \hline 74 \end{array}$$

Mike has 74 pages to read.

Remember you can use a strip diagram to show subtraction or addition.

In **1** and **2**, draw strip diagrams and write equations to solve.

1. A total of 312 people are participating in a marathon. So far, 215 people have finished. How many are still running?

2. There are 113 boys, 149 girls, and 195 adults at the zoo. How many more children are there than adults?

© Pearson Education, Inc. 3

1. Jorge is finding the sum of 337 + 281 by breaking it into smaller problems. He uses place value and finds the sums of the hundreds, tens, and ones. What is the sum of the tens?

   A 11

   B 12

   C 110

   D 118

2. Bill used place-value blocks to model a subtraction problem. What regrouping did Bill show?

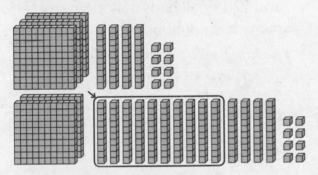

   A 3 hundreds 4 tens 8 ones as 2 hundreds 14 tens 8 ones

   B 3 hundreds 4 tens 8 ones as 2 hundreds 3 tens 18 ones

   C 2 hundreds 4 tens 8 ones as 1 hundreds 14 tens 8 ones

   D 3 hundreds 4 tens 8 ones as 2 hundreds 14 tens 7 ones

3. When finding 433 − 249 using place value, Marci began by subtracting 49. Which number should she have subtracted first?

   A 150   C 240

   B 200   D 400

4. A play began at 7:00 P.M. By 6:40, the first 176 people had arrived. By 6:50, another 204 people arrived. At 7:00, the last 59 people arrived. How many people attended the play?

   A 329   C 429

   B 339   D 439

5. Alana used place-value blocks to model a problem. Which problem did she model?

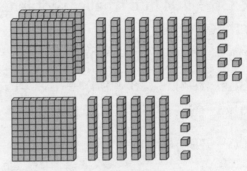

   A 215 + 111 = 326

   B 278 + 156 = 434

   C 287 + 165 = 452

   D 187 + 165 = 352

6. The girls' volleyball team raised $276 during a fundraiser. The boys' basketball team raised $289. Each team worked 28 hours to raise the money. How much did the two teams raise?

   A $465   C $565

   B $555   D $566

7. Tricia had 302 prize tickets. She traded 237 of the tickets for a stuffed animal and 20 tickets for a drink. How many prize tickets does Tricia have left?

A 155

B 145

C 55

D Not here

8. Which is the correct way Sarah could break 536 + 194 into smaller problems using place value?

A $(500 + 100) + (30 + 90) + (6 + 4)$

B $(536 + 194) + (36 + 94) + (6 + 4)$

C $(530 + 190) + (60 + 70) + (6 + 4)$

D $(500 + 200) + (40 + 90) + (6 + 4)$

9. Chickens at the Lapp chicken farm laid 300 eggs this morning. So far the Lapps have sold 168 of these eggs and are hoping to sell another 100 eggs later in the day. How many of the eggs do they have left to sell?

A 32

B 122

C 132

D 142

10. Luisa wants to use place-value blocks to show 367 + 215. How many tens blocks will she need to show the sum by regrouping?

A 9

B 8

C 7

D 6

11. A restaurant supply store has 211 large bags of flour, 166 medium bags of flour, and 228 small bags of flour in stock. How many bags of flour does the store have?

A 595

B 596

C 605

D 705

12. The residents of Elm City own 346 cats. They own 268 dogs and 37 birds. How many more cats than dogs do the residents own?

A 78

B 88

C 122

D 614

© Pearson Education, Inc. 3

13. The Green Dragon restaurant made a profit of $825 on Friday. The Tasty Bistro made a profit of $647 the same day. Find how much more profit the Green Dragon made.

Green Dragon profit	$825	

	$647	?
	Tasty Bistro profit	More profit

A $78

B $82

C $128

D $178

14. Which is the first step Fred could use in solving 318 − 121 if he was using place value to break the problem into smaller problems?

A Subtract 10 from 218

B Subtract 20 from 218

C Subtract 100 from 100

D Subtract 100 from 318

15. Yasmin earned $283 one summer from her babysitting job and $45 from walking dogs. She spent $139 of this money on a wedding present for her aunt. Which of the following is **NOT** a way to find how much money Yasmin had left?

A Add $45 and $283, then subtract $139

B Subtract $139 from $283, then add $45

C Add $283 and $45, then subtract $139

D Not here

16. Gregor has $165 to spend at a sporting goods store. He sees a pair of hockey pants for $76 and a jersey for $82. Will Gregor be able to buy both items? If so, how much money will he get back in change?

A No; Gregor does not have enough money.

B Yes; $7 back in change.

C Yes; $17 back in change.

D Yes; no change back.

17. Ali wants to find the sum of 173 + 25 using place value. She breaks the problem into smaller problems and writes 100 + (70 + 20) + (3 + 5). What is the sum?

A 200

B 199

C 198

D 189

18. Mitch is finding the difference between 255 − 124 using place value. He has subtracted the hundreds and tens so far. What are the amounts he has subtracted? How much does Mitch still need to subtract?

A 200; 50; He needs to subtract 4.

B 100; 20; He needs to subtract 3.

C 100; 20; He needs to subtract 4.

D 100; 20; He needs to subtract 5.

19. Which of the following are two steps Eli should follow to find $756 - 345$ using place value?

A $756 - 300$ and then $456 - 40$.

B $700 - 300$ and then $40 + 50$.

C $756 - 300$ and then $356 - 40$.

D $756 - 300$ and then $456 - 30$.

20. Joshua has 323 pennies in his piggy bank, and Lula has 255 pennies in hers. Draw a strip diagram and write an equation to find how many fewer pennies Lula has than Joshua.

21. Maggie makes jewelry out of beads. She buys 108 red beads, 240 green beads, and 259 blue beads. How many more red and green beads does Maggie buy than blue beads? Mark your answer in the grid below.

22. The Smith family spent $457 on groceries last month. The Wilson family spent $291. The Moore family spent $338. How much less did the Moores spend on groceries than the Smiths?

A $109

B $119

C $121

D $129

23. Describe how Janna will have to regroup to solve the subtraction problem below. What is the difference?

$$\begin{array}{r} 316 \\ -\ 226 \end{array}$$

24. Edison School has 332 students. Du Bois School has 246 students. Turner School has 199 students. How many more students does Edison School have than Du Bois School? Mark your answer in the grid below.

© Pearson Education, Inc. 3

TOPIC 4

Multiplication Meanings

Essential Question: What are different meanings of multiplication, including how addition and multiplication are related?

Many birds migrate during the winter.

Their survival depends on having enough to eat.

That's why I'm always on time for lunch! Here's a project on birds and multiplication.

Math and Science Project: Birds

Do Research Many kinds of birds fly south each year. Use the Internet, or another source, to discover which kinds of birds fly south in the winter. How far do they fly? What time of year do they fly? Where do they start and end their migration?

Journal: Write a Report Include what you found. Also include in your report:

- Information about why some birds fly in groups. For example, scientists believe one reason is for protection.

- Other factors influencing bird migration. Include weather, seasons, and climate.

- Make up and solve multiplication problems based on the data in your report.

Review What You Know

Vocabulary

Choose the best term from the box. Write it on the blank.

> • place value
>
> • round
>
> • order
>
> • equation

1. To _____, replace a number with a number that tells about how many.

2. A number sentence that includes an equal sign is an _____.

3. _____ is the value of a place a digit has in a number.

Adding 3-Digit Numbers

Find each sum.

4. 352
   + 234

5. 125
   + 289

6. 605
   + 347

7. 586
   + 234

8. 412
   + 324

9. 212
   + 888

Adding 3 or More Numbers

Find each sum.

10. 25
    32
    + 65

11. 503
    58
    + 116

12. Ramón read 25 pages of his book last week. He read 96 pages this week. He still has 110 pages to read. How long is the book?

    A 331 pages
    B 231 pages
    C 221 pages
    D 131 pages

Subtracting 3-Digit Numbers

13. **Communicate** Explain how to find $245 - 172$. Use the place-value blocks to help.

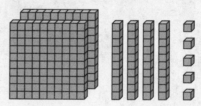

14. 356
    − 211

15. 712
    − 504

© Pearson Education, Inc. 3

My Word Cards

Use the examples for each word on the front of the card to help complete the definitions on the back.

A-Z

multiplication

$4 \times 3 = 12$

factors

$7 \times 3 = 21$

factors

product

$7 \times 3 = 21$

product

array

3 columns

2 rows

Commutative (Order) Property of Multiplication

$5 \times 7 = 35$

My Word Cards

The numbers that are multiplied together to give a product are called

_____.

_____ is an operation that gives the total number when you join equal groups.

An _____ is a way of displaying objects in equal rows and columns.

The answer to a multiplication problem

is called the _____.

Numbers can be multiplied in any order and the product will be the same

because of the _____

_____

_____.

© Pearson Education, Inc. 3

Name _____

Solve & Share

Ms. Witt bought 3 boxes of paint with 5 jars of paint in each box. What is the total number of jars Ms. Witt bought? *Solve this problem any way you choose.*

TEKS 3.4D Determine the total number of objects when equally-sized groups of objects are combined or arranged in arrays up to 10 by 10. Also, 3.4E, 3.5B. **Mathematical Process Standards** 3.1A, 3.1B, 3.1C, 3.1D, 3.1G

Digital Resources at PearsonTexas.com

Solve   Learn   Glossary   Check   Tools   Games

You can **connect.** Can you connect this problem to other problems you have come across in everyday life?

Look Back!

Draw a Picture How can you use a picture to show the math you did in the problem?

How Can You Find the Total Number of Objects in Equal Groups?

A Jessie used 3 bags to bring home the goldfish she won at the Fun Fair. She put the same number of goldfish in each bag. How many goldfish did she win?

I can use counters to show the groups.

8 goldfish in each bag

B The counters show 3 groups of 8 goldfish.

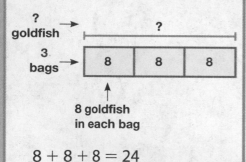

You can use addition to join equal groups.

? goldfish

3 bags → | 8 | 8 | 8 |

8 goldfish in each bag

$8 + 8 + 8 = 24$

C Multiplication is an operation that gives the total number when you join equal groups.

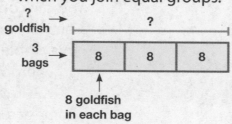

? goldfish

3 bags → | 8 | 8 | 8 |

8 goldfish in each bag

3 times 8 equals 24

$$3 \times 8 = 24$$

factor   factor   product

Factors are the numbers that are being multiplied. The product is the answer to a multiplication problem.

D Addition sentence:

$$8 + 8 + 8 = 24$$

Multiplication sentence:

$$3 \times 8 = 24$$

So, $8 + 8 + 8 = 3 \times 8$.

Jessie won 24 goldfish.

Do You Understand?

Convince Me! Suppose Jessie won 5 bags of 8 goldfish. Draw a picture or strip diagram to show the goldfish she won. Write an addition sentence and a multiplication sentence to represent the problem.

© Pearson Education, Inc. 3

Guided Practice

In **1** and **2**, use the pictures to complete the number sentences.

1.

2 groups of ____

4 + 4 = ____

2 × ____ = ____

2.

____ groups of 6

6 + ____ + ____ = ____

3 × ____ = ____

3. Reason Can you write 5 + 5 + 5 + 5 as a multiplication sentence? Explain.

4. Reason Can you write 3 + 4 + 7 = 14 as a multiplication sentence? Explain.

5. Number Sense Write an addition sentence and a multiplication sentence to solve this problem. Jessie bought 4 packages of colorful stones to put in the fish bowl. There are 6 stones in each package. How many stones did Jessie buy?

Independent Practice

Leveled Practice Complete **6** and **7**. Use the pictures to help.

6.

2 groups of ____

5 + ____ = ____

2 × ____ = ____

7.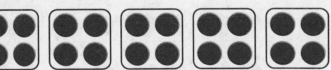

5 groups of ____

4 + 4 + 4 + ____ + ____ = ____

5 × ____ = ____

For **8** through **11**, complete each number sentence. Use counters or draw a picture to help.

8. 2 + 2 + 2 + 2 = 4 × ____

9. ____ + ____ + ____ = 3 × 7

10. 9 + ____ + ____ = 3 × ____

11. 6 + 6 + 6 + 6 + 6 = ____ × ____

Problem Solving

12. Communicate Luke says you can always add or multiply to join groups. Is he correct? Explain why or why not.

13. Extend Your Thinking Lois says any addition sentence where the addends are all the same can be written as a multiplication sentence. Is Lois correct? Explain why or why not.

14. Analyze Information The bar graph shows the favorite fruits of students in Ramón's class. Did more students choose bananas or apples as their favorite fruit? Explain how you know.

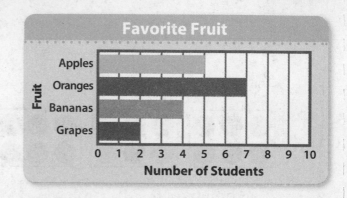

15. Jenna drew a picture to show 4 groups of 2. Which picture did Jenna draw?

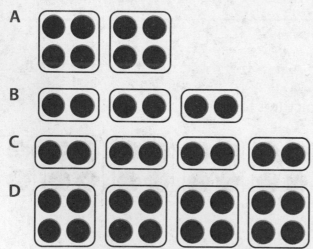

A

B

C

D

16. Number Sense Maria has 6 new flashlights. Each flashlight takes 3 batteries. How many batteries will Maria need for all the flashlights? Write an addition sentence and a multiplication sentence. Explain how the sentences are related.

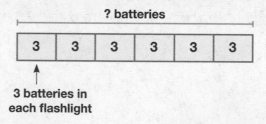

? batteries

| 3 | 3 | 3 | 3 | 3 | 3 |

3 batteries in each flashlight

17. Analyze Information Mark drew this picture to show 2 groups of 4. Is Mark's picture correct? Explain.

18. Personal Financial Literacy Jenna saves $5 each week. How much money will Jenna save after 6 weeks? Write an addition sentence and a multiplication sentence to solve.

© Pearson Education, Inc. 3

Another Look!

Each group below has the same number of squares.
There are 5 groups of 4 squares.

There are 20
squares in all.

20 squares

| 4 | 4 | 4 | 4 | 4 |

An addition sentence or multiplication sentence
can represent the total number of squares:

$4 + 4 + 4 + 4 + 4 = 20$

$5 \times 4 = 20$

In **1** and **2**, complete the addition and multiplication sentences.

1.

4 groups of ____

$4 + 4 + 4 + 4 =$ ____

$4 \times$ ____ $=$ ____

2.

32

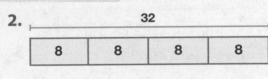

| 8 | 8 | 8 | 8 |

____ groups of 8

___ $+$ ___ $+$ ___ $+$ ___ $= 32$

___ $\times 8 =$ ___

In **3** and **4**, write the addition sentence as a multiplication sentence.

3. $1 + 1 + 1 + 1 + 1 = 5$

4. $7 + 7 + 7 = 21$

In **5** through **8**, write the multiplication sentence as an addition sentence.

5. $5 \times 5 = 25$

6. $6 \times 2 = 12$

7. $4 \times 4 = 16$

8. $5 \times 6 = 30$

9. **Number Sense** Jan bought 3 bags of beads. Each bag contains 7 beads. Draw a strip diagram and write an addition sentence and a multiplication sentence to show how many beads Jan bought. How are the two number sentences related?

10. ⭐ Misha bought 4 boxes of 6 markers each. He wrote this addition sentence to show how many markers he bought: $6 + 6 + 6 + 6 = 24$. Which multiplication sentence could Misha have written?

A $2 \times 12 = 24$

B $1 \times 24 = 24$

C $4 \times 6 = 24$

D $3 \times 8 = 24$

These multiplication sentences show different ways to find 24.

11. **Explain** Debra drew this shape on the back of her notebook.

What is the name of the shape Debra drew? How do you know?

12. **Math and Science** A clutch is the number of eggs a bird lays. A woodpecker's clutch has 4 eggs. Draw a picture to show how many eggs there would be in 3 woodpecker clutches. Write an addition sentence and a multiplication sentence for your picture.

13. **Analyze Information** Carrie drew this picture to show 3 groups of 3.

Is Carrie's picture correct? Why or why not?

14. **Extend Your Thinking** Marion has 4 cards, Jake has 4 cards, and Sam has 3 cards. Can you write a multiplication sentence to find how many cards they have in all? Explain your answer.

15. Martin has 3 piles of coins. Each pile has 5 dimes. Write a multiplication sentence to show how many dimes Martin has. Then, find how much money Martin has.

16. Snazzy Sneakers is having a shoe sale. Anthony buys 4 pairs of shoes. How many individual shoes did he buy? Write an addition sentence and a multiplication sentence that shows your solution.

© Pearson Education, Inc. 3

Name _____

☆ ☆
Solve & Share

Mark put sports cards in an album. He put 4 rows of cards on each page. He put 3 cards in each row. How many cards are on each page? *Solve this problem any way you choose.*

You can **formulate a plan.** Sometimes drawing a picture can help you solve a problem. *Show your work in the space below!*

⭐ **TEKS 3.4D** Determine the total number of objects when equally-sized groups of objects are combined or arranged in arrays up to 10 by 10. Also, 3.4E, 3.5B.
Mathematical Process Standards 3.1A, 3.1B, 3.1C, 3.1D, 3.1F, 3.1G

Digital Resources at PearsonTexas.com

 Solve   Learn   Glossary   Check   Tools   Games

Look Back!

Explain Will your answer be the same if Mark puts 3 rows of 4 cards on each page? Explain.

A

Dana keeps her swimming medal collection in a display on the wall.

The display has 4 rows. Each row has 5 medals. How many medals are in Dana's collection?

The medals are in an array. An array shows objects in equal rows.

B The counters show 4 rows and 5 columns.

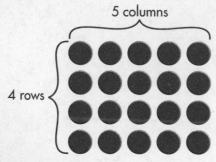

5 columns

4 rows

Each row is a group. You can use addition to find the total.

$5 + 5 + 5 + 5 = 20$

C Multiplication can also be used to find the total in an array.

You say, "4 times 5 equals 20."

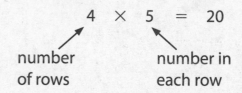

$$4 \times 5 = 20$$

number of rows   number in each row

There are 20 medals in Dana's collection.

Do You Understand?

Convince Me! Jason also has a swimming medal collection. His display has 5 rows with 5 medals in each row. Who has more medals, Jason or Dana? Draw an array and write an addition sentence and a multiplication sentence to show your work.

© Pearson Education, Inc. 3

☆ Guided Practice ☆

In **1** and **2**, write a multiplication sentence for each array.

1.

2.

Remember, an array shows objects in equal rows.

3. **Connect** Look at the example about Dana's medals on page 214. What does the first factor in the multiplication sentence tell you about the array?

4. **Draw a Picture** Mia puts 4 rows with 7 muffins in each row on a platter. Draw an array to find the total number of muffins.

Independent Practice ☆

Leveled Practice In **5** through **7**, write a multiplication sentence for each array.

5.

6.

7.

In **8** through **11**, draw an array to show each multiplication fact. Write the product.

8. $5 \times 6 =$ _____

9. $2 \times 9 =$ _____

10. $5 \times 3 =$ _____

11. $4 \times 2 =$ _____

12. Reason Liza drew these two arrays. How are the arrays alike? How are they different?

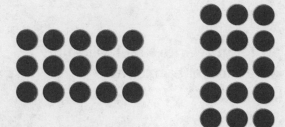

13. Analyze Information How many more oak trees are there than pine trees? Explain how you know.

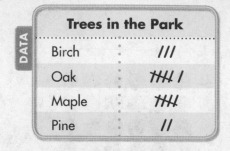

DATA	Trees in the Park	
	Birch	///
	Oak	⊬⊬ /
	Maple	⊬⊬
	Pine	//

14. ⭐ Dan bought the stickers shown below. Which number sentence shows one way to find how many stickers Dan bought?

A 5 + 5 = ?

B 5 × 4 = ?

C 5 + 4 = ?

D 5 − 4 = ?

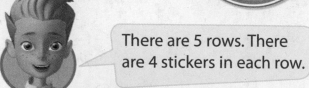

There are 5 rows. There are 4 stickers in each row.

15. Use a Strip Diagram Delbert puts 5 nickels in each of his 3 empty piggy banks. How many nickels did Delbert put in the banks? Write a multiplication sentence to solve.

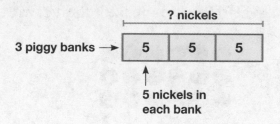

? nickels

3 piggy banks → | 5 | 5 | 5 |

5 nickels in each bank

16. Number Sense Mr. Lopez planted 8 rows of apple trees on his farm. He planted 5 trees in each row. Write an addition sentence and a multiplication sentence to find the total number of trees Mr. Lopez planted. How are the two number sentences related?

17. Extend Your Thinking Margo has 23 pictures. Can she use all the pictures to make an array with exactly two equal rows? Why or why not?

© Pearson Education, Inc. 3

Name _____

Another Look!

Scott arranged some apples in an array.
He made 4 rows with 3 apples in each row.
How many apples does Scott have?

Multiplication can be used to find the total in an array.

Scott's array

The array shows 4 rows of 3 apples.

$3 + 3 + 3 + 3 = 12$

Say, 4 times 3 equals 12.

Write, $4 \times 3 = 12$.

For **1** through **3**, write an addition sentence and a multiplication sentence for each array.

1.

$3 + \underline{} + \underline{} = 9$

$3 \times \underline{} = 9$

2.

$4 + \underline{} = \underline{}$

$2 \times \underline{} = \underline{}$

3.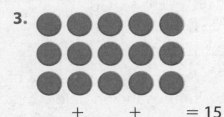

$\underline{} + \underline{} + \underline{} = 15$

$\underline{} \times \underline{} = 15$

In **4** through **7**, draw an array. Write an addition sentence and a multiplication sentence for your array.

4. 3×4

5. 2×3

6. 2×5

7. 3×6

8. Draw a Picture Paula arranged her stamps in an album. The album has 3 rows of stamps, with 7 stamps in each row. How many stamps does Paula have? Draw an array to solve the problem. Write an addition sentence and a multiplication sentence for the array.

9. Communicate Shelly wants to plant 6 rows of flowers, with 7 flowers in each row. What addition sentence and what multiplication sentence can she write to find how many flowers she needs to plant? Which number sentence do you find easier to use? Why?

10. ★ Jana made the array at the right to show how she wants to arrange some pictures. Which multiplication sentence describes the array Jana made?

A $3 \times 12 = 36$
B $2 \times 18 = 36$
C $6 \times 6 = 36$
D $4 \times 9 = 36$

11. Reason Marie has one of the solid figures shown below.

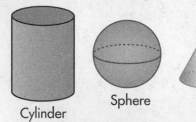

Cylinder   Sphere   Cone

Marie's solid figure has 2 flat surfaces, 0 edges, and 0 vertices. Which solid figure does Marie have?

12. Carole has a 7×8 array of pennies. David has a 3×4 array of nickels. Find the value of each array. Which array has a greater value?

13. Personal Financial Literacy Frank spends $10 each week on school lunches. How much does Frank spend on school lunches for 9 weeks?

14. Extend Your Thinking Vince has 16 beads. How many different arrays can Vince draw to represent the total number of beads he has? Explain

© Pearson Education, Inc. 3

Name _____

Solve & Share

Harvey the Hop Toad jumps 4 times in the same direction. He jumps 5 inches in each jump. How can you show how far he goes on a number line?

You can **connect ideas.** You can show addition on a number line.

⭐ TEKS 3.4E Represent multiplication facts by using a variety of approaches such as repeated addition, equal-sized groups, arrays, area models, equal jumps on a number line, and skip counting. **Mathematical Process Standards** 3.1B, 3.1D, 3.1E, 3.1F, 3.1G

Digital Resources at PearsonTexas.com

Solve Learn Glossary Check Tools Games

0 1 2 3 4 5 6 7 8 9 10 11 12 13 14 15 16 17 18 19 20 21 22

Look Back!

Connect How are Harvey's jumps on the number line like repeated addition? How are they like skip counting?

A

Clara is making gift bags for her 5 friends. She wants to put 3 glitter pens in each gift bag. How many glitter pens does Clara need?

You can use a number line and skip counting to show multiplication.

Glitter Pens Glitter Pens Glitter Pens Glitter Pens Glitter Pens

B

Draw arrows on the number line to show the number of glitter pens for each gift bag.

3 pens   6 pens   9 pens   12 pens   15 pens

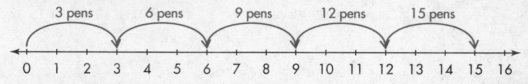

0 1 2 3 4 5 6 7 8 9 10 11 12 13 14 15 16

Skip counting: 3, 6, 9, 12, 15

Multiplication: $5 \times 3 = 15$

Clara needs 15 glitter pens.

Do You Understand?

Convince Me! What would skip counting by 6 look like on the number line?

© Pearson Education, Inc. 3

☆ Guided Practice *

In **1**, complete the number line and fill in the blanks.

1. Jim ran 3 miles a day for 4 days in a row. How many miles did he run?

   Draw jumps on the number line. Skip count by 3s.

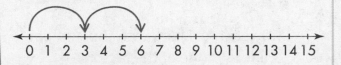

   ← 0 1 2 3 4 5 6 7 8 9 10 11 12 13 14 15 →

   Number of jumps: _____

   Jim ran _____ miles.

2. **Explain** Why do you skip count by 3s on the number line?

3. **Explain** Why do you make four jumps on the number line?

4. **Communicate** How would the jumps on the number line look different if Jim ran 2 miles each day?

☆ Independent Practice ☆

Leveled Practice In **5**, show how you found the solution on the number line.

5. Judy wants to put 2 apples into each of 6 fruit baskets. How many apples will she need? Draw jumps on the number line to show how many apples Judy will need.

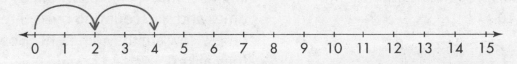

   0 1 2 3 4 5 6 7 8 9 10 11 12 13 14 15

   Judy will need _____ apples.

In **6** and **7**, show the multiplication fact on the number line. Write the product.

6. $7 \times 2 =$ _____   ← 0 1 2 3 4 5 6 7 8 9 10 11 12 13 14 15 →

7. $3 \times 3 =$ _____   ← 0 1 2 3 4 5 6 7 8 9 10 11 12 13 14 15 →

Problem Solving

8. Represent Suki invited 5 friends to a party. She gave each friend 2 party favors. How many party favors did Suki give away? Draw jumps on the number line to find the answer.

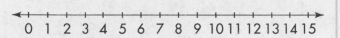

9. Stan drew this number line.

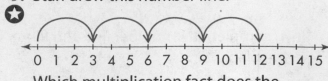

Which multiplication fact does the number line show?

A 4 × 12 = 48
B 4 × 4 = 16
C 2 × 7 = 14
D 4 × 3 = 12

There are 4 jumps on the number line. 4 is one of the factors.

10. Nikki wants to use 3 glass beads in a necklace she is making. She wants to make 6 necklaces. How many glass beads will Nikki need?

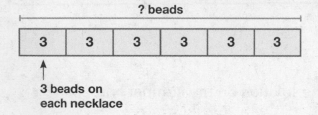

? beads

| 3 | 3 | 3 | 3 | 3 | 3 |

3 beads on each necklace

11. Draw a Picture Raj drew a plane shape with 5 straight sides and 5 vertices. What is the name of the shape Raj drew? Draw a similar shape.

12. Analyze Information Tim drew this number line to show the multiplication fact 5 × 2 = 10.

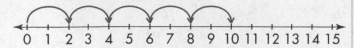

Which parts of the number line represent the factors? Which part shows the product?

13. Extend Your Thinking Draw a number line to compare skip counting by 3s four times and skip counting by 4s three times. How are they different? How are they alike?

© Pearson Education, Inc. 3

Name _____

Another Look!

There are 4 fruit bars in a package. Abby buys 5 packages. How many fruit bars does she buy?

Use a number line. Skip count by 4s, five times.

You can use a number line to show $5 \times 4 = 20$.

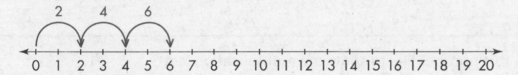

Number of jumps: 5   Number in each jump: 4

$5 \times 4 = 20$ Abby buys 20 fruit bars.

Use the number line for **1** through **3**.

1. Jack put 2 photos on each of 7 pages of his photo album. How many photos did he use? Complete the jumps on the number line.

Number of jumps: _____   Number in each jump: _____

_____ × _____ = _____

Jack used _____ photos.

2. Why do you skip count by 2s on the number line?

3. Why do you make 7 jumps on the number line?

4. Tony bought 7 packages of mini-muffins. There were 3 mini-muffins in each package. How many mini-muffins did Tony buy altogether? Use the number line to help find the answer.

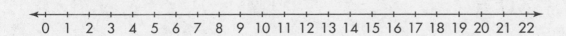

5. Represent Diane used 5 feet of ribbon to decorate each gift she was wrapping. She wrapped 5 gifts. How many feet of ribbon did she use?

Show how to find the answer using the number line.

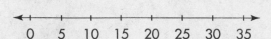

6. Jerry drew this number line.

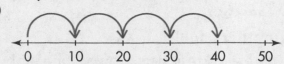

Which multiplication fact does the number line show?

A $4 \times 10 = 40$
B $8 \times 5 = 40$
C $2 \times 20 = 40$
D $2 \times 10 = 20$

7. Extend Your Thinking Draw a number line to compare skip counting by 4s four times to skip counting by 8s two times. How are they alike? How are they different? Explain.

8. Alyssa has saved $232 from mowing lawns. She spends $189 on back-to-school shopping. How much of her savings does Alyssa have left?

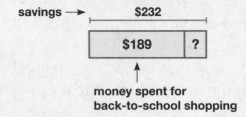

money spent for back-to-school shopping

9. Explain Tina drew this number line to show the multiplication fact $5 \times 3 = 15$.

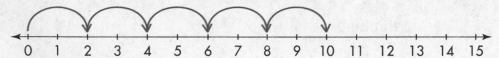

Is her number line correct? Why or why not?

10. Analyze Information Timmy surveyed his classmates to see what their favorite season was. The pictograph shows the results of the survey. How many students chose spring? If 4 students had chosen spring, how would the graph look different?

Favorite Season

Spring	𝑥 𝑥 𝑥 𝑥 𝑥
Summer	𝑥 𝑥 𝑥 𝑥 𝑥 𝑥 𝑥
Fall	𝑥 𝑥 𝑥
Winter	𝑥 𝑥 𝑥 𝑥 𝑥 𝑥

Each 𝑥 = 2 votes

© Pearson Education, Inc. 3

Name _____

☆ ☆
Solve & Share

Cathy arranged seashells in two different arrays. One array has 2 rows with 6 shells in each row. The other array has 6 rows with 2 shells in each row. Do both arrays have the same number of shells? Draw the arrays, then write a multiplication sentence for each.

You can **communicate.** What do you notice is the same in each array?

 TEKS 3.4F Recall facts to multiply up to 10 by 10 with automaticity and recall the corresponding division facts. Also, 3.4E, 3.4K. **Mathematical Process Standards** 3.1B, 3.1D, 3.1G

Digital Resources at PearsonTexas.com

 Solve   Learn   Glossary   Check Tools   Games

Look Back!

Reason What happens when you change the order of the factors in a multiplication problem?

Does Order Matter When You Multiply?

A

Libby and Sydney each say her poster has more stickers. Which poster has more stickers?

Sydney's poster

Remember, an array shows objects in equal rows.

Libby's poster

B Libby's Poster

On Libby's poster, there are 4 rows with 3 stickers in each row. There are two ways to write this:

$3 + 3 + 3 + 3 = 12$

and

$4 \times 3 = 12$

C Sydney's Poster

On Sydney's poster, there are 3 rows with 4 stickers in each row. There are two ways to write this:

$4 + 4 + 4 = 12$

and

$3 \times 4 = 12$

D Both posters have the same number of stickers.

The Commutative (Order) Property of Multiplication says you can multiply numbers in any order and the product is the same. So, $4 \times 3 = 3 \times 4$.

Do You Understand?

Convince Me! Circle the pair of number sentences that shows the Commutative (Order) Property of Multiplication. Explain your answer.

$2 \times 4 = 8$ $2 \times 4 = 8$ $2 + 2 + 2 + 2 = 8$

$2 \times 8 = 16$ $4 \times 2 = 8$ $4 \times 2 = 8$

© Pearson Education, Inc. 3

Name _____

For **1** and **2**, draw an array and give the product for each fact.

1. $5 \times 2 =$ _____ $2 \times 5 =$ _____

2. $3 \times 8 =$ _____ $8 \times 3 =$ _____

For **3** and **4**, complete the number sentence.

3. $5 \times 2 =$ _____ $\times 5$

4. $6 \times 1 = 1 \times$ _____

5. Complete the following statement.

$6 \times 4 = 24$, so $4 \times 6 =$ _____.

6. Connect What multiplication fact can be paired with 2×6 to make a pair of facts showing the Commutative Property of Multiplication?

7. Communicate Why is the Commutative Property of Multiplication sometimes called the *order* property?

Independent Practice

Leveled Practice For **8** and **9**, write a multiplication sentence for each array in the pair.

8.

9.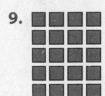

For **10** and **11**, draw an array to show each multiplication fact. Write the products.

10. $2 \times 3 =$ _____ $3 \times 2 =$ _____

11. $5 \times 6 =$ _____ $6 \times 5 =$ _____

For **12** through **14**, fill in the missing number.

12. $5 \times 3 =$ _____ $\times 5$

13. $8 \times$ _____ $= 4 \times 8$

14. _____ $\times 6 = 6 \times 7$

Problem Solving

15. Explain How do the arrays at the right show the Commutative Property of Multiplication?

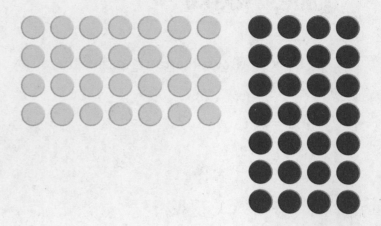

16. Draw a Picture Effie earned $146 from babysitting, $120 from her allowance, and $245 from mowing lawns this year. Draw a strip diagram to find how much Effie earned.

> A strip diagram can show 3 or more addends.

17. ⭐ Chen arranged 32 berries in the array shown below.

What other array can he use to show the same number of berries?

A 3 rows of 4 berries
B 5 rows of 4 berries
C 3 rows of 8 berries
D 8 rows of 4 berries

18. Extend Your Thinking Ramón says he can use the Commutative Property of Multiplication to show the product of 4×6 is the same as the product of 3×8. Is he correct? Why or why not?

19. Draw a Picture Matt drew a plane shape by tracing the flat surface of a cube.

Draw and label the shape Matt drew.

© Pearson Education, Inc. 3

Name _____

Another Look!

This array shows 2 rows of 3 pennies.

This array shows 3 rows of 2 pennies.

An array shows objects in equal rows.

$2 \times 3 = 6$

$3 \times 2 = 6$

You can use the **Commutative Property of Multiplication** to multiply the numbers in any order.

$2 \times 3 = 6$ so $3 \times 2 = 6$

For **1** and **2**, draw an array to show each multiplication fact. Write the products.

1. $2 \times 8 =$ ____ $8 \times 2 =$ ____

2. $4 \times 4 =$ ____

For **3** through **12**, complete each multiplication sentence. You may use counters or draw pictures to help.

3. $3 \times 4 = 12$, so ____ $\times 3 = 12$.

4. $5 \times 6 = 30$, so ____ $\times 5 = 30$.

5. $5 \times 2 = 10$, so $2 \times$ ____ $= 10$.

6. $4 \times 8 = 32$, so ____ $\times 4 = 32$.

7. $8 \times 6 = 48$, so $6 \times 8 =$ ____ .

8. $7 \times 6 = 42$, so ____ $\times 7 = 42$.

9. $7 \times 9 = 63$, so ____ $\times$ ____ $= 63$.

10. $7 \times 8 = 56$, so ____ $\times$ ____ $= 56$.

11. $3 \times 8 = 24$, so ____ $\times$ ____ $= 24$.

12. $5 \times 3 = 15$, so ____ $\times$ ____ $= 15$.

13. Use the Commutative Property of Multiplication to draw the second array and write multiplication sentences.

$3 \times \underline{\hspace{1cm}} = \underline{\hspace{1cm}}$

$7 \times 3 = \underline{\hspace{1cm}}$

14. Analyze Information Taylor made these arrays to show the Commutative Property of Multiplication. Is that what the arrays show? Why or why not?

15. Explain Scott puts some sports stickers in rows. He makes 6 rows with 5 stickers in each row. If he put the same stickers in 5 equal rows, how many stickers would be in each row? How do you know?

A good math explanation can include words, numbers, and symbols.

16. Karen bought 24 star stickers arranged in the array shown below.

What other array could the same number of stickers have been arranged in?

A 3 rows of 4 stickers

B 6 rows of 4 stickers

C 4 rows of 5 stickers

D 4 rows of 8 stickers

17. Extend Your Thinking Ed arranged some tiles in different arrays. One array has 3 rows with 7 tiles in each row. The other array has 7 rows with 3 tiles in each row. Can you use the Commutative Property to show the two arrays have the same number of tiles? Explain.

18. Communicate Mike built this box to hold his hobby tools. What solid figure is the box shaped like? How many faces, edges, and vertices does the box have?

© Pearson Education, Inc. 3

Name _____

Solve & Share

Write and solve a multiplication story about 4 × 5. Choose one of the phrases below to use in your multiplication story.

Phrases

- 4 equal groups of 5
- 4 rows of 5
- (Name) has 5 _____.
  (Name) has 4 times as many _____.

⭐ **TEKS 3.5C** Describe a multiplication expression as a comparison such as 3 × 24 represents 3 times as much as 24. Also, 3.4K, 3.5B.
Mathematical Process Standards 3.1B, 3.1D, 3.1E, 3.1G

Digital Resources at PearsonTexas.com

 Solve   Learn   Glossary   Check   Tools   Games

You can **communicate.** You can write multiplication stories about objects in your classroom.

Look Back!

Communicate Why is the answer to your classmate's story the same as the answer to your story?

A-Z

A

Write a multiplication story for 3 × 6.

Stories can be written to describe multiplication facts.

B ## Equal Groups

Randy has 3 packs of 6 buttons. How many buttons does he have?

3 × 6 = 18

Randy has 18 buttons.

C ## An Array

Eliza planted 6 lilies in each of 3 rows. How many lilies did she plant?

3 × 6 = 18

Eliza planted 18 lilies.

D ## Times as Many

Kanisha has 6 carrots. Jack has 3 times as many. How many carrots does Jack have?

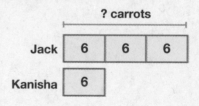

3 × 6 = 18

Jack has 18 carrots.

Do You Understand?

Convince Me! Write a "Times as Many" story for 10 × 3 = ☐.

© Pearson Education, Inc. 3

Name _____

In **1** and **2**, write a multiplication story for the problem. Use the picture or use objects to find the product.

1. $3 \times 5 =$ _____

2. $2 \times 4 =$ _____

3. Explain How would the story on page 232 about Randy and the buttons change if the multiplication sentence $2 \times 6 = \square$ were used?

4. Justify Could the story about the carrots on page 232 be an addition story? Explain.

5. What multiplication sentence could be written if Eliza planted 6 lilies in each of 2 rows?

Independent Practice

Leveled Practice In **6** through **9**, write a multiplication story for each picture or equation. Use the picture or equation to find the product.

6.

7.

8. $7 \times 3 =$ _____

9. $5 \times 5 =$ _____

Problem Solving

10. Represent 5 students went to the school store and bought 2 pencils each. What multiplication sentence describes this story?

You can draw loops around the pencils to show groups.

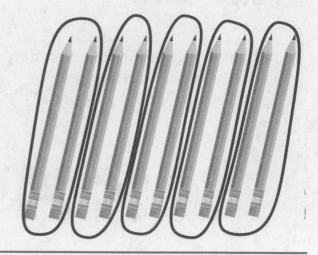

11. Check for Reasonableness Brian said 42 + 35 + 16 is greater than 150. Explain why his answer is not reasonable.

12. A soccer team traveled to a game in 4 vans. Each van held 6 players. Which multiplication sentence describes the story?

A $3 \times 8 = 24$
B $4 \times 6 = 24$
C $2 \times 12 = 24$
D $4 \times 4 = 16$

13. Extend Your Thinking A group of 12 monarch butterflies is getting ready to migrate. How many wings does the group have? Explain how you found the answer.

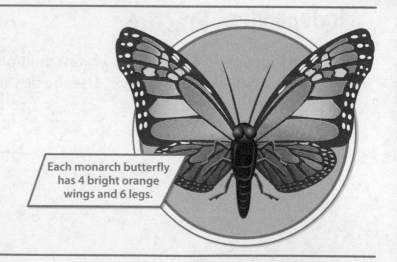

Each monarch butterfly has 4 bright orange wings and 6 legs.

14. Draw a Picture Steve has some packages of balloons. There are 8 balloons in each package. He has 24 balloons in all. Draw a picture to find how many packages of balloons Steve has. What multiplication fact does the story describe?

15. Seven teams played in the tournament. There were 6 players on each team. Write a multiplication sentence for this story.

© Pearson Education, Inc. 3

Another Look!
Write a story for 4 × 9.

Josephine had 4 friends over for a snack. She gave each friend 9 cherries. How many cherries did Josephine give in all?

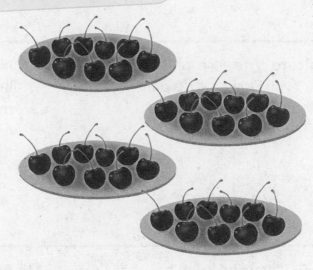

4 × 9 = 36

Josephine gave 36 cherries in all.

In **1** through **6**, write a multiplication story for each multiplication fact. Draw a picture to find the product.

1. 4 × 3 = ____

2. 5 × 2 = ____

3. 4 × 6 = ____

4. 7 × 5 = ____

5. 8 × 5 = ____

6. 9 × 4 = ____

7. Represent Four tennis players got 3 balls each from their coach to practice. How many tennis balls did the players receive in all? What multiplication sentence describes this story? Circle groups of tennis balls in the picture to show your answer.

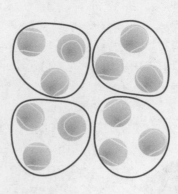

8. Communicate Write a multiplication story for 6 × 7. Draw a strip diagram for your story.

9. Math and Science There are 5 bluebirds in the backyard. Later, 10 times as many cardinals arrive. Write and solve a multiplication sentence to show how many cardinals there are.

10. There are 9 players on each baseball ⭐ team. Four teams are playing at the park. How many players are at the park? Which multiplication sentence does the story describe?

    A 2 × 18 = 36
    B 6 × 6 = 36
    C 3 × 12 = 36
    D 4 × 9 = 36

11. Analyze Information Mrs. Foster needs to order 400 pencils. A large box of pencils has 250 pencils. A small box of pencils has 125 pencils. Will one large box and one small box be enough? Explain.

12. Extend Your Thinking Judy is a dog walker. She walks 4 dogs at a time. Including Judy's legs, how many legs are in the group each time Judy walks the dogs? Explain how you found the answer.

© Pearson Education, Inc. 3

Name _____

☆ **Solve & Share** ☆

At the craft store, Nan bought 3 bottles of glitter that cost $5 each. She also bought twice as many bottles of glue that cost $2 each. How much did Nan spend? Do you have enough information to solve the problem? *If so, solve this problem any way you choose.*

 TEKS 3.1A Apply mathematics to problems arising in everyday life, society, and the workplace. Also, 3.4K, 3.5B. **Mathematical Process Standards** 3.1B, 3.1C, 3.1D, 3.1G

Digital Resources at PearsonTexas.com

Solve   Learn   Glossary   Check   Tools   Games

You can **formulate a plan.** What information do you need to solve the problem? You can use arrays to help solve the problem. *Show your work in the space below!*

Look Back!

Formulate a Plan Describe the plan you used to solve the problem.

A Analyze

Keisha plans to make 3 puppets. Tanya will make 3 times as many puppets as Keisha. Each puppet needs 2 buttons for its eyes. How many buttons will Tanya need?

Some word problems have hidden questions that need to be answered before you can solve the problem.

B Plan and Solve

Find and solve the hidden question.
How many puppets will Tanya make?

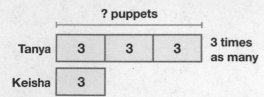

? puppets

Tanya | 3 | 3 | 3 | 3 times as many

Keisha | 3

3 × 3 puppets = 9 puppets

Tanya will make 9 puppets.

C Justify and Evaluate

Use the answer to the hidden question to solve the problem.
How many buttons will Tanya need?

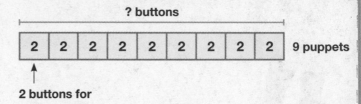

? buttons

2 2 2 2 2 2 2 2 2   9 puppets

2 buttons for each puppet

9 × 2 buttons = 18 buttons

Tanya will need 18 buttons.

Do You Understand?

Convince Me! The longest part of a hiking trail is two times the combined length of the other parts of the trail. What is the total length of the trail? Explain your solution.

2 miles   2 miles   3 miles

© Pearson Education, Inc. 3

Name _____

☆ Guided Practice *

> In **1**, use the answer to the hidden question to solve the problem.

1. Keisha bought glue for $3, sequins for $6, and lace for $4 to decorate her puppets. She paid for these items with a $20 bill. How much change should she get?

   Hidden Question: What is the total cost of the three items?

   $3 + $6 + $4 = ____

   $20 − $13 = ____

> Remember to answer any hidden questions first when solving multi-step problems.

2. **Communicate** Write a problem that has a hidden question. Then, solve your problem.

Independent Practice ☆

> Leveled Practice Use the pictures for **3** through **5**.

3. Craig bought 2 bags of oranges. After he ate 3 of the oranges, how many oranges were left?

   Hidden Question: How many oranges did Craig buy?

   ? oranges

10	10

   20 oranges

3	?

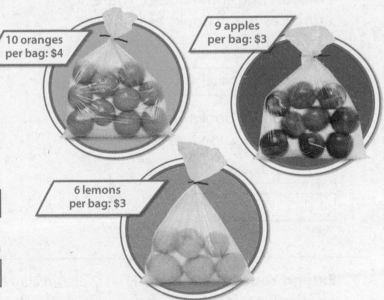

10 oranges per bag: $4

9 apples per bag: $3

6 lemons per bag: $3

4. Delia bought 2 bags of lemons and 3 bags of apples. How much did she spend on fruit?

5. Mr. Day bought a bag each of apples, oranges, and lemons. He paid with a $20 bill. What change should he get?

Problem Solving

6. **Explain** Trish bought 2 yards of rope to make a swing. Judy bought 6 yards of rope. The rope cost $3 a yard. How much did the two girls spend? Explain how you found your answer.

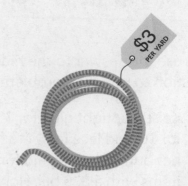
$3 PER YARD

7. **Number Sense** Karen saved 1,235 pennies. Mario saved 1,253 pennies and Leslie saved 1,301 pennies. Write the names in order from greatest to least number of pennies saved.

8. Al had $38. He spent $4 on an action figure and $10 on a board game. Which number sentence shows how much money Al has left?

   A $38 + $4 + $10 = ?
   B $38 − ($4 + $10) = ?
   C $38 − $4 = ?
   D $38 + $10 = ?

9. **Analyze Information** The library has 4 movies and some books. There are 5 times as many books as movies.

   ? books

   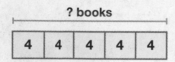

   | 4 | 4 | 4 | 4 | 4 |

   After 3 of the books were checked out, how many books were left?

   _____ books

   | 3 | ? |

10. **Explain** José has 4 action figures. His brother has 3 times as many action figures. How many action figures do the boys have? Explain how you found your answer.

11. **Extend Your Thinking** Carl has 2 dozen clay beads. He makes one necklace. Does Carl have enough beads left to make a bracelet? Explain how you found your answer.

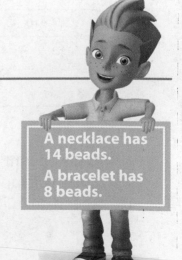

A necklace has 14 beads.

A bracelet has 8 beads.

© Pearson Education, Inc. 3

Name _____

Another Look!

Enzo's puts 3 meatballs in each of its meatball subs.
Tony's uses 2 times as many meatballs for its meatball subs.
Mr. Kerwin orders 4 meatball subs from Tony's.
How many meatballs will be in all of his subs?

> Find the hidden question to help you solve the problem.

How many meatballs does Tony's put in each meatball sub?	Use the answer to the hidden question to solve the problem.
? meatballs in a sub	**? meatballs**
3 | 3	6 | 6 | 6 | 6
$3 \times 2 = 6$	$6 \times 4 = 24$
Tony's puts 6 meatballs in each of its meatball subs.	Mr. Kerwin will have 24 meatballs all together in his 4 meatball subs.

In **1**, use the strip diagrams to solve the hidden question and the problem.

1. Barbara bought a book for $8, a magazine for $5, and bottled water for $2. She paid with a $20 bill. How much change should she get?

   Hidden Question: What is the total cost of the three items?

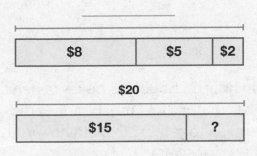

For **2** and **3**, find and solve the hidden question. Then, solve the problem.

2. Lee bought 4 posters for $6 each. He paid with a $50 bill. How much change should Lee get back?

3. Mika bought 3 notebooks for $2 each. She paid with a $10 bill. How much change should Mika get back?

4. **Communicate** Carla collected 328 shells. Dan collected 176 shells. How could you use compatible numbers to estimate how many shells they collected?

5. ⭐ Ben has $50 in his wallet. He buys two T-shirts for $14 each. How much money does he have left?

   A $12
   B $22
   C $26
   D $37

6. Sheila arranged her dimes in 4 rows with 10 dimes in each row. How many dimes does Sheila have? What is the value of Sheila's array?

7. Martha saves $30 each month for 3 months to buy a $75 coat. After buying the coat, how much will Martha have left of her savings?

In **8** through **10**, use the picture at the right.

8. **Justify** Teri bought 3 boxes of pencils and 2 notebooks. She paid with a $20 bill. How much change did she receive? What hidden question helped you solve the problem?

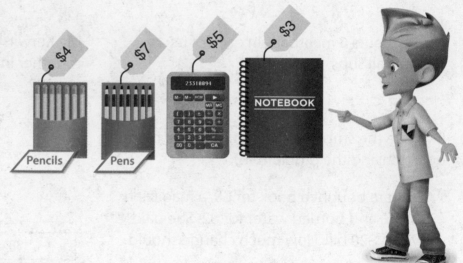

9. **Explain** Martin bought 3 boxes of pens and a calculator. How much money did he spend all together? Explain how you found your answer.

10. **Extend Your Thinking** Joey bought 2 notebooks and 2 boxes of pencils. How much money did he spend all together? Show two ways you could find the answer.

© Pearson Education, Inc. 3

Name _____

1. **Number Sense** Janet has 4 packages of markers. Each package contains 5 markers. Draw a strip diagram. Then, write an addition sentence and a multiplication sentence to show how many markers Janet has.

Applying Math Processes
- How does this problem connect to previous ones?
- What is my plan?
- How can I use tools?
- How can I use number sense?
- How can I communicate and represent my thinking?
- How can I organize and record information?
- How can I explain my work?
- How can I justify my answer?

2. **Explain** How do the arrays show the Commutative Property of Multiplication?

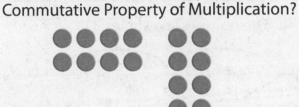

3. **Extend Your Thinking** Sandy has 12 glass beads, 16 clay beads, and 10 wood beads. She uses 24 of them to make a necklace. Are there at least 12 beads left to make a bracelet?

4. **Reason** How are these arrays alike? How are they different?

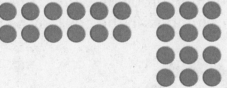

5. **Number Sense** Sanjay bought 3 boxes of energy bars. Each box contains 5 bars. He wrote $5 + 5 + 5 = 15$ to show how many energy bars he bought. What multiplication sentence could Sanjay have written? Explain.

6. **Represent** Collin put 3 photos on each of 3 pages in his photo album. How many photos did Collin use? Use the number line to find your answer.

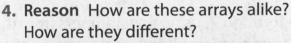

0 1 2 3 4 5 6 7 8 9 10 11 12 13 14 15

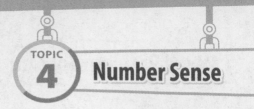

TOPIC 4 Number Sense

Error Search

For **1** through **4**, circle each statement that is not correct. Then, tell why it is not correct.

1. The array shows 4 × 4 = 16.

2. 6 + 6 + 6 = 18 is the same as 3 × 6 = 18.

3. 4 × 8 = 8 × 4 is an example of the Commutative Property of Multiplication.

4. The number line shows 3 × 2 = 6.

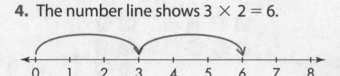

Target Number

For **5** through **7**, using any numbers from the box as addends, list as many addition problems with a sum equal to the Target Number as you can. Numbers in the box may be used more than once.

5.

24

2	3	4
5	6	7
8	10	12

6.

12

2	3	4
5	6	8
9	10	12

7.

18

2	3	4
5	6	8
9	10	12

© Pearson Education, Inc. 3

Set A pages 207–212

How many is 3 groups of 4?

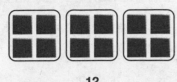

12

| 4 | 4 | 4 |

$4 + 4 + 4 = 12$

$3 \times 4 = 12$

$4 + 4 + 4 = 3 \times 4$

Remember that you can use addition or multiplication to join equal groups.

Complete each number sentence. Use counters or draw a picture to help.

1. $2 + 2 + 2 = 3 \times$ ____

2. ____ + ____ + ____ $= 3 \times 6$

3. $8 +$ ____ $+$ ____ $=$ ____ $\times 8$

Set B pages 213–218

Find 4×6.

The array shows 4 rows of 6 counters.

Each row is a group. You can use addition or multiplication to find the total.

$6 + 6 + 6 + 6 = 24$

$4 \times 6 = 24$

Remember that an array shows objects in equal rows.

Write an addition sentence and a multiplication sentence for each array.

1.

2.

Set C pages 219–224

Skip count by 4s three times.

4   8   12

You can use a number line to find 3×4.

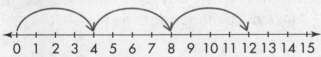

0 1 2 3 4 5 6 7 8 9 10 11 12 13 14 15

Number of jumps: 3
Number in each jump: 4

$3 \times 4 = 12$

Remember that you can show repeated addition on a number line.

Use the number line to complete each multiplication fact.

1. $2 \times 3 =$ ____

0 1 2 3 4 5 6 7 8 9 10 11 12 13 14 15

2. $4 \times 3 =$ ____

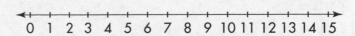

0 1 2 3 4 5 6 7 8 9 10 11 12 13 14 15

Set D pages 225–230

This array shows
3 rows of 4.

$3 \times 4 = 12$

This array shows 4 rows of 3.

$4 \times 3 = 12$

So, $3 \times 4 = 4 \times 3$.

Remember that the Commutative Property of Multiplication says you can multiply numbers in any order and the product is the same.

Draw an array to show each multiplication fact. Write the products.

1. $2 \times 4 = $ _____ $4 \times 2 = $ _____

2. $3 \times 5 = $ _____ $5 \times 3 = $ _____

Set E pages 231–236

Write a story for $3 \times 6 = \square$.

Tim has 3 bunches of flowers. Each bunch has 6 flowers. How many flowers does Tim have?

$3 \times 6 = 18$

Tim has 18 flowers.

Remember that when you write a multiplication story, end with a question.

Write a multiplication story for the multiplication fact. Draw a picture to go with the story.

1. $3 \times 9 = $ _____

Set F pages 237–242

Kimberly bought 3 apples for $4 each. She paid for them with a $20 bill. How much change should she get back?

$3 \times 4 = 12$
$\$20 - \$12 = \$8$

Kimberly should get $8 in change.

Remember that some word problems have hidden questions that need to be answered before you can solve the problem.

Solve each problem. Use arrays or strip diagrams to solve.

1. Ken has $25. He buys two caps for $7 each. How much money does he have left?

2. Maria went on a 25-mile hike. She hiked 8 miles the first day. She hiked 9 miles the second day. How many miles are left for her to hike?

© Pearson Education, Inc. 3

Name _____

1. Jace drew a picture. Which number sentence goes with Jace's picture?

A $1 + 2 + 1 + 2 = 1 \times 6$

B $2 + 2 + 8 = 3 \times 4$

C $2 + 2 + 2 + 2 = 4 \times 2$

D $4 + 6 = 2 \times 5$

2. Aidan put 2 turtles in each of 4 aquariums. How would you show Aidan's multiplication problem on a number line?

$4 \times 2 = \square$

A Start at 4. Skip count by 4s two times.

B Start at 0. Skip count by 2s four times.

C Start at 4. Skip count by 4s one time.

D All of the above

3. Maya said, "According to the Commutative Property of Multiplication, you can write $6 \times 4 = 24$ another way." If $6 \times 4 = 24$, then

A $6 + 6 + 6 + 6 = 24$.

B $6 \times 2 = 12$.

C $4 + 4 + 4 + 4 + 4 + 4 = 24$.

D $4 \times 6 = 24$.

4. Megan organized her photos in an array. Which multiplication sentence matches Megan's array?

A $4 \times 3 = 12$

B $12 + 0 = 12$

C $3 \times 3 = 9$

D $4 + 3 = 7$

5. Josiah made six 3-point baskets in his last basketball game. How could you write the addition sentence as a multiplication sentence?

$3 + 3 + 3 + 3 + 3 + 3 = 18$

A $6 \times 3 = 18$

B $3 + 18 = 21$

C $3 \times 3 = 9$

D $6 + 6 + 6 = 18$

6. Mr. Singh has 2 potatoes, and Ms. Miller has 7 times as many. Which multiplication fact shows how many potatoes Ms. Miller has?

A $7 + 2 = 9$

B $2 \times 2 = 7 - 3$

C $7 \times 2 = 14$

D $2 \times 2 = 7$

7. Jennifer was moving her comic book collection. She created 4 piles of comic books. Each pile had 5 comic books. Which multiplication sentence shows the total number of comic books in her collection?

A $4 \times 5 = 9$

B $4 + 5 = 9$

C $4 + 4 = 8$

D $4 \times 5 = 20$

---

8. In a community garden, Teresa is growing 2 rows of tomato plants, with 4 plants in each row. How could you show the same number of plants by using the Commutative Property?

---

9. To paint 3 medium-sized rooms, Minh needs 2 gallons of paint. How many gallons of paint does he need to paint 12 medium-sized rooms? Mark your answer in the grid below.

---

10. William wanted to write a multiplication story that had 12 as the answer. Which group could William **NOT** use in the story?

A 2 rows of 6 plates

B 3 cartons of a dozen eggs

C 4 boxes of 3 golf balls

D 3 cars with 4 people

---

11. Crystal drew jumps on a number line to solve a multiplication fact. Which multiplication fact does her number line show?

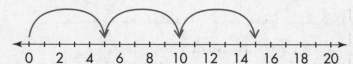

---

12. There are 7 houses on Carson Lane. Linden Boulevard has 3 times as many houses. How many more houses are on Linden Boulevard than Carson Lane? Mark your answer in the grid below.

© Pearson Education, Inc. 3

Multiplication Facts: Use Patterns and Known Facts

Essential Question: How can unknown multiplication facts be found using patterns? How can unknown multiplication facts be found using known facts?

> Animals have adaptations that help them survive in their environment.

> You can often tell what type of food an animal eats just by looking at its teeth.

> That's why lions have sharp teeth! Here's a project on animal adaptations and multiplication.

Math and Science Project: Animal Adaptations

Do Research Look up your favorite animal on the Internet, or observe it in its environment. Identify different adaptations the animal has. How do adaptations help the animal get food and stay safe?

Journal: Write a Report Include what you found. Also in your report:

- Tell how adaptations help animals survive changes in weather, build homes, and attract mates.

- Tell why some animals travel in a herd. Include pictures of animals in herds. Write multiplication problems about the animals in your pictures.

Name _____

Review What You Know

Vocabulary

Choose the best term from the box. Write it on the blank.

> - multiplication
> - array
> - factors
> - product

1. The _____ is the answer to a multiplication problem.

2. Numbers that are being multiplied

are _____.

3. An operation that gives the total when you join equal groups is

_____.

Multiplication as Repeated Addition

Complete each number sentence. Use counters or draw a picture to help.

4. $4 + 4 + 4 + 4 = 4 \times$ ____

5. $7 +$ ____ $+$ ____ $=$ ____ $\times 3$

6. ___ $+$ ___ $+$ ___ $+ 5 =$ ___ $\times$ ____

7. $3 \times 6 =$ ____ $+$ ____ $+$ ____

Skip Counting on the Number Line

8. Marty drew this number line.

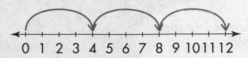

Which multiplication fact does the number line show?

A $3 \times 5 = 15$
B $3 \times 4 = 12$
C $3 \times 3 = 9$
D $3 \times 6 = 18$

9. If you continue skip counting, what is the next number on the number line?

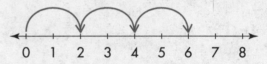

A 8
B 10
C 12
D 14

The Commutative Property

10. **Explain** How do the arrays below model the Commutative Property of Multiplication?

© Pearson Education, Inc. 3

My Word Cards

Use the examples for each word on the front of the card to help complete the definitions on the back.

A-Z

multiple

0, 4, 8, 12, and 16 are multiples of 4.

Identity (One) Property of Multiplication

$4 \times 1 = 4$

Zero Property of Multiplication

$4 \times 0 = 0$

Distributive Property

$7 \times 4 = (5 \times 4) + (2 \times 4)$

Associative (Grouping) Property of Multiplication

$(3 \times 2) \times 4 = 24$

$3 \times (2 \times 4) = 24$

$(3 \times 2) \times 4 = 3 \times (2 \times 4)$

Complete each definition. Extend learning by writing your own definitions.

The _____

_____

_____

states that the product of any number and 1 is that number.

The product of a given number and any other whole number is called a

_____.

The _____

says that a multiplication fact can be broken apart into the sum of two other multiplication facts.

The _____

_____ states that the product of any number and zero is zero.

The _____

_____

_____ says that you can change the grouping of the factors and the product will be the same.

© Pearson Education, Inc. 3

Name _____

Solve & Share

Each chicken has 2 legs. How can you find out how many legs there are in a group of 9 chickens?

⭐ **TEKS 3.4F** Recall facts to multiply up to 10 by 10 with automaticity and recall the corresponding division facts. Also, 3.4E, 3.4K.
Mathematical Process Standards 3.1B, 3.1C, 3.1D, 3.1F, 3.1G

Digital Resources at PearsonTexas.com

Solve   Learn   Glossary   Check   Tools   Games

You can **analyze relationships.** You can use a data table to record and analyze information.

Look Back!

Communicate Explain another way you could solve this problem.

A

How many socks are in 7 pairs of socks? Find 7 × 2.

1 pair	2 pairs	3 pairs	4 pairs	5 pairs	6 pairs	7 pairs
1 × 2	2 × 2	3 × 2	4 × 2	5 × 2	6 × 2	7 × 2
2	4	6	8	10	12	14

There are 14 socks in 7 pairs.

B How many fingers are on 7 gloves?

Find 7 × 5.

C

1 × 5 = 5
2 × 5 = 10
3 × 5 = 15
4 × 5 = 20
5 × 5 = 25
6 × 5 = 30
7 × 5 = 35

You can use skip counting or patterns to find the number of fingers on 7 gloves.

There are 35 fingers on 7 gloves.

Do You Understand?

Convince Me! Use skip counting or patterns to answer these questions:

How many socks are in 9 pairs? 10 pairs?

How many fingers are on 9 gloves? 10 gloves?

© Pearson Education, Inc. 3

Another Example

Multiples are the products of a number and other whole numbers.

DATA

2s Facts	
$0 \times 2 = 0$	$5 \times 2 = 10$
$1 \times 2 = 2$	$6 \times 2 = 12$
$2 \times 2 = 4$	$7 \times 2 = 14$
$3 \times 2 = 6$	$8 \times 2 = 16$
$4 \times 2 = 8$	$9 \times 2 = 18$

DATA

5s Facts	
$0 \times 5 = 0$	$5 \times 5 = 25$
$1 \times 5 = 5$	$6 \times 5 = 30$
$2 \times 5 = 10$	$7 \times 5 = 35$
$3 \times 5 = 15$	$8 \times 5 = 40$
$4 \times 5 = 20$	$9 \times 5 = 45$

The products for the 2s facts are multiples of 2. Multiples of 2 end in 0, 2, 4, 6, or 8.

The products for the 5s facts are multiples of 5. Multiples of 5 end in 0 or 5.

☆ Guided Practice *

For **1** through **3**, find each product.

1. $2 \times 4 = $ _____
$2 \times 1 = 2$
$2 \times 2 = 4$
$2 \times 3 = $ _____
$2 \times 4 = $ _____

2. $\begin{array}{r} 8 \\ \times\ 2 \\ \hline \end{array}$

3. $\begin{array}{r} 5 \\ \times\ 8 \\ \hline \end{array}$

4. Communicate Is 25 a multiple of 2 or 5? How do you know?

5. Number Sense Bert says 2×8 is 15. How can you use patterns to show Bert's answer is wrong?

☆ Independent Practice ☆

For **6** through **12**, find each product.

6. $2 \times 2 = $ _____

7. $3 \times 5 = $ _____

8. $7 \times 2 = $ _____

9. $\begin{array}{r} 6 \\ \times\ 5 \\ \hline \end{array}$

10. $\begin{array}{r} 2 \\ \times\ 4 \\ \hline \end{array}$

11. $\begin{array}{r} 9 \\ \times\ 2 \\ \hline \end{array}$

12. $\begin{array}{r} 5 \\ \times\ 7 \\ \hline \end{array}$

*For another example, see Set A on page 333.

Problem Solving

For **13** and **14**, use the table at the right.

13. Analyze Information Maru rented some bowling shoes. She also bowled 2 games. How much money did Maru spend? How did you find the answer?

Bowling	
Cost per game	$5
Daily shoe rental	$2

14. Mental Math Wendy paid for 2 games with a twenty-dollar bill. How much change should she get back?

15. Reason Eric has some nickels. He says they are worth exactly 34 cents. Can you tell if Eric is correct or not? Why or why not?

16. Check for Reasonableness Brian said 78 + 92 + 85 is greater than 300. Explain why Brian's answer is not reasonable.

17. Shannon traded 6 nickels in for dimes. How many dimes did Shannon receive?

18. Rachel has 8 pairs of earrings. How many earrings does Rachel have?

19. April has the coins shown below.

April counted the value of her coins in cents. Which list shows numbers April would have named?

A 5, 10, 16, 20, 25, 26

B 5, 10, 15, 22, 25, 32

C 5, 10, 15, 20, 25, 30

D 10, 15, 22, 25, 30, 35

20. Extend Your Thinking Jake went bowling. On his first turn, he knocked down 2 pins. On his second turn, he knocked down 2 times as many. So far, how many pins has Jake knocked down? How do you know?

© Pearson Education, Inc. 3

Name _____

Another Look!

When you multiply by 2, you can use a doubles fact. For example, 2 × 6 is the same as adding 6 + 6. Both equal 12.

When you multiply by 5, you can use a pattern to find the product.

2s Facts	
2 × 0 = 0	2 × 5 = 10
2 × 1 = 2	2 × 6 = 12
2 × 2 = 4	2 × 7 = 14
2 × 3 = 6	2 × 8 = 16
2 × 4 = 8	2 × 9 = 18

5s Facts	
5 × 0 = 0	5 × 5 = 25
5 × 1 = 5	5 × 6 = 30
5 × 2 = 10	5 × 7 = 35
5 × 3 = 15	5 × 8 = 40
5 × 4 = 20	5 × 9 = 45

Each multiple of 2 ends in 0, 2, 4, 6, or 8. All multiples of 2 are even.

Each multiple of 5 ends in 0 or 5.

For **1** through **17**, find each product.

1. 2 × 5 = ?

  5 + 5 = _____

  2 × 5 = _____

2. 2 × 4 = ?

  4 + 4 = _____

  2 × 4 = _____

3. 1 × 2 = ?

  1 + 1 = _____

  2 × 1 = _____

4. 5 × 5 = _____

5. 3 × 5 = _____

6. 5 × 7 = _____

7. 2 × 8 = _____

8. 5 × 9 = _____

9. 2 × 7 = _____

10. 5
   × 4

11. 1
   × 5

12. 2
   × 0

13. 8
   × 2

14. What is 9 times 2? _____

15. What is 5 times 8? _____

16. What is 6 times 2? _____

17. What is 5 times 0? _____

For **18** and **19**, use the table at the right.

18. **Analyze Information** Dana bought 3 tuna sandwiches and 3 fruit punch drinks. How much money did Dana spend? How do you know?

Daily Specials	
Tuna Sandwiches	$5
Fruit Punch Drinks	$2

DATA

19. Aidan bought 5 tuna sandwiches. How much did Aidan spend?

20. **Personal Financial Literacy** Georgia is making sock puppets. Each pair of socks costs $2. Georgia bought 6 pairs of socks. How much did she spend?

21. **Explain** Tara walks 2 miles each day. How many miles does Tara walk in a week? How did you find the answer?

22. **Explain** There are 5 days in each school week. How many school days are in 9 weeks? Explain.

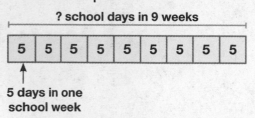

? school days in 9 weeks

| 5 | 5 | 5 | 5 | 5 | 5 | 5 | 5 | 5 |

5 days in one school week

23. The ones digit of a number greater than 1 is 0. Which factor or factors must that number have?

   A   2 only

   B   5 only

   C   2 and 5

   D   neither 2 nor 5

24. **Analyze Information** Mika drew this shape. What is the name of the shape Mika drew? Mika then drew a shape that has 2 fewer sides. What is the name of that shape?

25. **Extend Your Thinking** How can adding doubles help you multiply by 2? Give an example.

© Pearson Education, Inc. 3

Name _____

Solve & Share

Maria bought 4 packages of bottled water. There are 9 bottles in each package. How many bottles did Maria buy? *Solve this problem any way you choose.*

⭐ **TEKS 3.4F** Recall facts to multiply up to 10 by 10 with automaticity and recall the corresponding division facts. Also, 3.4, 3.4K.
Mathematical Process Standards 3.1A, 3.1B, 3.1C, 3.1D, 3.1E, 3.1F, 3.1G

Digital Resources at PearsonTexas.com

Solve Learn Glossary Check Tools Games

You can **use representations.** How can an array or a data table help?

Look Back!

Justify If Maria bought 9 packages of bottled water and there were 4 bottles in each package, would the number of bottles she bought be the same or different? Explain.

How Can Patterns Be Used to Find 9s Facts?

The owner of a flower shop puts 9 roses in each package. How many roses are in 8 packages?

You can use patterns to find 8 × 9.

DATA

9s Facts

$0 \times 9 = 0$

$1 \times 9 = 9$

$2 \times 9 = 18$

$3 \times 9 = 27$

$4 \times 9 = 36$

$5 \times 9 = 45$

$6 \times 9 = 54$

$7 \times 9 = 63$

$8 \times 9 = \blacksquare$

$9 \times 9 = \blacksquare$

B One Way

Use these patterns. Start with $1 \times 9 = 9$.

The ones digit decreases by 1 each time. So, the ones digit in the product after 63 in the facts table above is 2.

The tens digit increases by 1 each time.

So, the tens digit in the product after 63 in the facts table above is 7.

$8 \times 9 = 72$

There are 72 roses in 8 packages.

C Another Way

Use these patterns to find the product.

The tens digit is 1 less than the factor being multiplied by 9.

$$8 - 1 = 7$$

$$8 \times 9 = 72$$

$$7 + 2 = 9$$

The digits of the product have a sum of 9 or a multiple of 9.

Do You Understand?

Use the patterns above to find 9×9. Explain how you found the product.

© Pearson Education, Inc. 3

Name _____

In **1** through **8**, find each product.

1. $9 \times 2 =$ _____

2. $5 \times 9 =$ _____

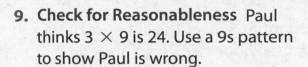
You can use patterns to solve multiplication facts with 9s.

3. $7 \times 9 =$ _____

4. $4 \times 9 =$ _____

5. $2 \times 9 =$ _____

6. $6 \times 9 =$ _____

7. $\begin{array}{r} 3 \\ \times\ 9 \\ \hline \end{array}$ **8.** $\begin{array}{r} 8 \\ \times\ 9 \\ \hline \end{array}$

9. **Check for Reasonableness** Paul thinks 3×9 is 24. Use a 9s pattern to show Paul is wrong.

10. **Communicate** Look at the table of 9s facts on page 260. Describe a number pattern in the multiples of 9.

☆ **Independent Practice** ☆

For **11** through **22**, find each product.

11. $9 \times 0 =$ _____   **12.** $2 \times 9 =$ _____   **13.** $8 \times 9 =$ _____   **14.** $9 \times 9 =$ _____

15. $\begin{array}{r} 4 \\ \times\ 9 \\ \hline \end{array}$ **16.** $\begin{array}{r} 9 \\ \times\ 5 \\ \hline \end{array}$ **17.** $\begin{array}{r} 9 \\ \times\ 7 \\ \hline \end{array}$ **18.** $\begin{array}{r} 9 \\ \times\ 1 \\ \hline \end{array}$

19. What is 9×3? _____   **20.** What is 9×6? _____

21. What is 0×9? _____   **22.** What is 9×8? _____

Problem Solving

For **23** through **25**, use the table to the right.

23. Number Sense The library is having a used book sale. How much do 4 hardcover books cost? What are two ways to find the answer?

Library Book Sale	
Paperback Books	$5
Hardcover Books	$9
Magazines	$2

24. Extend Your Thinking How much more would Chico spend if he bought 3 hardcover books rather than 3 paperback books? Show how you found the answer.

25. Justify Maggie bought only magazines. The clerk told her she owed $15. How does Maggie know the clerk made a mistake?

26. The owner of a flower shop put 9 sunflowers in each of 6 vases. Then, he counted the flowers by 9s. Which list shows the numbers he named?

A 9, 19, 29, 39, 49, 59

B 6, 12, 18, 24, 36, 42

C 18, 27, 36, 45, 56, 65

D 9, 18, 27, 36, 45, 54

27. Estimation Chris and Jerome played a video game. Their scores are listed in the table below. How can you use compatible numbers to estimate how many points they scored in all?

Player	Points
Chris	437
Jerome	398

© Pearson Education, Inc. 3

Name _____

Another Look!

You can use patterns to help remember 9s facts.

9s Facts
$0 \times 9 = 0$
$1 \times 9 = 9$
$2 \times 9 = 18$
$3 \times 9 = 27$
$4 \times 9 = 36$
$5 \times 9 = 45$
$6 \times 9 = 54$
$7 \times 9 =$
$8 \times 9 =$
$9 \times 9 =$

DATA

1. The tens digit will be 1 less than the factor being multiplied by 9.
2. The sum of the digits of the product will always be 9 or a multiple of 9, unless the other factor is 0.

Find 9×7.

The tens digit must be 1 less than 7.
The tens digit is 6.

The sum of the digits is 9.
$6 + 3 = 9$, so the ones digit is 3.

The product is 63.

For **1** through **13**, find each product.

1. $3 \times 9 = ?$

Tens digit: $3 - 1 =$ _____

Sum of digits:
_____ + _____ = 9

$3 \times 9 =$ _____

2. $2 \times 9 = ?$

Tens digit: $2 - 1 =$ _____

Sum of digits:
_____ + _____ = 9

$2 \times 9 =$ _____

3. $1 \times 9 = ?$

Tens digit: $1 - 1 =$ _____

Sum of digits:
_____ + _____ = 9

$1 \times 9 =$ _____

4. $0 \times 9 =$ _____

5. $6 \times 9 =$ _____

6. $9 \times 9 =$ _____

7.
$$\begin{array}{r} 9 \\ \times\ 8 \\ \hline \end{array}$$

8.
$$\begin{array}{r} 7 \\ \times\ 9 \\ \hline \end{array}$$

9.
$$\begin{array}{r} 4 \\ \times\ 9 \\ \hline \end{array}$$

10.
$$\begin{array}{r} 2 \\ \times\ 9 \\ \hline \end{array}$$

11. Find 6 times 9.

12. Find 5 times 9.

13. Find 0 times 9.

14. Connect Paula's hair was put into 9 braids. Each braid used 4 beads. How many beads were used? Explain how you found the product.

15. Connect A standard baseball game has 9 innings. A doubleheader is 2 games in the same day. How many innings are there in a doubleheader?

16. Reason Sasha says if she knows the product of 9×8, she also knows the product of 8×9. Is Sasha correct? Why or why not?

17. Personal Financial Literacy Dustin had $502 in the bank. He made a deposit of $49, and a day later, he made a withdrawal of $166. How much money does Dustin have in the bank now?

18. Analyze Information Mary, Carrie, and Jerry are in line for lunch. Mary is in front of Carrie and Jerry is in front of Mary. Who is first in line? Who is last in line?

Draw a picture to help solve the problem.

19. Explain Rita bought 5 pairs of socks. Each pair cost $4. How much did Rita spend on socks? Explain how you know.

$4.00

20. Tony has 9 sets of baseball cards. Each set contains 6 cards. Which number sentence did Tony write to find how many cards he has?

A $9 \times 9 = 81$

B $9 \times 6 = 54$

C $9 + 9 + 9 + 9 = 36$

D $9 + 6 = 15$

21. Extend Your Thinking Jordan received 9 text messages last week. She received 3 times as many this week. How many text messages did Jordan receive in all?

© Pearson Education, Inc. 3

Name _____

Carlos said $6 \times 0 = 6$. Do you agree? Explain your thinking.

Lesson 5-3
Multiplying with 0 and 1

TEKS 3.4F Recall facts to multiply up to 10 by 10 with automaticity and recall the corresponding division facts. Also, 3.4E, 3.4K.
Mathematical Process Standards 3.1B, 3.1C, 3.1D, 3.1E, 3.1G

Digital Resources at PearsonTexas.com

Solve   Learn   Glossary   Check   Tools   Games

You can **create and use representations,** such as a picture, to help you.

Look Back!

Connect Draw a picture to show $5 \times 0 = 0$.

A

Kira has 8 plates with 1 orange on each plate. How many oranges does Kira have?

You can use patterns to find 8×1.

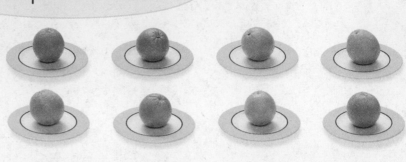

B

8 groups with 1 in each group equals 8 in all.

$$8 \times 1 = 8$$

Kira has 8 oranges.

1 plate with 8 oranges also equals 8 oranges.

$$1 \times 8 = 8$$

The Identity (One) Property of Multiplication: When you multiply a number and 1, the product is that number.

C

If Kira has 4 plates with 0 oranges on each plate, she has 0 oranges.

$$4 \times 0 = 0$$

If $4 \times 0 = 0$, then $0 \times 4 = 0$.

The Zero Property of Multiplication: When you multiply a number and 0, the product is 0.

Do You Understand?

Write multiplication stories for 7×1 and 5×0. Include pictures, number sentences, and solutions.

© Pearson Education, Inc. 3

☆ Guided Practice*

For **1** through **6**, find each product.

1.

$3 \times 1 =$ ___

 You can use the Identity and Zero Properties of Multiplication to find these products.

2. ☐ ☐ ☐

$3 \times 0 =$ ___

3. $1 \times 7 =$ ___

4. $5 \times 0 =$ ___

5.   4
  $\times\,0$

6.   2
  $\times\,1$

7. Draw a Picture Draw an array to show $1 \times 8 = 8$.

8. Analyze Information Chad has 6 plates. There is 1 apple and 0 grapes on each plate. How many apples are there? How many grapes are there?

Independent Practice ☆

For **9** through **15**, find each product.

9. $0 \times 4 =$ ___

10. $1 \times 6 =$ ___

11. $4 \times 1 =$ ___

12.   9
  $\times\,1$

13.   0
  $\times\,2$

14.   1
  $\times\,1$

15.   6
  $\times\,0$

For **16** through **21**, complete each number sentence. Write $<$, $>$, or $=$ in each ◯.

16. 1×6 ◯ 8×0

17. 0×654 ◯ 346×0

18. 0×754 ◯ 5×1

19. 0×0 ◯ 0×9

20. 1×7 ◯ 5×1

21. 1×4 ◯ 4×1

*For another example, see Set C on page 333.

Problem Solving

22. Reason Brent drew this model to show 5 groups of 1 is the same as 1 group of 5. Is Brent correct? Explain how you know.

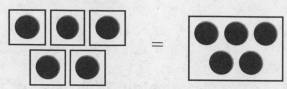

23. Check for Reasonableness Troy says 632 rounds to 600. Rick says 632 rounds to 630. Who is correct? Explain.

24. Number Sense A unicycle relay team has 4 riders. Each rider has one unicycle. If each unicycle has 1 wheel, how many wheels does the team have? What property of multiplication can you use to find the answer?

25. Reason Why do you think the Identity Property of Multiplication is sometimes called the One Property of Multiplication?

26. Tickets for a school concert are free to students. The cost is $1 for each adult. What is the total cost of tickets for 2 adults and 5 students?

A $7   C $2

B $5   D $1

27. Extend Your Thinking The product of two factors is 0. One of the factors is 0. Can you tell what the other factor is? Explain your answer.

28. Explain The children in the third-grade classes are having a bike parade. There are 3 rows of bikes with 5 bikes in each row. How many bikes are in the parade? Explain how you know.

© Pearson Education, Inc. 3

Name _____

Another Look!

Zero and one have special multiplication properties.

The Identity (One) Property of Multiplication	The Zero Property of Multiplication
When you multiply a number and 1, the product is that number.	When you multiply a number and 0, the product is 0.
Examples:	Examples:
$4 \times 1 = 4$ $16 \times 1 = 16$	$5 \times 0 = 0$ $123 \times 0 = 0$
$1 \times 9 = 9$ $13 \times 1 = 13$	$17 \times 0 = 0$ $0 \times 58 = 0$
$251 \times 1 = 251$ $1 \times 48 = 48$	$0 \times 51 = 0$ $74 \times 0 = 0$

For **1** through **6**, draw a picture to represent the multiplication fact and then solve.

1. $1 \times 3 =$ _____

2. $0 \times 6 =$ _____

3. $9 \times 0 =$ _____

4. $5 \times 0 =$ _____

5. $1 \times 7 =$ _____

6. $0 \times 4 =$ _____

For **7** through **10**, find each product.

7. $\begin{array}{r} 1 \\ \times\ 7 \\ \hline \end{array}$

8. $\begin{array}{r} 8 \\ \times\ 0 \\ \hline \end{array}$

9. $\begin{array}{r} 8 \\ \times\ 1 \\ \hline \end{array}$

10. $\begin{array}{r} 10 \\ \times\ 0 \\ \hline \end{array}$

For **11** through **13**, complete each number sentence. Write $<$, $>$, or $=$ in each $\bigcirc$.

11. $0 \times 4 \bigcirc 0 \times 4$

12. $1 \times 8 \bigcirc 6 \times 1$

13. $1 \times 5 \bigcirc 5 \times 1$

14. Number Sense Chen says the product of 4 × 0 is the same as the sum of 4 + 0. Is Chen correct? Explain.

15. Which multiplication equation has the ⭐ greatest product?

A 4 × 2 = ☐

B 5 × 0 = ☐

C 10 × 0 = ☐

D 10 × 1 = ☐

16. Explain Sara put 4 boxes in her closet. Each box is for holding a different type of seashell. So far, there are 0 shells in each box. Write a multiplication sentence to show how many shells Sara has. What property of multiplication can you use? Explain.

17. Personal Financial Literacy Sally and her sister, Patsy, want to save money to buy their mom a birthday present. Sally plans to save $3 a week for 6 weeks. Patsy plans to save $4 a week for 4 weeks. Who will save more money? How do you know?

18. Analyze Information Bob made a pictograph of the marbles he has. How many more red marbles does Bob have than green marbles? Explain how you found the answer.

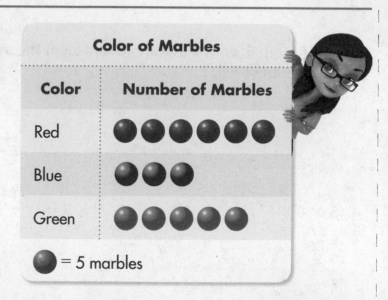

Color of Marbles

Color	Number of Marbles
Red	●●●●●●
Blue	●●●
Green	●●●●●

● = 5 marbles

19. Use a Strip Diagram Kirsten puts 6 coins in each of 3 envelopes. How many coins did Kirsten put in the envelopes? Use the strip diagram to help you solve.

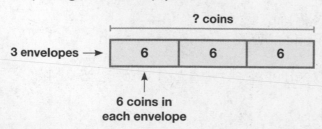

? coins

3 envelopes → | 6 | 6 | 6 |

6 coins in each envelope

20. Extend Your Thinking Chef Morgan's restaurant has 24 tables. Fifteen of the tables each have one flower in a vase. The remaining tables have 5 flowers in each vase. How many flowers are there? Show how you found the answer.

© Pearson Education, Inc. 3

Name _____

⭐ **Solve & Share**　Max used patterns to draw shapes around the numbers in the chart below. What patterns did Max use? Explain.

⬦ **TEKS 3.4F** Recall facts to multiply up to 10 by 10 with automaticity and recall the corresponding division facts. Also, 3.4E, 3.4K.
Mathematical Process Standards 3.1A, 3.1B, 3.1C, 3.1D, 3.1F, 3.1G

Digital Resources at PearsonTexas.com

Solve　Learn　Glossary　Check　Tools　Games

1	②	3	④	5	⑥	7	⑧	△9	⑩
11	⑫	13	⑭	15	⑯	17	△⑱	19	⑳
21	㉒	23	㉔	25	㉖	△27	㉘	29	㉚
31	㉜	33	㉞	35	△㊱	37	㊳	39	㊵
41	㊷	43	㊹	△45	㊻	47	㊽	49	㊿
51	㊾...	53	△54	55	56	57	58	59	60
61	62	△63	64	65	66	67	68	69	70
71	△72	73	74	75	76	77	78	79	80
△81	82	83	84	85	86	87	88	89	△90
91	92	93	94	95	96	97	98	△99	100

You can **connect ideas.** You can use patterns to make connections.

Look Back!

Tools How can tools such as a hundred chart help you find patterns?

What Are the Patterns for Multiples of 2, 5, and 9?

The product of a given number and any other whole number is called a multiple.

1	②	3	④	5	⑥	7	⑧	△9	⑩
11	⑫	13	⑭	15	⑯	17	⑱	19	⑳
21	㉒	23	㉔	25	㉖	△27	㉘	29	㉚
31	㉜	33	㉞	35	㊱	37	㉘38	39	㊵

◯ multiples of 2   ▢ multiples of 5   △ multiples of 9

You can use a hundred chart to find patterns in multiples of 2, 5, and 9.

B To find multiples of 2, skip count by 2s.

②, ④, ⑥, ⑧, ⑩, ⑫, ⑭, ⑯...

All multiples of 2 are even numbers.

C To find multiples of 5, skip count by 5s.

5, 10, 15, 20, 25, 30, 35, 40...

All multiples of 5 have a 0 or 5 in the ones place.

D To find multiples of 9, skip count by 9s.

△9, △18, △27, △36, △45, △54, △63, △72...

The digits of multiples of 9 add to 9 or a multiple of 9.

For 99, for example, $9 + 9 = 18$, and 18 is a multiple of 9.

Do You Understand?

Tell how you would use patterns to find each product shown in the table.

Fact	Pattern
$6 \times 2 =$ ___	
$5 \times 5 =$ ___	
$9 \times 6 =$ ___	

© Pearson Education, Inc. 3

Name _____

In **1** through **4**, skip count to find the number that comes next.

1. 2, 4, 6, 8, _____, _____

2. 20, 25, 30, _____, _____

3. 20, 22, 24, _____, _____

4. 10, 15, 20, _____, _____

5. **Analyze Information** In the chart on page 272, what pattern do you see for the numbers that have both red circles and green squares?

6. **Explain** Why is 63 not a multiple of 2?

Independent Practice

In **7** through **14**, skip count to find the number that comes next.

7. 18, 27, 36, _____

8. 5, 10, 15, _____

9. 88, 90, 92, _____

10. 36, 45, 54, _____

11. 24, 26, 28, _____

12. 20, 25, 30, _____

13. 9, 18, 27, _____

14. 10, 12, 14, _____

In **15** through **30**, find each product.

15. $2 \times 6 =$ _____

16. $9 \times 9 =$ _____

17. $2 \times 3 =$ _____

18. $5 \times 7 =$ _____

19. $5 \times 6 =$ _____

20. $9 \times 3 =$ _____

21. $9 \times 6 =$ _____

22. $5 \times 3 =$ _____

23. $\begin{array}{r} 5 \\ \times\ 8 \\ \hline \end{array}$

24. $\begin{array}{r} 9 \\ \times\ 4 \\ \hline \end{array}$

25. $\begin{array}{r} 7 \\ \times\ 5 \\ \hline \end{array}$

26. $\begin{array}{r} 5 \\ \times\ 5 \\ \hline \end{array}$

27. $\begin{array}{r} 4 \\ \times\ 5 \\ \hline \end{array}$

28. $\begin{array}{r} 9 \\ \times\ 2 \\ \hline \end{array}$

29. $\begin{array}{r} 2 \\ \times\ 7 \\ \hline \end{array}$

30. $\begin{array}{r} 5 \\ \times\ 2 \\ \hline \end{array}$

Problem Solving

31. Number Sense How many arms do 9 starfish have if…

a each starfish has 6 arms? Write a multiplication sentence to solve.

b each starfish has 7 arms? Write a multiplication sentence to solve.

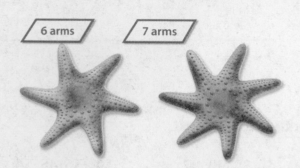

6 arms 7 arms

32. Extend Your Thinking In wheelchair basketball, players use sports chairs that have 2 large wheels and 5 small wheels. If there are 9 players, how many…

a large wheels are there? Write a multiplication sentence to solve.

b small wheels are there? Write a multiplication sentence to solve.

c wheels of any size are there? Write an addition sentence to solve.

33. Number Sense Use the digits 3, 4, and 6 to make as many 3-digit numbers as you can. Put the numbers in order from least to greatest.

34. Explain Karen is making 5 necklaces. She uses 12 beads in each necklace. Devin is making 12 bracelets. He uses 5 beads in each bracelet. Who uses the most beads? How many beads do they each use? Explain.

35. Jody is working on her model train. She adds 9 pieces of track. Each piece of track is attached with 4 screws. Which of the following does **NOT** show a way to find how many screws Jody needs?

A Skip count by 4s nine times

B 4 + 4 + 4 + 4 + 4 + 4 + 4 + 4 + 4

C Add 9 + 4

D Multiply 9 × 4

36. Reason Pedro is making a poster for each of his 4 friends. Each poster will have 5 stickers. How many stickers will Pedro need? Skip count by 5s to find the answer. Then, write the multiplication sentence. What other way could you use to find the answer?

© Pearson Education, Inc. 3

Name _____

Another Look!

Pattern	Example
All multiples of 2 are even numbers.	2, 8, 16, 24
All multiples of 5 end in 0 or 5.	5, 10, 15, 20
For all multiples of 9, the sum of the digits is always a multiple of 9.	$27: 2 + 7 = 9$ $63: 6 + 3 = 9$

Look for patterns to find multiples of 2, 5, and 9.

In **1** through **8**, use patterns to find each product.

1. 5
    $\times\ 8$

2. 2
    $\times\ 7$

3. 9
    $\times\ 8$

4. 5
    $\times\ 7$

5. 6
    $\times\ 5$

6. 7
    $\times\ 9$

7. 5
    $\times\ 9$

8. 2
    $\times\ 9$

For **9** through **16**, skip count to find the number that comes next.

9. 30, 32, 34, _____

10. 30, 35, 40, _____

11. 27, 36, 45, _____

12. 12, 14, 16, _____

13. 40, 45, 50, _____

14. 9, 18, 27, _____

15. 18, 20, 22, _____

16. 10, 15, 20, _____

In **17** through **24**, find each product.

17. $3 \times 5 =$ _____

18. $3 \times 9 =$ _____

19. $3 \times 2 =$ _____

20. $2 \times 8 =$ _____

21. $1 \times 2 =$ _____

22. $9 \times 1 =$ _____

23. $9 \times 4 =$ _____

24. $9 \times 6 =$ _____

25. Connect Teresa bought 3 boxes of gourmet chocolate. Each box has 9 pieces of chocolate inside. How many pieces of chocolate does Teresa have in all?

26. Margie bought 6 lamps that cost $5 each. How much did Margie spend on lamps?

27. Phil is making 9 name tags. Each name tag is decorated with 6 stickers. How many stickers does Phil need?

A 15 stickers

B 18 stickers

C 54 stickers

D 81 stickers

The solution is a multiple of 9.

28. Reason A package of baseball cards includes 5 cards. How many baseball cards are in 7 packages? Skip count by 5s to find the answer. Then, write a multiplication sentence.

29. Draw a Picture Ruth volunteers at an animal shelter. There are 6 rows of dog pens with 5 pens in each row. Draw a strip diagram to find the number of dog pens at the shelter.

30. Explain Chris needs to find the product of two numbers. One of the numbers is 10. The answer also needs to be 10. How will Chris solve this problem? Explain.

31. Extend Your Thinking Mrs. Cartland is buying bouquets for table decorations. She buys 6 bouquets with 3 flowers in each. She also buys 5 bouquets with 6 flowers in each. How much does Mrs. Cartland spend? Explain how you found the answer.

Bouquets with 3 Flowers
$2

Bouquets with 6 Flowers
$6

© Pearson Education, Inc. 3

Name _____

Solve & Share

Duke runs 10 miles each week. How many miles will he run in 6 weeks? 7 weeks? 8 weeks? *Solve these problems any way you choose.* Describe patterns you find.

⬦ **TEKS 3.4F** Recall facts to multiply up to 10 by 10 with automaticity and recall the corresponding division facts. Also, 3.4, 3.4K.
Mathematical Process Standards 3.1A, 3.1B, 3.1C, 3.1D, 3.1F, 3.1G

Digital Resources at PearsonTexas.com

Solve   Learn   Glossary   Check   Tools   Games

You can use **number sense.** How can you use number sense or mental math to solve the problems?

Look Back!

Connect How are the patterns when multiplying by 10 related to the patterns when multiplying by 5?

What Are the Patterns in Multiples of 10?

A

Greg wants to train for a race that is 10 weeks away. The chart shows his training schedule. How many miles will Greg run to train for the race?

You can use patterns to find 10 × 10.

Weekly Training Schedule	
Activity	**Miles**
Swimming	4 miles
Running	10 miles
Biking	9 miles

B

10s Facts	
0 × 10 = 0	5 × 10 = 50
1 × 10 = 10	6 × 10 = 60
2 × 10 = 20	7 × 10 = 70
3 × 10 = 30	8 × 10 = 80
4 × 10 = 40	9 × 10 = 90
	10 × 10 = ?

Use patterns to find the product.

- Write the factor you are multiplying by 10.

- Write a zero to the right of that factor. A multiple of 10 will always have a 0 in the ones place.

$$10 \times 10 = 100$$

Greg will run 100 miles.

Do You Understand?

How many miles will Greg swim in 10 weeks? Write a number sentence and use a pattern to find the product.

© Pearson Education, Inc. 3

Another Example

You can skip count by 10s three times on a number line to find 3×10.

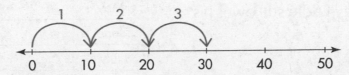

$3 \times 10 = 30$

☆ Guided Practice *

In **1** through **4**, find each product.

1. $2 \times 10 =$ ____0

2. $6 \times 10 =$ ____0

3. $8 \times 10 =$ ____

4. $9 \times 10 =$ ____

You can look at the ones place to tell if a number is a multiple of 10.

5. Justify Is 91 a multiple of 10? Explain.

Independent Practice ☆

In **6** and **7**, use the number lines to help find the product.

6. $1 \times 10 =$ ____

7. $5 \times 10 =$ ____

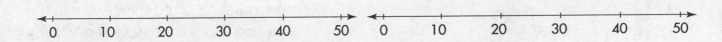

In **8** through **13**, find each product.

8. $10 \times 10 =$ ____0

9. $9 \times 10 =$ ____0

10. $7 \times 10 =$ ____0

11. $3 \times 10 =$ ____

12. $5 \times 10 =$ ____

13. $8 \times 10 =$ ____

Problem Solving

14. **Personal Financial Literacy** Eddie borrowed $65 from his dad. Every month, he pays back $12. Complete the table to find how much money Eddie still owes his dad after 4 months.

Month	Amount Eddie Owes
April	$65 – $12 = _____
May	_____ – $12 = _____
June	_____ – _____ = _____
July	_____ – _____ = _____

15. Kimmy bought 7 tickets to a concert. Each ticket costs $10. Which number sentence shows the total cost of the tickets Kimmy bought?

A $7 + 10 = \$17$

B $4 \times 10 = \$40$

C $7 \times 10 = \$70$

D $10 \times 10 = \$100$

16. **Number Sense** Write an addition sentence and a multiplication sentence for the array below.

⬤ ⬤ ⬤ ⬤ ⬤
⬤ ⬤ ⬤ ⬤ ⬤
⬤ ⬤ ⬤ ⬤ ⬤

17. **Draw a Picture** Mai had 3 packs of pens. Each pack had 10 pens. She gave 5 pens to Ervin and 8 pens to Sara. How many pens did Mai have left? Draw a picture to help solve the problem.

18. **Reason** Raul has only dimes in his pocket. Could he have exactly 45 cents? Explain.

19. **Analyze Information** Use the table to find the total number of juice boxes bought for a school picnic.

Food Item	Number of Packages	Number in Each Package
Hot dogs	8	10
Rolls	10	9
Juice boxes	7	10

Juice boxes: _____

20. **Extend Your Thinking** Look at the table at the top of page 278. Greg multiplied 5×10 to find how many more miles he biked than swam in the 10 weeks. Does that make sense? Why or why not?

© Pearson Education, Inc. 3

Name _____

Another Look!

The table shows multiplication facts for 10.

10s Facts	
$10 \times 0 = 0$	$10 \times 5 = 50$
$10 \times 1 = 10$	$10 \times 6 = 60$
$10 \times 2 = 20$	$10 \times 7 = 70$
$10 \times 3 = 30$	$10 \times 8 = 80$
$10 \times 4 = 40$	$10 \times 9 = 90$
	$10 \times 10 = 100$

All multiples of 10 end with zero.

Find 5×10.

To find the answer, you can skip count by 10s five times on a number line or you can write a zero after the 5.

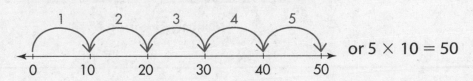

or $5 \times 10 = 50$

In **1** and **2**, use the number lines to help find the product.

1. $2 \times 10 = $ _____

2. $4 \times 10 = $ _____

For **3** through **12**, find the product.

3. $10 \times 6 = $ _____

4. $10 \times 10 = $ _____

5. $0 \times 10 = $ _____

6. $1 \times 10 = $ _____

7. $10 \times 3 = $ _____

8. $9 \times 10 = $ _____

9. $\begin{array}{r} 10 \\ \times\ 1 \\ \hline \end{array}$

10. $\begin{array}{r} 10 \\ \times\ 3 \\ \hline \end{array}$

11. $\begin{array}{r} 10 \\ \times\ 8 \\ \hline \end{array}$

12. $\begin{array}{r} 10 \\ \times\ 7 \\ \hline \end{array}$

13. Connect If you know $8 \times 10 = 80$, what other related multiplication fact do you know? Use the Commutative (Order) Property of Multiplication to explain.

14. Sarah told Tom to write a multiplication fact that does **NOT** have a product that is a multiple of 10. Which fact did Tom write?

A 10×8

B 7×5

C 5×6

D 8×5

15. Analyze Information Joey made this graph to show how many incorrect answers students got on a test. How many students got 3 answers incorrect? How do you know?

16. Justify Mary Ann earns $10 each day walking the neighborhood dogs. How much will she earn in 7 days? Explain why the answer will be a multiple of ten.

17. Write 89,607 in expanded and word form.

18. Connect There are 3 games of basketball being played at the park. Each game has 10 players. Greg says there are a total of 35 players. Use what you've learned about multiples of 10 to explain why Greg is incorrect.

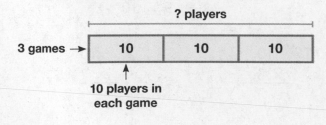

? players

3 games → | 10 | 10 | 10 |

10 players in each game

19. Extend Your Thinking Junior says the product of 25×10 is 250. How can you use patterns to check Junior's answer?

© Pearson Education, Inc. 3

Name _____

Solve & Share

Find two ways to break the array below into two smaller arrays. What multiplication sentence can you write for each array? What is the total? Tell how you decided.

⊕ **TEKS 3.4K** Solve … problems involving multiplication … within 100 using strategies based on objects; pictorial models, including arrays, … and equal groups; properties of operations; or recall of facts. Also, 3.4F, 3.4E.
Mathematical Process Standards 3.1B, 3.1C, 3.1D, 3.1F

You can **analyze relationships.** You can analyze the relationship between the large array and the two smaller arrays.

Digital Resources at PearsonTexas.com

Solve Learn Glossary Check Tools Games

Look Back!

Reason Find and compare the total of the smaller arrays and the large array. Why are the totals the same even though the arrays are different?

How Can You Break Up a Multiplication Fact?

Maria wants to set up 7 rows of 4 chairs for a meeting. She wants to know how many chairs she needs but does not know the product of 7 × 4.

You can use known facts to help find the product of unknown facts.

B **What You Think**

Maria thinks of **7** rows of 4 chairs as **5** rows of 4 chairs and another **2** rows of 4 chairs.

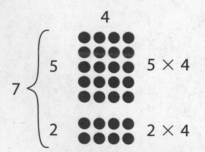

C **What You Write**

The Distributive Property says that a multiplication fact can be broken apart into the sum of two other multiplication facts.

Maria knows the two new facts.

7 × 4 = (5 × 4) + (2 × 4)
7 × 4 = 20 + 8
7 × 4 = 28

So, 7 × 4 = 28.

Maria needs 28 chairs.

Do You Understand?

What is another way Maria could break up the array for 7 × 4? Draw a picture of the two new arrays and write the new facts.

© Pearson Education, Inc. 3

☆ Guided Practice*

In **1** and **2**, use the smaller arrays and the Distributive Property to find each missing factor. You may use counters to help.

1.

4×8

___ $\times 8 = ($ ___ $\times 8) + (2 \times 8)$

2.

3×5

___ $\times$ ___ $= ($ ___ $\times 5) + (1 \times$ ___ $)$

3. **Reason** Rafael broke up an array for 6×3 into two new arrays that both look the same. What were the two arrays?

4. **Reason** Ann broke up a large array into two smaller arrays. The two smaller arrays show 1×8 and 4×8. What was the large array that Ann started with?

☆ Independent Practice ☆

For **5** and **6**, separate the rows in the large array into two smaller arrays. Write the new facts.

5.

$4 \times 5 = ($ ___ $\times$ ___ $) + ($ ___ $\times$ ___ $)$

6.

$5 \times 6 = ($ ___ $\times$ ___ $) + ($ ___ $\times$ ___ $)$

For **7** through **10**, use the Distributive Property to find each missing factor. Use counters and arrays to help.

7. $6 \times 8 = (4 \times$ ___ $) + (2 \times 8)$

8. $10 \times 3 = ($ ___ $\times 3) + (2 \times 3)$

9. $($ ___ $\times 7) = (3 \times 7) + (2 \times$ ___ $)$

10. $(8 \times$ ___ $) = ($ ___ $\times 8) + (4 \times 8)$

*For another example, see Set F on page 334.

Topic 5 | Lesson 5-6

285

Problem Solving

11. Use a Strip Diagram Paige has 7 toy horses. Lexi has 5 times as many. How many toy horses does Lexi have? Write a number sentence to solve the problem.

? toy horses

Lexi	7	7	7	7	7

Paige	7

12. Check for Reasonableness Fred wants to separate the rows of the array below into a 2 × 4 array and a 3 × 4 array. Can Fred do this? Explain.

13. Use the Distributive Property to find 11 × 5. Write a multiplication sentence.

14. Write 23,482 in expanded form.

15. Communicate Explain how you can break a 9 × 6 array into two smaller arrays. What are the new facts?

16. Extend Your Thinking How can you use 3 × 5 = 15 to help you find 6 × 5?

17. Which shows a way to separate the rows of the array below?

A (2 × 7) + (5 × 7)

B (7 × 7) + (7 × 7)

C (2 × 7) + (3 × 7)

D (2 × 5) + (5 × 7)

18. Number Sense David has 10 packs of juice boxes. Each pack contains 9 juice boxes. Kara gives David 2 more packs of 9 juice boxes. How many juice boxes does David have now? Show how you found the answer.

© Pearson Education, Inc. 3

Name _____

Another Look!

With the Distributive Property, you can break apart a multiplication fact into the sum of two other facts.

The array below shows 6 × 4 or 6 rows of 4 circles.

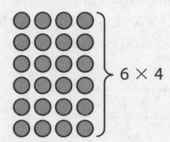

6 × 4

You can draw a line to break **6** rows of 4 circles into **2** rows of 4 circles and **4** rows of 4 circles.

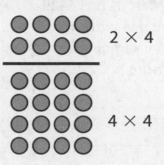

2 × 4

4 × 4

In **1** and **2**, draw a line to separate each array into two smaller arrays. Write the new facts.

1.

● ● ●
● ● ●
● ● ●
● ● ●

4 × 3 = (___ × ___) + (___ × ___)

2.

● ● ● ● ● ●
● ● ● ● ● ●
● ● ● ● ● ●
● ● ● ● ● ●
● ● ● ● ● ●

5 × 6 = (___ × ___) + (___ × ___)

For **3** through **10**, use the Distributive Property to find each missing factor.

3. 4 × 6 = (1 × 6) + (___ × 6)

4. 5 × 8 = (___ × 8) + (2 × 8)

5. 4 × 5 = (___ × 5) + (2 × ___)

6. 7 × 6 = (3 × ___) + (___ × ___)

7. 3 × 8 = (___ × 8) + (2 × ___)

8. 5 × 7 = (2 × ___) + (3 × ___)

9. 4 × 7 = (___ × ___) + (2 × ___)

10. 5 × 5 = (___ × 5) + (4 × ___)

11. Communicate Don breaks a 4 × 7 array into a 2 × 7 array and another array. What is the fact for Don's second array? Write a number sentence that shows the relationship of the 4 × 7 array to the other two arrays.

12. Draw a Picture Tony broke a larger array into a 2 × 3 array and a 4 × 3 array. What did the larger array look like? Draw a picture. Write a number sentence to show the relationship between the larger array and the two smaller arrays.

13. Use a Strip Diagram Marcus has $429 in his checking account. He withdraws $126. How much money remains in Marcus's checking account?

$429

| $126 | ? |

14. Use a Strip Diagram Lulu buys a dress for $67, a hat for $35, and shoes for $49. How much did Lulu spend?

?

| $67 | $35 | $49 |

15. Analyze Information Akela drew these smaller arrays to find the product of a larger array. What did the larger array look like? Write a number sentence to show the relationship between the larger array and the two smaller arrays. What is the product?

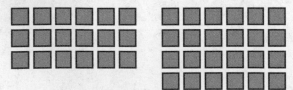

16. Extend Your Thinking Rosa says she can break this array into 3 different sets of smaller arrays. Is Rosa correct? Explain.

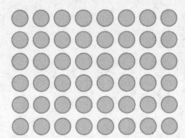

17. ⭐ Which number makes this number sentence true?

$7 \times 5 = (\boxed{} \times 5) + (2 \times 5)$

A 2

B 3

C 4

D 5

18. Reason Todd says he can find 3 × 9 by adding the products of 3 × 5 and 3 × 4. Is Todd correct?

© Pearson Education, Inc. 3

Name _____

Solve & Share

There are 3 rows of pictures on a wall. Each row has 6 pictures. How many pictures are on the wall? *Solve this problem any way you choose.*

✪ **TEKS 3.4F** Recall facts to multiply up to 10 by 10 with automaticity and recall the corresponding division facts. Also, 3.4E, 3.4K.
Mathematical Process Standards 3.1B, 3.1C, 3.1D, 3.1F, 3.1G

Digital Resources at PearsonTexas.com

Solve   Learn   Glossary   Check   Tools   Games

You can **select and use tools.** You can use tools such as counters, drawings, and arrays to help solve the problem. *Show your work!*

Look Back!

Connect How can you use multiplication facts for the 1s and 2s to solve multiplication facts for the 3s?

How Can You Break Apart Arrays to Multiply with 3?

The Park District stores canoes in 3 rows. There are 6 canoes in each row. What is the total number of canoes stored?

You can multiply to find the total for an array.

B What You Show

Find 3 × 6.

Use 1s facts and 2s facts to help you multiply with 3.

Make an array for each multiplication sentence.

⎫
⎬ 2 × 6 = 12
⎭

12 + 6 = 18

⎫
⎬ 1 × 6 = 6

C What You Think

3 × 6 is 3 rows of 6. That is 2 sixes plus 1 more six.

2 sixes are 12.
1 six is 6.

12 + 6 = 18

3 × 6 = 18

There are 18 canoes.

Do You Understand?

Suppose there were 7 canoes in each of 3 rows. How can 2 × 7 = 14 help you find the total number of canoes?

© Pearson Education, Inc. 3

☆ Guided Practice *

For **1** through **6**, multiply. Use counters or draw pictures to help.

1. $3 \times 10 =$ _____   **2.** $3 \times 6 =$ _____

3.   3
    $\times\,1$

4.   3
    $\times\,2$

5.   3
    $\times\,7$

6.   3
    $\times\,3$

7. Analyze Information Selena arranged plants in 3 rows in her garden. She put 6 plants in each row. How many plants did Selena arrange?

8. Reason Alicia has 3 vases. She wants 9 flowers in each vase. She buys enough flowers for 2 vases. For the third vase, she cuts 9 flowers from her garden. How can Alicia use $2 \times 9 = 18$ to find how many flowers she needs?

Independent Practice ☆

Leveled Practice For **9** and **10**, multiply. Use the pictures to help.

9. 3×4

$2 \times 4 =$ _____

$1 \times 4 =$ _____

$8 + 4 =$ _____

10. 3×5

$2 \times 5 =$ _____

$1 \times 5 =$ _____

$10 + 5 =$ _____

For **11** through **20**, find the product. Use counters or draw pictures to help.

11. $2 \times 3 =$ _____   **12.** $9 \times 3 =$ _____   **13.** $10 \times 3 =$ _____

14. $8 \times 3 =$ _____   **15.** $5 \times 3 =$ _____   **16.** $0 \times 3 =$ _____

17.   7
    $\times\,3$

18.   3
    $\times\,8$

19.   3
    $\times\,3$

20.   4
    $\times\,3$

Problem Solving

For **21** and **22**, use the table at the right.

21. **Analyze Information** What is the total number of stamps in a package of car stamps and a package of outer space stamps? Show how you found the answer.

Number of Stamps in Different Packages

Kind of Stamp	Number of Rows	Number in Each Row
Dinosaur	3	7
Car	3	9
Outer Space	3	8
Reptile	5	6

22. **Draw a Picture** Cara bought 1 package of reptile stamps. What is the total number of reptile stamps Cara bought? Draw an array.

23. **Check for Reasonableness** Allison bought 10 packages of energy bars. Each package contains 6 bars. Allison says she has a total of 65 energy bars. Is her answer reasonable? Why or why not?

24. Tanji has a paper clip chain. His chain has 426 paper clips. He breaks his chain into 2 parts. One part has 293 paper clips. How many paper clips are in the other part?

426 paper clips

293	?

25. **Number Sense** Mr. Torres has packages of tomatoes on the counter. Each package has 3 tomatoes. If Mr. Torres counts the tomatoes in groups of 3, which list shows numbers he would name?

    A 6, 12, 16, 19

    B 6, 9, 12, 15

    C 3, 6, 10, 13

    D 3, 7, 11, 15

26. **Extend Your Thinking** What two multiplication facts can help you find 3 × 9? How could you use 3 × 9 to find 9 × 3?

© Pearson Education, Inc. 3

Name _____

Another Look!

3s Facts	
$3 \times 0 = 0$	$3 \times 5 = 15$
$3 \times 1 = 3$	$3 \times 6 = 18$
$3 \times 2 = 6$	$3 \times 7 = 21$
$3 \times 3 = 9$	$3 \times 8 = 24$
$3 \times 4 = 12$	$3 \times 9 = 27$

Find 2×3.

$2 \times 3 = 6$

You can use arrays to show 3s facts.

You can also use a 2s and a 1s fact to find a 3s fact.

Find 7×3.
$7 \times 3 = (7 \times 2) + (7 \times 1)$
$7 \times 3 = 14 + 7$
$7 \times 3 = 21$

For **1** through **4**, use arrays or the Distributive Property to find each product.

1.

   $3 \times 4 =$ _____

2. Find 3×5.

   $3 \times 5 = ($____$\times 5) + (1 \times$____$)$

   $3 \times 5 =$ ____ $+$ ____

   $3 \times 5 =$ ____

3. Find 4×3.

   $4 \times 3 = (4 \times$____$) + ($____$\times 1)$

   $4 \times 3 =$ ____ $+$ ____

   $4 \times 3 =$ ____

4. Find 3×6.

   $3 \times 6 = (2 \times 6) + ($____$\times$____$)$

   $3 \times 6 =$ ____ $+$ ____

   $3 \times 6 =$ ____

For **5** through **11**, find each product.

5. $6 \times 3 =$ _____

6. $3 \times 7 =$ _____

7. $3 \times 3 =$ _____

8. $\begin{array}{r} 3 \\ \times 8 \\ \hline \end{array}$

9. $\begin{array}{r} 3 \\ \times 0 \\ \hline \end{array}$

10. $\begin{array}{r} 3 \\ \times 2 \\ \hline \end{array}$

11. $\begin{array}{r} 9 \\ \times 3 \\ \hline \end{array}$

12. Communicate How can you use a 2s fact and a 1s fact to find 3 × 8?

13. Construct Arguments Maria said 7 × 3 = 21. Connie said 3 × 7 = 21. Who is correct? Explain.

14. A bicycle store also sells tricycles. It has ⭐ 6 tricycles in stock. How many wheels do the tricycles have in all?

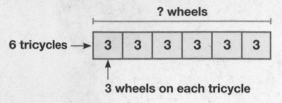

? wheels

6 tricycles → | 3 | 3 | 3 | 3 | 3 | 3 |

3 wheels on each tricycle

A 21 wheels

B 18 wheels

C 12 wheels

D 6 wheels

15. Draw a Picture Five people bought tickets to a football game. They bought 3 tickets each. How many tickets were bought? Draw an array.

16. Estimation How many small squares are needed to cover the figure below?

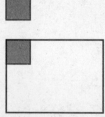

17. Extend Your Thinking Sid says 26 is a multiple of 3. Is Sid correct? Why or why not?

18. Represent Use a 2s fact and a 1s fact to find 3 × 3. Make an array for each multiplication sentence to illustrate your answer.

19. Kenichi's jump rope team is competing in a tournament. There are 10 teams in the tournament. How many players are in the tournament?

Jump Rope Tournament Teams of 3 Only

© Pearson Education, Inc. 3

Name _____

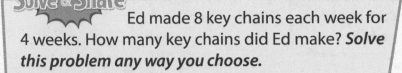

Solve & Share

Ed made 8 key chains each week for 4 weeks. How many key chains did Ed make? *Solve this problem any way you choose.*

⬦ **TEKS 3.4F** Recall facts to multiply up to 10 by 10 with automaticity and recall the corresponding division facts. Also, 3.4E, 3.4K.
Mathematical Process Standards 3.1B, 3.1C, 3.1D, 3.1F, 3.1G

Digital Resources at PearsonTexas.com

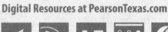

Solve   Learn   Glossary   Check   Tools   Games

You can **select and use tools.** You can use tools such as counters, drawings, and arrays, or known facts to help solve the problem. *Show your work in the space below!*

Look Back!

Connect How can you use multiplication facts for the 2s to solve multiplication facts for the 4s?

How Can You Use Doubles to Multiply with 4?

A-Z

Anna painted piggy banks to sell at the student art show. She painted a bank on each of the 7 days of the week for 4 weeks. How many piggy banks did Anna paint?

You can multiply to find the total for an array.

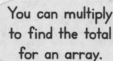

B ## What You Show

Find 4 × 7.

To multiply by 4, you can think of a 2s fact and then double it.

You can make arrays.

 } 2 × 7 = 14

 } 2 × 7 = 14
14 + 14 = 28

C ## What You Think

4 × 7 is 4 rows of 7. That is 2 sevens plus 2 sevens.

2 sevens are 14.

14 + 14 = 28
So, 4 × 7 = 28.

Anna painted 28 piggy banks.

Do You Understand?

You know 2 × 8 = 16. How can you find 4 × 8?

© Pearson Education, Inc. 3

☆ Guided Practice*

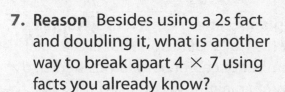

In **1** through **6**, multiply. Use counters or draw pictures to help.

1. 3 × 4 = ____   **2.** 5 × 4 = ____

3. 4 × 9 = ____   **4.** 1 × 4 = ____

5.   2
    × 4

6.   10
    × 4

7. Reason Besides using a 2s fact and doubling it, what is another way to break apart 4 × 7 using facts you already know?

8. Number Sense Nolan made lamps to sell at the school art show. He made 9 lamps each week for 4 weeks. How many lamps did Nolan make?

☆ Independent Practice ☆

Leveled Practice For **9** and **10**, multiply. Use the pictures to help.

9. Find 4 × 6.

2 × 6 = ____

2 × 6 = ____

12 + 12 = ____

So, 4 × 6 = ____.

10. Find 4 × 9.

2 × 9 = ____

2 × 9 = ____

18 + 18 = ____

So, 4 × 9 = ____.

In **11** through **17**, find the product. You may draw pictures to help.

11. 4 × 8 = ____   **12.** 4 × 3 = ____   **13.** 6 × 4 = ____

14.   7
    × 4

15.   9
    × 4

16.   4
    × 5

17.   4
    × 2

Problem Solving

For **18** and **19**, use the table at the right.

18. Explain James needs to buy supplies for his Trail Walk Trip. What is the total number of cereal bars James needs to buy? Explain how you used the table to find the answer.

19. Communicate How many more apples than juice drinks does James need? Show how you found the answer.

DATA

Trail Walk Trip Supplies

Item	Number of Packages Needed	Number of Items in Each Package
Apples	2	8
Cereal Bars	4	6
Juice Drinks	4	3

20. Math and Science Martin studied slugs in science class. He learned each slug has 4 feelers. That evening, he saw 7 slugs. How many feelers did all the slugs have? What are two strategies you can use to find the answer?

21. Reason Rachel says the first 8 is ten times as great as the second 8 in 18,852. Is Rachel correct? Why or why not?

22. Bess had boxes of candles on the table. ☆ Each box had 4 candles. If Bess counted the candles in groups of 4, which list shows numbers she would have named?

A 8, 12, 16, 20

B 8, 12, 14, 18

C 4, 6, 12, 14

D 4, 8, 10, 14

23. Extend Your Thinking Lila had 9 weeks of rock climbing lessons. She had 4 lessons each week. Explain why Lila can use 4 × 9 to find the product of 9 × 4.

© Pearson Education, Inc. 3

Name _____

Another Look!

If you know a 2s multiplication fact, you can find a 4s multiplication fact.

4s Facts	
$4 \times 0 = 0$	$4 \times 5 = 20$
$4 \times 1 = 4$	$4 \times 6 = 24$
$4 \times 2 = 8$	$4 \times 7 = 28$
$4 \times 3 = 12$	$4 \times 8 = 32$
$4 \times 4 = 16$	$4 \times 9 = 36$

DATA

Find 4×3. Draw an array.

$\left. \begin{array}{} \bullet\bullet\bullet \\ \bullet\bullet\bullet \end{array} \right\} 2 \times 3 = 6$

$\left. \begin{array}{} \bullet\bullet\bullet \\ \bullet\bullet\bullet \end{array} \right\} 2 \times 3 = 6$

$6 + 6 = 12$

So, $4 \times 3 = 12$.

In **1** and **2**, use a 2s fact to find the product of the 4s fact.

1. Find 4×9.

$\left. \begin{array}{} \bullet\bullet\bullet\bullet\bullet\bullet\bullet\bullet\bullet \\ \bullet\bullet\bullet\bullet\bullet\bullet\bullet\bullet\bullet \end{array} \right\}$ ___ $\times 9 =$ ___

$\left. \begin{array}{} \bullet\bullet\bullet\bullet\bullet\bullet\bullet\bullet\bullet \\ \bullet\bullet\bullet\bullet\bullet\bullet\bullet\bullet\bullet \end{array} \right\} 2 \times$ ___ $=$ ___

___ $+ 18 =$ ___

So, $4 \times 9 =$ ___.

2. Find 4×2.

$\left. \begin{array}{} \bullet\bullet \\ \bullet\bullet \end{array} \right\}$ ___ $\times 2 =$ ___

$\left. \begin{array}{} \bullet\bullet \\ \bullet\bullet \end{array} \right\} 2 \times$ ___ $=$ ___

___ $+ 4 =$ ___

So, $4 \times 2 =$ ___.

In **3** through **14**, find the product.

3. $4 \times 6 =$ ___

4. $8 \times 4 =$ ___

5. $4 \times 9 =$ ___

6. $2 \times 4 =$ ___

7. $4 \times 1 =$ ___

8. $4 \times 7 =$ ___

9. $0 \times 4 =$ ___

10. $4 \times 4 =$ ___

11. $4 \times 10 =$ ___

12. $3 \times 4 =$ ___

13. $5 \times 4 =$ ___

14. $4 \times 0 =$ ___

For **15** and **16**, use the table at the right.

15. **Analyze Information** Jero and Max rented a canoe for 4 hours. They each rented a life jacket. How much money did they spend? How did you find the answer?

Canoeing	
Cost per hour	$4
Life jacket rental	$6

16. Tina paid for 6 hours of canoeing and 1 life jacket rental with two twenty-dollar bills. How much change did Tina get back? Show your work.

17. **Reason** Rob says he can use 2 × 5 to find 4 × 5. Is he correct? Explain.

18. **Number Sense** Texas became the 28th state in 1845. How can you write the year of Texas's statehood in word form?

19. **Extend Your Thinking** Mark is having a party. He invited 35 people. Mark set up 8 tables with 4 chairs at each table. Does Mark have enough tables and chairs for all his guests? Explain.

20. Jillian bought 4 boxes of crayons for party favors. Each box had the same number of crayons. How many crayons did Jillian buy?

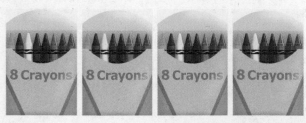

A 16

B 24

C 32

D 36

© Pearson Education, Inc. 3

Name _____

☆ ★ ☆
Solve & Share

Students set up 6 rows of seats for a music concert. They put 6 seats in each row. What is the total number of seats? *Solve this problem any way you choose.*

 TEKS 3.4F Recall facts to multiply up to 10 by 10 with automaticity and recall the corresponding division facts. Also, 3.4E, 3.4K.
Mathematical Process Standards 3.1B, 3.1C, 3.1D, 3.1E, 3.1G

Digital Resources at PearsonTexas.com

Solve Learn Glossary Check Tools Games

You can **create and use representations.** Use counters to build and break apart arrays. *Show your work in the space below!*

Look Back!

Number Sense How can 3s facts help you solve 6s facts?

How Can You Break Apart Arrays to Multiply?

The members of the band march in 6 equal rows. There are 8 band members in each row. How many are in the band?

You can multiply to find the total for an array.

B What You Show

Find 6 × 8.

Use 5s facts and 1s facts.

Make an array for each multiplication sentence.

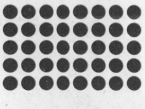

$5 \times 8 = 40$

$1 \times 8 = 8$

C What You Think

6 × 8 is 6 rows of 8. That is 5 eights plus 1 more eight.

5 eights are 40.
8 more is 48.
$40 + 8 = 48$

So, $6 \times 8 = 48$.

The band has 48 members.

Do You Understand?

Convince Me! Use a 5s fact and a 1s fact to find 6 × 9. Draw two arrays. Explain your drawings.

 © Pearson Education, Inc. 3

Another Example

Find 7×8. Use 5s facts and 2s facts to help you multiply by 7.

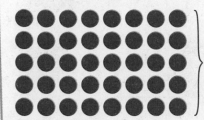

$5 \times 8 = 40$

$2 \times 8 = 16$

7×8 is 7 rows of 8.
That is 5 eights plus 2 eights.

5 eights are 40.
2 eights are 16.

$40 + 16 = 56$

So, $7 \times 8 = 56$.

☆ Guided Practice*

In **1** through **6**, multiply. Draw pictures or use counters to help.

1. $6 \times 10 =$ ____

2. $7 \times 6 =$ ____

3. $\begin{array}{r} 7 \\ \times\ 7 \\ \hline \end{array}$

4. $\begin{array}{r} 9 \\ \times\ 7 \\ \hline \end{array}$

5. Find 4 times 7. ____

6. Multiply 6 and 5. ____

7. **Number Sense** The students who are graduating are standing in 7 equal rows. There are 9 students in each row. How many students are graduating? Use a 5s fact and a 2s fact.

8. **Analyze Information** Chrissy bakes 3 cherry pies. She cuts each pie into 6 slices. How many slices does Chrissy have?

☆ Independent Practice ☆

In **9** through **16**, find the product. Draw pictures to help.

9. $\begin{array}{r} 5 \\ \times\ 7 \\ \hline \end{array}$

10. $\begin{array}{r} 3 \\ \times\ 6 \\ \hline \end{array}$

11. $\begin{array}{r} 7 \\ \times\ 8 \\ \hline \end{array}$

12. $\begin{array}{r} 1 \\ \times\ 7 \\ \hline \end{array}$

13. $\begin{array}{r} 10 \\ \times\ 6 \\ \hline \end{array}$

14. $\begin{array}{r} 4 \\ \times\ 7 \\ \hline \end{array}$

15. $\begin{array}{r} 7 \\ \times\ 3 \\ \hline \end{array}$

16. $\begin{array}{r} 8 \\ \times\ 6 \\ \hline \end{array}$

Problem Solving

17. Analyze Information The National Toy Train Museum has 5 large layouts for trains. One day, each layout had the same number of trains. Use the picture on the right to find how many trains were on display at the museum that day. Write a number sentence to solve the problem.

The museum has model trains that date back to the 1800s!

6 trains in each layout

---

18. Draw a Picture Nan made the arrays shown to find 6 × 3. Explain how to change the arrays to find 7 × 3.

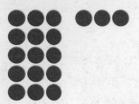

19. The dance team lines up with 4 rows of 6 dancers each. How many dancers are on the dance team?

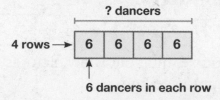

? dancers

4 rows → | 6 | 6 | 6 | 6 |

6 dancers in each row

---

20. Miguel had the baskets of oranges shown at the right. Each basket held 6 oranges. If Miguel counted the oranges in groups of 6, which list shows the numbers he would have named?

A 6, 12, 21, 26, 32

B 6, 11, 16, 21, 26

C 12, 16, 20, 24, 28

D 6, 12, 18, 24, 30

---

21. Extend Your Thinking Marge says 7 × 0 is equal to 7 + 0. Is Marge correct? Why or why not?

22. Estimation One train has 377 seats. Another train has 345 seats. Use rounding to the nearest ten to find about how many seats are on the two trains.

© Pearson Education, Inc. 3

Name _____

Another Look!

You can use multiplication facts you already know to find other multiplication facts.

Find 6 × 9. Use a 3s fact.

$$3 \times 9 = 27$$
$$3 \times 9 = 27$$
$$27 + 27 = 54$$

So, 6 × 9 = 54.

Find 7 × 5. Use a 2s fact.

$$2 \times 5 = 10$$
$$5 \times 5 = 25$$
$$10 + 25 = 35$$

So, 7 × 5 = 35.

For **1** and **2**, use a known fact.

1. 6 × 4 = ?

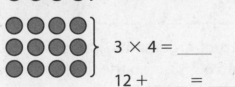

$$3 \times 4 = \underline{\hspace{1cm}}$$
$$3 \times 4 = \underline{\hspace{1cm}}$$
$$12 + \underline{\hspace{1cm}} = \underline{\hspace{1cm}}$$

So, 6 × 4 = ____.

2. 7 × 4 = ?

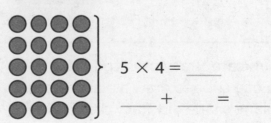

$$2 \times 4 = \underline{\hspace{1cm}}$$
$$5 \times 4 = \underline{\hspace{1cm}}$$
$$\underline{\hspace{1cm}} + \underline{\hspace{1cm}} = \underline{\hspace{1cm}}$$

So, 7 × 4 = ____.

In **3** through **11**, find each product.

3. 2 × 7 = ____

4. 6 × 7 = ____

5. 7 × 9 = ____

6. 6 × 4 = ____

7. 6 × 8 = ____

8. 7 × 7 = ____

9. 6 × 2 = ____

10. 8 × 7 = ____

11. 3 × 7 = ____

In **12** and **13**, use the table at the right.

12. **Analyze Information** Sam's Café is having a special on salad platters. Al buys 4 chicken salad platters and 3 tuna salad platters for his garden crew. How much money did Al spend? How did you find the answer?

13. Emmet buys 7 egg salad platters. How much did Emmet spend?

Salad Platters	
Tuna Salad	$6
Egg Salad	$4
Chicken Salad	$7

DATA

14. Emily has 7 apples. She cuts each apple ⭐ into 6 slices. How many slices does Emily have?

   A   13

   B   36

   C   42

   D   49

15. **Explain** At a picnic, 6 tables are set up. Each table can seat 8 people. How many people can be seated at the tables? Use a 3s fact to find the answer.

16. **Communicate** Tracy used the flat surface of a cube to draw a plane shape. What plane shape did Tracy draw? How do you know?

17. **Construct Arguments** Harold says, "To find 6 × 8, I can use the facts for 5 × 4 and 1 × 4." Do you agree? Explain.

18. The chicken eggs that Raul's science class is watching take 3 weeks to hatch. There are 7 days in each week. How many days will it be until the eggs hatch?

19. What multiplication fact can be found by using the arrays for 2 × 9 and 5 × 9?

© Pearson Education, Inc. 3

Name _____

Solve & Share There are 8 rows of prizes. There are 6 prizes in each row. How many prizes are there? *Solve this problem any way you choose.*

⭐ **TEKS 3.4F** Recall facts to multiply up to 10 by 10 with automaticity and recall the corresponding division facts. Also, 3.4E, 3.4K.
Mathematical Process Standards 3.1A, 3.1D, 3.1F, 3.1G

Digital Resources at PearsonTexas.com

Solve   Learn   Glossary   Check   Tools   Games

You can **connect ideas.** Can you use known facts to solve unknown facts? *Show your work!*

Look Back!

Communicate Tell how you can use 2s, 3s, or 4s facts to solve the problem.

A

At a school fun fair, students try to toss a table tennis ball into a bowl. There are 8 rows of bowls. There are 8 bowls in each row. How many bowls are there?

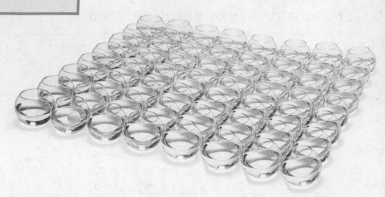

You can multiply to find the total for an array.

B ## One Way

Use 2s facts to find 8×8.

8×8 is 4 groups of 2 eights.

$\left.\begin{array}{l}\bullet\bullet\bullet\bullet\bullet\bullet\bullet\bullet \\ \bullet\bullet\bullet\bullet\bullet\bullet\bullet\bullet\end{array}\right\} 2 \times 8 = 16$

$\left.\begin{array}{l}\bullet\bullet\bullet\bullet\bullet\bullet\bullet\bullet \\ \bullet\bullet\bullet\bullet\bullet\bullet\bullet\bullet\end{array}\right\} 2 \times 8 = 16$

$\left.\begin{array}{l}\bullet\bullet\bullet\bullet\bullet\bullet\bullet\bullet \\ \bullet\bullet\bullet\bullet\bullet\bullet\bullet\bullet\end{array}\right\} 2 \times 8 = 16$

$\left.\begin{array}{l}\bullet\bullet\bullet\bullet\bullet\bullet\bullet\bullet \\ \bullet\bullet\bullet\bullet\bullet\bullet\bullet\bullet\end{array}\right\} 2 \times 8 = 16$

$16 + 16 + 16 + 16 = 64$

C ## Another Way

Double a 4s fact to find 8×8.

8×8 is 4 eights plus 4 eights.

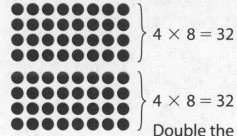

$4 \times 8 = 32$

$4 \times 8 = 32$

Double the product.

So, $8 \times 8 = 64$. $\quad 32 + 32 = 64$

There are 64 bowls in all.

Do You Understand?

Convince Me! How could $5 \times 8 = 40$ help you find 8×8?

© Pearson Education, Inc. 3

Name_____

In **1** through **6**, multiply. You may draw pictures or use counters to help.

1. $8 \times 7 =$ _____

2. $8 \times 4 =$ _____

3. $6 \times 8 =$ _____

4. $10 \times 8 =$ _____

5. $\begin{array}{r} 9 \\ \times\ 8 \\ \hline \end{array}$ 6. $\begin{array}{r} 8 \\ \times\ 3 \\ \hline \end{array}$

7. **Number Sense** Multiply 8 and 3. Write and solve the multiplication sentence.

8. Find 5 times 8. Write and solve the multiplication sentence.

9. Multiply 8 and 1. Write and solve the multiplication sentence.

☆ **Independent Practice** ☆

In **10** through **23**, find the product. You may draw pictures to help.

10. $8 \times 4 =$ _____   11. $1 \times 8 =$ _____   12. $2 \times 8 =$ _____

13. $5 \times 8 =$ _____   14. $8 \times 2 =$ _____   15. $8 \times 6 =$ _____

16. $\begin{array}{r} 8 \\ \times\ 8 \\ \hline \end{array}$ 17. $\begin{array}{r} 8 \\ \times\ 5 \\ \hline \end{array}$ 18. $\begin{array}{r} 0 \\ \times\ 8 \\ \hline \end{array}$ 19. $\begin{array}{r} 4 \\ \times\ 8 \\ \hline \end{array}$

20. $\begin{array}{r} 10 \\ \times\ 8 \\ \hline \end{array}$ 21. $\begin{array}{r} 8 \\ \times\ 1 \\ \hline \end{array}$ 22. $\begin{array}{r} 3 \\ \times\ 8 \\ \hline \end{array}$ 23. $\begin{array}{r} 7 \\ \times\ 8 \\ \hline \end{array}$

Problem Solving

In **24** and **25**, use the table at the right.

24. **Explain** Ming bought 8 belts for gifts. How much money did Ming spend? Show how you can use a 4s fact to find the answer.

Clothing Sale	
Shirt	$23
Belt	$9
Sweater	$38
Pair of jeans	$42

25. **Reason** Willa bought a shirt and a sweater. She had $14 left. How much money did Willa start with? How do you know?

---

26. Mr. Garner spends $112 on groceries, $72 on fuel, and $347 on bills. How much did Mr. Garner spend?

?		
$112	$72	$347

27. Tom spent $48 more than Jill. Jill spent $167. How much did Tom spend?

---

28. Mischa bought 8 boxes of orange tiles. There are 8 tiles in each box. How many tiles did Mischa buy? Write an equation and solve.

29. Aaron bought 6 boxes of yellow tiles. There are 7 tiles in each box. How many tiles did Aaron buy? Write an equation and solve.

---

30. **Extend Your Thinking** Sophi says, "To find 8×8, I can find 2×8 and double it." Do you agree? Explain.

31. ★ Ms. Vero has boxes of crayons in her classroom closet. Each box has 8 crayons in it. If Ms. Vero counts the crayons in groups of 8, which list shows the numbers she would have named?

   A 8, 16, 28, 32, 40, 48

   B 8, 14, 18, 24, 32, 40

   C 16, 20, 24, 28, 32, 36

   D 8, 16, 24, 32, 40, 48

© Pearson Education, Inc. 3

Name _____

Another Look!

You can double a 4s fact to multiply with 8.

Find 8 × 6. Double a 4s fact.

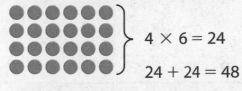

4 × 6 = 24

4 × 6 = 24

24 + 24 = 48

So, 8 × 6 = 48.

8s Facts	
8 × 0 = 0	8 × 5 = 40
8 × 1 = 8	8 × 6 = 48
8 × 2 = 16	8 × 7 = 56
8 × 3 = 24	8 × 8 = 64
8 × 4 = 32	8 × 9 = 72

For **1** and **2**, double a 4s fact.

1. 8 × 5 = ?

4 × 5 = _____

4 × 5 = _____

20 + _____ = _____

So, 8 × 5 = _____.

2. 8 × 3 = ?

4 × 3 = _____

4 × 3 = _____

_____ + _____ = _____

So, 8 × 3 = _____.

For **3** through **9**, find the products.

3. 2 × 8 = _____

4. 4 × 8 = _____

5. 8 × 5 = _____

6.　　7
　　× 8

7.　　9
　　× 8

8.　　1
　　× 8

9.　　6
　　× 8

10. **Explain** Luis made the arrays shown at the right to find 5 × 8. Explain how he could change the arrays to find 7 × 8. Add to Luis's drawing to show your solution.

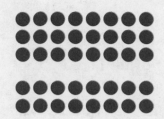

---

11. **Math and Science** An octopus has 8 arms. At the aquarium there are 3 octopuses in one tank. How many arms do the octopuses have all together? What are two strategies you can use to find the answer?

12. Jana has 43 books. Her brother has 20 books. How many books do they have in all?

? books

43	20

---

13. ⭐ Ted bought 6 packages of rolls. Each package contains 8 rolls. How many rolls did Ted buy?

   A 42
   B 48
   C 49
   D 54

14. **Reason** During the California Gold Rush, miners sometimes paid $10 for a glass of water. What was the total cost if 8 miners each bought one glass of water? How can you use a 4s fact to find the answer?

---

15. How many pints are in 5 gallons?

1 gallon = 8 pints

16. **Extend Your Thinking** Lani said all of the multiples of 8 are also multiples of 2. Jamila said all of the multiples of 8 are also multiples of 4. Who is correct? Explain.

© Pearson Education, Inc. 3

Name_____

Solve & Share

Gina has 2 quilts. Each quilt has 5 rows with 3 squares in each row. How many squares are in both quilts? *Solve this problem any way you choose.* Then, find another way to solve the problem.

⬥ TEKS 3.4K Solve … problems involving multiplication … within 100 using strategies based on objects; pictorial models, including arrays, … and equal groups; properties of operations; or recall of facts. Also, 3.5C.
Mathematical Process Standards 3.1B, 3.1C, 3.1D, 3.1G

Digital Resources at PearsonTexas.com

Solve   Learn   Glossary   Check   Tools   Games

You can **formulate a plan.** You can solve this problem in more than one way. *Show your work!*

Look Back!

Explain Gina multiplied 2 × 5 × 3. Jake multiplied 5 × 3 × 2. They both found 30 squares. Explain why.

How Can You Multiply 3 Numbers?

A-Z

Drew is joining 3 sections of a quilt. Each section has 2 rows with 4 squares in each row. How many squares are in these 3 sections? Find 3 × 2 × 4.

You can multiply to find the total for an array.

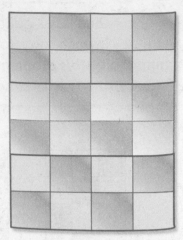

B One Way

Find 3 × 2 first.

(3 × 2) × 4

6 × 4 = 24

6 rows, 4 squares in each row

There are 24 squares in all.

C Another Way

Find 2 × 4 first.

3 × (2 × 4)

3 × 8 = 24

3 sections, 8 squares in each section

There are 24 squares in Drew's quilt.

The Associative (Grouping) Property of Multiplication says that you can change the grouping of the factors and the product will be the same.

Do You Understand?

Convince Me! Here is a problem with 3 factors: 5 × 2 × 3. Use the Associative (Grouping) Property of Multiplication to show two different ways to find the answer. Did you get the same answer both ways?

© Pearson Education, Inc. 3

Name _____

In **1** through **4**, use the Associative Property of Multiplication to find the missing number. You may use objects or draw a picture to help.

1. $2 \times (4 \times 2) = (2 \times 4) \times$ _____

2. $(3 \times 4) \times 3 = 3 \times ($ _____ $\times 3)$

3. $2 \times (2 \times 3) = (2 \times 2) \times$ _____

4. $(3 \times 2) \times 4 =$ _____ $\times (2 \times 4)$

5. **Analyze Information** Sarah has 4 pages of stickers in an album. Each page has 3 rows with 2 stickers in each row. How many stickers are in Sarah's album? Use objects to help.

6. **Explain** Billy concludes the product of $(2 \times 3) \times 5$ is not equal to the product of $2 \times (3 \times 5)$. Is Billy correct? Explain.

☆ **Independent Practice** ☆

In **7** through **12**, use the Associative Property of Multiplication to find the missing number. You may use objects or draw a picture to help.

7. $8 \times (3 \times 6) = (8 \times 3) \times$ _____

8. $5 \times (6 \times 9) = (5 \times 6) \times$ _____

9. $5 \times (7 \times 2) = (5 \times 7) \times$ _____

10. $5 \times (2 \times 9) = (5 \times$ _____ $) \times 9$

11. $3 \times (2 \times 5) = (3 \times 2) \times$ _____

12. $4 \times (2 \times 2) = (4 \times$ _____ $) \times 2$

In **13** through **18**, use the Associative Property of Multiplication to find the product. You may use objects or draw a picture to help.

13. $2 \times 3 \times 2 =$ _____

14. $3 \times 6 \times 1 =$ _____

15. $2 \times 6 \times 2 =$ _____

16. $5 \times 2 \times 4 =$ _____

17. $5 \times 2 \times 2 =$ _____

18. $3 \times 3 \times 2 =$ _____

Problem Solving

In **19** and **20**, use the picture at the right.

19. **Analyze Information** There are 4 mockingbird nests at a park. Each nest has 5 eggs. How many eggs are there?

20. **Number Sense** At another park, there are 3 mockingbird nests with 4 eggs in each nest and 2 more nests with 3 eggs each. How many eggs are there?

Mockingbirds lay 3 to 5 eggs.

21. Maria says she can find the product for $2 \times 3 \times 4$ by solving $3 \times 2 \times 4$. Is Maria correct? Explain.

22. **Construct Arguments** Anita says the product of $5 \times 2 \times 3$ is less than 20. Do you agree? Explain.

23. ⭐ Which number makes both number sentences true?

$$4 \times (3 \times 2) = (4 \times \,?) \times 2$$

$$3 \times (5 \times 2) = (? \times 5) \times 2$$

  A 7   **C** 3
  B 5   **D** 2

24. **Extend Your Thinking** How do you know $4 \times 2 \times 2$ is the same as 4×4? Explain.

In **25** and **26**, use the table at the right.

25. **Analyze Information** Ellis bought 3 packs of baseball cards and 2 times as many packs of basketball cards. How many cards did Ellis buy?

26. Frederick bought 3 packs of hockey cards and 2 packs of football cards. How many cards did Frederick buy?

DATA

Sports Card Sale

Kind of Cards	Number of Cards in Each Pack
Baseball	8
Basketball	5
Football	7
Hockey	6

© Pearson Education, Inc. 3

Name _____

Another Look!

Use the Associative Property of Multiplication to find the product of $2 \times 3 \times 2$.

The Associative Property states that the way the factors are grouped does not change the product.

One Way
$2 \times 3 \times 2$
$(2 \times 3) \times 2$
$\downarrow$
$6 \times 2 = 12$

Another Way
$2 \times 3 \times 2$
$2 \times (3 \times 2)$
$\downarrow$
$2 \times 6 = 12$

1. Find the product of $4 \times 2 \times 3$ two different ways.

$4 \times 2 \times 3$ $4 \times 2 \times 3$

$(4 \times 2) \times 3$ $4 \times (2 \times 3)$

    $\downarrow$ $\downarrow$

____ $\times\ 3 =$ ____ $4 \times$ ____ $=$ ____

In **2** through **16**, find each product. You may draw a picture to help.

2. $3 \times 2 \times 1 =$ ____   **3.** $2 \times 3 \times 5 =$ ____   **4.** $4 \times 3 \times 2 =$ ____

5. $4 \times 2 \times 7 =$ ____   **6.** $3 \times 3 \times 2 =$ ____   **7.** $2 \times 4 \times 5 =$ ____

8. $2 \times 2 \times 6 =$ ____   **9.** $4 \times 1 \times 5 =$ ____   **10.** $5 \times 1 \times 3 =$ ____

11. $6 \times 1 \times 5 =$ ____   **12.** $3 \times 3 \times 4 =$ ____   **13.** $4 \times 2 \times 6 =$ ____

14. $5 \times 5 \times 2 =$ ____   **15.** $2 \times 2 \times 5 =$ ____   **16.** $3 \times 2 \times 2 =$ ____

17. Communicate Mrs. Stokes bought 3 packages of fruit juice. Each package has 2 rows with 6 boxes in each row. How many boxes of fruit juice did Mrs. Stokes buy? Write a number sentence with your answer.

18. Which number makes both number sentences true?

$8 \times 2 \times 4 = 8 \times (? \times 4)$

$4 \times 6 \times 2 = (4 \times 6) \times ?$

A 2
B 4
C 6
D 8

These number sentences show the Associative (Grouping) Property of Multiplication.

19. Formulate a Plan Jesse bought 3 sheets of stamps and Marco bought 2 times as many sheets of stamps. On each sheet there are 4 rows of stamps with 3 stamps in each row. How many stamps did Marco buy?

20. Construct Arguments Jill says the product of $4 \times 2 \times 3$ is more than 20. Do you agree? Explain.

21. Analyze Information Amy has 3 bags of marbles, and Ron has 2 bags of marbles. There are 6 marbles in each of their bags. How many marbles do they have?

22. Tools Matt has a block. He uses one of the flat surfaces of the block to trace a triangle. What type of solid figure is Matt's block?

23. What is 12,438 rounded to the nearest ten thousand? What is it rounded to the nearest thousand?

24. Extend Your Thinking Write two different multiplication number sentences for the arrays shown. Find the product of each one.

© Pearson Education, Inc. 3

Name _____

Solve & Share

Alfredo buys 6 bags of oranges. Each bag contains 5 oranges. How many oranges does Alfredo buy? **Solve this problem any way you choose.**

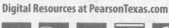

TEKS 3.4F Recall facts to multiply up to 10 by 10 with automaticity and recall the corresponding division facts. Also, 3.4K, 3.5C.
Mathematical Process Standards 3.1B, 3.1C, 3.1F, 3.1G

Digital Resources at PearsonTexas.com

Solve   Learn   Glossary   Check   Tools   Games

You can **select and use tools.** You can use tools such as patterns, counters, drawings, skip counting, and arrays, or known facts to help solve the problem. **Show your work in the space below!**

Look Back!

Tools How do tools such as skip counting, using known facts, and arrays help you solve multiplication facts?

How Do You Use Strategies to Multiply?

A

A scientist on a boat is studying hammerhead sharks. The length of the boat is 6 times the length of a hammerhead shark like the one shown at the right. How long is the boat?

An adult hammerhead shark is about 5 yards long.

You can multiply to put together equal groups.

B One Way

Use a pattern to find 6 × 5.

6 × 5 means 6 groups of 5.
Count by 5s.

5	5	5	5	5	5

5   10   15   20   25   30

So, 6 × 5 = 30.

The boat is 30 yards long.

C Another Way

Use known facts to find 6 × 5.

Use 2s facts and 4s facts to help.

$2 × 5 = 10$

$4 × 5 = 20$

$10 + 20 = 30$

The boat is 30 yards long.

Do You Understand?

Convince Me! What other known facts could you use to find 6 × 5? Give two pairs of facts.

© Pearson Education, Inc. 3

☆ **Guided Practice** *

In **1** through **6**, multiply.

1. $6 \times 4 =$ _____

2. $4 \times 5 =$ _____

3. $9 \times 3 =$ _____

4. $3 \times 2 =$ _____

5. $\begin{array}{r} 1 \\ \times\,4 \\ \hline \end{array}$

6. $\begin{array}{r} 9 \\ \times\,8 \\ \hline \end{array}$

7. Connect What known facts can you use to find 3×5?

8. Explain To find 9×5, how could knowing $7 \times 5 = 35$ help you?

☆ Independent Practice ☆

Leveled Practice In **9** through **25**, use a pattern or known facts to find the product.

9. $5 \times 5 =$ _____

10. $9 \times 2 =$ _____

11. $5 \times 9 =$ _____

12. $8 \times 7 =$ _____

13. $3 \times 6 =$ _____

14. $8 \times 4 =$ _____

15. $\begin{array}{r} 10 \\ \times\,4 \\ \hline \end{array}$

16. $\begin{array}{r} 7 \\ \times\,6 \\ \hline \end{array}$

17. $\begin{array}{r} 6 \\ \times\,5 \\ \hline \end{array}$

18. $\begin{array}{r} 2 \\ \times\,8 \\ \hline \end{array}$

19. $\begin{array}{r} 9 \\ \times\,0 \\ \hline \end{array}$

20. $\begin{array}{r} 10 \\ \times\,6 \\ \hline \end{array}$

21. $\begin{array}{r} 4 \\ \times\,9 \\ \hline \end{array}$

22. $\begin{array}{r} 9 \\ \times\,7 \\ \hline \end{array}$

23. What is 6×4? _____

24. What is 5×8? _____

25. What is 10×1? _____

Problem Solving

For **26** and **27**, use the pictures below.

26. Mr. Marks is studying 3 blacktip sharks and 4 tiger sharks. Estimate the length of the 7 sharks.

27. **Construct Arguments** Ms. Kent estimates the total length of 14 blacktip sharks is greater than the total length of 7 tiger sharks. Is Ms. Kent correct? Explain your thinking.

Blacktip Shark
About 2 yards long

Tiger Shark
About 4 yards long

28. ★ Hal counted the number of fish in 3 fish tanks. There were 7 fish in each. How many fish were in the 3 fish tanks?

  A 21

  B 24

  C 27

  D 37

29. **Formulate a Plan** Bob has a collection of 230 sports cards. If he buys 5 packages of sports cards with 9 sports cards in each package, how many sports cards will Bob have?

30. Cecilia wants to buy a used flute and a used piccolo. The flute costs $575. The piccolo costs $420. How much money does Cecilia need to buy the flute and the piccolo?

?	
$575	$420

31. **Extend Your Thinking** Show how you can use known facts to find 6 × 9. Explain how you chose the known facts.

© Pearson Education, Inc. 3

Name _____

Another Look!

Find 6×4.

You can use a pattern or known facts to find 6×4.

Pattern

6×4 means 6 groups of 4.

?					
4	4	4	4	4	4
4	8	12	16	20	24

So, $6 \times 4 = 24$.

Known Facts

Use 3s facts to help.

$3 \times 4 = 12$

$3 \times 4 = 12$
$12 + 12 = 24$

So, $6 \times 4 = 24$.

For **1** and **2**, use a pattern or known facts to find the product.

1. $3 \times 5 = ?$

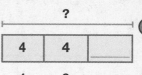

?		
5	5	
5	10	

$2 \times 5 =$ _____

$1 \times 5 =$ _____

$3 \times 5 =$ _____

$10 +$ _____ $=$ _____

2. $3 \times 4 = ?$

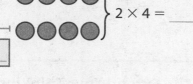

?		
4	4	
4	8	

$2 \times 4 =$ _____

$1 \times 4 =$ _____

$3 \times 4 =$ _____

$8 +$ _____ $=$ _____

For **3** through **8**, multiply.

3. $7 \times 2 =$ _____

4. $8 \times 5 =$ _____

5. $6 \times 8 =$ _____

6. $9 \times 7 =$ _____

7. $4 \times 8 =$ _____

8. $7 \times 3 =$ _____

9. **Analyze Information** The home team had 3 touchdowns, 2 field goals, and 1 safety. The visiting team scored 4 touchdowns. Which team scored more points? Explain.

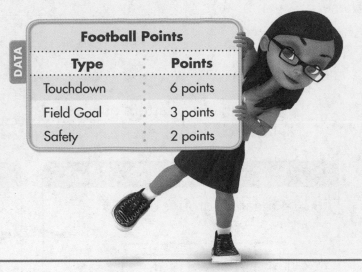

DATA

Football Points	
Type	**Points**
Touchdown	6 points
Field Goal	3 points
Safety	2 points

10. Tia counted the campers and beds in 7 cabins. There were 9 campers and 12 beds in each cabin. How many campers were in the 7 cabins?

A 84   C 63

B 72   D 35

11. Use the array to complete the problem.

$2 \times \underline{\hspace{1cm}} = 10$

$10 \div 2 = \underline{\hspace{1cm}}$

12. **Explain** Rick says to find 2×5, he can use counting by 5s: 5, 10, 15, 20, 25. Explain what Rick did wrong.

13. **Number Sense** Without multiplying, which product will be greater, 4×3 or 4×5? Explain.

14. **Extend Your Thinking** Jill has 4 bags of marbles. There are 3 red, 5 green, 2 yellow, and 6 black marbles in each bag. How many marbles does Jill have? Show how you found the answer.

15. Robert will drive a total of 561 miles to his vacation cabin. He has driven 128 miles so far. How many more miles does Robert need to drive to get to his cabin?

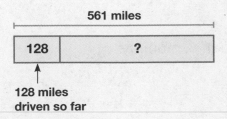

561 miles

| 128 | ? |

128 miles driven so far

© Pearson Education, Inc. 3

☆ ⭐ ☆
Solve & Share

At the pet store, Sam bought 3 hamsters that cost $10 each. He bought twice as many mice that cost $4 each. How much did Sam spend? *Solve this problem any way you choose.*

You can **formulate a plan.** What information do you need to solve the problem?

⭐ **TEKS 3.1D** Communicate mathematical ideas, reasoning, and their implications using multiple representations, including symbols, diagrams, graphs, and language as appropriate. Also, 3.4K, 3.5B. **Mathematical Process Standards** 3.1B, 3.1F

Digital Resources at PearsonTexas.com

Solve   Learn   Glossary   Check   Tools   Games

Look Back!

Check for Reasonableness Describe a strategy for checking your solution's reasonableness.

A **Analyze**

How Do You Solve Multi-Step Problems Using Strip Diagrams and Equations?

Keisha bought 2 yards of felt to make some puppets. Tanya bought 6 yards of felt. The felt cost $3 a yard. How much did the two girls spend on felt?

Some word problems have hidden questions that need to be answered before you can solve the problem.

$3 per yard

B **Plan**

Find and solve the hidden question.

How many yards of felt did the girls buy?

? yards

2 yards	6 yards

Write and solve an equation.

$2 + 6 = \boxed{}$ $2 + 6 = 8$

The girls bought 8 yards of felt.

C **Solve**

Use the answer to the hidden question to solve the problem.

How much did the girls spend?

? total cost

$3	$3	$3	$3	$3	$3	$3	$3

Write and solve an equation.

$8 \times \$3 = \boxed{}$ $8 \times \$3 = \$24$

The girls spent $24 on felt.

Do You Understand?

Convince Me! Suppose Keisha bought 3 yards of felt, and Tanya bought 5 yards of felt. The felt costs $2 a yard. How much did the girls spend on felt? Is the hidden question the same? Explain.

In **1** and **2**, use the strip diagrams to find the answer.

1. Megan has 2 dolls. Heather has 4 times as many dolls as Megan. How many dolls does Heather have? Use the strip diagram to write and solve an equation.

Megan	2

| Heather | 2 | 2 | 2 | 2 | **4 times as many** |

? dolls

_____ × _____ = ?

Heather has _____ dolls.

2. A store has 4 different televisions. The store also has 5 times as many cell phones as televisions. How many cell phones does the store have? Use the strip diagram to write and solve an equation.

TVs	4

| Cell Phones | 4 | 4 | 4 | 4 | 4 | **5 times as many** |

? cell phones

_____ × _____ = ?

The store has _____ cell phones.

Independent Practice

3. There are 3 tennis balls in each can. Phil had 7 cans of tennis balls before he lost 2 of the balls. How many tennis balls does Phil now have? Draw a strip diagram and write an equation to solve the problem.

One Can	3

| Phil's Cans | 3 | 3 | 3 | 3 | 3 | 3 | 3 | **7 times as many** |

? tennis balls

4. Jen bought 4 marbles. Amber bought 5 marbles. The marbles cost $2 each. How much did the marbles cost?

a. What is the hidden question?

b. Draw a strip diagram and write an equation to solve the problem.

Strip diagrams can help you answer the hidden question.

Problem Solving

5. Connect Ron is going fishing. He bought hooks for $2, line for $4, and bait for $6. How much did Ron spend? Use the strip diagram to write an equation, and then solve the problem.

? money spent

$2	$4	$6

6. Sarah had a collection of 10 stickers. She bought enough stickers to have twice as many, then she gave 3 stickers to a friend. Which equation shows how many stickers Sarah has left?

A $10 + 2 - 3 = ?$
B $(10 - 10) + 3 = ?$
C $10 - (2 \times 3) = ?$
D $(10 + 10) - 3 = ?$

7. Draw a Picture The desks in a classroom are arranged in groups of 6. If there are 4 groups of desks, how many desks are in the classroom? Draw a strip diagram and write an equation to solve the problem.

8. Jen said the value of the 4 in 24,299 is 4. Mark said the value of the 4 is 4,000. Who is correct? Explain.

9. Reason There are 8 chairs at the lunch table. There are 4 legs on each chair. Jon says there are 34 legs on all of the chairs. Is Jon correct? Use the strip diagram to help.

? chair legs

4	4	4	4	4	4	4	4

10. Extend Your Thinking Vic has 5 video games. Joe has 3 times as many video games as Vic. Joe lets one of his friends borrow 2 of his video games. How many video games does Joe have now? Show all of your equations.

11. Use a Strip Diagram The coffee shop has 4 sizes of cups and some types of drinks. There are 5 times as many types of drinks as there are cup sizes. If the coffee shop sells 3 types of its drinks, how many other types of drinks have not been sold? The strip diagram helps you answer the hidden question. Draw another strip diagram to solve the problem.

cup sizes | 4

types of drinks | 4 | 4 | 4 | 4 | 4 | 5 times as many

? types of drinks

© Pearson Education, Inc. 3

Name _____

Another Look!

You can draw strip diagrams and write equations to help solve problems.

Ron has 6 bags and puts 2 red, 3 yellow, and 4 green marbles in each bag. How many marbles does Ron have?

Find and solve the hidden question. How many marbles does Ron put in each bag?

? marbles in a bag

2	3	4

$2 + 3 + 4 = 9$

Ron puts 9 marbles in each bag.

Now use the answer to the hidden question to solve the problem.

? marbles

9	9	9	9	9	9

$6 \times 9 = 54$

Ron has 54 marbles.

For **1**, use the strip diagrams to answer the hidden question and solve the problem.

1. Paul has 7 piles of sports cards. There are 3 basketball, 3 football, and 4 baseball cards in each pile. How many sports cards does Paul have?

   Hidden Question: How many sports cards are in each pile?

   ? sports cards in each pile

3	3	4

   ? sports cards

10	10	10	10	10	10	10

For **2** and **3**, use the strip diagram to write an equation and then solve.

2. There are 6 buttons on each shirt. How many buttons are on 8 shirts?

   ? buttons

6	6	6	6	6	6	6	6

3. Sue is sorting 9 pairs of shoes. How many shoes is Sue sorting?

   ? shoes

2	2	2	2	2	2	2	2	2

4. Sophia measured her colored pencils and made a table. Use Sophia's table to complete the bar graph.

Sophia's Pencils	
Color	Length in Inches
Red	4
Blue	3
Green	7
Yellow	9

DATA

Sophia's Pencils

Length in Inches

10
9
8
7
6
5
4
3
2
1
0

Red   Blue   Green   Yellow
Color

5. **Draw a Picture** A farmer owned 9 chickens, each of which laid 3 eggs. His neighbor owned 5 chickens, each of which laid 4 eggs. How many eggs did all the chickens lay? Draw a strip diagram and write an equation to solve the problem.

6. Josie has $50. She buys 3 pairs of sandals for $8 each. How much money does she have left?

A $11
B $24
C $26
D $29

In **7** and **8**, use the picture at the right.

7. **Analyze Information** Beth bought 3 boxes of pens. She paid with a $50 bill. How much change did Beth receive? What hidden question helped you solve the problem?

8. **Extend Your Thinking** Erin bought 1 calculator, 1 box of pens, and 2 notebooks. How much money did Erin spend? Show two ways you could find the answer.

$4

$3

$5

$7

Pencils

Pens

© Pearson Education, Inc. 3

Name _____

1. **Communicate** Explain how you can break an 8 × 6 array into two smaller arrays. What are the new facts?

Applying Math Processes

- How does this problem connect to previous ones?
- What is my plan?
- How can I use tools?
- How can I use number sense?
- How can I communicate and represent my thinking?
- How can I organize and record information?
- How can I explain my work?
- How can I justify my answer?

2. **Reason** Michael has only nickels in his pocket. Could he have exactly 39 cents? Explain.

3. **Use a Strip Diagram** Marsha has 4 apples. Alicia has 6 times as many apples. How many apples does Alicia have?

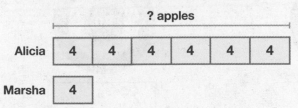

? apples

| Alicia | 4 | 4 | 4 | 4 | 4 | 4 |

| Marsha | 4 |

4. **Check for Reasonableness** Marcus says the product of 5 × 8 × 2 is less than 100. Is Marcus correct? Explain.

5. **Draw a Picture** Emilio made the array shown to find 2 × 7. Explain how to change the array to find 2 × 9. Draw a picture to solve the problem.

6. **Extend Your Thinking** Which costs more, 20 potatoes or 20 red onions? How much more? Explain how you found your answer.

10 potatoes per bag: $4

4 red onions per bag: $3

Error Search

For **1** through **4**, find each problem that is not correct. Circle the problems that are wrong and rewrite the problems so they are correct.

1. 2 × 7 = 15

2. 8 × 9 = 72

3. 5 × 7 = 30

4. 10 × 9 = 100

Target Number

For **5** through **7**, using any numbers from the box as factors, list as many multiplication problems with a product equal to the Target Number as you can. Numbers in the box may be used more than once.

5.

20

2	3	4
5	6	7
8	9	10

6.

60

2	3	4
5	6	7
8	9	10

7.

80

2	3	4
5	6	7
8	9	10

© Pearson Education, Inc. 3

ed to find

. Use

ng. Draw 6 curved
th arrow should

= _____

4 = _____

5 = _____

5 = _____

9 = _____

11 12 13 14 15

h number

Reteaching

Remember that mutiples of 2
are even numbers. Multiples
of 5 end in 0 or 5.

1. $2 \times 3 =$ _____   2. $5 \times 3 =$ _____

3. $5 \times 5 =$ _____   4. $2 \times 6 =$ _____

5. $8 \times 2 =$ _____   6. $7 \times 5 =$ _____

7. $\begin{array}{r} 2 \\ \times 2 \\ \hline \end{array}$ 8. $\begin{array}{r} 7 \\ \times 2 \\ \hline \end{array}$

9. $\begin{array}{r} 8 \\ \times 5 \\ \hline \end{array}$ 10. $\begin{array}{r} 9 \\ \times 5 \\ \hline \end{array}$

er is multiplied
the ones place.

0 $\times$ 10 = _____

$\times$ 10 = _____

1 $\times$ 10 = _____

find

Remember that the last digits in the products
of 9 form a pattern: 0, 9, 18, 27, 36, 45, 54, 63,
72, 81.

1. $9 \times 5 =$ _____   2. $9 \times 7 =$ _____

3. $6 \times 9 =$ _____   4. $8 \times 9 =$ _____

5. $9 \times 9 =$ _____   6. $9 \times 11 =$ _____

Property says that
broken apart into
iplication facts.

ssing value.
erty.

+ (2 $\times$ 4)

$\times$ 5)

+ (3 $\times$ 2)

(_____ $\times$ 7)

6) + (5 $\times$ 6)

3) + (6 $\times$ 3)

Remember that the product of 0 and any other
number is 0. When you multiply a number by
1, the product is that same number.

1. $0 \times 4 =$ _____   2. $1 \times 9 =$ _____

3. $0 \times 9 =$ _____   4. $1 \times 6 =$ _____

5. $10 \times 0 =$ _____   6. $9 \times 0 =$ _____

7. $3 \times 1 =$ _____   8. $8 \times 1 =$ _____

0 $\times$ 2 = _____   10. $1 \times 0 =$ _____

Set D | pages 271–276

Find 9 × 3. Use the hundred chart to skip count. Start at the upper left and count every number with a triangle around it until you get to the 3rd triangle.

1	②	3	④	5	⑥	7	⑧	△9	⑩
11	⑫	13	⑭	15	⑯	17	△18	19	⑳
21	㉒	23	㉔	25	㉖	△27	㉘	29	㉚
31	㉜	33	㉞	35	△36	37	㉞	39	㊵

$9 \times 3 = 27$

Remember that patterns can be use the products of the same factor.

In **1** through **10**, find each product the hundred chart to skip count.

1. $2 \times 7 = $ ____   **2.** 5×8

3. $2 \times 10 = $ ____   **4.** 5×4

5. $3 \times 5 = $ ____   **6.** $6 \times$

7. $9 \times 3 = $ ____   **8.** $5 \times$

9. $2 \times 3 = $ ____   **10.** $1 \times$

Set E | pages 277–282

Find 10 × 6.

> When multiplying a number by 10, add a zero to the right of the number.

$10 \times 6 = 60$

Remember that when a numb by 10, the product has a zero i

1. $10 \times 7 = $ ____   **2.** 1

3. $3 \times 10 = $ ____   **4.** 9

5. $10 \times 0 = $ ____   **6.**

Set F | pages 283–288

Will set up 8 rows of 6 tables. How many tables did Will set up?

Use a known fact to help find the product of unknown facts.

$8 \times 6 = (4 \times 6) + (4 \times 6)$
$8 \times 6 = 24 + 24$
$8 \times 6 = 48$

So, $8 \times 6 = 48$.

Will set up 48 tables.

Remember the Distributive a multiplication fact can be the sum of two other mult

In **1** through **6**, find the m Use the Distributive Prope

1. ____ $\times 4 = (2 \times 4)$

2. $6 \times 5 = (4 \times 5) + ($

3. $8 \times 2 = ($ ____ $\times 2$

4. $5 \times 7 = (4 \times 7) +$

5. ____ $\times 6 = (4 \times$

6. $8 \times 3 = ($ ____ $\times$

Name _____

Set G pages 289–300

Find 3 × 4.

3 × 4 is 3 rows of 4. You can use a 2s fact to find 3 × 4.

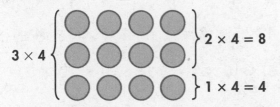

$$3 \times 4 = 12$$

Remember that to find the product of a 3s fact, you can add a 2s fact and a 1s fact. To find the product of a 4s fact, you can double the product of a 2s fact.

1. 3 × 7 = _____   **2.** 4 × 9 = _____

3. 4 × 10 = _____   **4.** 3 × 10 = _____

5. 3 × 8 = _____   **6.** 8 × 4 = _____

7. 9 × 3 = _____   **8.** 10 × 4 = _____

Set H pages 301–306

Find 6 × 9.

When you have 6 as a factor in a multiplication problem, you can use a 5s fact to help.

$$6 \times 9 = (5 \times 9) + (1 \times 9)$$
$$6 \times 9 = 45 + 9$$
$$6 \times 9 = 54$$

You can also use a 5s fact to help when you have 7 as a factor.

Remember that when you have a multiplication problem with two factors, you can break the problem into two smaller problems.

1. 6 × 6 = _____   **2.** 7 × 9 = _____

3. 7 × 7 = _____   **4.** 6 × 8 = _____

5. 1 × 7 = _____   **6.** 10 × 6 = _____

7.   6
   × 5   **8.**   6
   × 3   **9.**   10
   × 7

Set I pages 307–312

Find 8 × 9.

You can use 2s facts.

$$8 \times 9 = (2 \times 9) + (2 \times 9) + (2 \times 9) + (2 \times 9)$$
$$8 \times 9 = 18 + 18 + 18 + 18$$
$$8 \times 9 = 72$$

You can use 4s facts.

$$8 \times 9 = (4 \times 9) + (4 \times 9)$$
$$8 \times 9 = 36 + 36$$
$$8 \times 9 = 72$$

Remember that in addition to 2s facts and 4s facts, you can use 5s facts to find 8s facts.

1. 8 × 6 = _____   **2.** 8 × 8 = _____

3. 8 × 7 = _____   **4.** 8 × 10 = _____

5. 1 × 8 = _____   **6.** 0 × 8 = _____

7.   8
   × 5   **8.**   8
   × 3   **9.**   8
   × 2

A nursery is selling vegetable plants in rectangular containers. Each container has two rows of 8 plants. How many plants are in three containers?

Write the multiplication sentence: 2 × 8 × 3. Use the Associative (Grouping) Property of Multiplication to help solve the problem.

(2 × 8) × 3   2 × (8 × 3)

16 × 3 = 48   2 × 24 = 48

Remember that the Associative (Grouping) Property says that you can change the grouping of the factors and the product will be the same.

1. 3 × 5 × 7 = _____   **2.** 6 × 2 × 6 = _____

3. 4 × 5 × 3 = _____   **4.** 8 × 3 × 4 = _____

5. 3 × 10 × 4 = _____ **6.** 9 × 10 × 2 = _____

7. 2 × 3 × 4 = _____   **8.** 0 × 2 × 8 = _____

Find 6 × 7.

You can use a pattern or known facts to find products.

Use a pattern: 7, 14, 21, 28, 35, 42

Use known facts:

3 × 7 = 21

21 + 21 = 42

Remember that you can use patterns, known facts, or skip counting to find products.

1. 5 × 9 = _____   **2.** 8 × 10 = _____

3. 4 × 10 = _____ **4.** 9 × 8 = _____

5. 6 × 9 = _____   **6.** 7 × 3 = _____

7. 6 × 5 = _____   **8.** 4 × 9 = _____

Kit bought 2 tennis balls for $3 each and three times as many golf balls for $7 each. How much money did Kit spend?

?

| $3 | $3 |

↑
$3 for each tennis ball

?

| $7 | $7 | $7 | $7 | $7 | $7 |

↑
$7 for each golf ball

2 × 3 = $6

6 × 7 = $42

6 + 42 = $48

Remember to find and solve the hidden question first in a multi-step problem.

1. A store has 4 packs of sunflower seeds that sell for $3 each. There are twice as many packs of dried cranberries that sell for $8 each. What is the total cost of the seeds and cranberries?

2. Antwan has 3 packs of regular pencils with 6 pencils in each pack. He has 4 packs of colored pencils with 8 pencils in each pack. How many pencils does Antwan have?

© Pearson Education, Inc. 3

Name _____

1. A building has 9 rows of mailboxes. There are 6 mailboxes in each row. How many mailboxes are there?

A 15

B 45

C 54

D 63

2. Tickets to a juggling show cost $5 for each adult and $2 for each child. How much do tickets for 4 adults and 3 children cost?

A $10

B $14

C $23

D $26

3. Krista arranged her buttons in an array. Which shows a way to break Krista's array into two smaller arrays?

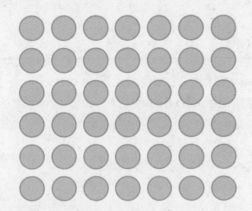

A $(3 \times 6) + (3 \times 1)$

B $(3 \times 7) + (3 \times 7)$

C $(3 \times 6) + (3 \times 6)$

D $(3 \times 7) + (4 \times 7)$

4. Mr. Blonski wrote four statements on the board. Which of the statements is **NOT** true?

A $24 \times 0 = 0$

B $45 \times 1 = 45$

C $67 \times 1 = 1 \times 67$

D $38 \times 0 = 38$

5. Mark said, "I am thinking of a number that is a multiple of 9." Which of the following could be Mark's number?

A 37

B 49

C 67

D Not here

6. A bakery uses 3 cups of flour to make each loaf of bread. There are 6 loaves of bread on a tray. There are 3 trays on a cart. How many cups of flour are used to make a full cart of bread?

A 18

B 27

C 54

D 63

7. Casey has 3 tennis balls. Lee has twice as many tennis balls as Casey. Nikko has 6 times as many tennis balls as Lee. How many tennis balls does Nikko have?

A 11

B 18

C 30

D 36

8. Gabe has 4 pet birds. The pet store has 8 times as many birds. Use the strip diagram below. Which number sentence can you use to find how many birds the pet store has?

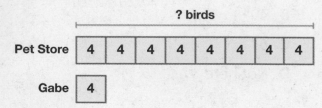

A 4 × 4 = 16

B 4 × 6 = 24

C 4 × 8 = 32

D 4 × 9 = 36

9. A set of blocks has 4 different types of blocks. There are 10 of each type of block. How many blocks are in the set?

A 14

B 30

C 40

D 44

10. Ava has 3 baskets. Each basket has 8 apples. How many apples does Ava have?

A 16

B 24

C 27

D 36

11. Tim's family rented a kayak and a canoe for 6 hours. How much did they spend?

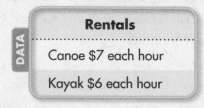

A $36

B $42

C $78

D $85

12. Dawn has 2 bananas. She cuts each banana into 8 slices. How many slices of banana does Dawn have?

A 16

B 24

C 27

D 32

© Pearson Education, Inc. 3

Name _____

13. A T-shirt costs $10. Jeff bought 2 T-shirts for himself. He bought 3 more T-shirts to give as gifts. How much money did Jeff spend?

   A $20

   B $30

   C $50

   D $60

16. Ben says the product of 2 and 5 is 8. Is his answer reasonable? Choose the best explanation.

   A Yes. When you multiply by 2, the ones digit of the product could be 8.

   B No. When you multiply by 5, the ones digit of the product must be 0 or 5.

   C No. The sum of the digits of the product must be a multiple of 5.

   D None of the above reasons is correct.

---

14. Amy arranged her counters into an array. Which number sentence shows how Amy's array can be broken into smaller arrays?

   A $(3 \times 9) = (3 \times 3) + (3 \times 3)$

   B $(3 \times 9) = (1 \times 9) + (2 \times 9)$

   C $(3 \times 9) = (1 \times 9) + (3 \times 9)$

   D $(3 \times 9) = (3 \times 9) + (9 \times 9)$

17. Vance has 6 pencils. He has 8 times as many markers. Which number sentence can you use to find how many markers Vance has? Use the strip diagram to help.

   A $6 \times 6 = 36$

   B $6 \times 8 = 48$

   C $6 \times 9 = 54$

   D $8 \times 8 = 64$

---

15. April lives on a farm that has 4 sheep. The farm has 5 times as many chickens as sheep. How many chickens and sheep are on the farm?

   A 16

   B 20

   C 24

   D 25

18. Haley said, "I used a multiplication property to find $39 \times 1 = 39$." Which property of multiplication did Haley use?

   A Identity (One) Property of Multiplication

   B Zero Property of Multiplication

   C Distributive Property

   D Associative (Grouping) Property of Multiplication

19. Ed said, "I am thinking of a number that is a multiple of both 2 and 5." Which of the following numbers could be Ed's number?

A 15

B 16

C 25

D 30

20. Alex has 5 dimes in his pocket. How much money does Alex have?

21. Art has 4 stacks of paper. There are 8 sheets of paper in each stack. How many sheets of paper does Art have? Mark your answer in the grid below.

22. Mrs. Kinne wrote 4 number sentences on the board. Which of Mrs. Kinne's number sentences shows the Associative (Grouping) Property of Multiplication?

A $4 \times 8 = (2 \times 8) + (2 \times 8)$

B $4 \times 8 \times 1 = 4 \times 8$

C $(4 \times 8) \times 3 = 4 \times (8 \times 3)$

D $4 \times 8 \times 0 = 0$

23. Adam wrote an equation. Fill in the blank to make Adam's equation true.
$(3 \times 4) + (3 \times 4) = $ _____.

24. Jake has 7 times as many tools this year as he had last year. Last year Jake had 2 tools. How many tools does Jake have this year? Mark your answer in the grid below.

© Pearson Education, Inc. 3

TOPIC
6

Meanings of Division

Essential Question: What are different meanings of division, including how division is related to other operations?

We depend on energy in its many forms every day.

Did you know that both living and non-living things use energy?

I need energy just to think about that! Here's a project on energy use and division.

Math and Science Project: Energy Everywhere

Do Research There is energy all around us, and there are many types of energy. For example, electrical energy helps run an escalator. Use the Internet or another resource to look up the types of energy. Give examples for each type of energy.

Journal: Write a Report Include what you found. Also in your report:

• Make a list of the things in your home that use energy. Be sure to include the type of energy each one uses.

• Make up and solve division problems based on your list. Draw strip diagrams and write equations.

Review What You Know

Vocabulary

Choose the best term from the box. Write it on the blank.

> - The Identity Property of Multiplication
> - The Zero Property of Multiplication
> - The Distributive Property
> - The Associative Property of Multiplication

1. _____ says that a multiplication fact can be broken apart into the sum of two other multiplication facts.

2. _____
   _____ says that when you multiply a number and 1, the product is that number.

3. _____
   _____ says that you can change the grouping of the factors and the product will be the same.

Multiplying with 0 and 1

Find each product.

4. $6 \times 0 =$ _____   5. $6 \times 1 =$ _____

6. $10 \times 1 =$ _____   7. $10 \times 0 =$ _____

8. $11 \times 1 =$ _____   9. $11 \times 0 =$ _____

10 as a Factor

Find each product.

10. $3 \times 10 =$ _____   11. $8 \times 10 =$ _____

12. **Reason** Paul has only dimes in his bank. Could he have exactly 55 cents?

13. Alex bought 9 tickets to a play. Each ticket costs $10. Which equation shows the total cost of the tickets Alex bought?

    A $9 + 10 = \$19$
    B $9 \times 10 = \$90$
    C $4 \times 10 = \$40$
    D $4 + 10 = \$14$

The Distributive Property

14. **Explain** Steve broke an array into two smaller arrays. The two smaller arrays show 1×4 and 4×4. What was the array that Steve started with?

© Pearson Education, Inc. 3

My Word Cards

Use the examples for each word on the front of the card to help complete the definitions on the back.

A-Z

division

$$12 \div 3 = 4$$

Total   Number of equal groups   Number in each group

My Word Cards

Complete each definition. Extend learning by writing your own definitions.

_____ is an operation that tells how many equal groups there are or how many are in each group.

© Pearson Education, Inc. 3

Name _____

Solve & Share

Four friends picked 20 apples. They want to share them equally. How many apples should each person get? *Solve this problem any way you choose.*

⭐ **TEKS 3.4H** Determine the number of objects in each group when a set of objects is partitioned into equal shares or a set of objects is shared equally. Also, 3.4K, 3.5B.
Mathematical Process Standards 3.1A, 3.1B, 3.1C, 3.1D, 3.1E, 3.1G

Digital Resources at PearsonTexas.com

Solve   Learn   Glossary   Check   Tools   Games

You can **create and use representations.** Drawing a picture that represents the problem can help you solve it. *Show your work!*

Look Back!

Draw a Picture How can you use a picture to show how the counters helped you solve this problem?

A

Three friends have 12 toys to share equally. How many toys will each friend get?

Think of arranging 12 toys into 3 equal groups.

Division is an operation that is used to find how many equal groups there are or how many are in each group.

B

What You Think

Put one toy at a time in each group.

12 toys

↑
4 toys for each friend

When all the toys are grouped, there will be 4 in each group.

C

What You Write

You can write a division sentence to find the number in each group.

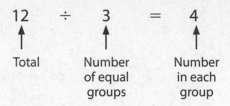

$$12 \div 3 = 4$$

Total — Number of equal groups — Number in each group

Each friend will get 4 toys.

Do You Understand?

Convince Me! What would happen if 3 friends tried to share 13 toys equally?

© Pearson Education, Inc. 3

Name _____

☆ Guided Practice *

In **1** through **3**, draw a picture to solve.

1. 15 bananas are divided equally into 3 boxes. How many bananas are in each box?

2. 16 plants are divided equally into 4 pots. How many plants are in each pot?

3. 20 kids are divided equally into 5 cars. How many kids are in each car?

4. Represent 18 eggs are divided into 3 rows. How many eggs are in each row? Solve the equation. Use the strip diagram to solve.

18

?	?	?

$18 \div 3 =$ _____

5. Explain Can 12 grapes be shared equally among 5 children with no grapes remaining? Why or why not?

Independent Practice ☆

Leveled Practice In **6** and **7**, draw a picture to solve.

6. 18 marbles are divided equally into 6 sacks. How many marbles are in each sack?

7. 16 crayons are shared equally by 2 people. How many crayons does each person have?

In **8** through **11**, complete each equation.

8. $12 \div 2 =$ ☐

12

?	?

9. $16 \div 8 =$ ☐

16

?	?	?	?	?	?	?	?

10. $9 \div 3 =$ _____

11. $14 \div 7 =$ _____

Problem Solving

12. Max has the stickers shown at the right. He wants to put an equal number of stickers on each of 2 posters. Which shows how to find the number of stickers Max should put on each poster?

Max has 14 stickers.

A $14 + 2 = ?$

B $14 \times 2 = ?$

C $14 - 2 = ?$

D $14 \div 2 = ?$

13. Construct Arguments Jim is putting 18 pens into equal groups. He says there will be more pens in each of 2 equal groups than in each of 3 equal groups. Is Jim correct? Explain.

14. Reason Ms. Terry's class is hosting a fundraising challenge. The students in her class are divided into 4 teams. Each team has an equal number of students. Do you have enough information to find how many students are on each team? Explain.

15. Represent Erika draws a hexagon. Maria draws a pentagon. Who draws the shape with more sides? How many more sides does that shape have?

16. Number Sense The flag bearers in a parade march in 9 rows with 5 people in each row. Each person is carrying 1 flag. Write a number sentence to show how many flags there are.

17. Justify Andrew is solving the problem $30 \div 6$. He reasons that, because 6 is twice as big as 3, then $30 \div 6$ must be twice as big as $30 \div 3$. What mistake is Andrew making?

18. Extend Your Thinking Joy has 12 shells. She gives 2 shells to her mom. Then she and her sister share the other shells equally. How many shells does Joy get? How many shells does her sister get? How do you know?

© Pearson Education, Inc. 3

Another Look!

A.J. has 15 T-shirts. He sorted them equally into 5 laundry bins. How many T-shirts did A.J. put in each bin? You can use a strip diagram to solve.

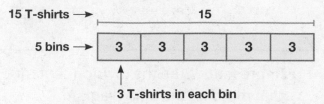

15 T-shirts → 15

5 bins → | 3 | 3 | 3 | 3 | 3 |

↑
3 T-shirts in each bin

There are 15 T-shirts. There are 5 groups.
There are 3 T-shirts in each group.
So, $15 \div 5 = 3$.

A.J. put 3 T-shirts in each laundry bin.

Division can show how many items are in each group.

For **1**, use the strip diagram to help divide.

1. There are 12 tennis balls that need to be packaged equally into 4 cans.
   How many tennis balls will be in each can?

   12 tennis balls → 12

   4 cans → | ? | ? | ? | ? |

   ↑
   ? tennis balls in each can

   There are ____ tennis balls.

   There are ____ groups.

   There are ____ tennis balls in each group.

   $12 \div$ ____ = ____

For **2** through **7**, put an equal number of objects in each group. Use counters or draw a picture to solve.

2. Sort 16 apples equally into 2 baskets. How many apples are in each basket?

3. Arrange 20 chairs equally at 4 tables. How many chairs are at each table?

4. 7 rabbits share 21 carrots equally. How many carrots does each rabbit get?

5. 25 dimes shared by 5 children. How many dimes for each child?

6. Divide 14 books equally on 2 shelves. How many books are on each shelf?

7. 24 people divide among 3 elevators equally. How many people are in each elevator?

8. **Explain** Can you divide 14 shirts into 2 equal piles? Why or why not?

9. **Connect** In February 1981, there were ⭐ 28 days, all in complete weeks. There are 7 days in a complete week. How many weeks were there in February 1981?

    A 3   **C** 5
    B 4   **D** 7

10. **Communicate** Ron and Pam each have 20 pennies. Ron puts his pennies into 4 equal groups. Pam puts her pennies into 5 equal groups. Who has more pennies in each group? Explain.

11. **Represent** Write the division sentence that matches the strip diagram.

		16	
?	?	?	?

12. There are 90 third-grade students and 72 fourth-grade students at Johnsonville Elementary. Write and solve a number sentence to show how many more third graders there are than fourth graders. Then write and solve a number sentence to show the total number of students.

13. **Extend Your Thinking** Kyra has a rock collection. When she puts her rocks into 2 equal piles, there are no rocks left over. When she puts her rocks into 3 equal piles, there are still no rocks left over. When she puts her rocks into 4 equal piles, there are still no rocks left over. How many rocks could Kyra have?

14. **Formulate a Plan** Sam, Clara, and Dylan are each going to make a necklace. They will divide the beads equally. Look at the table on the right. How will you find how many beads each person receives for his or her necklace? Are any beads left over?

Beads for Necklaces

Color	Number
Blue	5
Red	9
White	12

© Pearson Education, Inc. 3

Name _____

☆ ★ ☆
Solve & Share

Li made 12 tacos. He wants to give some of his friends 2 tacos each. If Li does not get any of the tacos, how many of his friends will get tacos? *Solve this problem any way you choose.*

⭐ **TEKS 3.4H** Determine the number of objects in each group when a set of objects is partitioned into equal shares or a set of objects is shared equally. Also, 3.4K, 3.5B.
Mathematical Process Standards 3.1A, 3.1B, 3.1C, 3.1D, 3.1G

Digital Resources at PearsonTexas.com

Solve   Learn   Glossary   Check   Tools   Games

You can use **number sense.** How can what you know about sharing help you solve the problem? *Show your work in the space below!*

Look Back!

Tools How can counters or drawings help you show your work?

How Can You Divide Using Repeated Subtraction?

A

June has 10 strawberries to serve to her guests. If each guest eats 2 strawberries, how many guests can June serve?

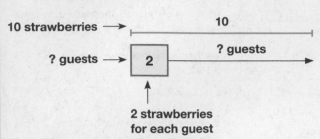

10 strawberries → |—————— 10 ——————|

? guests → [**2**] ? guests →

↑
2 strawberries
for each guest

B ## One Way

You can use repeated subtraction to find how many groups of 2 are in 10.

$10 - 2 = 8$
$8 - 2 = 6$
$6 - 2 = 4$
$4 - 2 = 2$
$2 - 2 = 0$

You can subtract 2 five times. There are five groups of 2 in 10.

There are no strawberries left.

June can serve 5 guests.

C ## Another Way

You can write a division equation to find the number of groups.

Write: $10 \div 2 = ?$

Read: Ten divided by 2 equals what number?

Solve: $10 \div 2 = 5$

June can serve 5 guests.

Do You Understand?

Convince Me! In the example above, what if each guest ate 5 strawberries? How many guests could June serve? Write and solve a division equation, use repeated subtraction, or draw a strip diagram to solve the problem.

© Pearson Education, Inc. 3

☆ Guided Practice *

In **1** and **2**, use counters or draw a picture to solve.

1. The bell choir has 16 gloves. There are 2 gloves in each pair. How many pairs of gloves are there?

2. Ruth has 15 dog treats. She gives each of her dogs 3 treats. How many dogs does Ruth have?

3. **Explain** Show how you can use repeated subtraction to find how many groups of 4 there are in 20. Then write the division sentence for the problem.

Independent Practice ☆

Leveled Practice In **4** through **7**, use counters or draw a picture to solve.

4. Ruth picked 8 apples. She placed 4 apples in each bag. How many bags did Ruth have?

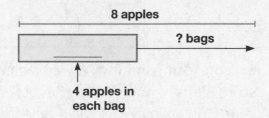

8 apples

? bags

4 apples in each bag

5. The wagons on the farm have 4 wheels each. There are 12 wheels. How many wagons are on the farm?

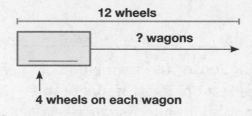

12 wheels

? wagons

4 wheels on each wagon

6. Shirley bought 30 markers that came in packages of 5 markers each. How many packages did Shirley buy?

7. Marcus had 18 pencils. He distributed 2 pencils to each desk. How many desks are there?

Problem Solving

For **8** and **9**, use the table at the right.

8. Analyze Information The chart shows the amount of money three friends have in their pockets. If Jenna has only nickels in her pockets, how many nickels does she have?

9. If Zoe has 5 coins in her pocket, what coins does she have?

Money in Pockets	
Claudia	78 cents
Zoe	42 cents
Jenna	35 cents

10. Communicate Raymond has 16 model planes that he wants to display. Will he need more shelves if he puts 8 planes on a shelf or 4 planes on a shelf? Explain.

11. To solve a problem in her math book, Jacqui writes the following:

$$24 - 8 = 16$$
$$16 - 8 = 8$$
$$8 - 8 = 0$$

Which problem is Jacqui trying to solve?

A $24 \div 8$ C $24 - 16$

B $24 \div 6$ D 24×3

12. Number Sense The population of College Station, Texas, is ninety-three thousand, eight hundred fifty-seven. Write the number in standard form.

13. Extend Your Thinking An ice cream store plans to make 8 new flavors each year. How many years will it take for the store to make 80 flavors? Write and solve an equation.

14. Personal Financial Literacy Kiara owed Hazel $20. She paid Hazel back in 5 months. If she gave Hazel the same amount of money each month, how much did Kiara pay back each month?

You can draw a strip diagram to help you solve!

© Pearson Education, Inc. 3

Name _____

Another Look!

Layla has 20 raffle tickets.
There are 5 tickets in each book.
How many books of raffle tickets
does Layla have? Find $20 \div 5 = \boxed{}$.

$\left.\begin{array}{l} 20 - 5 = 15 \\ 15 - 5 = 10 \\ 10 - 5 = 5 \\ 5 - 5 = 0 \end{array}\right\}$ There are four groups of 5 in 20.

Subtract 5 tickets each time.

You subtracted 5 four times. So, $20 \div 5 = 4$.

Layla has 4 books of raffle tickets.

In **1**, use repeated subtraction to help you solve.

1. Ryan has 10 markers.
   There are 5 markers in each box.
   How many boxes of markers are there?
   Find $10 \div 5 = \boxed{}$.

   $10 - 5 = $ _____

   $5 - $ _____ $ = $ _____

   You subtracted 5 two times.

   So, _____ $\div$ _____ $=$ _____.

   Ryan has _____ boxes of markers.

In **2** and **3**, use strip diagrams or counters or draw a picture to solve.

2. There are 16 books. The librarian arranged
   4 books on each shelf. How many shelves
   are there?

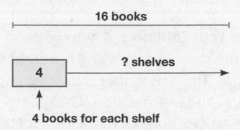

   16 books

   4   ? shelves

   4 books for each shelf

3. Joseph had 28 paintbrushes to give to
   4 members of the Art Club. He wanted to
   give an equal number of brushes to each
   member. How many brushes did each
   member get?

4. Daniel has to carry 32 boxes to his room. He can carry 4 boxes on each trip. How many trips will Daniel take?

A 6
B 7
C 8
D 9

5. Reason The store clerk has 21 mugs to display on shelves. Will she need more shelves if she puts 7 mugs on a shelf or 3 on a shelf? Explain.

6. Construct Arguments Tamara says that $20 \div 5 = 4$. Is she correct? Use repeated subtraction to explain your answer.

7. Connect The United States Mint released five state quarters every year. There are 50 states. How many years did it take for all 50 state quarters to be released? Write and solve an equation.

8. Use a Strip Diagram Write a division sentence that represents the strip diagram below.

40				
8	8	8	8	8

9. Justify Derek is thinking of a number. When he rounds his number to the nearest 10, he gets 580. When he rounds his number to the nearest 100, could he get 500? Why or why not?

10. Extend Your Thinking A newspaper has more than 30 pages and fewer than 40 pages. The newspaper is divided into sections, and each section has 8 pages. How many sections does the newspaper have?

© Pearson Education, Inc. 3

Name _____

Find 18 ÷ 3 any way you choose.

You can **connect ideas.** How can you use what you know about multiplication to help you find 18 ÷ 3?

Lesson 6-3
Finding Missing Numbers in a Multiplication Table

⭐ **TEKS 3.4J** Determine a quotient using the relationship between multiplication and division. Also, 3.4K, 3.5D.
Mathematical Process Standards 3.1A, 3.1C, 3.1D, 3.1F, 3.1G

Digital Resources at PearsonTexas.com

Solve   Learn   Glossary   Check   Tools   Games

×	0	1	2	3	4	5	6	7	8	9	10
0	0	0	0	0	0	0	0	0	0	0	0
1	0	1	2	3	4	5	6	7	8	9	10
2	0	2	4	6	8	10	12	14	16	18	20
3	0	3	6	9	12	15	18	21	24	27	30
4	0	4	8	12	16	20	24	28	32	36	40
5	0	5	10	15	20	25	30	35	40	45	50
6	0	6	12	18	24	30	36	42	48	54	60
7	0	7	14	21	28	35	42	49	56	63	70
8	0	8	16	24	32	40	48	56	64	72	80
9	0	9	18	27	36	45	54	63	72	81	90
10	0	10	20	30	40	50	60	70	80	90	100

Look Back!

Connect Describe how you can use multiplication to find 18 ÷ 3.

How Can You Use a Multiplication Table to Solve Division Problems?

Write a missing factor equation and then use the multiplication table to find 15 ÷ 3.

×	0	1	2	3	4	5
0	0	0	0	0	0	0
1	0	1	2	3	4	5
2	0	2	4	6	8	10
3	0	3	6	9	12	15

$15 ÷ 3 = ?$

$3 × ? = 15$

3 times what number equals 15?

You can use a multiplication table to solve a division problem.

B Step 1

You know one factor is 3. Find the 3 in the first column of this multiplication table.

×	0	1	2	3	4	5
0	0	0	0	0	0	0
1	0	1	2	3	4	5
2	0	2	4	6	8	10
3	0	3	6	9	12	15

C Step 2

You know the product is 15. Follow the row the 3 is in until you come to 15.

×	0	1	2	3	4	5
0	0	0	0	0	0	0
1	0	1	2	3	4	5
2	0	2	4	6	8	10
3	0	3	6	9	12	15

D Step 3

Look straight up to the top of that column of the table. The number on the top of the column is 5. The missing factor is 5.

$3 × 5 = 15$ $15 ÷ 3 = 5$

×	0	1	2	3	4	5
0	0	0	0	0	0	0
1	0	1	2	3	4	5
2	0	2	4	6	8	10
3	0	3	6	9	12	15

Do You Understand?

Convince Me! Write a missing factor equation and use the multiplication table above to solve each division problem.

$6 ÷ 3 = ?$ $12 ÷ 3 = ?$ $9 ÷ 3 = ?$

© Pearson Education, Inc. 3

Name _____

☆ **Guided Practice**

In **1** through **8**, find the value that makes the equation true. Use the multiplication table on page 357 to help.

1. 24 ÷ 6 = ____
6 × ____ = 24

2. 63 ÷ 9 = ____
9 × ____ = 63

3. 25 ÷ 5 = ____
5 × ____ = 25

4. 42 ÷ 7 = ____
7 × ____ = 42

5. 45 ÷ 5 = ____
5 × ____ = 45

6. 15 ÷ 3 = ____
3 × ____ = 15

7. 12 ÷ 6 = ____
6 × ____ = 12

8. 40 ÷ 5 = ____
5 × ____ = 40

9. Tools Where on a multiplication table do you find the two factors in a multiplication problem?

10. Communicate How can you rephrase 35 ÷ 7 so you can solve it with a multiplication table?

11. Explain Explain how to use a multiplication table to solve a missing factor equation.

☆ **Independent Practice** ☆

Leveled Practice For **12** through **23**, find the value that makes the equations true. Use the multiplication table on page 357 to help.

12. 45 ÷ 9 = ____
9 × ____ = 45

13. 21 ÷ 3 = ____
3 × ____ = 21

14. 36 ÷ 6 = ____
6 × ____ = 36

15. 32 ÷ 4 = ____
4 × ____ = 32

16. 20 ÷ 5 = ____
5 × ____ = 20

17. 21 ÷ 7 = ____
7 × ____ = 21

18. 18 ÷ 9 = ____

19. 35 ÷ 5 = ____

20. 56 ÷ 8 = ____

21. 28 ÷ 4 = ____

22. 14 ÷ 7 = ____

23. 40 ÷ 5 = ____

Problem Solving

24. Connect Some members of the Bird Club used a tally chart to record how many different birds they each saw one day. Fill in the blanks below to make the sentence true. Then complete the chart to show that Mr. Molina saw 6 more species of birds than Mr. Dobbs.

_____ saw 4 more species

of birds than _____.

Number of Different Birds Seen	
Ms. Chester	THI II
Mr. Dobbs	IIII
Miss Simmons	THI THI I
Mr. Molina	_____

25. Justify Bill used a multiplication table to find the value of 12 ÷ 6. His answer was 3. Do you agree? Why or why not?

×	0	1	2	3	4	5	6	7
0	0	0	0	0	0	0	0	0
1	0	1	2	3	4	5	6	7
2	0	2	4	6	8	10	12	14
3	0	3	6	9	12	15	18	21
4	0	4	8	12	16	20	24	28
5	0	5	10	15	20	25	30	35
6	0	6	12	18	24	30	36	42
7	0	7	14	21	28	35	42	49
8	0	8	16	24	32	40	48	56
9	0	9	18	27	36	45	54	63

26. Find the value that makes the equation true.

$30 \div$ ____ $= 5$

27. Reason ★ Find the 2-digit odd numbers in a multiplication table. What is true about the factors of all of these numbers?

A They are all even.

B They are all odd.

C Some of them are odd and some of them are even.

D They are all greater than 5.

28. Write 2 division facts and two multiplication facts using the numbers 7, 6, and 42.

You can use the multiplication table to help you solve.

29. Extend Your Thinking Mr. Baker had a basket of apples. He made 5 pies with the apples. He used 5 apples to make each pie. When he was done, he had 3 apples left over. How many apples were in the basket before Mr. Baker started baking?

© Pearson Education, Inc. 3

Another Look!

Find 24 ÷ 6.

You can think of a division problem as a multiplication fact with a missing factor.

missing factor

A. Find the factor you already know in the first column of the table. In **6 × ? = 24**, that factor is **6**.

B. Go across the row until you get to the product. In 6 × ? = **24**, the product is **24**.

C. Go straight to the top of that column. The number at the top of the column is 4. So, the missing factor is 4. 24 ÷ 6 = 4

×	0	1	2	3	4
0	0	0	0	0	0
1	0	1	2	3	4
2	0	2	4	6	8
3	0	3	6	9	12
4	0	4	8	12	16
5	0	5	10	15	20
6	0	6	12	18	**24**

factor   product

For **1** through **15**, find the value that makes the equations true. Use the multiplication table on page 357 to help.

1. 8 ÷ 2 = _____

2 × _____ = 8

2. 12 ÷ 4 = _____

4 × _____ = 12

3. 16 ÷ 8 = _____

8 × _____ = 16

4. 18 ÷ 6 = _____

6 × _____ = 18

5. 27 ÷ 3 = _____

3 × _____ = 27

6. 36 ÷ 4 = _____

4 × _____ = 36

7. 48 ÷ 8 = _____

8 × _____ = 48

8. 35 ÷ 7 = _____

7 × _____ = 35

9. 30 ÷ 5 = _____

5 × _____ = 30

10. 24 ÷ 8 = _____

11. 49 ÷ 7 = _____

12. 54 ÷ 6 = _____

13. 14 ÷ 2 = _____

14. 24 ÷ 3 = _____

15. 32 ÷ 8 = _____

16. Explain Christina has these two tiles. Draw a new shape she can create with the tiles. Then name the shape and how many sides the new shape has.

17. There are 3 drawers in Mona's dresser. Each drawer has the same number of shirts. Mona has 27 shirts. How many shirts are in each drawer?

For **18** through **20**, use the multiplication table at the right.

18. A pet shop has 24 fish in 8 tanks, with an equal number of fish in each tank. Which multiplication fact can you use to find how many fish are in each tank?

A $2 \times 4 = 8$

B $4 \times 6 = 24$

C $8 \times 3 = 24$

D $9 \times 8 = 72$

×	0	1	2	3	4	5	6	7
0	0	0	0	0	0	0	0	0
1	0	1	2	3	4	5	6	7
2	0	2	4	6	8	10	12	14
3	0	3	6	9	12	15	18	21
4	0	4	8	12	16	20	24	28
5	0	5	10	15	20	25	30	35
6	0	6	12	18	24	30	36	42
7	0	7	14	21	28	35	42	49
8	0	8	16	24	32	40	48	56
9	0	9	18	27	36	45	54	63

19. Math and Science Together 3 new homes have 18 solar panels. There is an equal number of panels on each home. How many solar panels does each home have? Explain how to use the multiplication table to solve the problem.

20. Extend Your Thinking Hana uses the multiplication table to find the value of $\square$ in $49 \div 7 = \square$. She says the answer is 6. Is Hana correct? Why or why not?

For **21** and **22**, use the graph at the right.

21. Make a Graph Ethan went to the farmers market. He bought 5 pears, 2 apples, and 4 peaches. Use this information to complete the bar graph.

22. How many pieces of fruit did Ethan buy?

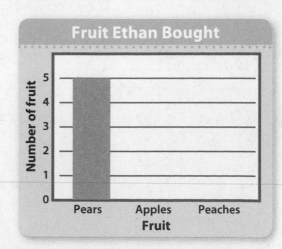

© Pearson Education, Inc. 3

Name _____

Solve & Share

Write a real-world division story for 8 ÷ 2. Then write another real-world story that shows a different way to think about division.

You can **communicate.** How can the words in the story help you solve 8 ÷ 2?

⭐ **TEKS 3.4K** Solve ... problems involving ... division within 100 using strategies based on objects; pictorial models, including arrays, ... and equal groups; properties of operations; or recall of facts. Also, 3.4, 3.5B.
Mathematical Process Standards 3.1B, 3.1C, 3.1D, 3.1E, 3.1G

Digital Resources at PearsonTexas.com

 Solve   Learn   **A-Z** Glossary   Check   Tools   Games

Look Back!

Use a Strip Diagram Draw a strip diagram that can be used with your division story.

A

Mrs. White asked her students to write a division story for 15 ÷ 3.

Mike and Kia decided to write stories about putting roses in vases.

Mike's Story	**Kia's Story**

B I have 15 roses. I want to put an equal number of roses in each of 3 vases. How many roses should I put in each vase?

Find $15 ÷ 3 = \boxed{}$.

15 roses

3 vases → | 5 | 5 | 5 |

↑
5 roses in each vase

$15 ÷ 3 = 5$

I should put 5 roses in each vase.

The main idea is "How many are in each group?"

The main idea is "How many groups are there?"

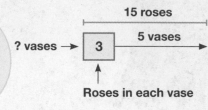

C I have 15 roses to put into vases. I want to put 3 roses in each vase. How many vases will I need?

Find $15 ÷ 3 = \boxed{}$.

15 roses

? vases → | 3 | 5 vases →

↑
Roses in each vase

$15 ÷ 3 = 5$

I will need 5 vases.

Do You Understand?

Convince Me! How are Mike's and Kia's stories alike? How are the two stories different?

© Pearson Education, Inc. 3

☆ **Guided Practice** ☆

In **1** through **3,** plan a division story for the equation. Then, write the story.

1. $8 \div 4 =$ _____

I will write about 8 _____.
They will be in 4 equal groups.

2. $10 \div 2 =$ _____

3. $20 \div 5 =$ _____

4. Formulate a Plan When you write a division story, what two pieces of information do you need to include?

5. When you write a division story, what kind of information do you ask for?

☆ **Independent Practice** ☆

Leveled Practice In **6** through **9,** plan and write a division story for each equation. Then use counters or draw a picture to solve.

6. $18 \div 3 =$ _____

I will write about 18 _____.
I will put them in 3 equal groups.

7. $14 \div$ _____ $= 2$

8. $24 \div 8 =$ _____

9. $30 \div$ _____ $= 3$

Problem Solving

For **10** through **13**, use the table at the right. There are 36 third-graders who want to play on different teams.

10. Represent If all the third-graders want to play baseball, how many teams will there be?

DATA

Sports Team	Number
Baseball	9 players
Basketball	5 players
Doubles Tennis	2 players

11. Can half of the 36 third-graders play baseball and the other half play doubles tennis without any students left over?

12. ★ Suppose that 20 third-graders went swimming and the rest played doubles tennis. How many doubles tennis teams would there be?

A 16
B 10
C 8
D 6

13. Explain Could all 36 third-graders play in basketball games at the same time? Explain your answer.

14. Extend Your Thinking Hector wrote this division story problem to go with the division sentence 24 ÷ 4:

"There are 24 bears in the woods. Each bear has 4 legs. How many legs are on all the bears in the woods?"

What mistake did Hector make? Explain.

15. Number Sense Steve cares for 18 cats at a shelter. If he places 3 cats in each playpen, how many playpens will Steve need? Write and solve a division equation.

16. Personal Financial Literacy Kara earned $40 babysitting. She deposited $25 in the bank and spent the rest on activity books. How many activity books did Kara buy?

$3 each

© Pearson Education, Inc. 3

Name _____

Another Look!

Eddie was asked to write a division story using $12 \div 4 = \square$.

This is Eddie's story:

Cami has 12 crayons and some cans.
She puts 4 crayons into each can.
How many cans did Cami use?

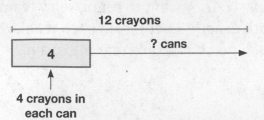

12 crayons

? cans

4

4 crayons in each can

You can draw a picture to show Eddie's story this way.

$12 \div 4 = 3$. So Cami used 3 cans.

In **1** and **2**, write the missing information and plan a division story for each equation. Write the story. Use counters or draw a picture to solve.

1. $10 \div \underline{\hspace{0.5cm}} = 5$

I will write about 10 _____.
I will put them in groups of 5.

2. $21 \div 7 = \underline{\hspace{0.5cm}}$

I will write about 21 _____.
I will put them in 7 equal groups.

In **3** through **6**, write a division story for each equation. Use counters or draw a picture to solve.

3. $48 \div 6 = \underline{\hspace{0.5cm}}$

4. $56 \div \underline{\hspace{0.5cm}} = 8$

5. $36 \div \underline{\hspace{0.5cm}} = 9$

6. $49 \div 7 = \underline{\hspace{0.5cm}}$

7. Reason Sheila wrote a division story. She wrote about how to divide 24 flowers into equal groups. What information must she give about the groups?

8. Draw a Picture Write a division story for the equation $36 \div 9 = \square$. Then use counters or draw a picture to solve.

9. Check for Reasonableness ⭐ Angela rides her bike to school 3 to 5 times a week. What is a good estimate of the number of times Angela rides her bike to school in 4 weeks?

A More than 28
B From 12 to 20
C From 6 to 10
D Less than 6

10. Communicate There are 16 people at a party. They want to set up relay teams with exactly 3 people on each team. Will each person be on a team? Explain.

11. Tools Vera uses place-value blocks to model adding two numbers. What addition sentence can Vera write using this model?

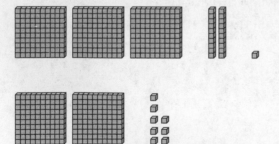

12. Write a division story for $16 \div 8$. Draw a strip diagram for your story.

13. Extend Your Thinking Complete the sentences with numbers that make sense. Do not use the number 1. Then write the division sentence that matches the story, and draw to solve.

"There are 35 rabbits at the fair. The rabbits are kept in _____ hutches with _____ rabbits in each hutch."

State Fair
35 Rabbits on Display!

© Pearson Education, Inc. 3

Name _____

Solve & Share

Kenny handed out 24 crayons to the 4 students at his table. Each student receives the same number of crayons. How many crayons should each student get? Write an equation to help you solve the problem. *Solve this problem any way you choose.*

You can **create and use representations.** Remember, you can use a symbol such as ? to represent an unknown in your equation. *Show your work in the space below!*

TEKS 3.1D Communicate mathematical ideas, reasoning, and their implications using multiple representations, … as appropriate. Also, 3.5B.
Mathematical Process Standards 3.1B, 3.1C, 3.1D, 3.1E, 3.1F, 3.1G

Digital Resources at PearsonTexas.com

Solve   Learn   Glossary   Check   Tools   Games

Look Back!

Connect Is there more than one equation possible? Use what you know about addition, subtraction, multiplication, and division to write another equation.

Analyze

How Can You Use a Strip Diagram and an Equation to Solve a Problem?

Kara handed out 12 sheets of paper equally to the 6 students at her table. How many sheets of paper did each student get?

You can write an equation and draw a strip diagram to find how many sheets of paper each student got.

Plan

Draw a strip diagram to show what you know.

12 sheets ⟶ | 12 |

6 students ⟶ | ? | ? | ? | ? | ? | ? |

↑

? sheets for each student

You know how many in all and the number of groups.

You need to find the size of each group.

A strip diagram shows division as sharing.

Solve

Write an equation for your strip diagram. Then solve.

$12 \div 6 = \boxed{}$

Because $6 \times 2 = 12$, then $12 \div 6 = 2$.

Each student got 2 sheets of paper.

Do You Understand?

Convince Me! Suppose Kara had the same 12 sheets of paper to hand out, but each student needs 3 sheets of paper for an art project. Will Kara have enough paper for the 6 students at her table? Draw a strip diagram and write an equation to explain your thinking.

 © Pearson Education, Inc. 3

Name _____

In **1**, use the strip diagram and complete the sentences. Then write an equation to solve the problem.

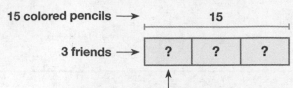

15 colored pencils ⟶   15

3 friends ⟶ | ? | ? | ? |

↑
? colored pencils for each friend

1. Kayla has 15 colored pencils to give equally to 3 friends. How many colored pencils will each friend get?

   There are ____ colored pencils. Kayla puts the colored pencils into ____ equal groups.

   Each friend gets ____ colored pencils.

2. **Explain** Explain how you can use the strip diagram to help you solve Exercise 1.

3. Robert has 18 muffins to share equally with 6 friends. How many muffins will each friend get? Draw a strip diagram and write an equation to solve.

Independent Practice ☆

Leveled Practice In **4** through **7**, Draw a strip diagram and write an equation to solve.

4. There are 18 students in Ms. Muhammad's class. She divides them into teams of 6. How many teams are there?

5. There are 32 actors in the play. Each scene is played out by 4 different actors. How many scenes are in the play?

6. Mya has a book of 12 crossword puzzles. She solves the same number of puzzles each day for 4 days. Then she is done with the book. How many puzzles does Mya solve each day?

7. Padma is playing a game that has 42 levels. She completes the same number of levels each day for 6 days. Then she is done with the game. How many levels does Padma complete each day?

Problem Solving

8. Represent Draw a strip diagram and write an equation to solve. Mario has 14 socks. He puts them in pairs. How many pairs does Mario have?

9. Draw a strip diagram and write an equation to solve. Glenda has 24 water bottles to distribute equally to 6 marathon runners. How many water bottles should each runner receive?

10. Represent Draw a strip diagram and write an equation to solve. There are 14 chairs. Henry puts the chairs into 2 equal rows. How many chairs are in each row?

11. Julia has 114 bracelets. 57 of them are gold. How many bracelets are not gold?

114 bracelets →

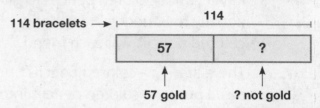

12. Mental Math Molly wants to make one array with 4 rows of 7 tiles and another array with 6 rows of 3 tiles. How many tiles does Molly need?

13. Justify Gregory drew this diagram to model the equation $36 \div \square = 4$. What error did Gregory make?

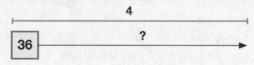

A He should replace 36 with 9.
B He should replace both numbers with 8.
C He should replace 4 with 9.
D He should switch the numbers.

14. Janet has a solid figure with 2 flat surfaces and 0 vertices. Circle the figure that Janet could have.

15. Extend Your Thinking Look at Exercises 8 and 10. How are the problems alike? How are they different?

© Pearson Education, Inc. 3

Name _____

Another Look!

Nora has 10 marbles. She puts the same number of marbles into 2 bags. How many marbles does she put in each bag? You need to find out how many in each group.

Draw a line and label it with the total.
You know there are 2 groups.
Draw 2 boxes of the same size to show that there are 2 groups.

Draw a picture to show what you know.

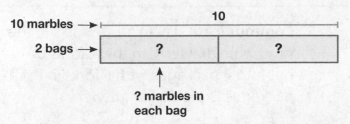

Write an equation. Then solve.

10 ÷ 2 = ?

Since 2 × 5 = 10, then 10 ÷ 2 = 5. Nora puts 5 marbles in each bag.

In **1** and **2**, write the equation to answer the question and solve.

1. Kali has 15 cards. She makes 3 stacks of cards with the same number of cards in each stack. How many cards are in each stack?

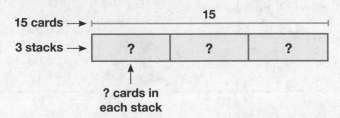

2. The pet shop has 25 fish. There are 5 fish in each tank. How many tanks are there? Draw a strip diagram.

3. **Use a Strip Diagram** Choose the strip diagram that shows the
★ problem. "Mr. Kay has 12 eggs. He uses them to make
omelets. Each omelet needs 4 eggs. How many omelets can he make?"

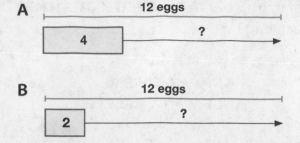

A
12 eggs
| 4 | ?

B
12 eggs
| 2 | ?

C
12 omelets
| ? | ? | ? | ? |

D
12 eggs
| ? | ? |

4. **Justify** Marco has 36 stamps. He puts
9 stamps on each page of an album.
How many pages has he filled so far?
Write an equation to show your answer.

5. **Communicate** There are 16 forks in the
silverware drawer. Can these forks be
put into 4 packages with 5 forks in each
package? Explain your answer.

6. The chart shows the populations of
Smallville and Largeburg when written in
word form. How many more people live
in Largeburg than in Smallville? Record
your answer in standard form.

7. Write the populations of Smallville and
Largeburg in expanded form.

Town	Population
Smallville	six thousand, nine hundred seven
Largeburg	twenty-one thousand, four hundred eighteen

8. **Extend Your Thinking** Use the numbers below to complete
the 3 equations. Use each number exactly once.

2   3   4   5   6   8   9   27   30

____ ÷ ____ = ____

____ ÷ ____ = ____

____ ÷ ____ = ____

© Pearson Education, Inc. 3

Name _____

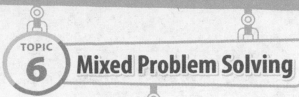

1. **Use a Strip Diagram** Scott has 20 apples to give equally to 5 friends. How many apples will each friend get? Write an equation that shows the problem.

20 apples

?	?	?	?	?

Applying Math Processes
- How does this problem connect to previous ones?
- What is my plan?
- How can I use tools?
- How can I use number sense?
- How can I communicate and represent my thinking?
- How can I organize and record information?
- How can I explain my work?
- How can I justify my answer?

2. **Explain** Allison has 10 hair ribbons. She gives 4 to her cousin. Then she and her sister share the rest equally. How many ribbons does Allison get? How many ribbons does her sister get?

3. **Reason** Lydia had a bouquet of flowers. There were 7 vases on the table. She put 3 flowers in each vase. When she was done, she had 3 flowers left. Before Lydia put the flowers in the vases, how many flowers were in the bouquet?

4. How are the 4s related in 44,268?

5. **Communicate** Use the multiplication table to explain how you could find the answer to $14 \div 2$.

×	0	1	2	3	4	5	6	7
0	0	0	0	0	0	0	0	0
1	0	1	2	3	4	5	6	7
2	0	2	4	6	8	10	12	14
3	0	3	6	9	12	15	18	21
4	0	4	8	12	16	20	24	28
5	0	5	10	15	20	25	30	35
6	0	6	12	18	24	30	36	42
7	0	7	14	21	28	35	42	49
8	0	8	16	24	32	40	48	56
9	0	9	18	27	36	45	54	63

6. **Extend Your Thinking** Derek has 12 swimming trophies that he wants to display. Will he need more shelves if he puts 4 on a shelf or 3 on a shelf? Show how you found the answer.

Error Search

For **1** through **4**, circle each problem that is not correct. Rewrite the problem so it is correct.

1. $28 \div 7 = 4$ | **2.** $40 \div 5 = 9$ | **3.** $36 \div 8 = 6$ | **4.** $63 \div 7 = 9$

Over or Under?

Estimation For **5** through **16**, circle the better estimate.

5. 23×9

over 170

under 170

6. 8×89

over 730

under 730

7. 3×67

over 190

under 190

8. 6×32

over 200

under 200

9. 75×5

over 410

under 410

10. 5×61

over 290

under 290

11. 58×2

over 100

under 100

12. 27×4

over 90

under 90

13. 6×81

over 500

under 500

14. 3×48

over 130

under 130

15. 88×5

over 460

under 460

16. 9×18

over 190

under 190

© Pearson Education, Inc. 3

Name _____

Set A pages 345–350

Jacqueline has 6 fruit snacks to share with 2 friends.

How many fruit snacks does each friend get if the friends share equally?

$6 \div 2 = 3$ fruit snacks

Bert bought 8 muffins that were in 4 packages.

How many muffins are in each package?

$8 \div 4 = 2$ muffins

Remember that division is an operation to find the number of equal groups or the number in each equal group.

| In **1** through **4**, divide to show equal groups. |

1. 4 sandwiches shared by 2 adults
   ☐ sandwiches

2. 9 raisin boxes shared by 3 children
   ☐ raisin boxes

3. $12 \div 2 =$ _____   4. $10 \div 5 =$ _____

Set B pages 351–356

Find $8 \div 2$. Use repeated subtraction.

$8 - 2 = 6$
$6 - 2 = 4$ You must subtract 2 from
$4 - 2 = 2$ 8 four times to reach zero.
$2 - 2 = 0$

$8 \div 2 = 4$

Remember that when you use repeated subtraction to divide, you should not stop subtracting until you reach zero.

| In **1** through **4**, solve by using repeated subtraction. |

1. $25 \div 5 =$ _____   2. $16 \div 4 =$ _____

3. $15 \div 5 =$ _____   4. $24 \div 4 =$ _____

Set C pages 357–362

Use a multiplication table to find $16 \div 4$.

×	0	1	2	3	4	5	6	7
0	0	0	0	0	0	0	0	0
1	0	1	2	3	4	5	6	7
2	0	2	4	6	8	10	12	14
3	0	3	6	9	12	15	18	21
4	0	4	8	12	16	20	24	28
5	0	5	10	15	20	25	30	35
6	0	6	12	18	24	30	36	42
7	0	7	14	21	28	35	42	49
8	0	8	16	24	32	40	48	56
9	0	9	18	27	36	45	54	63

Find 4 in the first column of the table.

Follow the 4s row until you come to 16.

Then look to the top of that column to find the missing factor: 4.

$16 \div 4 = 4$

Remember that you can rewrite a division problem as a multiplication problem.

| In **1** through **14**, find each quotient. Use the multiplication table. |

1. $20 \div 5 =$ _____   2. $28 \div 4 =$ _____

3. $32 \div 8 =$ _____   4. $48 \div 8 =$ _____

5. $49 \div 7 =$ _____   6. $54 \div 9 =$ _____

7. $63 \div 9 =$ _____   8. $56 \div 8 =$ _____

9. $45 \div 9 =$ _____   10. $40 \div 8 =$ _____

11. $35 \div 7 =$ _____   12. $36 \div 6 =$ _____

13. $30 \div 5 =$ _____   14. $9 \div 3 =$ _____

Write and solve the division equation shown by the story.

Mr. Kim had 24 apple slices. He wanted his 3 children to share the apple slices equally. How many apple slices should each child get?

$$24 \div 3 = \boxed{}$$
$$24 \div 3 = 8$$

Each child gets 8 apple slices.

Remember that the word *share* shows division.

In **1** and **2**, write and solve the division equation for each story. Find the quotient.

1. The workers at a seafood restaurant forgot to put 32 spoons on the customers' tables. If there should be 4 spoons on each table, how many tables are missing spoons?

2. Michael and two friends are playing with 15 toy cars. Each friend wants the same number of cars. How many cars should each friend get?

Linh bought 16 plums at a farmers market. She wants to give her 4 nieces an equal number of plums. How many plums should Linh give to each of her nieces?

You can write an equation and draw a strip diagram to solve a division problem.

$$16 \div 4 = \boxed{}$$

16 plums

| 4 | 4 | 4 | 4 |

$$16 \div 4 = 4$$

Each niece should receive 4 plums.

Remember that when drawing a strip diagram to show division, the number of units in the strip is equal to the second number in the equation.

Write the answer to each word problem. You can draw a strip diagram to help you.

1. Mr. Jones is making holiday cookies for his friends. He is planning to make 6 different kinds of cookies. He has a dozen eggs. There are 12 eggs in a dozen. Each cookie recipe calls for 2 eggs. Does Mr. Jones have enough eggs?

2. Mrs. Dominguez has 20 students in her class. She wants students to work in groups of 4 to complete a project, with an equal number of students in each group. How many students will be in each group?

© Pearson Education, Inc. 3

Name _____

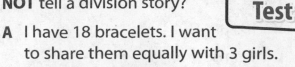

1. A class has 80 glue sticks. There are 10 students in the class. If the glue sticks are shared equally among all of the students, how many glue sticks does each student get?

A 3

B 8

C 9

D 10

2. Saima has 14 muffins. She wants to give 2 muffins to each friend at her party. How many friends can Saima invite to her party?

A 5

B 6

C 7

D 8

3. Beth has 72 buttons to sort in 8 piles. Which multiplication equation can help you find 72 ÷ 8? Use the multiplication table below to help.

×	0	1	2	3	4	5	6	7	8	9	10
0	0	0	0	0	0	0	0	0	0	0	0
1	0	1	2	3	4	5	6	7	8	9	10
2	0	2	4	6	8	10	12	14	16	18	20
3	0	3	6	9	12	15	18	21	24	27	30
4	0	4	8	12	16	20	24	28	32	36	40
5	0	5	10	15	20	25	30	35	40	45	50
6	0	6	12	18	24	30	36	42	48	54	60
7	0	7	14	21	28	35	42	49	56	63	70
8	0	8	16	24	32	40	48	56	64	72	80
9	0	9	18	27	36	45	54	63	72	81	90
10	0	10	20	30	40	50	60	70	80	90	100

A $7 \times 8 = ?$ **C** $8 \times ? = 64$

B $7 \times 9 = ?$ **D** $8 \times ? = 72$

4. Natalie wrote 4 stories. Which of Natalie's stories below does **NOT** tell a division story?

A I have 18 bracelets. I want to share them equally with 3 girls.

B I have 20 bracelets. I want to give 2 girls the same number of bracelets.

C There are 4 girls. Each girl has 5 bracelets.

D I will divide 24 bracelets equally among 6 girls.

5. Lupe has 63 crackers to share equally with 6 friends. If Lupe also gets crackers, how many crackers will each person get?

A 7

B 9

C 10

D 10 with 3 left over

6. Al needs to put 9 basketballs in each bin. He has 45 basketballs. Which equation will help you find how many bins Al can fill?

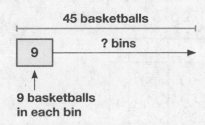

45 basketballs

9   ? bins

9 basketballs in each bin

A $45 \div 9 = ?$

B $45 \times 5 = ?$

C $45 \div 8 = ?$

D $9 \div 45 = ?$

7. Ann has 27 tennis balls. She wants to put them in cans that hold 3 balls each. How many cans can Ann fill?

   A 11 cans

   B 10 cans

   C 9 cans

   D Not here

8. Rory has 81 rocks to sort into 9 varieties. Which multiplication equation can help Rory find 81 ÷ 9? Use the multiplication table below to help.

×	0	1	2	3	4	5	6	7	8	9	10
0	0	0	0	0	0	0	0	0	0	0	0
1	0	1	2	3	4	5	6	7	8	9	10
2	0	2	4	6	8	10	12	14	16	18	20
3	0	3	6	9	12	15	18	21	24	27	30
4	0	4	8	12	16	20	24	28	32	36	40
5	0	5	10	15	20	25	30	35	40	45	50
6	0	6	12	18	24	30	36	42	48	54	60
7	0	7	14	21	28	35	42	49	56	63	70
8	0	8	16	24	32	40	48	56	64	72	80
9	0	9	18	27	36	45	54	63	72	81	90
10	0	10	20	30	40	50	60	70	80	90	100

9. Holly has 40 hats. The hats come in 2 different styles. If she divides the hats equally into 5 boxes, how many hats are in each box?

10. Zak is using repeated subtraction to find 48 ÷ 8. How many times will Zak subtract 8?

   A 6

   B 7

   C 8

   D 9

11. A kennel has 9 dogs. The kennel has 18 treats to give out equally to the dogs. Write and solve an equation to find how many treats each dog gets.

18 treats

| ? | ? | ? | ? | ? | ? | ? | ? | ? |

12. Eric had 72 dimes. He divided them equally into 8 piles. How many dimes were in each pile? Mark your answer in the grid below.

© Pearson Education, Inc. 3

Division Facts

Essential Question: How can unknown divisio[n]
found using known multiplication facts?

Landforms are natural features of the Earth's landscape. Mountains, valleys, and plains are some examples.

Did you know that Pikes Peak is the most visited mountain in North America?

Let's get g[o]
meantime, he[re]
on landforms

Math and Science Project: Landforms

Do Research Use the Internet or some other source to find information about two landforms. How were they formed? What forces are shaping them today? How are the two landforms alike and different? What makes them special?

Journal: Write a Report Inclu[de]
Also in your report:

- List 5 to 10 examples of each

- Find the areas of the landfor[m]
  Make up and solve division p[roblems]
  your data.

Name

⭐ Review

Vocabula[ry]

Choose th[e]
it on the b[lank]

1. _____
   give a[

2. Use _____
   equa[
   each

3. _____
   gives
   put t[o]

Division

Use coun[
complete

4. There
   in 3 b[
   each

5. There
   share
   muff[

ry

e best term from the box. Write
lank.

- division
- equation
- factors
- multiplication

____ are multiplied together to
product.

_____ to find how many
groups or how many are in
group.

_____ is an operation that
the total number when you
gether equal groups.

as Sharing

ers or draw a picture to
the problem.

are 18 apples, divided equally
askets. How many apples are in
basket?

apples

are 32 muffins. Eight people
them equally. How many
ns does each person get?

muffins

Use Multiplication to Solve Division

Find each product. Use the multiplication
table to help.

×	0	1	2	3	4	5	6	7
0	0	0	0	0	0	0	0	0
1	0	1	2	3	4	5	6	7
2	0	2	4	6	8	10	12	14
3	0	3	6	9	12	15	18	21
4	0	4	8	12	16	20	24	28
5	0	5	10	15	20	25	30	35
6	0	6	12	18	24	30	36	42
7	0	7	14	21	28	35	42	49
8	0	8	16	24	32	40	48	56
9	0	9	18	27	36	45	54	63

6. $12 \div 3 =$ _____   **7.** $28 \div 4 =$ _____

8. $36 \div 6 =$ _____   **9.** $48 \div 8 =$ _____

Division Stories

10. Marcus has 42 markers. He puts the
same number of markers into each
of 7 boxes. Which number sentence
shows how many markers are in
each box?

A $42 + 7 = 49$

B $42 \div 7 = 6$

C $42 \div 6 = 7$

D $6 \times 7 = 42$

11. Explain Sara has 32 flowers.
She wants to put 6 flowers into
each bouquet. Can Sara make
6 bouquets? Explain your answer.

© Pearson Education, Inc. 3

My Word Cards

Use the examples for each word on the front of the card to help complete the definitions on the back.

A-Z

fact family

$2 \times 3 = 6$

$3 \times 2 = 6$

$6 \div 2 = 3$

$6 \div 3 = 2$

dividend

$63 \div 9 = 7$

↑

dividend

divisor

$63 \div 9 = 7$

↑

divisor

quotient

$63 \div 9 = 7$

↑

quotient

divisible

$$\begin{array}{r} 9 \ \text{R0} \\ 2\overline{)18} \end{array}$$

18 is divisible by 2, since it can be divided by 2 without leaving a remainder.

divisibility rules

The divisibility rule for 2:

If a number has a 0, 2, 4, 6, or 8 in the ones place, it is divisible by 2.

even number

Even numbers have a 0, 2, 4, 6, or 8 in the ones place.

odd number

Odd numbers have a 1, 3, 5, 7, or 9 in the ones place.

My Word Cards

The _____ is the number to be divided.

A _____ is a group of related facts using the same numbers.

The _____ is the answer to a division problem.

The number by which another number is divided is called the _____.

The rules that state when a number can be divided by another number without a remainder are called

_____.

A number is _____ if it can be divided by another number without leaving a remainder.

A number that is not divisible by 2 is an

_____.

A number that is divisible by 2 is an

_____.

© Pearson Education, Inc. 3

Name _____

☆ ☆
Solve & Share

Use 24 counters to make an array with 3 equal rows. Write a multiplication and a division sentence to describe the array.

You can **analyze relationships.** What is the relationship between multiplication and division in each of your sentences?
Show your work in the space below!

⭐ TEKS 3.5D Determine the unknown whole number in a multiplication or division equation relating to three whole numbers when the unknown is either a missing factor or product. Also, 3.4J, 3.5B. **Mathematical Process Standards** 3.1B, 3.1C, 3.1D, 3.1F, 3.1G

Digital Resources at PearsonTexas.com

Solve   Learn   Glossary   Check   Tools   Games

Look Back!

Analyze Relationships Marisol arranged the same 24 counters into an array with 6 counters in each row. Write a multiplication and a division sentence to describe this array.

This array can show the relationship between multiplication and division.

Multiplication
3 rows of 10 drums
$3 \times 10 = 30$
30 drums

Division
30 drums in 3 equal rows
$30 \div 3 = 10$
10 drums in each row

B A fact family shows how multiplication and division are related.

Fact family for 3, 10, and 30:

$3 \times 10 = 30 \quad 30 \div 3 = 10$

$10 \times 3 = 30 \quad 30 \div 10 = 3$

dividend   divisor   quotient

A fact family is a group of related facts using the same numbers.

C The **dividend** is the number of objects to be divided.

The **divisor** is the number by which another number is divided.

The **quotient** is the answer to a division problem.

Remember, a product is the answer to a multiplication problem.

Do You Understand?

Convince Me! $4 \times 7 = 28$ is one fact in a fact family. Draw an array for this fact. Write the other three facts in the fact family.

☆ Guided Practice ☆

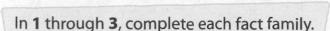
In **1** through **3**, complete each fact family.

1. 3 × ____ = 21   7 × ____ = 21

21 ÷ 3 = ____   21 ÷ 7 = ____

2. 2 × ____ = 18   9 × ____ = 18

18 ÷ 2 = ____   18 ÷ 9 = ____

3. 2 × ____ = 20   10 × ____ = 20

20 ÷ 2 = ____   20 ÷ 10 = ____

4. Look at the fact family for 3, 10, and 30 on page 386. What do you notice about the products and the dividends?

5. Connect Is 4 × 6 = 24 part of the fact family for 3, 8, and 24? Explain.

Independent Practice ☆

Leveled Practice In **6** and **7**, complete each fact family.

6. 2 × ____ = 16

16 ÷ 2 = ____

8 × ____ = 16

16 ÷ 8 = ____

7. 8 × ____ = 56

56 ÷ 8 = ____

7 × ____ = 56

56 ÷ 7 = ____

Some fact families have only 2 facts. The fact family for 2, 2, and 4 has 2 × 2 = 4 and 4 ÷ 2 = 2.

For **8** through **13**, write the fact family.

8. Write the fact family for 6, 7, and 42.

9. Write the fact family for 9, 10, and 90.

10. Write the fact family for 2, 3, and 6.

11. Write the fact family for 1, 5, and 5.

12. Write the fact family for 3, 8, and 24.

13. Write the fact family for 5, 6, and 30.

Problem Solving

14. Reason Write a multiplication and division sentence for the array.

$4 \times$ ___ $= 20$

$20 \div$ ___ $= 5$

15. Complete the fact family.

$8 \times 5 =$ ___

$5 \times 8 =$ ___

$40 \div 8 =$ ___

___ $\div$ ___ $=$ ___

16. Mental Math How many inches shorter is the red pencil than the green and yellow pencil combined?

DATA

Sophia's Pencils	
Color	**Length in Inches**
Red	4
Blue	3
Green	7
Yellow	9

17. Carla picked 9 apples a day for three days. Which number tells you how many apples she picked in three days and makes this equation true?

☐ $\div 3 = 9$

A 3

B 12

C 18

D 27

18. Write 21,212 in word and expanded forms.

19. While harvesting, an apple picking crew filled 3 carts with apples. One cart had 674 apples. Another cart had 656 apples. The third cart had 647 apples. Write the number of apples in the carts in order from least to greatest.

20. Explain Write the fact family for 3, 3, and 9.

21. Extend Your Thinking How many arrays of equal-length rows could you build with 10 counters? Draw the arrays you could build.

© Pearson Education, Inc. 3

Name _____

Another Look!

Multiplication	**Division**
6 rows of 4 glue sticks	24 glue sticks in 6 equal rows
$6 \times 4 = 24$	$24 \div 6 = 4$
24 glue sticks	4 glue sticks in each row

Multiplication facts can help you learn division facts!

Here is the fact family for 4, 6, and 24:

$4 \times 6 = 24$ $24 \div 4 = 6$

$6 \times 4 = 24$ $24 \div 6 = 4$

For **1** and **2**, complete each fact family.

1. $2 \times \underline{\quad} = 14$ $7 \times \underline{\quad} = 14$

$14 \div 2 = \underline{\quad}$ $14 \div 7 = \underline{\quad}$

2. $9 \times \underline{\quad} = 81$

$81 \div 9 = \underline{\quad}$

In **3** and **4**, write the fact family.

3. There are 28 days in 4 weeks. What fact family would you use to find the number of days in 1 week?

4. There are 12 inches in 1 foot. What fact family would you use to find the number of inches in 2 feet?

5. **Mental Math** Use the array to write a multiplication and division sentence.

6. An array has twice as many columns as rows. The dividend for a division sentence that describes the array is 18. How many rows and columns does the array have?

   A 2 and 9
   B 3 and 9
   C 3 and 6
   D 1 and 18

7. **Math and Science** Letchworth State Park in upstate New York is often called the "Grand Canyon of the East." Last year, the Mendoza family visited the park. Each person hiked 3 miles. What fact family represents the total miles hiked by the Mendoza family?

Name	Miles Hiked
Julio	3
Rosa	3
Miguel	3
Clara	3

8. **Formulate a Plan** There are 3 pairs of scissors in one package. What fact family would you use to find the number of scissors in 5 packages?

9. **Analyze Information** Serena has a set of toy trains. She has 3 passenger cars. What is the total length of her passenger cars?

Serena's Train Cars	
Color	Length in Inches
Engine	4
Tender	3
Passenger Car	9
Caboose	7

10. **Extend Your Thinking** You have 3 boxes of 6 pencils. You will use 2 pencils each week. How many weeks of school will you have pencils? How do you know?

11. **Extend Your Thinking** Evan told his class that he has 14 socks. Quinton said that Evan must have 7 pairs of socks. Is Quinton correct? Explain.

© Pearson Education, Inc. 3

Name _____

☆ **Solve & Share** ☆

Kara puts 30 toys into 5 party bags. She puts the same number of toys into each bag. How many toys are in each bag? *Solve this problem any way you choose.*

You can use **number sense.** How can a fact family that uses 30 and 5 help you solve the problem? *Show your work in the space below!*

⊕ **TEKS 3.4F** Recall facts to multiply up to 10 by 10 with automaticity and recall the corresponding division facts. Also, 3.4J, 3.5D.
Mathematical Process Standards 3.1B, 3.1C, 3.1D, 3.1F, 3.1G

Digital Resources at PearsonTexas.com

Solve   Learn   Glossary   Check   Tools   Games

Look Back!

Draw a Picture Show two pictures you might draw to represent 30 ÷ 5.

What Multiplication Fact Can You Use?

A

Dee has 14 noisemakers. She puts the same number on each of 2 tables. How many noisemakers are on each table?

What You Think	What You Write
2 times what number is 14? $2 \times 7 = 14$	$14 \div 2 = 7$ 7 noisemakers are on each table.

Using Multiplication to Divide

B Dee has 40 stickers. If she puts 5 stickers on each bag, how many bags can Dee decorate?

Find $40 \div 5$.

What You Think	What You Write
What number times 5 is 40? $8 \times 5 = 40$	$40 \div 5 = 8$ Dee can decorate 8 bags.

You can use multiplication to help divide.

C Dee wants to put 15 cups in 3 equal stacks on the table. How many cups will Dee put in each stack?

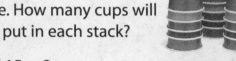

Find $15 \div 3$.

What You Think	What You Write
3 times what number is 15? $3 \times 5 = 15$	$15 \div 3 = 5$ Dee will put 5 cups in each stack.

You can use multiplication to help divide.

Do You Understand?

Convince Me! Write and solve a division story using the numbers 20, 4, and 5. Write the division fact and the related multiplication fact you use to help solve the problem.

© Pearson Education, Inc. 3

Another Example

There are two ways to write a division problem.

24 ÷ 4 = 6

↑ dividend   ↑ divisor   ↑ quotient

6 ← quotient
divisor → 4)24 ← dividend

✰ Guided Practice*

In 1 and 2, complete each fact family.

1. 3 × 6 = 18 _____
   18 ÷ 3 = 6 _____

2. 9 × 4 = 36 _____
   36 ÷ 4 = 9 _____

For 3 through 6, find each quotient.

3. 36 ÷ 4 = ____   4. 15 ÷ 5 = ____

5. 2)18   6. 3)30

7. **Number Sense** How can 5 × 3 = 15 help you divide 15 by 3?

8. **Analyze Information** Dena has 3 children. She buys 30 pencils to share equally among her children for the school year. How many pencils will each of her children get? Write the answer and the fact family you used.

✰ Independent Practice ✰

For 9 through 20, find each quotient.

9. 12 ÷ 2 = ____   10. 12 ÷ 3 = ____   11. 16 ÷ 4 = ____   12. 35 ÷ 5 = ____

13. 14 ÷ 2 = ____   14. 20 ÷ 4 = ____   15. 24 ÷ 4 = ____   16. 45 ÷ 5 = ____

17. 3)27   18. 4)40   19. 5)40   20. 3)21

Problem Solving

21. Number Sense Joey says, "I can't solve 8 ÷ 2 by using the fact 2 × 8 = 16." Do you agree or disagree? Explain.

22. Anna wants to make one array with 2 rows of 8 tiles and another array with 3 rows of 5 tiles. How many tiles does Anna need all together?

23. How many individual squares are inside the rectangle below? Write a multiplication sentence that represents the number of squares.

24. Explain Sammy wants to buy one remote control car for $49 and three small cars for $5 each. What is the total amount Sammy will spend? Explain.

25. Mike bought 3 bags of marbles holding 5 marbles each. He gave 4 marbles to Marsha. How many marbles does Mike have left?

A 11 **C** 19
B 15 **D** 21

26. Connect Bob has 15 pennies and 3 dimes. Miko has the same amount of money, but she only has nickels. How many nickels does Miko have?

27. Collette has 12 swimming medals from 3 swim meets. If Collette won the same number of medals at each meet, how many medals did she win at each meet?

28. Extend Your Thinking Chris gives 18 pretzels equally to 3 friends. Martha gives 20 pretzels equally to 4 friends. Whose friends got more pretzels? Write number sentences to explain.

© Pearson Education, Inc. 3

Name _____

Another Look!

You can use multiplication facts to help with division.

Example 1

Darren and Molly have 16 sheets of paper to share. Each will get the same number of sheets of paper. How many sheets will Darren and Molly each get?

What You Think	What You Write
2 times what number equals 16? $2 \times 8 = 16$	$16 \div 2 = 8$ Darren and Molly will each get 8 sheets of paper.

Example 2

Peter has 24 pennies. He puts the pennies into 4 equal rows. How many pennies are in each row?

What You Think	What You Write
4 times what number equals 24? $4 \times 6 = 24$	$24 \div 4 = 6$ Peter has 6 pennies in each row.

For **1** through **16**, find each quotient.

1. $14 \div 2 =$ _____

2. $35 \div 5 =$ _____

3. $15 \div 3 =$ _____

4. $32 \div 4 =$ _____

5. $9 \div 3 =$ _____

6. $18 \div 2 =$ _____

7. $16 \div 2 =$ _____

8. $21 \div 3 =$ _____

9. $2\overline{)12}$

10. $3\overline{)27}$

11. $5\overline{)25}$

12. $4\overline{)20}$

13. $5\overline{)30}$

14. $5\overline{)45}$

15. $2\overline{)10}$

16. $4\overline{)28}$

17. Analyze Information You have 18 erasers and use 3 erasers each month. How many months will your erasers last? Identify the quotient, dividend, and divisor.

18. Number Sense Write a fact family using the numbers 5, 6, and 30.

19. Reason Franklin says that if he divides 40 by 5, he will get 8. Jeff says he should get 9. Who is correct? Explain.

20. Estimation Round each addend to the nearest hundred to estimate the sum: $264 + 127$.

21. ⭐ You have 2 dollars. You have the money changed into nickels. How many nickels should you receive?

A 5   **C** 20

B 10   **D** 40

22. Use a Strip Diagram Megan arranges 25 chairs into 5 equal rows. How many chairs are in each row?

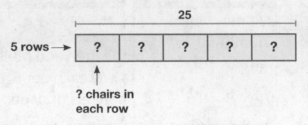

23. Extend Your Thinking Carl has 16 rubber balls to share with his 2 brothers and 1 sister. If Carl and his brothers and sister each get the same number of rubber balls, how many rubber balls will each of them get?

© Pearson Education, Inc. 3

Name _____

Solve & Share

There are 18 children in a ballet class. They are standing in rows of 6 for a dance recital. How many rows of children are there? *Solve the problem any way you choose.*

⭐ **TEKS 3.4F** Recall facts to multiply up to 10 by 10 with automaticity and recall the corresponding division facts. Also, 3.4J, 3.5D.
Mathematical Process Standards 3.1C, 3.1D, 3.1E, 3.1G

Digital Resources at PearsonTexas.com

Solve   Learn   Glossary   Check   Tools   Games

You can **create and use representations.** Can drawing a picture with counters help you solve the problem? *Show your work!*

Look Back!

Draw a Picture Draw a strip diagram to represent the problem.

How Do You Divide with 6 and 7?

There are 48 dogs entered in a dog show. The judge wants 6 dogs in each group. How many groups will there be?

You can divide to find how many groups of dogs there will be.

Using Multiplication to Divide

B Find $48 \div 6$.

What You Think	What You Write
What number times 6 is 48?	$48 \div 6 = 8$
$8 \times 6 = 48$	There will be 8 groups.

You can use multiplication to help divide.

C Another dog was entered in the show. There will now be 7 dogs in each group. How many groups will there be?

Find $49 \div 7$.

What You Think	What You Write
What number times 7 is 49?	$49 \div 7 = 7$
$7 \times 7 = 49$	There will be 7 groups.

Do You Understand?

Convince Me! Write and solve a division story using the numbers 36, 6, and 6. Write the division fact and the related multiplication fact you use to help solve the problem.

© Pearson Education, Inc. 3

Name _____

In **1** through **6**, write the related multiplication fact, then find each quotient.

1. $36 \div 6 =$ _____   **2.** $42 \div 6 =$ _____

3. $42 \div 7 =$ _____   **4.** $18 \div 6 =$ _____

5. $6\overline{)24}$ **6.** $6\overline{)30}$

7. Reason How can you tell without dividing that $42 \div 6$ will be greater than $42 \div 7$?

8. Number Sense How can $8 \times 6 = 48$ help you divide 48 by 6?

Independent Practice *

Leveled Practice In **9** through **20**, use related multiplication and division facts to find the quotient.

9. $6 \times \square = 12$
$12 \div 6 = \square$

10. $3 \times \square = 21$
$21 \div 3 = \square$

11. $6 \times \square = 30$
$30 \div 6 = \square$

12. $2\overline{)14}$

13. $7\overline{)49}$

14. $6\overline{)60}$

15. $6\overline{)54}$

16. $6\overline{)6}$

17. $7\overline{)28}$

18. Find 49 divided by 7.

19. Divide 54 by 6.

20. Find 35 divided by 7.

Problem Solving

21. Julia has 8 buttons on her coat. $\frac{1}{4}$ of the buttons are yellow. How many buttons are yellow?

    A 8

    B 7

    C 2

    D 1

22. **Personal Financial Literacy** Gloria mowed 7 lawns and earned $56. She was paid the same amount for each lawn. How much money did Gloria earn for mowing each lawn?

23. **Mental Math** Explain the mistake in the fact family below. Give the correct fact.

    $4 \times 7 = 28$ $7 \times 4 = 28$

    $7 \div 4 = 28$ $28 \div 7 = 4$

24. There are 35 new tires. Each truck will get 6 tires plus 1 tire for a spare. How many trucks will get new tires?

For **25** through **28**, use the picture below.

1 package of 7 red beads: $1

1 package of 6 green beads: $2

1 package of 5 gold beads: $3

25. Martha bought 1 package of each color bead. How much did Martha spend?

26. Cassidy bought 2 packages of red beads, 1 package of green beads, and 5 packages of gold beads. How much did Cassidy spend?

27. **Explain** Guy bought 28 red beads and 18 green beads. How many packages did Guy buy? Explain how you solved the problem.

28. **Extend Your Thinking** Andy bought exactly 35 beads, all the same color. Which color beads could Andy have bought? Explain.

© Pearson Education, Inc. 3

Name _____

Another Look!

You have 63 pine trees to plant on a plot of land. The owner wants 7 rows of trees. How many trees should you plant in each row?

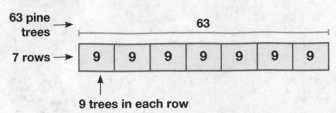

63 pine trees →

7 rows →

63

| 9 | 9 | 9 | 9 | 9 | 9 | 9 |

↑
9 trees in each row

You can divide to find how many trees are in each row.

What You Think
What number times 7 is 63?
$9 \times 7 = 63$

What You Write
$63 \div 7 = 9$
There will be 9 trees in each row.

In **1** and **2**, draw a strip diagram to find the quotient.

1. Find $56 \div 7$.

2. Find $36 \div 6$.

For **3** through **13**, find the quotient.

3. $30 \div 6 =$ _____

4. $28 \div 7 =$ _____

5. $42 \div 6 =$ _____

6. $54 \div 6 =$ _____

7. $6\overline{)48}$

8. $7\overline{)56}$

9. $7\overline{)70}$

10. $7\overline{)49}$

11. Divide 60 by 6.

12. Divide 7 by 7.

13. Find 21 divided by 7.

For **14** and **15**, use the picture at the right.

14. Willa is building birdhouses. Each side of the birdhouse will need 9 nails. How many nails does Willa need for each birdhouse?

15. Number Sense Willa changes the design of her birdhouse so she only uses 7 nails on each side. How will this change the number of nails she uses?

There are 7 sides on the birdhouse.

---

16. Use a Strip Diagram Teachers at a school in Houston are taking 24 students in 4 equal groups on a trip to the zoo. How many students are in each group?

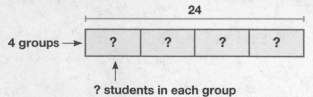

24

4 groups → ? | ? | ? | ?

? students in each group

17. Estimation It takes 10 minutes to bake a batch of cookies. You need to bake 7 batches of cookies. How long will it take to bake all the cookies?

A less than 1 hour
B more than 1 hour
C exactly 2 hours
D more than 2 hours

---

18. There are 48 states in the contiguous United States. If you put 6 states in each group, how many groups will there be? Show the fact family.

19. Manny has 28 chapters in a book to read. He reads 7 chapters each week. How many weeks will it take for Manny to read the book?

---

20. The third grade at Johnson Grade School is having a pizza party. Class 1 has 22 students, Class 2 has 20 students, and Class 3 has 18 students. Each pizza will feed 6 students. How many pizzas will be needed?

21. Extend Your Thinking There are 42 roses in the garden. Diane picks 7 roses for each bouquet of flowers. How many bouquets can she make? How many more bouquets can Diane make if she uses 6 roses in each bouquet?

© Pearson Education, Inc. 3

Name _____

Solve & Share

An art teacher has 72 crayons. The crayons came in boxes with 8 crayons in each box. How many boxes of crayons were there? *Solve this problem any way you choose.*

You can **analyze relationships.** Which fact family uses the numbers 72 and 8 and could help you solve the problem? *Show your work in the space below!*

⭐ **TEKS 3.4F** Recall facts to multiply up to 10 by 10 with automaticity and recall the corresponding division facts. Also, 3.4J, 3.5D.
Mathematical Process Standards 3.1A, 3.1B, 3.1C, 3.1D, 3.1F, 3.1G

Digital Resources at PearsonTexas.com

Solve   Learn   Glossary   Check   Tools   Games

Look Back!

Draw a Picture Draw at least one picture you could use to help solve the problem.

A

John has 56 straws. He needs 8 straws to make a spider. How many spiders can John make? Find 56 ÷ 8.

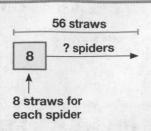

56 straws

8 | ? spiders →

↑
8 straws for
each spider

What number
times 8 is 56?

To make each spider,
you need 8 straws.

7 × 8 = 56

John can make 7 spiders.

Using Multiplication to Divide

B

Luz made 9 animals. She used 54 straws. She used the same number of straws for each animal. How many straws did Luz use for each animal?

Find 54 ÷ 9.

You can divide to
find the number of
straws Luz used for
each animal.

54 straws

| ? | ? | ? | ? | ? | ? | ? | ? | ? |

↑
? straws
for one animal

What You Think	What You Write
9 times what number is 54? 9 × 6 = 54	54 ÷ 9 = 6 Luz used 6 straws for each animal.

Do You Understand?

Convince Me! Write the related multiplication sentence that can be used to complete each division fact.

Division Fact	Related Multiplication Sentence
72 ÷ 8 = _____	_____ × _____ = _____
48 ÷ 6 = _____	_____ × _____ = _____
63 ÷ 7 = _____	_____ × _____ = _____

© Pearson Education, Inc. 3

☆ Guided Practice *

In **1** and **2**, use the multiplication equation to help find each quotient.

1. $16 \div 8 = ?$

What number times 8 is 16?

____ $\times 8 = 16$

So, $16 \div 8 =$ ____.

2. $64 \div 8 = ?$

What number times 8 is 64?

____ $\times 8 = 64$

So, $64 \div 8 =$ ____.

3. **Number Sense** What multiplication fact can you use to find $18 \div 9$?

4. **Reason** Carla and Jeff each use 72 straws. Carla makes animals with 9 legs. Jeff makes animals with 8 legs. Who makes more animals? Explain your answer.

Independent Practice ☆

Leveled Practice In **5** through **16**, find each quotient.

5. $24 \div 8 = ?$

What number times 8 is 24?

____ $\times 8 = 24$

$24 \div 8 =$ ____

6. $45 \div 9 = ?$

What number times 9 is 45?

____ $\times 9 = 45$

$45 \div 9 =$ ____

7. $27 \div 9 = ?$

What number times 9 is 27?

____ $\times 9 = 27$

$27 \div 9 =$ ____

8. $48 \div 8 =$ ____

9. $72 \div 9 =$ ____

10. $8 \div 8 =$ ____

11. $54 \div 9 =$ ____

12. $72 \div 8 =$ ____

13. $90 \div 9 =$ ____

14. $8\overline{)80}$

15. $8\overline{)32}$

16. $9\overline{)9}$

Problem Solving

17. **Analyze Information** Charlie and his friend Richard went on a ski trip. On the first day, Charlie skied 8 times as many minutes as Richard. Charlie skied for 64 minutes. Use the strip diagram below to write and solve a number sentence to find how long Richard skied.

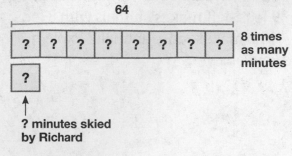

18. **Math and Science** After visiting Bracken Cave in Texas, Maria and 7 friends decide to make bats from chenille sticks. They need 4 chenille sticks for each bat, so Maria buys a package of 40 sticks. Does Maria have enough for everyone?

19. ⭐ Which number sentence is **NOT** in the same fact family as the others?

    A $56 \div 8 = 7$
    B $7 \times 8 = 56$
    C $56 \div 7 = 8$
    D $64 \div 8 = 8$

20. **Number Sense** Callie drove 268 miles on Saturday and 323 miles on Sunday. Write and solve a number sentence to find how far Callie drove.

21. What is the value of the 2 in 26,491?

22. Christopher earned $528 and spent $216. How much money does Christopher have left?

23. **Explain** Mr. Stern bought 4 child tickets and 2 adult tickets. How much more did Mr. Stern spend for the adult tickets than for the child tickets? Explain.

Playhouse Ticket Prices	
Type of Ticket	Price of Ticket
Child	$4
Youth	$8
Adult	$9

© Pearson Education, Inc. 3

Name _____

Another Look!

Multiplication facts can help you to find division facts when 8 or 9 is the divisor.

There are 32 counters. There are 8 rows of counters. How many counters are in each row?

There are 45 counters. There are 9 equal groups. How many counters are in each group?

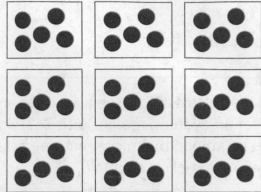

What You Think	**What You Write**
8 times what number equals 32? $8 \times 4 = 32$	$32 \div 8 = 4$ There are 4 counters in each row.

What You Think	**What You Write**
9 times what number equals 45? $9 \times 5 = 45$	$45 \div 9 = 5$ There are 5 counters in each group.

In **1** through **3**, use the multiplication equation to help find each quotient.

1. $54 \div 9 = ?$

$9 \times$ _____ $= 54$

So, $54 \div 9 =$ _____.

2. $24 \div 8 = ?$

$8 \times$ _____ $= 24$

So, $24 \div 8 =$ _____.

3. $56 \div 8 = ?$

$8 \times$ _____ $= 56$

So, $56 \div 8 =$ _____.

In **4** through **12**, find each quotient.

4. $36 \div 9 =$ _____

5. $63 \div 9 =$ _____

6. $80 \div 8 =$ _____

7. $9\overline{)72}$

8. $8\overline{)48}$

9. $9\overline{)81}$

10. $8\overline{)8}$

11. $9\overline{)90}$

12. $9\overline{)27}$

13. Connect Maluwa has 9 identical tiles. ★ When she counts the total number of sides on the tiles, she gets 72. Which could be one of her tiles?

A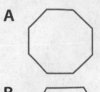

B

C

D

14. Check for Reasonableness Earl has saved $153 in his bank account. He wants to buy a camera that costs $299. He says that if he gets another $50, he will have enough to buy the camera. Does Earl's thinking make sense? Why or why not?

15. Justify It costs $7 to see a matinee and $9 for an evening movie. With $63, would you be able to buy more matinee tickets or evening tickets? Explain.

DATA	Movie Prices	
Matinee		$7
Evening Movie		$9

16. Personal Financial Literacy Andy had $66 in the bank. For 3 months, he deposited $7 a month and did not make any withdrawals. How much money did Andy have in the bank after 3 months?

17. Write 4,219 in expanded form.

18. James has two 5-dollar bills, one quarter, and two pennies. How much money does James have?

19. Analyze Information Teri scored 64 points in the first 8 basketball games she played in. She scored the same number of points in each game. Write and solve a number sentence to find the number of points Teri scored in each game.

20. Extend Your Thinking Adam made 19 paper cranes on Monday and 8 more on Tuesday. He gave all the cranes away to 9 friends so that all the friends had an equal number of cranes. How many cranes did each friend receive? Explain your answer.

© Pearson Education, Inc. 3

Solve & Share

Maria and Gil want pancakes for breakfast. How many pancakes can their mother make for them so that each of them has the same number with none left over? Name at least 6 different numbers. Tell how you know.

TEKS 3.4I Determine if a number is even or odd using divisibility rules. **Mathematical Process Standards** 3.1B, 3.1C, 3.1D, 3.1F, 3.1G

Digital Resources at PearsonTexas.com

| Solve | Learn | Glossary | Check | Tools | Games |

You can **reason.** Think about numbers that can be separated into two equal groups.

Look Back!

Construct Arguments How are the numbers that work alike? How are they different from numbers that don't work?

How Can You Tell Whether a Number Is Even or Odd?

Ahmed and Nita take turns choosing what the family eats for dinner. Can they each choose dinner the same number of days in April? In May?

A whole number is divisible by 2 if it can be divided by 2 with none left over.

Numbers that are divisible by 2 have a 0, 2, 4, 6, or 8 in the ones place. This is a divisibility rule for 2.

You can use a divisibility rule to tell whether a number is even or odd.

Numbers Divisible by 2

1	2	3	4	5	6	7	8	9	10
11	12	13	14	15	16	17	18	19	20
21	22	23	24	25	26	27	28	29	30
31	32	33	34	35	36	37	38	39	40

B There are 30 days in April. Decide whether 30 is an even or odd number.

APRIL						
S	M	T	W	T	F	S
		1	2	3	4	5	6
7	8	9	10	11	12	13
14	15	16	17	18	19	20
21	22	23	24	25	26	27
28	29	30				

A whole number is even if it is divisible by 2.

30 has a 0 in the ones place, so it is divisible by 2.

30 is even.

Ahmed and Nita can each choose the dinner menu the same number of days in April.

C There are 31 days in May. Decide whether 31 is an even or odd number.

MAY						
S	M	T	W	T	F	S
				1	2	3	4
5	6	7	8	9	10	11
12	13	14	15	16	17	18
19	20	21	22	23	24	25
26	27	28	29	30	31	

A whole number is odd if it is not divisible by 2.

31 has a 1 in the ones place, so it is not divisible by 2.

31 is odd.

Ahmed and Nita cannot each choose the dinner menu the same number of days in May.

Do You Understand?

Convince Me! In a leap year, February has 29 days. In a regular year, February has 28 days. Can Ahmed and Nita choose dinner the same number of days in February when it is a leap year? When it is not a leap year? Tell how you know, including how you know whether each number is even or odd.

Name _____

For **1** and **2**, write or circle to complete the sentences. Use divisibility rules to tell if the number is even or odd.

1. 24

24 has a ____ in the ones place.

It   is
     is not   divisible by 2.

24 is   even
        odd   .

2. 33

33 has a ____ in the ones place.

It   is
     is not   divisible by 2.

33 is   even
        odd   .

Numbers Divisible by 2									
1	2	3	4	5	6	7	8	9	10
11	12	13	14	15	16	17	18	19	20

3. Number Sense Charlie is thinking of a number. It has a 7 in the ones place. Is the number that comes right after Charlie's number even or odd? Explain how you know.

4. Ava's house number is odd. It is greater than 30 and less than 40. Name two possible numbers that could be Ava's house number.

Independent Practice ☆

Leveled Practice For **5** through **7**, write *yes* or *no* to tell if each number is divisible by 2. Then, write *even* or *odd*.

5. 45

Is 45 divisible by 2?

_____

45 is _____.

6. 70

Is 70 divisible by 2?

_____

70 is _____.

7. 121

Is 121 divisible by 2?

_____

121 is _____.

For **8** through **15**, write *even* or *odd*.

8. 46 is _____.   **9.** 79 is _____.   **10.** 372 is _____.   **11.** 290 is _____.

12. 188 is _____.   **13.** 647 is _____.   **14.** 800 is _____.   **15.** 799 is _____.

Problem Solving

For **16** through **18**, use the table at the right.

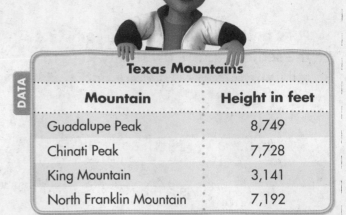

Texas Mountains

Mountain	Height in feet
Guadalupe Peak	8,749
Chinati Peak	7,728
King Mountain	3,141
North Franklin Mountain	7,192

16. **Analyze Information** Is the height of Guadalupe Peak an even number or an odd number? Explain your answer.

17. **Construct Arguments** Callie says if King Mountain were 10 feet taller, it would be an odd number of feet high. Do you agree or disagree? Why?

18. Complete the sentence: The difference in height between _____ and _____ is an odd number.

19. **Communicate** Explain why 1,286 is an even number.

20. Which number is **NOT** divisible by 2?

  A 2,780
  B 4,681
  C 5,902
  D 9,926

21. **Draw a Picture** Draw a shape with an odd number of angles. Then, write the name of the shape.

22. **Extend Your Thinking** The bakery has 208 muffins. After Ms. Craig buys some muffins, the bakery has just 184 muffins. Did Ms. Craig purchase an even number of muffins or an odd number of muffins? Explain your answer.

© Pearson Education, Inc. 3

Name _____

Another Look!

Think about the numbers 1, 3, 5, 7, and 9. When you divide these numbers by 2, there is 1 left over. These numbers are not divisible by 2. They are odd.

Think about the numbers 0, 2, 4, 6, and 8. When you divide these numbers by 2, nothing is left over. These numbers are divisible by 2. They are even.

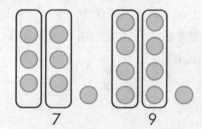

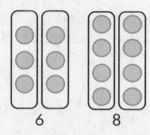

To find if a multidigit number is even or odd, check the digit in the ones place.

479
There is a 9 in the ones place.
9 is not divisible by 2.
9 is odd. So, 479 is odd.

356
There is a 6 in the ones place.
6 is divisible by 2.
6 is even. So, 356 is even.

For **1** through **4**, circle the digit in the ones place. Then write *even* or *odd*.

1. 36 is _____.   **2.** 18 is _____.   **3.** 83 is _____.   **4.** 40 is _____.

For **5** through **7**, write *yes* or *no*, then write *even* or *odd*.

5. 29

   Is 29 divisible by 2?

   _____

   29 is _____.

6. 544

   Is 544 divisible by 2?

   _____

   544 is _____.

7. 4,321

   Is 4,321 divisible by 2?

   _____

   4,321 is _____.

For **8** through **15**, write *even* or *odd*.

8. 39 is _____.   **9.** 48 is _____.   **10.** 300 is _____.   **11.** 411 is _____.

12. 895 is _____.   **13.** 602 is _____.   **14.** 5,650 is _____.   **15.** 1,961 is _____.

16. Reason The addition chart has 3 even numbers in the left column and 3 odd numbers in the top row. Complete the chart by writing the remaining sums. Shade all the sums that are even. Then, describe what you see in the chart about the sum of an odd number and an even number.

+	33	51	79
42	75		
58			
60			

---

17. Explain There are 58 children at a summer camp. The counselors want to divide them into two equal teams for an activity. Is this possible? Explain your answer.

18. ★ Logan has some baseball cards. If he had 1 more baseball card, he would have an odd number of cards. Which could be the number of baseball cards in Logan's collection?

A 433
B 456
C 517
D 809

---

19. Connect Use the digits 4, 5, 6, 7, and 8 once each to write an odd five-digit number. Write it both in standard form and in word form.

20. Extend Your Thinking Explain why every other number is an even number.

---

21. Communicate Describe how you would decide if 2,018 is odd or even. Draw a picture to show your answer.

22. Represent Sandra has 18 bags of peanuts to hand out to 9 friends. Can she give each friend an equal number of bags? Draw a strip diagram to help you solve.

© Pearson Education, Inc. 3

Name _____

Use counters to find 5 ÷ 1 and 5 ÷ 5. Make a sketch of your work.

You can **analyze relationships.** Use what you know about multiplying by 1 to solve the problems and sketch your work. *Show your work in the space below!*

⭐ **TEKS 3.4F** Recall facts to multiply up to 10 by 10 with automaticity and recall the corresponding division facts. Also, 3.4J, 3.5D.
Mathematical Process Standards 3.1A, 3.1B, 3.1C, 3.1D, 3.1F, 3.1G

Digital Resources at PearsonTexas.com

Solve   Learn   Glossary   Check   Tools   Games

Look Back!

Number Sense Use your understanding of multiplying by 1 to find 8 ÷ 1 and 8 ÷ 8.

How Do You Divide with 1 or 0?

A

Neil has 3 goldfish. He puts 1 goldfish in each bowl. How many bowls did Neil use? Find 3 ÷ 1.

Any number divided by 1 is itself.

What number times 1 is 3?

$3 \times 1 = 3$
So, $3 \div 1 = 3$.

Neil used 3 bowls.

3 put into groups of 1

---

1 as a Quotient

B Find 3 ÷ 3.

3 times what number equals 3?

$3 \times 1 = 3$

So, $3 \div 3 = 1$.

Rule: Any number (except 0) divided by itself is 1.

Dividing 0 by a Number

C Find 0 ÷ 3.

3 times what number equals 0?

$3 \times 0 = 0$

So, $0 \div 3 = 0$.

Rule: 0 divided by any number (except 0) is 0.

Dividing by 0

D Find 3 ÷ 0.

0 times what number equals 3?

There is no such number. So, $3 \div 0$ can't be done.

Rule: You cannot divide any number by 0.

Do You Understand?

Convince Me! Sue wrote 9 invitations. She put 1 invitation in each mailbox on her street. How many mailboxes got invitations? Which number sentence shows the problem and the solution? Explain your thinking.

$0 \div 9 = 0$ $9 \div 1 = 9$

© Pearson Education, Inc. 3

Name _____

In **1** and **2**, solve the multiplication sentence to find each quotient.

1. Find 8 ÷ 8.

8 × ____ = 8

So, 8 ÷ 8 = ____.

2. Find 2 ÷ 1.

1 × ____ = 2

So, 2 ÷ 1 = ____.

Remember, you cannot divide any number by 0.

3. **Connect** How can you tell, without dividing, that 375 ÷ 375 = 1?

4. **Explain** Describe how you can find 0 ÷ 267 without dividing.

☆ Independent Practice ☆

Leveled Practice In **5** through **7**, solve the multiplication sentence to find each quotient.

5. Find 0 ÷ 7.

7 × ____ = 0

So, 0 ÷ 7 = ____.

6. Find 4 ÷ 4.

4 × ____ = 4

So, 4 ÷ 4 = ____.

7. Find 6 ÷ 1.

1 × ____ = 6

So, 6 ÷ 1 = ____.

For **8** through **18**, find each quotient.

8. 3 ÷ 3 = ____

9. 0 ÷ 8 = ____

10. 5 ÷ 5 = ____

11. 7 ÷ 1 = ____

12. 6)‾6

13. 1)‾5

14. 25)‾25

15. 1)‾13

16. Find 0 divided by 8.

17. Find 9 divided by 1.

18. Find 10 divided by 10.

Problem Solving

For **19** through **22**, use the picture at the right.

19. Reason Paul hiked one trail 3 times for a total distance of 12 miles. Which trail did he hike?

20. Analyze Information Marty hikes one of the trails 4 times. In all, he hikes more than 10 miles but less than 16 miles. Which trail does he hike? Explain your answer.

21. Reason Addie hiked 3 different trails for a total distance of 11 miles. Which trails did she hike?

22. Fiona hiked all the trails twice. How many miles did Fiona hike?

23. Anthony divided 0 by 6. Jessica used a different number sentence but got the same answer. Which could be the number sentence Jessica used?

A $6 \div 6$

B $4 \div 0$

C $0 \div 4$

D $6 \div 1$

24. Extend Your Thinking Bella had 12 crayons. She used one crayon for each picture she drew. How many pictures did Bella draw? Write the equation that shows the problem and the solution.

25. Personal Financial Literacy The Henderson children ran in a track-a-thon to raise money for a pet shelter. They collected $5 for each lap they ran. How much money did Gina and Craig raise together?

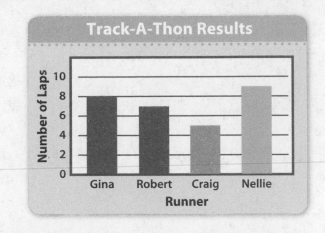

Track-A-Thon Results

© Pearson Education, Inc. 3

Name _____

Another Look!

There are special rules to follow when dividing with 0 or 1.

Rule	Example	What You Think	What You Write
When any number is divided by 1, the quotient is that number.	$7 \div 1 = ?$	1 times what number is 7? $1 \times 7 = 7$ So, $7 \div 1 = 7$.	$7 \div 1 = 7$ or $1\overline{)7}$ with 7 on top
When any number (except 0) is divided by itself, the quotient is 1.	$8 \div 8 = ?$	8 times what number is 8? $8 \times 1 = 8$ So, $8 \div 8 = 1$.	$8 \div 8 = 1$ or $8\overline{)8}$ with 1 on top
When zero is divided by a number (except 0), the quotient is 0.	$0 \div 5 = ?$	5 times what number is 0? $5 \times 0 = 0$ So, $0 \div 5 = 0$.	$0 \div 5 = 0$ or $5\overline{)0}$ with 0 on top
You cannot divide a number by 0.	$9 \div 0 = ?$	0 times what number is 9? There is no number that works, so $9 \div 0$ cannot be done.	$9 \div 0$ cannot be done

For **1** through **8**, write the quotient.

1. $5 \div 1 =$ ____

2. $9 \div 9 =$ ____

3. $0 \div 8 =$ ____

4. $6 \div 6 =$ ____

5. $4 \div 1 =$ ____

6. $1\overline{)7}$

7. $8\overline{)8}$

8. $7\overline{)0}$

In **9** and **10**, use the sign at the right.

9. **Analyze Information** Bob has $20. He spends $5 on a snack and spends the rest on ride tickets. How many ride tickets can Bob buy?

10. Tanji buys 8 ride tickets and shares them equally among 8 friends. Write an equation and solve to show the number of tickets each friend receives.

RIDE TICKETS
$1 each

---

11. Which of these has the greatest quotient?

   A $6 \div 6$
   B $5 \div 1$
   C $0 \div 3$
   D $8 \div 8$

12. **Number Sense** Place the numbers 0, 1, 3, and 3 in the blanks so the number sentence is true.

$$\underline{\hspace{1cm}} \div \underline{\hspace{1cm}} > \underline{\hspace{1cm}} \div \underline{\hspace{1cm}}$$

---

13. **Connect** There are 7 ducklings. They sleep in 1 large nest. Write and solve an equation to show how many ducklings sleep in the nest.

---

14. **Mental Math** The number of students at Netherwood Elementary School is an odd number. When this number is rounded to the nearest hundred, it is 300. When it is rounded to the nearest ten, it is 280. What could the number of students be?

15. **Extend Your Thinking** Write and solve a story problem that goes with $6 \div 6$.

© Pearson Education, Inc. 3

Name _____

☆ ☆
Solve & Share

A tour bus to a national park holds 56 people. There are 7 tour guides at the park to lead equal groups of people from the bus. How many people are in each tour group? *Solve this problem any way you choose.*

You can **create and use representations.** How can drawing an array or a picture help you find the number of people in each tour group? *Show your work in the space below!*

🌟 **TEKS 3.4F** Recall facts to multiply up to 10 by 10 with automaticity and recall the corresponding division facts. Also, 3.4J, 3.5D.
Mathematical Process Standards 3.1B, 3.1C, 3.1D, 3.1E, 3.1F

Digital Resources at PearsonTexas.com

Solve   Learn   Glossary   Check   Tools   Games

Look Back!

Connect How can $7 \times ? = 56$ help you find $56 \div 7 = ?$

A

Sabrina has 28 quarters in her bank. She wants to trade all of them for one-dollar bills. How many one-dollar bills will Sabrina get?

There are 4 quarters in one dollar.

B ## One Way

How many groups of 4 are in 28?

You can draw a strip diagram to help solve the problem.

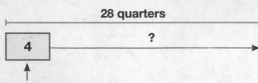

28 quarters

| 4 | ? |

↑
4 quarters in one dollar

$28 \div 4 = 7$

There are 7 groups of 4 in 28. Sabrina can trade 28 quarters for 7 one-dollar bills.

C ## Another Way

What number times 4 equals 28?

You can use multiplication facts to help solve the problem.

$? \times 4 = 28$

$7 \times 4 = 28$

Sabrina can trade 28 quarters for 7 one-dollar bills.

Do You Understand?

Convince Me! Why can both $28 \div 7 = ?$ and $? \times 7 = 28$ be used to solve the problem above?

© Pearson Education, Inc. 3

☆ Guided Practice *

In **1** through **5**, use a multiplication or a division fact to complete the equations.

1. 45 ÷ 5 = _____

5 × _____ = 45

> You can use multiplication to help divide.

2. 3 × _____ = 21

21 ÷ 3 = _____

3. 6 × _____ = 30

30 ÷ 6 = _____

4. 24 ÷ 6 = _____

6 × _____ = 24

5. 6 × _____ = 12

12 ÷ 6 = _____

6. Look back at the problem on page 422. Suppose Sabrina found 8 more quarters in her desk. Including the quarters that were in her bank, how many one-dollar bills can she trade for her quarters now?

7. Number Sense Calvin solves the number sentence 49 ÷ 7 = ☐. How does this help him complete the number sentence 7 × ☐ = 49?

Independent Practice *

Leveled Practice In **8** through **10**, use fact families to complete the equations.

8. 42 ÷ 7 = _____

7 × _____ = 42

9. 6 × _____ = 18

18 ÷ 6 = _____

10. 9 × _____ = 72

72 ÷ 9 = _____

For **11** through **19**, find the product or quotient.

11. 36 ÷ 4 = _____

12. 8 × 8 = _____

13. 15 ÷ 3 = _____

14. 6)‾36‾

15. 9)‾63‾

16. 9)‾54‾

17. Multiply 8 and 5. _____

18. Divide 18 by 9. _____

19. Divide 27 by 3. _____

Problem Solving

For **20** through **22**, use the recipe at the right.

20. Connect How many cups of peanuts would Eric need to make 5 batches of trail mix? Write an equation to show your thinking.

Eric's Trail Mix

Makes one batch
Ingredients:
4 cups peanuts
3 cups raisins
2 cups walnuts

21. Draw a Picture How many batches of trail mix can Eric make with 16 cups of peanuts, 12 cups of raisins, and 8 cups of walnuts? Draw a picture or a diagram to show your thinking.

22. Reason Eric spends $30 to buy the ingredients for 5 batches of trail mix. What is the cost of the ingredients Eric needs for one batch?

  A $150   **C** $6

  B $25   **D** $5

---

23. Write and solve a word problem that is modeled with the number line.

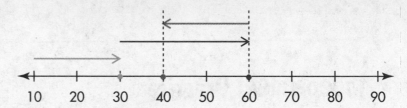

10 20 30 40 50 60 70 80 90

---

24. Communicate Emilia drew lines to divide these squares into parts. Explain how the divided squares are different. Then, explain how they are alike.

25. Extend Your Thinking Wilson is thinking of 2 one-digit numbers. When he multiplies them, the product is 27. What is the sum of the two numbers? Explain your answer.

© Pearson Education, Inc. 3

Name _____

Another Look!

A class is making popcorn for a carnival. Each batch makes 30 cups. The students put the popcorn in bags that hold 6 cups each. How many bags of popcorn does one batch make?

You can solve the problem using division or multiplication.

Division	Multiplication
How many groups of 6 are in 30?	What number times 6 equals 30?

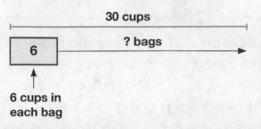

Divide the total number of cups by the number of cups in each bag:

$30 \div 6 = 5$ ← Number of bags

Each batch of popcorn makes 5 bags.

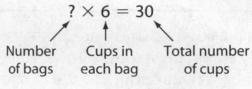

$5 \times 6 = 30$

Each batch of popcorn makes 5 bags.

For **1** through **9**, use multiplication and division to complete the fact family.

1. $21 \div 3 = $ _____

$3 \times $ _____ $= 21$

$21 \div $ _____ $= 3$

_____ $\times 3 = 21$

2. $36 \div 6 = $ _____

$6 \times $ _____ $= 36$

3. $18 \div 9 = $ _____

$9 \times $ _____ $= 18$

$18 \div $ _____ $= 9$

_____ $\times 9 = 18$

4. $54 \div 9 = $ _____

$9 \times $ _____ $= 54$

$54 \div $ _____ $= 9$

_____ $\times 9 = 54$

5. $18 \div 6 = $ _____

$6 \times $ _____ $= 18$

$18 \div $ _____ $= 6$

_____ $\times 6 = 18$

6. $40 \div 5 = $ _____

$5 \times $ _____ $= 40$

$40 \div $ _____ $= 5$

_____ $\times 5 = 40$

7. $14 \div 2 = $ _____

$2 \times $ _____ $= 14$

$14 \div $ _____ $= 2$

_____ $\times 2 = 14$

8. $25 \div 5 = $ _____

$5 \times $ _____ $= 25$

9. $32 \div 4 = $ _____

$4 \times $ _____ $= 32$

$32 \div $ _____ $= 4$

_____ $\times 4 = 32$

For **10** and **11**, use the table at the right.

10. **Analyze Information** Ellis asks some classmates to name their favorite color. He records the information in a tally chart. How many classmates answered the question?

DATA	Favorite Color	
	Red	⫪⫪ /
	Blue	////
	Green	⫪⫪ ///

11. Suppose Ellis asked more classmates to name their favorite color. If twice as many classmates named blue this time, how many classmates named blue?

---

12. At a music recital, there are 30 chairs. They are set up in 6 equal rows. What number sentence can you use to find the number of chairs in each row?

13. **Reason** A music store has 5 guitars for sale. Each guitar has 6 strings. The manager wants to replace all the strings. If new strings come in boxes of 10, how many boxes of strings does she need?

---

14. ⭐ Tolen has 18 dog treats. He gives the same number of treats to 6 dogs at the animal shelter where he works. Which two number sentences could be used to find the number of treats each dog gets?

   A $18 + 6 = 24$ and $24 - 6 = 18$

   B $18 \div 6 = 3$ and $6 \times 3 = 18$

   C $18 \div 18 = 1$ and $1 \times 18 = 18$

   D $6 \div 3 = 2$ and $6 \div 2 = 3$

15. **Mental Math** Jason has 3 bags with 5 mangoes in each bag. Maria has 5 bags with 4 mangoes in each bag. Who has more mangoes?

---

16. **Extend Your Thinking** A chessboard has 8 rows of squares with 8 squares in each row. At the beginning of the game each player puts 16 pieces on the board, with each piece on its own square. How many squares are empty at the beginning of the game? Explain your answer.

  © Pearson Education, Inc. 3

Name _____

☆ ☆
Solve & Share

Two girls and two boys went to the festival. The total cost of their tickets was $20. Each child paid the same amount for a ticket. What was the cost of each ticket? *Solve this problem any way you choose.*

⊕ **TEKS 3.1A** Apply mathematics to problems arising in everyday life, society, and the workplace. Also, 3.4K, 3.5B. **Mathematical Process Standards** 3.1B, 3.1C, 3.1D, 3.1E, 3.1F, 3.1G

You can **use representations** such as an array, to communicate and help solve this problem. *Show your work in the space below!*

Digital Resources at PearsonTexas.com

Solve   Learn   Glossary   Check   Tools   Games

Look Back!

Connect What multiplication fact can you use to solve the problem?

How Can You Solve a Two-Step Problem?

A Analyze

Remember, some problems have hidden questions to be answered before you can solve the problem.

A store has boxes of video games for sale. In each box, the video games are in 2 rows with 3 video games in each row. The total cost of a box of video games is $54. Each video game costs the same amount. What is the cost of each video game?

Solving a Two-Step Problem

B Plan

First, find and answer the hidden question.

You can use a strip diagram to show multiplication as joining equal groups.

What is the total number of video games in each box?

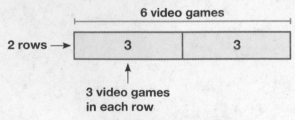

6 video games

2 rows → | 3 | 3 |

3 video games in each row

$2 \times 3 = 6$

There are 6 video games in each box.

C Solve

Use the answer to the hidden question to solve the problem.

You can use a strip diagram to show division as sharing.

What is the cost of each video game?

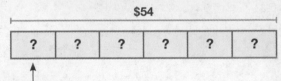

$54

| ? | ? | ? | ? | ? | ? |

? cost of each video game

$54 \div 6 = 9$

Each video game costs $9.

Do You Understand?

Convince Me! Suppose the same box of video games is on sale for $30. How much does each video game cost? Is the hidden question the same or different as the problem above?

© Pearson Education, Inc. 3

☆ **Guided Practice** *

Answer the hidden question. Then, solve.

1. Twelve friends went camping. All except 4 of them went on a hike. The hikers carried 32 water bottles. Each hiker carried the same number of water bottles. How many water bottles did each hiker carry?

   Hidden question: How many friends went on the hike? How do you know?

2. **Connect** What operations did you use to solve Exercise 1?

3. **Communicate** Write a problem that can be solved by finding and answering a hidden question.

You can use strip diagrams or arrays to help solve two-step problems.

☆ **Independent Practice** ☆

For **4** and **5**, answer the hidden question first. Then, solve.

4. Mrs. Lum bought 6 rolls of pink ribbon and some rolls of yellow ribbon. The total cost of the rolls of ribbon was $27. Each roll cost $3. How many rolls of yellow ribbon did Mrs. Lum buy?

   Hidden Question: What is the total number of rolls of ribbon Mrs. Lum bought? How do you know?

5. There are 32 students in a physical education class. Twelve of the students are playing soccer. The rest are playing volleyball. The teacher divides the volleyball players into groups of 5. How many groups of volleyball players are there?

   Hidden Question: How many volleyball players are there? How do you know?

Problem Solving

6. **Justify** Use the table. Mrs. Casey paid for an admission ticket for herself and then spent $20 in child admission tickets for her son and some of his friends. If all the children then went for a boat ride, how much did Mrs. Casey pay for the boat ride tickets? How do you know?

County Fair		
Kind of Ticket	Adult	Child
Admission	$8	$4
Boat Rides	$2	$1

7. **Formulate a Plan** Martin raked 3 lawns yesterday and 4 lawns today. He earned a total of $42. He earned the same amount of money for each lawn. What can you do to find how much Martin earned for each lawn he raked?

   A First, multiply 3 by $42. Then, add 4.
   B First, multiply 4 by 3. Then, subtract the result from $42.
   C First, add 3 and 4. Then, divide $42 by the result.
   D First, divide $42 by 4. Then, multiply the result by 3.

8. **Draw a Picture** Draw lines to divide this rectangle into four equal parts.

9. **Analyze Information** Mr. Alton wants to buy tickets to a show. The tickets are for seats in 3 rows with 3 seats in each row. The total cost of the tickets is $81. Each ticket costs the same amount. What is the cost of one ticket?

10. **Extend Your Thinking** Seven students went bowling. Four of the students bowled 1 game each, and three of the students bowled 2 games each. The cost was $5 per game. How much money did the students spend on bowling? Explain.

© Pearson Education, Inc. 3

Name _____

Another Look!

To solve a two-step problem, you may need to find the answer to a hidden question first. Then you can use that answer to solve the problem.

Sandra has $22 to spend on school supplies. She buys a backpack and spends the rest of her money on notebooks. How many notebooks does Sandra buy?

What do you know?	What do you need to do?
• Sandra has $22 and spends $10 on a backpack.	Subtract 10 from 22. 22 − 10 = $12
• Sandra has $12 left to spend on notebooks that cost $3 each.	Divide 12 by 3. 12 ÷ 3 = 4

Sandra buys 4 notebooks.

For **1** through **3**, answer the hidden question first. Then, solve.

1. A basketball team scored 34 points. The starters scored 18 points and the bench players scored the rest. The two players on the bench each scored the same number of points. How many did each of the bench players score?

   Hidden Question: How many points were scored in all by the bench players?

2. There are 45 students taking a trip to the museum. They form 3 groups with 7 students each. How many students still need to be placed in groups?

   Hidden Question: How many students are in the 3 groups of 7 students each?

3. Juan has $20 to spend. He spends $3 each day for 5 days. How much does Juan have left?

   Hidden Question: How much money does Juan spend?

4. Explain While sitting on a park bench, Marcus counted a total of 40 wheels on bicycles and tricycles. He counted 8 bicycles. How can you find how many tricycles Marcus saw?

5. Number Sense Bert bought 4 books for $7 each. He also bought a magazine, which cost $5. He paid with a $50 bill. How much money did Bert receive back from the cashier?

6. Analyze Information Julie bought 3 baseballs and some softballs. The total cost was $45. Each ball cost $5. First, find the amount of money Julie spent on baseballs. Then, use that information to find how many softballs Julie bought.

7. Reason The table shows the number of students in each third-grade class at Thomasville Elementary School. Which class has an even number of students? How do you know?

DATA

Classroom Teacher	Number of Students
Mr. Bell	27
Ms. Ridley	26
Ms. Holtz	29

8. ★ There are 48 students in the band. The boys and girls are in separate rows. There are 6 students in each row. There are 3 rows of boys. How many rows of girls are there?

A 5
B 8
C 18
D 30

9. Extend Your Thinking Rochelle reads the following problem:

"A community group bought 9 student tickets and 3 adult tickets to the movies. The total cost of the tickets was $78. Student tickets cost $6. How much money does an adult ticket cost?"

To solve the problem, Rochelle writes the three number sentences shown at the right. Write the number sentences in order to show which step Rochelle took first, second, and third.

$78 - 54 = \$24$

$24 \div 3 = \$8$

$9 \times 6 = \$54$

© Pearson Education, Inc. 3

Name _____

 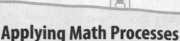
1. **Number Sense** Write two division facts and two multiplication facts using the numbers 3, 7, and 21.

_____

2. **Communicate** Sean has 32 pairs of socks. He puts 4 pairs of socks into each pile. How many piles of socks does Sean have? Show how you can use a multiplication sentence to find the answer.

Applying Math Processes
- How does this problem connect to previous ones?
- What is my plan?
- How can I use tools?
- How can I use number sense?
- How can I communicate and represent my thinking?
- How can I organize and record information?
- How can I explain my work?
- How can I justify my answer?

3. **Analyze Information** The array below can be used to model a multiplication and a division sentence. Write the sentences.

4. **Explain** Sam has 18 coupons he can trade for free movie tickets. He needs to trade 6 coupons for each free movie ticket. How many free movie tickets can Sam get? Explain how you know.

5. **Extend Your Thinking** Deb and Drew need to make 25 small paper birds to decorate a poster. Could they both make the same number of birds? Why or why not? How many birds will each person make if they make as close to the same number as possible?

6. **Use a Strip Diagram** Lizzie made 9 beaded necklaces. She used 63 beads. She used the same number of beads for each necklace. How many beads did Lizzie use for each necklace? How do you know?

63 beads

?	?	?	?	?	?	?	?	?

↑
? beads for one necklace

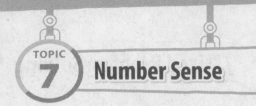

TOPIC 7 Number Sense

Error Search

For **1** through **6**, find each quotient that is not correct.
Circle the problem and rewrite the problem so it is correct.

1. $10 \div 2 = 5$

2. $9 \div 1 = 0$

3. $42 \div 7 = 7$

4. $20 \div 5 = 5$

5. $72 \div 9 = 8$

6. $32 \div 4 = 9$

Target Number

Mental Math For **7** through **12**, circle the numbers in the box that the Target Number is divisible by.

7.

1	2	3
4	5	6
7	8	9

8.

1	2	3
4	5	6
7	8	9

9.

1	2	3
4	5	6
7	8	9

10.

1	2	3
4	5	6
7	8	9

11.

1	2	3
4	5	6
7	8	9

12.

1	2	3
4	5	6
7	8	9

© Pearson Education, Inc. 3

Name _____

Set A pages 385–390

Monica has 24 chairs to arrange equally in 3 rows. You can use an array to find the number of chairs in each row.

This array shows the relationship between multiplication and division.

3 rows of 8   24 in 3 equal rows
  $3 \times 8 = 24$ $24 \div 3 = 8$

A fact family shows how multiplication and division are related.

Fact family for 3, 8, and 24:

  $3 \times 8 = 24$ $24 \div 3 = 8$
  $8 \times 3 = 24$ $24 \div 8 = 3$

Remember that a fact family is a group of related facts using the same numbers.

In **1** through **4**, write the other three facts in the fact family.

1. $3 \times 7 = 21$

2. $5 \times 3 = 15$

3. $8 \times 6 = 48$

4. $4 \times 5 = 20$

Set B pages 391–396

You can use multiplication to solve division problems. Hector has 24 oranges. He puts 4 oranges in each basket. How many baskets does Hector need for all the oranges?

4 times what number is 24?

  $4 \times 6 = 24$
  $24 \div 4 = 6$

Hector needs 6 baskets.

Remember that you can use multiplication to help divide.

In **1** and **2**, solve each problem. Write the multiplication fact and division fact you use to solve the problem.

1. Sally has 32 flowers. She puts 8 flowers in each vase. How many vases does Sally need for all the flowers?

2. Jon has 18 peaches. He uses 3 peaches to make a peach tart. How many peach tarts does Jon make if he uses all the peaches?

Brent is putting 42 books on shelves. He puts 6 books on each shelf. How many shelves will Brent need?

What number times 6 is 42?

$7 \times 6 = 42$

$42 \div 6 = 7$

Brent will need 7 shelves.

How many shelves would Brent need if he put 7 books on each shelf?

What number times 7 is 42?

$6 \times 7 = 42$

$42 \div 7 = 6$

Brent would need 6 shelves.

Remember that you can use multiplication facts for 6s and 7s to help you divide by 6s and 7s.

In **1** through **3**, solve each problem. Write the multiplication fact and division fact you use to solve the problem.

1. There are 42 runners entered in a marathon. They run in groups of 6. How many groups are there?

2. Lani has 35 bird stickers. There are 5 stickers on each sheet. How many sheets of bird stickers does she have?

3. Jake has 18 remote-controlled boats for 6 friends to share equally. How many boats will each friend get?

Lu made 9 bracelets. He used 72 beads. He used the same number of beads for each bracelet. How many beads did Lu use for each bracelet?

72 beads

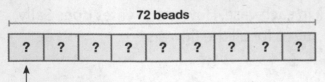

? beads for one bracelet

9 times what number is 72?

$9 \times 8 = 72$

$72 \div 9 = 8$

Lu used 8 beads for each bracelet.

Remember that you can use multiplication facts for 8s and 9s to help you divide by 8s and 9s.

For **1** through **5**, write the related multiplication fact that can be used to complete each division fact. Then, find the quotient.

1. $54 \div 9 = $ _____   _____ $\times$ _____ $=$ _____

2. $64 \div 8 = $ _____   _____ $\times$ _____ $=$ _____

3. $36 \div 9 = $ _____   _____ $\times$ _____ $=$ _____

4. $56 \div 8 = $ _____   _____ $\times$ _____ $=$ _____

5. $72 \div 8 = $ _____   _____ $\times$ _____ $=$ _____

© Pearson Education, Inc. 3

Name _____

Set E | pages 409–414

Which of these numbers is even?
Which of the numbers is odd?

34   57

A whole number is **even** if it is divisible by 2.

Numbers that are divisible by 2 have a 0, 2, 4, 6, or 8 in the ones place.

34 has a 4 in the ones place. So, 34 is an even number.

A whole number is **odd** if it is not divisible by 2.

57 has a 7 in the ones place, so it is not divisible by 2. So, 57 is an odd number.

Odd numbers have a 1, 3, 5, 7, or 9 in the ones place.

Remember that you can use a divisibility rule to tell whether a number is even or odd.

For **1** through **7**, circle even or odd.

1. 34   **even**   **odd**

2. 57   **even**   **odd**

3. 125   **even**   **odd**

4. 346   **even**   **odd**

5. 1,658   **even**   **odd**

6. 3,709   **even**   **odd**

7. 2,160   **even**   **odd**

Set F | pages 415–420

Find 5 ÷ 1. Five groups of 1.

What number times 1 is 5?

5 × 1 = 5   So, 5 ÷ 1 = 5.

Find 8 ÷ 8.

8 × 1 = 8   So, 8 ÷ 8 = 1.

Find 0 ÷ 8.

8 × 0 = 0   So, 0 ÷ 8 = 0.

Remember that any number divided by 1 is itself. Any number (except 0) divided by itself is 1. Zero divided by any number (except 0) is 0.

For **1** through **5**, use division to solve.

1. 0 ÷ 16 = ____

2. 8 ÷ 1 = ____

3. 10 ÷ 10 = ____

4. 7 ÷ 1 = ____

5. Leroy had 4 oranges. He gave one orange to each of his 4 friends. How many oranges did each friend get? Write a number sentence to show your answer.

Set G pages 421–426

How many groups of 4 are in 24?

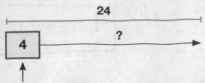

24

4

?

4 in each group

You can use a strip diagram to find out.

$24 \div 4 = ?$

You can use multiplication facts.

$? \times 4 = 24$

$6 \times 4 = 24$

There are 6 groups of 4 in 24.

Remember that you can use strip diagrams or multiplication facts to help solve a division problem.

In **1** through **8**, use related multiplication and division facts to solve.

1. $21 \div 7 = $ ____

$7 \times$ ____ $= 21$

2. $5 \times$ ____ $= 45$

$45 \div 5 = $ ____

3. $7 \times$ ____ $= 42$

$42 \div 7 = $ ____

4. $18 \div 6 = $ ____

$6 \times$ ____ $= 18$

5. $36 \div 6 = $ ____

$6 \times$ ____ $= 36$

6. $4 \times$ ____ $= 32$

$32 \div 4 = $ ____

7. $35 \div 5 = $ ____

$5 \times$ ____ $= 35$

8. $9 \times$ ____ $= 81$

$81 \div 9 = $ ____

Set H pages 427–432

A store has boxes of drinking glasses on sale. In each box, the glasses are in 2 rows with 2 glasses in each row. The total cost of a box of glasses is $12. Each glass costs the same amount. What is the cost of each glass?

First, find and answer the hidden question.

What is the total number of glasses in each box?

$2 \times 2 = 4$

There are 4 glasses in each box.

Then, use the hidden question to solve the problem. You can draw an array.

$\$12 \div 4 = \$3$

Each glass costs $3.

Remember that you should first find and answer the hidden question. Use the answer to solve the problem.

Find the hidden question, and then solve.

1. Marge bought 4 rolls of blue and 2 rolls of green wrapping paper. The cost of each roll was the same. The total cost of the rolls was $36. How much did each roll cost? Draw strip diagrams or use objects to solve.

© Pearson Education, Inc. 3

Name _____

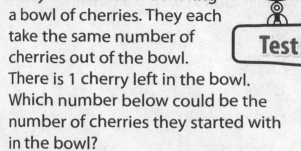

1. Heather wrote a multiplication fact and a division fact for the array below. Which shows a fact Heather could have written?

   A $5 \times 9 = 45$

   B $5 \times 5 = 25$

   C $9 \times 9 = 81$

   D $50 \div 5 = 10$

2. David solved a division problem. The dividend was 63. The quotient was 9. The divisor was 7. Which problem did David solve?

   A $63 \div 7 = 9$

   B $63 \div 9 = 7$

   C Both A and B are correct.

   D Neither A nor B is correct.

3. A balloon artist wants to make 6 different kinds of balloon animals. She needs 4 balloons to make each animal. If the balloons come in packs of 8, how many packs will she need to buy?

   A 2

   B 3

   C 4

   D 6

4. Betsy and Carlos are sharing a bowl of cherries. They each take the same number of cherries out of the bowl. There is 1 cherry left in the bowl. Which number below could be the number of cherries they started with in the bowl?

   A 37

   B 48

   C 24

   D 18

5. Mrs. Raspa wrote four number sentences. Which of Mrs. Raspa's number sentences is **NOT** true?

   A $0 \div 8 = 0$

   B $5 \div 1 = 5$

   C $7 \div 7 = 1$

   D $4 \div 0 = 0$

6. Mr. Vargas is buying used computer equipment. He buys 3 keyboards and 4 mice. He spends $42. If the items are all the same price, how much does each item cost?

   A $6

   B $7

   C $8

   D $10

7. Peter wrote four numbers. Which of Peter's numbers can be divided into 7 equal groups with 0 left over?

A 56

B 52

C 34

D 27

8. Barney stacked his pennies in 8 equal piles. There were no pennies left over. Which is the total number of pennies that Barney could have had?

A 26

B 32

C 43

D 57

9. Amber lives on a street where the house numbers are divisible by 6. Which house number could Amber have?

A 16

B 27

C 32

D Not here

10. Christina wrote three incorrect statements and one correct statement. Which of Christina's statements is correct?

A $72 \div 8 > 2 \times 5$

B $24 \div 4 > 1 \times 6$

C $0 \times 7 < 0 \div 3$

D $8 \times 1 = 64 \div 8$

11. Hina has 36 quarters. There are 4 quarters in one dollar. How much money does Hina have?

A $144

B $40

C $9

D $8

12. Which multiplication sentence can help Crystal find the answer to the division problem shown in the strip diagram?

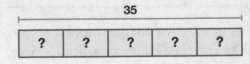

A $35 \div 5 = 7$

B $5 \times 7 = 35$

C $5 \times 5 = 25$

D $3 \times 5 = 15$

© Pearson Education, Inc. 3

Name _____

13. Xavier divided his action figure collection into 2 equal groups. There was 1 figure left over. Which choice describes the total number of action figures that Xavier has?

  A An even number

  B An odd number

  C Not enough information is given.

  D Both A and B could be true.

16. Cindy has 9 paper clips. She puts them in 1 pile. How many paper clips are in the pile?

  A 0 paper clips

  B 1 paper clip

  C 9 paper clips

  D It cannot be done.

14. Mandy is trying to find 6 ÷ 0. She says the answer is 0 because 6 × 0 = 0. Is Mandy correct? Choose the best explanation.

  A Yes, she is correct because 0 × 6 = 0.

  B No, she is not correct because 6 + 0 = 6.

  C No, she is not correct because no number times 0 can equal 6.

  D No, she is not correct because 6 is not part of the fact family for 0 and 0.

17. Kira has 63 sheets of recycled paper. She gives the same number of sheets to each of 9 friends. How many sheets does Kira give to each friend? Use the strip diagram to help.

63 sheets								
?	?	?	?	?	?	?	?	?

  A 6

  B 7

  C 8

  D 9

15. Luz has 36 pencil toppers. She sorts her pencil toppers into 6 groups. How many are in each group?

  A 5

  B 6

  C 7

  D 216

18. Amy wrote the fact family for 1, 4, and 4. Which does **NOT** belong to the fact family with 1, 4, and 4?

  A 1 × 4 = 4

  B 4 ÷ 4 = 1

  C 4 ÷ 1 = 4

  D 4 × 0 = 0

19. Gennaro wrote 4 statements about even and odd numbers. Which of Gennaro's statements is true?

 A All even numbers end in 0, 2, or 4.

 B All odd numbers are divisible by 3.

 C All even numbers are divisible by 2.

 D All odd numbers are not divisible by any other numbers.

20. Natalie completed 16 back handsprings in 4 tumble passes. She completes the same number of back handsprings in each pass. Which multiplication sentence can help you find 16 ÷ 4?

21. Gabby found 81 ÷ 9. Then, she multiplied the quotient by 7. What was the product? Mark your answer in the grid below.

22. A drum shop has 4 drumsticks in each of 5 packages. Some students show up and want to try out some of the drums in the shop. If each student gets 2 drumsticks, how many students can play drums?

 A 20

 B 10

 C 5

 D 4

23. "Here is a puzzle," said Mrs. Cho. "Which number will make both equations true?"

$$18 \div 9 = \underline{}$$

$$\underline{} \times 9 = 18$$

24. Mrs. Ortega found 70 ÷ 7. She multiplied the quotient by 8. What was the product? Mark your answer in the grid below.

© Pearson Education, Inc. 3

Number Sense: Multiplying 2-Digit by 1-Digit Numbers

Essential Question: How can products be estimated and found mentally?

Matter is all around us. Solids, liquids, and gases are three forms of matter.

The gases in the air are matter. We don't see them, but we know they are there.

I need to take a deep breath! Here's a project on properties of matter and multiplication.

Math and Science Project: Properties of Matter

Do Research Use the Internet or other sources to learn about properties of matter. Examples include shape, color, texture, and hardness. List 10–15 examples of matter. Describe the properties of each example you listed.

Journal: Write a Report Include what you found. Also in your report:

• Arrange your list of examples by their properties. How many properties did you include?

• Consider the size of matter. Measure the length of a small solid to the nearest inch. Find the length that is 10 times as long as your measure. Find the length that is 50 times as long as your measure.

Review What You Know

Vocabulary

Choose the best term from the box.
Write it on the blank.

- dividend
- divisor
- even number
- odd number
- quotient

1. The answer to a division problem is the _____.

2. The _____ is the number to be divided.

3. A whole number is an _____ if it is divisible by 2.

4. The number by which another number is divided is the _____.

Relating Multiplication and Division

Complete the facts represented by the array.

5. $4 \times 6 =$ ____

6. $24 \div 4 =$ ____

Division Facts

In **7** through **13**, find each quotient.

7. $18 \div 3 =$ ____   8. $28 \div 7 =$ ____

9. $72 \div 8 =$ ____   10. $35 \div 5 =$ ____

11. $6\overline{)48}$ 12. $8\overline{)64}$

13. There are 36 students in 4 computer classes. Each class is the same size. How many students are in each class?

14. There are 42 bottles of paint in 7 boxes. Each box contains the same number of bottles. Which equation can you solve to find the number of bottles in each box?

A $42 \times 7 = \square$ **C** $42 + 7 = \square$

B $42 \div 7 = \square$ **D** $42 - 7 = \square$

Money

15. **Explain** Mark has saved 32 quarters. He wants to spend them on a T-shirt that costs $8.50. Does Mark have enough money? Explain.

4 quarters = one dollar

© Pearson Education, Inc. 3

My Word Cards

Use the examples for each word on the front of the card to help complete the definitions on the back.

A-Z

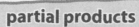

partial products

$$4 \times 24 = ?$$
$$(4 \times 20) + (4 \times 4)$$
$$4 \times 20 = 80$$
$$+ \, 4 \times 4 = 16$$
$$96$$

compensation

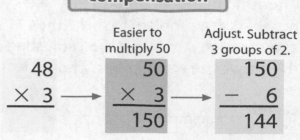

Easier to multiply 50

Adjust. Subtract 3 groups of 2.

$$48 \times 3 \longrightarrow \begin{array}{r} 50 \\ \times \quad 3 \\ \hline 150 \end{array} \longrightarrow \begin{array}{r} 150 \\ - \quad 6 \\ \hline 144 \end{array}$$

My Word Cards

Complete each definition. Extend learning by writing your own definitions.

Choosing numbers close to the numbers in a problem to make the computation easier and then adjusting the answer for the numbers chosen is

called _____.

Products found by breaking one factor in a multiplication problem into ones, tens, and hundreds, and then multiplying each of these by the other factor are

called _____.

© Pearson Education, Inc. 3

Name _____

Solve & Share

Find each product below. **Solve these problems any way you choose.**

$7 \times 30 =$ _____ $2 \times 40 =$ _____ $9 \times 20 =$ _____

⭐ **TEKS 3.4G** Use strategies … to multiply a two-digit number by a one-digit number. Strategies may include mental math … and the commutative, associative … properties. Also, 3.4.
Mathematical Process Standards 3.1B, 3.1C, 3.1D, 3.1F, 3.1G

Digital Resources at PearsonTexas.com

Solve   Learn   Glossary   Check   Tools   Games

You can **connect ideas.** How can multiplication facts and place value help you multiply by multiples of 10? *Show your work!*

Look Back!

Number Sense Describe any patterns you see in the problems and products.

What Is a Rule for Multiplying by a Multiple of 10?

A There are 5 boxes of crayons on a shelf.

Each box has 30 crayons. How many crayons are there?

Find 5×30.

? crayons →

?

5 boxes →

↑
30 crayons in each box

B Apply the Associative Property of Multiplication.

$5 \times 30 = 5 \times (3 \times 10)$
$5 \times 30 = (5 \times 3) \times 10$
$5 \times 30 = 15 \times 10$
$5 \times 30 = 150$

There are 150 crayons.

You can use basic multiplication facts to multiply by multiples of 10.

Use a shortcut to multiply.

C Find 5×30.

Multiply by the digit in the tens place.

$5 \times 3 = 15$

Write one zero after the product.

$5 \times 3\underline{0} = 15\underline{0}$

So, $5 \times 30 = 150$.

D Sometimes, the basic multiplication fact makes the rule look different.

Find 5×60.

Multiply by the digit in the tens place.

$5 \times 6 = 30$

Write one zero after the product.

$5 \times 6\underline{0} = 30\underline{0}$

So, $5 \times 60 = 300$.

When the product of a basic fact ends in zero, the answer will have two zeros.

Do You Understand?

Convince Me! Suppose there are 50 crayons in each of the 5 boxes. Find 5×50 using the Associative Property of Multiplication as shown above. How many crayons are in 5 boxes?

© Pearson Education, Inc. 3

Name _____

In **1** through **7**, complete each equation.

1. $2 \times 70 = 2 \times (\underline{\quad} \times \underline{\quad})$

$2 \times 70 = (2 \times \underline{\quad}) \times \underline{\quad}$

$2 \times 70 = 14 \times \underline{\quad}$

$2 \times 70 = \underline{\quad}$

2. $6 \times 6 = \underline{\quad}$ **3.** $7 \times 8 = \underline{\quad}$

$6 \times 60 = \underline{\quad}$ $70 \times 8 = \underline{\quad}$

4. $5 \times 4 = \underline{\quad}$ **5.** $8 \times 2 = \underline{\quad}$

$5 \times 40 = \underline{\quad}$ $80 \times 2 = \underline{\quad}$

6. $4 \times 9 = \underline{\quad}$ **7.** $3 \times 2 = \underline{\quad}$

$40 \times 9 = \underline{\quad}$ $3 \times 20 = \underline{\quad}$

8. Number Sense What basic fact can you use to find the product of 5×90? What is the product?

9. Reason Sue wants to find the product of 30×2, but knows only the product of 2×30. What property of multiplication could she use to help solve her problem? What basic facts could Sue use to find 30×2 and 2×30?

Independent Practice *

Leveled Practice In **10** through **26**, complete each equation.

10. $6 \times 70 = 6 \times (7 \times \underline{\quad})$

$6 \times 70 = (6 \times \underline{\quad}) \times \underline{\quad}$

$6 \times 70 = \underline{\quad} \times 10$

$6 \times 70 = \underline{\quad}$

11. $9 \times 50 = 9 \times (\underline{\quad} \times 10)$

$9 \times 50 = (9 \times \underline{\quad}) \times \underline{\quad}$

$9 \times 50 = 45 \times \underline{\quad}$

$9 \times 50 = \underline{\quad}$

12. $2 \times 6 = \underline{\quad}$ **13.** $5 \times 8 = \underline{\quad}$ **14.** $9 \times 4 = \underline{\quad}$

$2 \times 60 = \underline{\quad}$ $5 \times 80 = \underline{\quad}$ $9 \times 40 = \underline{\quad}$

15. $2 \times 30 = \underline{\quad}$ **16.** $60 \times 9 = \underline{\quad}$ **17.** $8 \times 20 = \underline{\quad}$

18. $80 \times 5 = \underline{\quad}$ **19.** $90 \times 2 = \underline{\quad}$ **20.** $30 \times 4 = \underline{\quad}$

21. $20 \times 5 = \underline{\quad}$ **22.** $5 \times 70 = \underline{\quad}$ **23.** $90 \times 9 = \underline{\quad}$

24. $7 \times 70 = \underline{\quad}$ **25.** $20 \times 4 = \underline{\quad}$ **26.** $8 \times 30 = \underline{\quad}$

Problem Solving

27. Check for Reasonableness Adam says the product of 2 × 50 equals 100. Dan says the product is 1,000. Who is correct? Explain.

?	
50	50

28. Communicate Debra bought 210 red beads, 137 green beads, and 190 orange beads. How many beads did Debra buy? Show how you can use the Associative Property of Addition to find the sum.

29. Tools What is the time that is halfway between the two times shown?

30. ⭐ A food supply store has 9 rows of boxes of cereal. Each row has the same number of boxes. There is a total of 630 boxes of cereal. How many boxes of cereal are in each row?

$$9 \times \boxed{} = 630$$

A 30
B 70
C 80
D 90

Think of a basic fact to solve.

31. Communicate Hanna has 9 spools of ribbon. Each spool has 60 yards of ribbon. How many yards of ribbon does Hanna have? What basic fact can you use to find the answer?

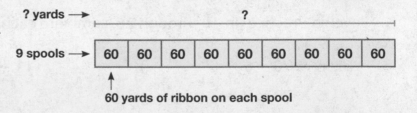

? yards →

9 spools →

60	60	60	60	60	60	60	60	60

60 yards of ribbon on each spool

32. Extend Your Thinking Ali and his family are going to the amusement park. If there are 2 adults and 5 children in the family, how much will the tickets cost? Show your work.

AMUSEMENT PARK
ADULT
$30

AMUSEMENT PARK
CHILD
$20

© Pearson Education, Inc. 3

Name _____

Another Look!

Find 9 × 70.

First, find the product of the basic multiplication fact, 9 × 7.

9 × 7 = 63

Then, write one zero after the product of the fact: **630**. So, 9 × 70 = 630.

Below are a couple more examples.

2 × 7 = 14	6 × 5 = 30
2 × 70 = 140	6 × 50 = 300

> You can use basic facts to help you multiply by multiples of 10.

In **1** and **2**, use basic facts to help you multiply.

1. Find 3 × 80.

Basic fact: 3 × _____ = _____

Show multiplication by 10 by writing a _____ after the product of the fact.

3 × 80 = _____

2. Find 9 × 50.

Basic fact: _____ × _____ = _____

Show multiplication by 10 by writing a _____ after the product of the fact.

9 × 50 = _____

For **3** through **17**, find each product.

3. 8 × 5 = _____
8 × 50 = _____

4. 7 × 3 = _____
70 × 3 = _____

5. 9 × 2 = _____
9 × 20 = _____

6. 7 × 9 = _____
7 × 90 = _____

7. 7 × 5 = _____
70 × 5 = _____

8. 2 × 4 = _____
2 × 40 = _____

9. 5 × 6 = _____
50 × 6 = _____

10. 8 × 7 = _____
80 × 7 = _____

11. 3 × 6 = _____
3 × 60 = _____

12. 30 × 9 = _____

13. 9 × 80 = _____

14. 60 × 6 = _____

15. 5 × 50 = _____

16. 7 × 60 = _____

17. 4 × 30 = _____

18. Communicate Show how the Associative Property of Multiplication can be used to find 3 × 70. Explain what the Associative Property of Multiplication lets you do to find the product.

19. Explain How can you use the basic multiplication fact 4 × 7 = 28 to find 4 × 70?

?			
70	70	70	70

20. Toby wrote a multiplication sentence ★ with 8 as one factor and 480 as the product. What is the other factor?

A 40   C 60

B 50   D 80

21. Communicate Explain why there are two zeros in the product of 5 × 40.

In **22** through **24**, use the tally chart at the right.

22. Analyze Information Sander took a survey of his classmates' favorite fruit. He recorded the data in a tally chart. Which fruit was the favorite? How do you know?

23. How many people took the survey? Explain how you can use skip counting to find the answer.

24. How many more students liked bananas and oranges than apples?

DATA

Favorite Fruits

Fruit	Tally
Apple	‖‖ ////
Banana	‖‖ ‖‖ //
Orange	‖‖ ‖‖ ////

25. Extend Your Thinking Yoshi made the two arrays shown at the right to find 4 × 8. Explain how he could change the arrays to find 5 × 8.

© Pearson Education, Inc. 3

Name _____

☆ **Solve & Share**

One part of Tina's vegetable garden has beans. Tina planted 3 rows of beans with 23 plants in each row. How many plants are in this part of Tina's garden? Think about place value and draw an array to help you solve this problem.

⭐ **TEKS 3.4G** Use strategies ... to multiply a two-digit number by a one-digit number. Strategies may include mental math, partial products, and the ... distributive properties.
Mathematical Process Standards 3.1B, 3.1C, 3.1D, 3.1E, 3.1F, 3.1G

You can **create and use representations.** You can use pictures of place-value blocks to make an array. *Show your work in the space below!*

Digital Resources at PearsonTexas.com

Solve · Learn · Glossary · Check · Tools · Games

Look Back!

Communicate When finding 3 × 23, how can breaking apart 23 by place value help you find the product?

A

How Can You Use Breaking Apart to Multiply?

A parking lot has the same number of spaces in each row. How many spaces are in the lot?

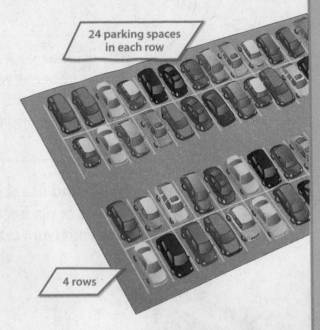

24 parking spaces in each row

4 rows

You can multiply to find the total for an array.

B
Step 1

Use an array to show 4×24.

Use the distributive property.
Break apart 24 into 20 and 4.
Think of 4×24 as

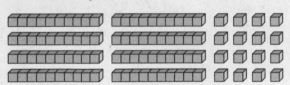

$(4 \times 20) + (4 \times 4)$.

80   16

C
Step 2

Add each part to find the total.

$80 + 16 = 96$

80 and 16 are called partial products because they are parts of the product.

$4 \times 24 = 96$

There are 96 spaces in the parking lot.

Do You Understand?

Convince Me! Suppose there are 6 rows of 24 cars. How would the partial products be similar to the partial products in the example above? How would they be different?

© Pearson Education, Inc. 3

Name _____

In **1** and **2**, complete each number sentence. You may use place-value blocks or drawings to help.

1. 4×32

   $4 \times 30 =$ ____

   $4 \times 2 =$ ____

   ____ + ____ = ____

2. 5×47

   $5 \times 40 =$ ____

   $5 \times 7 =$ ____

   ____ + ____ = ____

3. **Connect** In the parking lot example on page 454, what two place-value groups is the array broken into?

4. **Analyze Information** The new bicycles at a bicycle factory are stored in 3 equal rows. There are 24 bicycles in each row. How many new bicycles are stored at the factory?

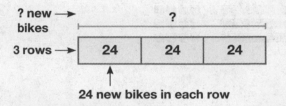

24 new bikes in each row

☆ **Independent Practice** ☆

Leveled Practice For **5** through **15**, find each product. You may use place-value blocks or drawings to help. Show your work in **8** through **15**.

5. 5×24

   $5 \times 20 =$ ____

   ____ × ____ = ____

   ____ + ____ = ____

6. 3×62

   $3 \times 60 =$ ____

   ____ × ____ = ____

   ____ + ____ = ____

7. 6×49

   $6 \times 40 =$ ____

   ____ × ____ = ____

   ____ + ____ = ____

8. $4 \times 16 =$ ____

9. $7 \times 25 =$ ____

10. $6 \times 32 =$ ____

11. $3 \times 87 =$ ____

12. $5 \times 43 =$ ____

13. $2 \times 54 =$ ____

14. $3 \times 58 =$ ____

15. $9 \times 64 =$ ____

Problem Solving

16. Reason Ryan wants to buy lamps that cost $68 each. If Ryan has $200, can he buy three lamps? Explain.

17. Tools Look at the time on the clock. Write two ways to say the time.

2:30

18. Check for Reasonableness Nina used place-value blocks to show how to find the product of 3 × 24. Is her model correct? Why or why not?

19. ⭐ Which shows how to break apart 4 × 42 by place value, and use the Distributive Property to find the partial products?

   A (4 × 4) + (4 × 2)

   B (4 × 40) + (4 × 2)

   C (4 × 40) + (4 × 1)

   D (4 × 40) + (2 × 2)

20. Extend Your Thinking Gina does 32 sit-ups every morning. Shirley does 6 fewer sit-ups each morning than Gina. How many sit-ups do Gina and Shirley do altogether in 4 days? Show how you found your answer using partial products.

21. Analyze Information Mr. Williams has three types of art in his gallery. He has 7 watercolor paintings. He has two times the number of oil paintings as watercolor paintings. He has 4 times as many sculptures as oil paintings. How many sculptures does Mr. Williams have in his gallery?

In **22** and **23**, use the table at the right.

22. Number Sense Brendan trained all summer for a bicycle race. How many miles did he bike?

23. Represent What is the difference between the greatest number of miles and the least number of miles Brendan biked? Draw a strip diagram and write an addition equation to solve.

Month	Miles Biked
June	150
July	198
August	212

© Pearson Education, Inc. 3

Name _____

Another Look!
Find 4 × 35.

Break apart 2-digit numbers by place value to multiply.

Break apart 35 into 30 + 5.

Multiply the tens.	Multiply the ones.
4 × 30 = 120	4 × 5 = 20

Add the partial products: 120 + 20 = 140.

So, 4 × 35 = 140.

For **1** through **14**, find each product. You may use place-value blocks or drawings to help. Show your work in **7** through **14**.

1. 5 × 32
5 × 30 = ____
5 × 2 = ____
____ + ____ = ____

2. 4 × 56
4 × 50 = ____
4 × 6 = ____
____ + ____ = ____

3. 6 × 73
6 × 70 = ____
6 × 3 = ____
____ + ____ = ____

4. 9 × 42
9 × 40 = ____
9 × 2 = ____
____ + ____ = ____

5. 5 × 57
5 × 50 = ____
5 × 7 = ____
____ + ____ = ____

6. 3 × 82
3 × 80 = ____
3 × 2 = ____
____ + ____ = ____

7. 7 × 24 = ____

8. 9 × 31 = ____

9. 6 × 64 = ____

10. 8 × 44 = ____

11. 4 × 48 = ____

12. 8 × 39 = ____

13. 7 × 27 = ____

14. 3 × 96 = ____

15. Communicate How can you find 8 × 42 by breaking apart one of the factors?

16. Construct Arguments Tani said, "To find 6 × 33, I can find (6 × 3) + (6 × 3). This will give me 18 + 18. Then, I can find the sum of the partial products." Do you agree with Tani? Why or why not?

17. Draw a Picture Draw an array to show 2 × 34. Break apart 34 by place value. What partial products does your array show? What is the answer to the problem?

18. Tools Steve had 75 pennies and gave 37 of them to his friend. Use the number line to find how many pennies Steve has left.

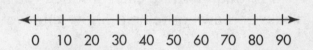

0 10 20 30 40 50 60 70 80 90

19. ⭐ Which shows how to break apart 5 × 78 by place value, and use the distributive property to find the partial products?

  A (5 × 7) + (5 × 8)
  B (5 × 5) + (5 × 8)
  C (5 × 70) + (5 × 7)
  D (5 × 70) + (5 × 8)

20. Extend Your Thinking April and Cora each jumped rope 6 times. April made 32 jumps each time. Cora made twice as many jumps as April. How many jumps did they make all together? Show how you can use partial products to find the answer.

21. Connect Marco made the shape at the right by putting together three other shapes. What shape did Marco make? What shapes did he use to make it?

Two-dimensional shapes can contain other shapes.

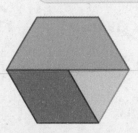

© Pearson Education, Inc. 3

Name _____

Solve & Share

Suppose you ride your bicycle 28 miles each week. How many miles would you ride in 4 weeks? Find the answer using mental math and explain your thinking.

TEKS 3.4G Use strategies ... to multiply a two-digit number by a one-digit number. Strategies may include mental math....
Mathematical Process Standards 3.1B, 3.1C, 3.1D, 3.1F, 3.1G

You can use **mental math.** Using a number that is compatible with 28 can help you multiply mentally.

Digital Resources at PearsonTexas.com

Solve   Learn   Glossary   Check   Tools   Games

Look Back!

Communicate Explain how you could use place value and partial products to find the product of 4 × 28 mentally.

What Are Some Ways to Multiply Mentally?

A

Evan rode his bicycle for 18 miles each day for 3 days. How many miles did Evan ride his bicycle?

Find 3 × 18 mentally.

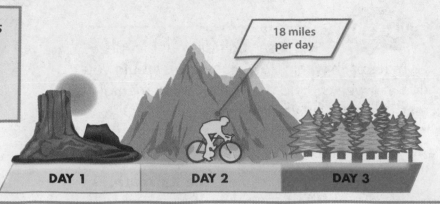

18 miles per day

DAY 1   DAY 2   DAY 3

B

One Way

Use compensation to find 3 × 18.

Substitute a number for 18 that is easy to multiply.

3 × 18

20 is 2 more than 18.

3 × 20 = 60

Now adjust. Subtract 3 groups of 2.

60 − 6 = 54
So, 3 × 18 = 54.

Evan rode his bicycle 54 miles.

C

Another Way

Pela rode her bicycle 32 miles each day for 3 days. How many miles did she ride?

Substitute a number for 32 that is easy to multiply.

3 × 32

30 is 2 less than 32.

3 × 30 = 90

Now adjust. Add 3 groups of 2.

90 + 6 = 96
So, 3 × 32 = 96.

Pela rode her bicycle 96 miles.

With compensation, you choose numbers close to the numbers in the problem to make the computation easier and then adjust the answer for the numbers chosen.

Do You Understand?

Convince Me! Explain how you would use mental math to find 4 × 56.

Name _____

 **Guided Practice**

In **1** through **3**, use compensation to find each product mentally.

1. 4×33

Substitute: $4 \times$ ____ $= 120$

Adjust: ____ $+ 12 =$ ____

2. $6 \times 37 =$ ____

3. $59 \times 3 =$ ____

4. Connect Why were 3 groups of 2 subtracted instead of added in the One Way example on page 460?

5. Explain Use compensation to find 73×3 mentally. Explain the process.

Independent Practice

Leveled Practice In **6** through **18**, use compensation to find each product.

6. 5×17 Substitute: $5 \times$ ____ $= 100$ Adjust: ____ $- 15 =$ ____

7. 3×43 Substitute: $3 \times$ ____ $= 120$ Adjust: ____ $+ 9 =$ ____

8. 7×29 Substitute: $7 \times$ ____ $= 210$ Adjust: $210 -$ ____ $=$ ____

9. 5×62 Substitute: $5 \times$ ____ $= 300$ Adjust: $300 +$ ____ $=$ ____

10. $7 \times 28 =$ ____

11. $61 \times 8 =$ ____

12. $64 \times 3 =$ ____

13. $4 \times 23 =$ ____

14. $44 \times 6 =$ ____

15. $9 \times 52 =$ ____

16. $9 \times 83 =$ ____

17. $2 \times 68 =$ ____

18. $95 \times 5 =$ ____

---

*For another example, see Set C on page 480.

Topic 8 | Lesson 8-3   **461**

Problem Solving

19. Personal Financial Literacy Felicia owed her cousin $12 for a T-shirt she bought. Then, Felicia borrowed another $15 from her cousin. If she pays back $9 each month, how long will it take Felicia to repay all of the money she borrowed?

20. A store clerk stacks soup cans on shelves. He decides to put 88 cans on each shelf. How many more cans will he put on 6 shelves than on 4 shelves?

A 880

B 276

C 236

D 176

21. Check for Reasonableness Eric says to find 3×67 using compensation, he can find 3×70 to get 210. Then, he can add 3 groups of 3 to get $210 + 9 = 219$. Is Eric correct? Why or why not? What is the product?

22. Number Sense Robin made 34 rings. She sold 8 rings on Monday and 6 rings on Tuesday. On Wednesday, Robin sold two times the number of rings she sold on Tuesday. How many rings does Robin have at the end of Wednesday?

23. Use a Strip Diagram Darren spent the same amount of time Wednesday and Thursday reading. On Friday he read for 10 minutes. If Darren read 40 minutes during the 3 days, how many minutes did he read on Wednesday? On Thursday?

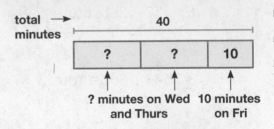

For **24** and **25**, use the table at the right.

24. Mental Math How much more money was spent for the number of pennants sold, than the number of caps sold?

25. Extend Your Thinking Mia and Nikki have been saving so they can each buy a cap, mug, and pennant. Together, the girls have $44 to spend. Will they be able to buy the items? Explain.

School Spirit Items		
Item	Cost	Number Sold
Caps	$8	39
Mugs	$6	41
Pennants	$7	56

© Pearson Education, Inc. 3

Name _____

Another Look!

Find 4 × 19 using compensation.

Step 1

Substitute a number for 19 that is easy to multiply by 4.

4 × 19
↓   Add 1 to make 20.
4 × 20

If you subtract when you substitute, you add to adjust. If you add when you substitute, you subtract to adjust.

Step 2

Find the new product.

4 × 20 = 80

Step 3

Now adjust. Subtract 4 groups of 1.

80 − 4 = 76   So, 4 × 19 = 76

For **1** through **13**, use compensation to find each product.

1. 5 × 32   Substitute: 5 × ____ = 150   Adjust: ____ + 10 = ____

2. 66 × 2   Substitute: 2 × ____ = 140   Adjust: ____ − 8 = ____

3. 7 × 82   Substitute: 7 × ____ = 560   Adjust: ____ + 14 = ____

4. 59 × 5   Substitute: 5 × ____ = 300   Adjust: ____ − 5 = ____

5. 69 × 8 = ____   **6.** 4 × 29 = ____   **7.** 2 × 47 = ____

8. 34 × 4 = ____   **9.** 53 × 7 = ____   **10.** 9 × 78 = ____

11. 7 × 91 = ____   **12.** 41 × 6 = ____   **13.** 17 × 5 = ____

14. Use a Strip Diagram Yolena and 3 friends bought tickets to a musical. The cost of each ticket was $43. How much did all of the tickets cost? Explain how you found the answer.

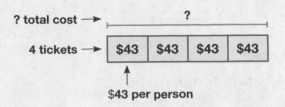

? total cost →

4 tickets →

| $43 | $43 | $43 | $43 |

↑
$43 per person

If you subtract to compensate, you add to adjust.

15. Communicate Use the picture at the right to find how many passengers 7 cabins can hold on the London Eye Ferris Wheel. Explain how you found the answer.

Each cabin can hold up to 25 passengers.

16. Check for Reasonableness Quinn used compensation to find the product of 37 × 4. First, she added 3 to 37 to get 40 and found 40 × 4 = 160. Then, she adjusted that product by adding 3 groups of 4 to get 172. Was Quinn's method reasonable? Why or why not?

17. ★ Davidson's Bakery uses 9 dozen eggs to make cookies each day. How many eggs are used at the bakery each day?

There are 12 eggs in 1 dozen.

A 90
B 98
C 108
D 112

18. Kevin drew the shape below. Name the shape and tell how many sides and vertices it has.

19. Extend Your Thinking Ms. Jacobs bought 4 cartons of markers. Each carton contained 18 boxes of markers, and each box contained 6 markers. How many markers did Ms. Jacobs buy?

© Pearson Education, Inc. 3

Solve & Share

Giant kelp is a water plant that grows about 18 inches in a day. Does this plant grow more than 100 inches in a week? Without finding an exact answer, explain how you can decide. **Solve this problem any way you choose.**

Lesson 8-4
Using Rounding to Estimate

TEKS 3.4G Use strategies … to multiply a two-digit number by a one-digit number. Strategies may include mental math … . **Mathematical Process Standards** 3.1A, 3.1B, 3.1C, 3.1D, 3.1G

Digital Resources at PearsonTexas.com

 Solve   Learn   Glossary   Check   Tools    Games

You can **select and use tools.** What tool can help you estimate?

Look Back!

Estimation Describe how rounding the number of inches giant kelp grows in one day to the nearest ten can help you estimate the number of inches this plant can grow in a week.

A

Bamboo is one of the fastest growing plants on Earth. It can grow up to 36 inches in a day. Can it grow more than 200 inches in a week?

You can estimate when you do not need an exact answer.

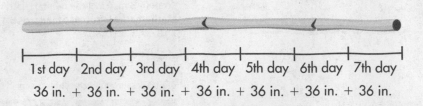

1st day 2nd day 3rd day 4th day 5th day 6th day 7th day
36 in. + 36 in. + 36 in. + 36 in. + 36 in. + 36 in. + 36 in.

B ## Step 1

An estimate is enough to find out if bamboo can grow more than 200 inches in a week.

Estimate 7 × 36.

Round 36 to the nearest ten.

halfway number
36

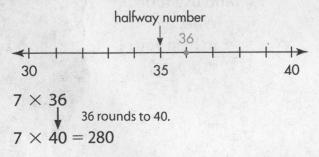

30   35   40

7 × 36
↓   36 rounds to 40.
7 × 40 = 280

7 × 36 is about 280.

C ## Step 2

Compare the estimate to 200 inches.

280 > 200

So, a bamboo plant can grow more than 200 inches in a week.

Did you know that 280 inches is about 23 feet?

Do You Understand?

Convince Me! Is the estimate in the example above greater than or less than the exact answer? Without finding the exact answer, how do you know?

© Pearson Education, Inc. 3

Name _____

For **1**, estimate the product.

1. 6 × 16

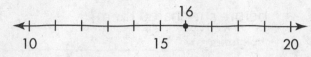

16 rounds to _____

6 × _____ = _____

2. Justify Is the exact answer for 6 × 16 greater than or less than your estimate in Exercise 1? How do you know, without finding the exact answer?

Independent Practice ☆

Leveled Practice In **3** through **20**, use rounding to estimate the product.

3. 2 × 46

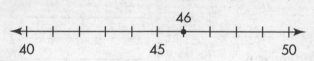

46 rounds to _____

2 × _____ = _____

4. 8 × 31

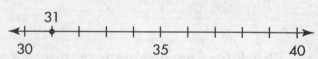

31 rounds to _____

8 × _____ = _____

5. 5 × 84   **6.** 7 × 26   **7.** 9 × 23   **8.** 3 × 67

9. 8 × 44   **10.** 9 × 47   **11.** 4 × 71   **12.** 6 × 85

13. 4 × 58   **14.** 6 × 18   **15.** 5 × 82   **16.** 7 × 97

17.   56   **18.**   73   **19.**   29   **20.**   47
     × 2   × 5   × 3   × 6

Problem Solving

21. Jamal is buying 5 books. Each book costs $19. Which number sentence shows the best estimate for the total cost of the books?

A 5 × $10 = $50

B $5 + $20 = $25

C 5 × $20 = $100

D 5 × $30 = $150

22. Number Sense Leslie had a number of pictures on Monday. On Tuesday, she and two friends shared the pictures equally. Each person got 8 pictures. How many pictures did Leslie have on Monday before she shared them?

? pictures ⟶   ?

3 people ⟶ | 8 | 8 | 8 |

↑ 8 pictures for each person

For **23** and **24**, use the bar graph at the right.

23. Communicate Does a Giant Bamboo plant grow more than 100 inches in 6 days? Explain how to round to estimate the answer.

24. Check for Reasonableness Jim says a eucalyptus tree grows more in 8 days than Callie grass grows in 2 days. Is Jim's statement reasonable? Explain.

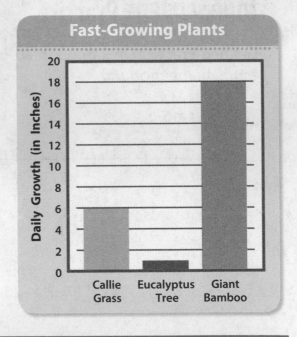

Fast-Growing Plants

---

25. Personal Financial Literacy David and Tammi work on web page designs. David worked 35 hours last week and Tammi worked 40 hours. David earns $9 per hour, and Tammi earns $8 per hour. Which person earned more money last week? How much more did that person earn?

26. Extend Your Thinking There are 18 rows of passenger seats on an airplane. Each row has 6 seats. Use rounding to estimate the total number of passenger seats on the plane. Draw a number line to show how you rounded.

© Pearson Education, Inc. 3

Name _____

Another Look!

You can use rounding to estimate products.

Estimate 6 × 22.

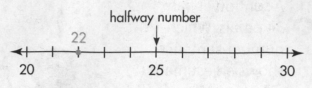

halfway number

22 rounds to 20.

6 × 20 = 120

So, 6 × 22 is about 120.

Estimate 8 × 37.

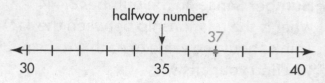

halfway number

37 rounds to 40.

8 × 40 = 320

So, 8 × 37 is about 320.

In **1** through **18**, use rounding to estimate the product.

1. Estimate 8 × 93.

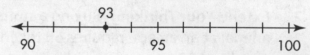

93 rounds to ____

8 × ____ = ____

2. Estimate 4 × 67.

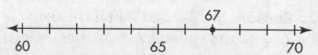

67 rounds to ____

4 × ____ = ____

3. 3 × 53

4. 7 × 69

5. 7 × 88

6. 8 × 39

7. 5 × 36

8. 8 × 53

9. 9 × 27

10. 6 × 31

11. 8 × 27

12. 3 × 54

13. 2 × 63

14. 5 × 98

15. 74
   × 6

16. 18
   × 3

17. 28
   × 9

18. 88
   × 5

19. **Connect** Audrey delivers 38 newspapers each day of the week except Sunday. About how many newspapers does Audrey deliver in a week? Explain how you rounded to estimate the answer.

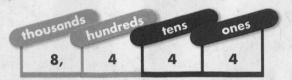

1st day	2nd day	3rd day	4th day	5th day	6th day

38 + 38 + 38 + 38 + 38 + 38

20. **Number Sense** In the number 8,444, what is the relationship between the 4s? Think about the value of each 4 to help you find your answer.

thousands hundreds tens ones

| 8, | 4 | 4 | 4 |

21. A sunflower has 34 petals. Which number sentence shows an estimate using rounding for about how many petals 9 sunflowers have?

A $9 + 34 = 43$

B $5 \times 25 = 125$

C $9 \times 30 = 270$

D $9 \times 50 = 450$

22. **Reason** Marcia said that if she uses 7×70 to estimate 7×73, her estimate will be less than the exact answer. Is Marcia correct? Explain.

23. **Extend Your Thinking** Buying a stuffed animal at an arcade requires 55 tokens. Tom has 100 tokens. He said he can buy 2 stuffed animals. Is Tom correct? Explain how he can use estimation with rounding to find the answer.

24. **Communicate** A basketball player scores an average of 32 points per game. About how many points will she score in 8 games? On the number line, show how you can round 32 to the nearest ten to estimate. Explain how you found your estimate.

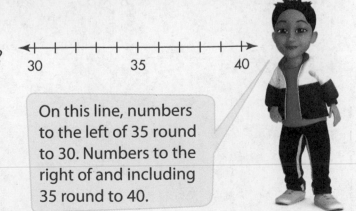

30   35   40

On this line, numbers to the left of 35 round to 30. Numbers to the right of and including 35 round to 40.

© Pearson Education, Inc. 3

Name _____

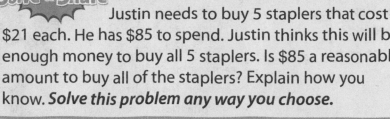

☆ ☆
Solve & Share

Justin needs to buy 5 staplers that cost $21 each. He has $85 to spend. Justin thinks this will be enough money to buy all 5 staplers. Is $85 a reasonable amount to buy all of the staplers? Explain how you know. *Solve this problem any way you choose.*

You can **check for reasonableness.** Can rounding help you check if the amount Justin has to buy the staplers is reasonable? *Show your work in the space below!*

⟳ **TEKS 3.1B** Use a problem-solving model that incorporates analyzing given information, … justifying the solution, … and the reasonableness of the solution. Also, 3.4G.
Mathematical Process Standards 3.1D, 3.1G

Digital Resources at PearsonTexas.com

Solve   Learn   Glossary   Check   Tools   Games

Look Back!

Check for Reasonableness If Justin had $110 to buy the 5 staplers, would this amount be more reasonable than $85? How do you know?

A Analyze

Karen glued sequins onto her project. She used 7 rows with 28 sequins in each row. How many sequins did Karen glue onto her project?

Ask yourself: Is my calculation reasonable? Did I answer the right question?

? sequins →

?

7 rows → | 28 | 28 | 28 | 28 | 28 | 28 | 28 |

↑
28 sequins in each row

Answer: Karen glued 155 sequins onto her project.

After you solve a problem, check to see if your answer is reasonable.

B Justify and Evaluate

Is my calculation reasonable?

I can use estimation.

To the nearest ten, 28 rounds to 30.

$7 \times 30 = 210$.

My answer is 155, but my estimate is 210. My answer is not reasonable. I should check my computation for 7×28.

C Did I answer the right question?

The question asks for the number of sequins Karen glued onto her project. I answered the right question, but my computation is incorrect.

The correct answer is 196 sequins.

Do You Understand?

Convince Me! Jeremy says that 5×48 equals 390. Use an estimate to decide if Jeremy's answer is reasonable. Justify your decision.

© Pearson Education, Inc. 3

Guided Practice

Decide if the given answer is reasonable. Justify your decision.

1. A pet shop had 5 empty fish tanks. After a delivery, 41 fish were put in each tank. How many fish were in the delivery?

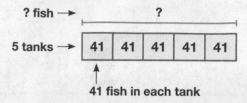

? fish → ?

5 tanks →

| 41 | 41 | 41 | 41 | 41 |

↑
41 fish in each tank

Answer: 205 fish were in the delivery.

2. In the example on page 472, how could you use mental math to find 7 × 28?

3. **Communicate** Write and solve a real-world multiplication problem. Exchange problems with a partner. Check answers for reasonableness.

Independent Practice

In **4** through **7**, decide if the given answer is reasonable. Justify your decision.

4. Malak bought 6 shirts that cost $22 each. How much did Malak pay?

   Answer: Malak paid $98.

5. A cook put 4 pecans on each of the 64 desserts she made for a party. How many pecans did she use?

   Answer: The cook used 256 pecans.

6. Jen has 39 glass beads. Mary has three times as many beads as Jen. How many beads does Mary have?

   Answer: Mary has 42 beads.

7. There were 482 concert tickets for sale. So far 129 tickets have sold. How many tickets have not sold?

   Answer: There are 611 tickets for sale.

Problem Solving

In **8** and **9**, use the table at the right.

8. **Check for Reasonableness** How many miles does a mail carrier walk in 8 weeks? Estimate first, then solve. Is your answer reasonable? Explain.

	Job	Distance Walked in 1 Week
DATA	Doctor	17 miles
	Mail carrier	21 miles
	Police officer	32 miles

9. **Analyze Information** How many more miles does a police officer walk than a doctor, in 6 weeks? Check your answer for reasonableness.

10. **Math and Science** Mass is the amount of matter in an object. Which is greater, the mass of 10 adult bowling balls or the mass of 23 bowling balls for children? How much greater is the mass?

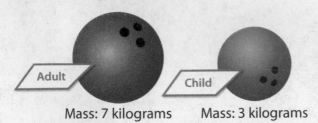

Adult — Mass: 7 kilograms   Child — Mass: 3 kilograms

11. **Communicate** The Colorado River is about 1,450 kilometers long. The Canadian River is about 1,457 kilometers long. Which of these estimated river lengths is an even number? Write the number. How do you know it is an even number?

12. **Extend Your Thinking** Derick created 12 drawings with a program on his computer. Janine created 5 times as many drawings as Derick. By the end of next month, Janine will create another 14 drawings. How many drawings will Janine have created by the end of next month? Explain how you can check for reasonableness.

13. Duane wants to use mental math to find 2 × 38. He can use compensation to find the product mentally. Duane begins by thinking of a number that is close to 38. What steps should Duane follow next?

A Multiply: 2 × 40 = 80;
   Subtract: 80 − 2 = 78

B Multiply: 2 × 30 = 60;
   Add: 60 + 8 = 68

C Multiply: 2 × 40 = 80;
   Subtract: 80 − 4 = 76

D Multiply: 2 × 40 = 80;
   Add: 80 + 4 = 84

© Pearson Education, Inc. 3

Name _____

Another Look!

Analyze   There are 5 animals on a farm. Each animal eats 85 pounds of food per week. How many pounds of food do the animals eat each week?

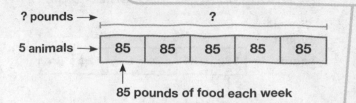

85 pounds of food each week

Answer: The animals eat 425 pounds of food each week.

Justify and Evaluate   To check for reasonableness, first, ask yourself, "Did I answer the right question?" Then, estimate to check your answer. $5 \times 90 = 450$. The answer is reasonable because 450 is close to 425.

After solving a problem, it is important to check your answer to see if it is reasonable.

In **1** through **4**, decide if the given answer is reasonable. Justify your decision.

1. Jaime practiced swimming for 8 hours each week for 12 weeks. How many hours did Jaime practice?

   Answer: Jaime practiced 66 hours.

   Was the right question answered? ____

   Estimate: $8 \times$ ____ $= 80$

   Is the estimate close to the answer? ____

   Is the answer reasonable? ____

2. Sue's family bought 6 tickets to a baseball game. Each ticket cost $28. How much did the family spend on tickets?

   Answer: The family spent $168.

   Was the right question answered? ____

   Estimate: ____ $\times 30 =$ ____

   Is the estimate close to the answer? ____

   Is the answer reasonable? ____

3. Mr. Dexter uses 9 rows of bricks for his patio. Each row has 77 bricks. How many bricks does Mr. Dexter use?

   Answer: Mr. Dexter uses 633 bricks.

4. Gianna had some colored pencils. She gave 29 of them to her friend and has 33 of the pencils left. How many colored pencils did Gianna have to begin with?

   Answer: Gianna had 62 colored pencils.

5. **Check for Reasonableness** Vernon is selling baseball cards for 12¢ each. He is selling 6 cards and says he will make $1.00. Is Vernon's answer reasonable? Explain.

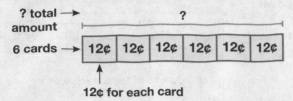

? total amount →

?

6 cards → | 12¢ | 12¢ | 12¢ | 12¢ | 12¢ | 12¢ |

12¢ for each card

6. **Explain** Nari wants to give 5 stickers to everyone in her class. Her class sits in 4 rows of 7 students. Nari says she'll need 140 stickers. Is Nari's statement reasonable? How do you know?

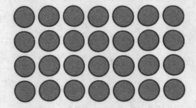

7. Victor has 7 stacks of coins with 63 coins in each stack. Which is the most reasonable number of coins Victor has?

   A 300, because 7 × 63 is about 7 × 40 = 280.

   B 360, because 7 × 63 is about 7 × 50 = 350.

   C 441, because 7 × 63 is about 7 × 60 = 420.

   D 500, because 7 × 63 is about 7 × 70 = 490.

8. **Math and Science** Stephie made a boat from a small piece of aluminum foil. She placed the boat in water, and dropped pennies in, one at a time. Her boat held 20 pennies and was able to float. She then made another boat that held 23 pennies and a third boat that held 45 pennies. How many pennies did the three boats hold? Write a number sentence that models the problem and shows the solution.

In **9** and **10**, use the table at the right.

9. **Analyze Information** Julie planted a sunflower and recorded its height in a table after each week. How tall will the sunflower be after the fifth week if it continues to grow the same number of inches each week? Explain.

Height of Sunflower	
Week	**Height (in Inches)**
1	16
2	32
3	48
4	64
5	

DATA

10. **Extend Your Thinking** The world's largest sunflower was about 300 inches tall. Julie says her sunflower will be that tall after 3 months. Is Julie's answer reasonable? Explain.

Remember, there are about 4 weeks in 1 month.

© Pearson Education, Inc. 3

Name _____

1. **Check for Reasonableness** Jeb says the product of 3 × 40 is 120. Ken says the product is 1,200. Who is correct? Explain.

_____

2. **Explain** Carrie made these two arrays to find 6 × 4. Explain how she can change the arrays to find 7 × 4.

Applying Math Processes

- How does this problem connect to previous ones?
- What is my plan?
- How can I use tools?
- How can I use number sense?
- How can I communicate and represent my thinking?
- How can I organize and record information?
- How can I explain my work?
- How can I justify my answer?

3. **Extend Your Thinking** Jack has 42 pennies. Tim has four times as many pennies as Jack. How many pennies will Tim have if he gives 50 pennies to his brother? Check your answer for reasonableness.

4. **Represent** A school store has 47 notebooks and five times as many pens as notebooks. How many of these supplies does the school store have? Draw a strip diagram to represent and solve this problem.

5. **Communicate** Ming runs an average of 22 miles a week. About how many miles will he run in 4 weeks? Explain how to use the number line to estimate the number of miles Ming will run.

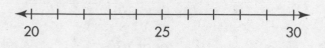

6. **Represent** Liza and her friends are making wristbands. Liza makes 8 wristbands. Stan makes 6 wristbands, and Cole makes 5 wristbands. Use pictures, numbers, or words to show two different ways to find the total number of wristbands that were made.

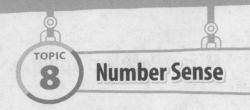

Error Search

In **1** through **6**, circle each problem that is not correct. Then, rewrite the problem so it is correct.

1. $9 \times 60 = 450$

2. $3 \times 42 = 162$

3. $70 \times 7 = 490$

4. $54 \times 6 = 423$

5. $5 \times 64 = 320$

6. $18 \times 9 = 226$

Over or Under?

In **7** through **18**, circle the better estimate.

7. 4×65

over 280

under 280

8. 9×32

over 270

under 270

9. 3×68

over 210

under 210

10. 5×74

over 350

under 350

11. 7×34

over 210

under 210

12. 8×47

over 400

under 400

13. 2×78

over 160

under 160

14. 6×63

over 360

under 360

15. 9×57

over 540

under 540

16. 4×51

over 200

under 200

17. 6×75

over 480

under 480

18. 3×39

over 120

under 120

© Pearson Education, Inc. 3

Name _____

Set A pages 447–452

Find 6 × 30. Apply the Associative Property of Multiplication.

$$6 \times 30 = 6 \times (3 \times 10)$$
$$6 \times 30 = (6 \times 3) \times 10$$
$$6 \times 30 = 18 \times 10$$
$$6 \times 30 = 180$$

You can use basic multiplication facts to multiply by multiples of 10.

Find 6 × 30.

Multiply by the digit in the tens place.

$$6 \times 3 = 18$$

Write one zero after the product of the basic fact.

$$6 \times 3\underline{0} = 18\underline{0}$$

Remember that some multiplication facts, such as 6 × 5, include a 0.

In **1** through **11**, use the Associative Property of Multiplication or basic facts to find each product.

1. 3 × 30   **2.** 50 × 9

3. 6 × 60   **4.** 5 × 80

5. 8 × 40   **6.** 80 × 7

7. 70 × 4   **8.** 8 × 30

9. 7 × 70   **10.** 90 × 5

11. Griffin bought 6 new songs online. Including the new songs, he now has 20 playlists with 5 songs in each playlist. How many songs does Griffin have?

Set B pages 453–458

Find 3 × 26. Use an array to show 3 × 26.

Break apart 26 into 20 and 6.

Think of 3 × 26 as:

$$(3 \times 20) + (3 \times 6)$$
$$60 \quad + \quad 18 = 78$$

So, 3 × 26 = 78.

You can use the Distributive Property to find products of 2-digit by 1-digit numbers.

Remember to break apart the 2-digit numbers by place value to multiply.

In **1** through **8**, find each product. You may use place-value blocks or drawings to help.

1. 6 × 17   **2.** 5 × 39

3. 7 × 82   **4.** 4 × 18

5. 8 × 43   **6.** 3 × 65

7. 9 × 54   **8.** 2 × 98

Topic 8 | Reteaching   **479**

Set C pages 459–464

Use compensation to find 4 × 28.

Substitute a number for 28 that is easier to multiply.

4 × 28
↓
          30 is 2 more than 28.
4 × 30 = 120

Now adjust. Subtract 4 groups of 2.

120 − 8 = 112   So, 4 × 28 = 112.

Remember that with compensation, you choose numbers close to the numbers in the problem to make the computation easier.

In **1** through **4**, use compensation to find each product mentally.

1. 21 × 8   **2.** 4 × 49

3. 7 × 62   **4.** 87 × 6

Set D pages 465–470

Estimate 4 × 67.

Round 67 to the nearest ten.

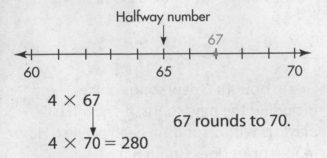

Halfway number

60   65   70

4 × 67
↓
          67 rounds to 70.
4 × 70 = 280

So, 4 × 67 is about 280.

Remember that you can use a number line and rounding to estimate products.

In **1** through **8**, estimate each product.

1. 3 × 63   **2.** 8 × 77

3. 6 × 57   **4.** 4 × 82

5. 7 × 75   **6.** 5 × 92

7. 2 × 68   **8.** 5 × 39

Set E pages 471–476

Ernesto is making 6 birdhouses. For each birdhouse he needs 28 nails. How many nails does he need?

Answer: Ernesto needs 148 nails.

I can check for reasonableness. I can estimate 6 × 30 = 180. 148 is not close to the estimate. The right question was answered in the problem, but the calculation is incorrect. The answer is not reasonable.

Remember to ask yourself if the right question was answered and if it is close to your estimate.

Decide if the given answer is reasonable. Justify your decision.

1. There are 48 marbles in each of 4 bags. How many marbles are in the bags?

Answer: There are 192 marbles in the bags.

© Pearson Education, Inc. 3

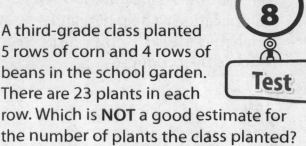

1. Hans does 25 jumping jacks every morning. Taylor does 2 times as many jumping jacks as Hans each day. How many jumping jacks do they both do in 5 days?

   A 125   **C** 275

   B 250   **D** Not here

2. The third-grade teachers at Jenny's school need 5 boxes of yellow folders and 4 boxes of red folders. Each box has 40 folders. How many folders do the teachers need?

   A 360

   B 400

   C 540

   D 800

3. Lily used compensation to find 3×26 mentally. Her answer is 90. Is Lily's answer correct? Which is the best explanation for why or why not?

   A Yes, she is correct because $26 + 4 = 30$, and $30 \times 3 = 90$.

   B Yes, she is correct because 90 is a close estimate for the exact answer.

   C No, she is incorrect because $3 \times 20 = 60$.

   D No, she is incorrect because she forgot to compensate by subtracting 3 groups of 4 from 90.

4. A third-grade class planted 5 rows of corn and 4 rows of beans in the school garden. There are 23 plants in each row. Which is **NOT** a good estimate for the number of plants the class planted?

   A About 180   **C** About 230

   B About 200   **D** About 300

5. Felicia wants to find how many counters are in 8 rows, with 37 counters in each row. She substitutes 40 for 37 by adding 3 to 37. Then she finds $8 \times 40 = 320$. What should Felicia do next?

   A Add 8 groups of 3 to 320.

   B Subtract 8 groups of 3 from 320.

   C Subtract 3 from 320.

   D Add 3 to 320.

6. Gil drew the array below to find 7×33.

   _____ _____ _____ ○ ○ ○
   _____ _____ _____ ○ ○ ○
   _____ _____ _____ ○ ○ ○
   _____ _____ _____ ○ ○ ○
   _____ _____ _____ ○ ○ ○
   _____ _____ _____ ○ ○ ○
   _____ _____ _____ ○ ○ ○

   Which shows the partial products Gil could use to find the product?

   A $7 \times 3 = 21$ and $7 \times 3 = 21$

   B $7 \times 30 = 210$ and $3 \times 3 = 9$

   C $7 \times 10 = 70$ and $7 \times 3 = 21$

   D $7 \times 30 = 210$ and $7 \times 3 = 21$

7. Tom uses the Associative Property of Multiplication to help him find 4×30. Tom writes $4 \times (3 \times 10) = (4 \times 3) \times 10$. Which is the product?

A 22

B 34

C 120

D 160

10. Jana has 22 nickels. She says that the value of all her nickels is more than $1. Which is the best estimate to help you decide if Jana's statement is reasonable?

A 22 rounds to 20. $5 \times 20 = 100$, so Jana has about 100 cents, or $1.

B 22 rounds to 30. $5 \times 30 = 150$, so Jana has about 150 cents, or $1.50.

C 22 rounds to 20. $1 \times 20 = 20$, so Jana has about $20.

D 22 rounds to 30. $1 \times 30 = 30$, so Jana has about $30.

8. Zane has 23 toy cars. Rasheed has twice as many toy cars as Zane. Zane says that combined, they have 89 toy cars. Is Zane's answer reasonable? Explain.

11. Jon wants to find 6×89. Show how he can find the product mentally. What is the product?

9. Pedro bought 3 bags of dog food at $23 for each bag. He also bought 1 case of cat food for $17. Use rounding to estimate how many dollars Pedro spent. Mark your answer in the grid below.

12. Marsha is finding 9×30. She uses a shortcut and finds the product of 9×3 before writing a 0 onto the end of the product. What is the product of the basic fact that Marsha finds first? Mark your answer in the grid below.

© Pearson Education, Inc. 3

Glossary

A.M. The time between midnight and noon.

acute angle An angle that is open less than a right angle.

acute triangle A triangle with 3 acute angles.

addends Numbers added together to give a sum.
Example: 2 + 7 = 9

Addend   Addend

angle A figure that is formed by 2 rays having the same endpoint.

angle measure The degrees of an angle.

area The number of square units needed to cover a region.

array A way of displaying objects in equal rows and columns.

Associative (Grouping) Property of Addition The grouping of addends can be changed and the sum will be the same.

Associative (Grouping) Property of Multiplication The grouping of factors can be changed and the product will be the same.

bar graph A graph using bars to show data.

base Flat surface of a solid that can roll.

benchmark fraction A commonly used fraction such as $\frac{1}{4}, \frac{1}{3}, \frac{1}{2}, \frac{2}{3},$ and $\frac{3}{4}$.

capacity (liquid volume) The amount a container can hold measured in liquid units.

centimeter (cm) A metric unit of length.

charity Giving money to help others.

Commutative (Order) Property of Addition Numbers can be added in any order and the sum will be the same.

Commutative (Order) Property of Multiplication Numbers can be multiplied in any order and the product will be the same.

compare To decide if one number is greater than or less than another number.

compatible numbers Numbers that are easy to add, subtract, multiply, or divide mentally.

compensation Choosing numbers close to the numbers in a problem to make computation easier and then adjusting the answer for the numbers chosen.

cone A solid figure with a circle as its base and a curved surface that meets at a point.

credit A way to buy something and pay for it later.

cube A solid figure with 6 same-size squares as its faces.

cup (c) A customary unit of capacity.

cylinder A solid figure with 2 circular bases.

data Pieces of information.

decagon A polygon with 10 sides.

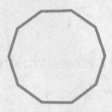

decimal A number with one or more digits to the right of the decimal point.

decimal point The dot used to separate dollars from cents in money.

decomposing Breaking a number into parts.
Example: $\frac{2}{5}$ can be broken into $\frac{1}{5} + \frac{1}{5}$.

degree (angle) A unit of measure for angles.

denominator The number below the fraction bar in a fraction, which shows the total number of equal parts.

difference The answer when subtracting one number from another.

© Pearson Education, Inc. 3

digits The symbols 0, 1, 2, 3, 4, 5, 6, 7, 8, and 9 used to write numbers.

Distributive Property A multiplication fact can be broken apart into the sum of two other multiplication facts.
Example: $5 \times 4 = (2 \times 4) + (3 \times 4)$

dividend The number to be divided.
Example: $63 \div 9 = 7$
↑
Dividend

divisible A number that can be divided by another number without leaving a remainder.

divisibility rules The rules that state when a number can be divided by another number without a remainder.

division An operation that tells how many equal groups there are or how many are in each group.

divisor The number by which another number is divided.
Example: $63 \div 9 = 7$
↑
Divisor

dollar sign A symbol ($) used to indicate money.

dot plot A way to organize data on a number line.

edge A line segment where 2 faces meet in a solid figure.

eighth One of 8 equal parts of a whole.

elapsed time The total amount of time that passes from the starting time to the ending time.

equal (equality) When the two sides of an equation have the same value.

equation A number sentence that uses an equal sign (=) to show that the value on its left side is the same as the value on its right side.

equilateral triangle A triangle with all sides the same length.

equivalent fractions Fractions that name the same part of a whole or the same location on a number line.

estimate To give an approximate number or answer.

even number A number that is divisible by 2.

expanded form A number written as the sum of the values of its digits.
Example: $2,476 = 2,000 + 400 + 70 + 6$

F

face A flat surface of a solid that cannot roll.

fact family A group of related facts using the same numbers.

factors Numbers that are multiplied together to give a product.
Example: $7 \times 3 = 21$

Factor   Factor

fifth One of 5 equal parts of a whole.

foot (ft) A customary unit of length. 1 foot equals 12 inches.

fourth One of 4 equal parts of a whole.

fraction A symbol, such as $\frac{1}{2}$, used to name a part of a whole, a part of a set, or a location on a number line.

frequency table A table used to show the number of times something occurs.

G

gallon (gal) A customary unit of capacity. One gallon equals 4 quarts.

gram (g) A metric unit of mass, the amount of matter in an object.

H

half (halves) One of 2 equal parts of a whole.

half hour A unit of time equal to 30 minutes.

hexagon A polygon with 6 sides.

hour A unit of time equal to 60 minutes.

hundredth One of 100 equal parts of a whole, written as 0.01 or $\frac{1}{100}$.

I

Identity (Zero) Property of Addition The sum of any number and zero is that same number.

Identity (One) Property of Multiplication The product of any number and 1 is that number.

inch (in.) A customary unit of length.

income Money earned from doing work.

interest Money you pay when you borrow money, or money you receive for lending money.

© Pearson Education, Inc. 3

intersecting lines
Lines that cross at
one point.

inverse operations Two operations that
undo each other.

isosceles triangle A triangle with at
least 2 sides the same length.

K

key The explanation for what each
symbol represents in a pictograph.

kilogram (kg) A metric unit of mass,
the amount of matter in an object. One
kilogram equals 1,000 grams.

kilometer (km) A metric unit of length.
One kilometer equals 1,000 meters.

L

line A straight path of points that is
endless in both directions.

line segment A part of a line that has
2 endpoints.

liter (L) A metric unit of capacity. One
liter equals 1,000 milliliters.

M

mass A measure of the amount of matter
in an object.

meter (m) A metric unit of length.
One meter equals 100 centimeters.

mile (mi) A customary unit of length.
One mile equals 5,280 feet.

milliliter (mL) A metric unit of capacity.

millimeter (mm) A metric unit of length.
1,000 millimeters equals 1 meter.

minute A unit of time equal to
60 seconds.

mixed number A number with a whole
number part and a fraction part.
Example: $2\frac{3}{4}$

multiple The product of a given number
and any other whole number.
Example: 0, 4, 8, 12, and 16 are multiples
of 4.

multiplication An operation that gives
the total number when you join equal
groups.

not equal When the two sides of an equation do not have the same value.

number line A line that shows numbers in order using a scale.
Example:

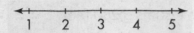

numerator The number above the fraction bar in a fraction, which shows how many equal parts are described.

obtuse angle An angle that is open more than a right angle.

obtuse triangle A triangle with one obtuse angle.

octagon A polygon with 8 sides.

odd number A number that is not divisible by 2.

order To arrange numbers from least to greatest or from greatest to least.

ounce (oz) A customary unit of weight.

P. M. The time between noon and midnight.

parallel lines Lines that never cross each other.

parallelogram A quadrilateral with 2 pairs of parallel sides.

partial products Products found by breaking one factor in a multiplication problem into ones, tens, and so on and then multiplying each of these by the other factor.

pentagon A polygon with 5 sides.

perimeter The distance around a figure.

period A group of 3 digits in a number, separated by a comma.

perpendicular Two lines, line segments, or rays that intersect to form right angles.

pictograph A graph using pictures or symbols to show data.

pint (pt) A customary unit of capacity. One pint equals 2 cups.

© Pearson Education, Inc. 3

place value The value given to the place a digit has in a number.
Example: In 3,946, the place value of the digit 9 is *hundreds*.

plane An endless flat surface.

planned spending Paying money for goods and services you expect.

point An exact position often marked by a dot.

polygon A closed figure made up of straight line segments.

pound (lb) A customary unit of weight. One pound equals 16 ounces.

product The answer to a multiplication problem.

quadrilateral A polygon with 4 sides.

quart (qt) A customary unit of capacity. One quart equals 2 pints.

quarter hour A unit of time equal to 15 minutes.

quotient The answer to a division problem.

ray A part of a line that has one endpoint and continues endlessly in one direction.

rectangle A parallelogram with 4 right angles.

rectangular prism A solid figure with 6 rectangular faces.

regroup (regrouping) To name a whole number in a different way.
Example: 28 = 1 ten 18 ones

remainder The number that is left over after dividing.
Example: 31 ÷ 7 = 4 R3
↑
Remainder

resources Things used to produce goods and services.

rhombus A parallelogram with all sides the same length.

right angle An angle that forms a square corner.

right triangle A triangle with one right angle.

round To replace a number with a number that tells about how much or how many to the nearest ten, hundred, thousand, and so on.
Example: 42 rounded to the nearest 10 is 40.

S

saving Putting money aside to use in the future.

scale The numbers that show the units used on a graph.

scalene triangle A triangle with no sides the same length.

second A unit of time. 60 seconds equal 1 minute.

side A line segment forming part of a polygon.

simplest form A fraction with a numerator and a denominator that cannot be divided by the same divisor, except 1.

sixth One of 6 equal parts of a whole.

solid figure A figure that has length, width, and height.

spending Paying money for goods such as food and clothes or services such as a haircut.

sphere A solid figure in the shape of a ball.

square A parallelogram with 4 right angles and all sides the same length.

square unit A square with sides 1 unit long, used to measure area.

standard form A way to write a number showing only its digits.
Example: 3,845

straight angle An angle that forms a straight line.

sum The answer to an addition problem.

survey To collect information by asking a number of people the same question and recording their answers.

© Pearson Education, Inc. 3

tally mark A mark used to record data on a tally chart.
Example: ~~HH~~ = 5

tenth One of 10 equal parts of a whole, written as 0.1 or $\frac{1}{10}$.

third One of 3 equal parts of a whole.

time interval An amount of time.

ton (T) A customary unit of weight. One ton equals 2,000 pounds.

trapezoid A quadrilateral with only one pair of parallel sides.

triangle A polygon with 3 sides.

triangular prism A solid figure with two triangular faces.

twelfth One of 12 equal parts of a whole.

unit angle An angle with a measurement of 1 degree.

unit fraction A fraction representing one part of a whole that has been divided into equal parts; it always has a numerator of 1.

unknown A symbol that stands for a number in an equation.

unplanned spending Paying money for goods and services you do not expect.

vertex of an angle The endpoint of 2 rays that form an angle.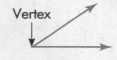

vertex of a polygon The point where two sides of a polygon meet.

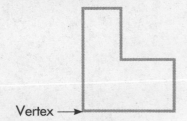

week A unit of time equal to 7 days.

weight A measure of how heavy an object is.

word form A number written in words. *Example:* 9,325 = nine thousand, three hundred twenty-five

yard (yd) A customary unit of length. One yard equals 3 feet or 36 inches.

Zero Property of Multiplication The product of any number and zero is zero.

© Pearson Education, Inc. 3